HARDPRESS.NET
HOME OF HARD-TO-FIND BOOKS

Decline and Fall of the Roman Empire
by Edward Gibbon

Address:
HardPress
8345 NW 66TH ST #2561
MIAMI FL 33166-2626
USA
Email: info@hardpress.net

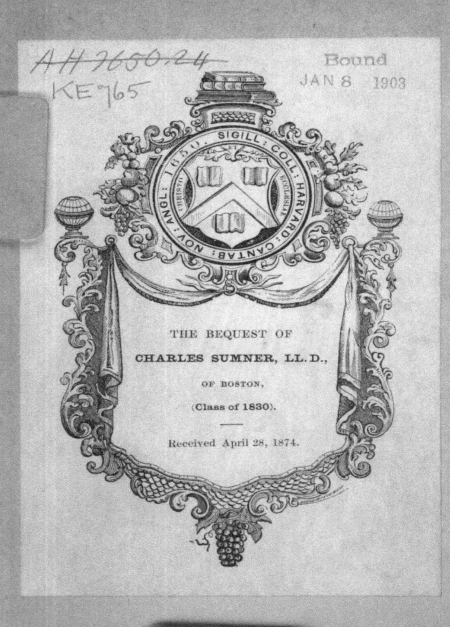

THE

HISTORY

OF THE

DECLINE AND FALL

OF THE

ROMAN EMPIRE.

BY

EDWARD GIBBON, ESQ.

IN TWELVE VOLUMES.
VOL. V.

A New Edition.

LONDON:

PRINTED FOR W. ALLASON; B. WHITROW AND CO.; C. CHAPPLE;
W. BARTON; J. EVANS AND SON; J. GREENHILL; J. HARWOOD;
R. HILL; G. HEBERT; W. HARRIS; T. MASON; R. SCHOLEY;
J. MAYNARD; T. BOHN; W. MASON; J. CARLISLE; T. FISHER;
J. BUMPUS; J. CRANWELL; I. PARSONS AND CO.; J. ROE;
T. LESTER;—ALSO W. AND P. JENKINS; AND E. KHULL AND CO.
GLASGOW; J. CUMMINS AND C. LA GRANGE, DUBLIN.

1820.

Plummer and Brewis, Printers, Lov--Lane, Little-Eastcheap.

CONTENTS

OF THE

FIFTH VOLUME.

CHAP. XXVII.

Death of Gratian—Ruin of Arianism—St. Ambrose—First civil war against Maximus—Character, administration, and penance of Theodosius—Death of Valentinian II.—Second civil war against Eugenius—Death of Theodosius.

CHAP. XXVIII

Final destruction of paganism—Introduction of the worship of saints and relics among the Christians.

CHAP. XXIX.

Final division of the Roman empire between the sons of Theodosius—Reign of Arcadius and Honorius—Administration of Rufinus and Stilicho—Revolt and defeat of Gildo in Africa.

CHAP. XXX.

Revolt of the Goths—They plunder Greece—Two great invasions of Italy by Alaric and Radagaisus—They are repulsed by Stilicho—The Germans over-run Gaul—Usurpation of Constantine in the West—Disgrace and death of Stilicho.

CHAP. XXXI.

Invasion of Italy by Alaric—Manners of the Roman senate and people—Rome is thrice besieged, and at length pillaged by the Goths—Death of Alaric—The Goths evacuate Italy—Fall of Constantine—Gaul and Spain are occupied by the barbarians—Independence of Britain.

CHAP. XXXII.

Arcadius emperor of the East—Administration and disgrace of Eutropius—Revolt of Gainas—Persecution of St. John Chrysostom—Theodosius II, emperor of the East—His sister Pulcheria—His wife Eudocia—The Persian war, and division of Armenia.

THE
HISTORY

OF THE

DECLINE AND FALL

OF THE

ROMAN EMPIRE.

CHAP. XXVII

Death of Gratian—Ruin of Arianism—St. Am-
brose—First civil war, against Maximus—
Character, administration, and penance, of
Theodosius—Death of Valentinian II.—Se-
cond civil war, against Eugenius—Death of
Theodosius.

THE fame of Gratian, before he had accomplished the twentieth year of his age, was
equal to that of the most celebrated princes.
His gentle and amiable disposition endeared him
to his private friends, the graceful affability of
his manners engaged the affection of the people:
the men of letters, who enjoyed the liberality,
acknowledged the taste and eloquence of their
sovereign; his valour and dexterity in arms
were equally applauded by the soldiers; and the

CHAP.
XXVII.
~~~~~~~~~~
Character
and con-
duct of the
emperor
Gratian.
A. D. 379-
383.

clergy considered the humble piety of Gratian as the first and most useful of his virtues. The victory of Colmar had delivered the West from a formidable invasion; and the grateful provinces of the East ascribed the merits of Theodosius to the author of *his* greatness, and of the public safety. Gratian survived those memorable events only four or five years; but he survived his reputation; and, before he fell a victim to rebellion, he had lost in a great measure, the respect and confidence of the Roman world.

His defects.

The remarkable alteration of his character or conduct, may not be imputed to the arts of flattery, which had besieged the son of Valentinian from his infancy; nor to the headstrong passions which that gentle youth appears to have escaped. A more attentive view of the life of Gratian, may perhaps suggest the true cause of the disappointment of the public hopes. His apparent virtues, instead of being the hardy productions of experience and adversity, were the premature and artificial fruits of a royal education. The anxious tenderness of his father was continually employed to bestow on him those advantages, which he might perhaps esteem the more highly, as he himself had been deprived of them; and the most skilful masters of every science, and of every art, had laboured to form the mind and body of the young prince.[*] The knowledge which they pain-

---

[*] Valentinian was less attentive to the religion of his son; since he intrusted the education of Gratian to Ausonius, a professed pagan, (Mem

fully communicated was displayed with ostentation, and celebrated with lavish praise. His soft and tractable disposition received the fair impression of their judicious precepts, and the absence of passion might easily be mistaken for the strength of reason. His preceptors gradually rose to the rank and consequence of ministers of state ;[b] and, as they wisely dissembled their secret authority, he seemed to act with firmness, with propriety, and with judgment, on the most important occasions of his life and reign. But the influence of this elaborate instruction did not penetrate beyond the surface; and the skilful preceptors, who so accurately guided the steps of their royal pupil, could not infuse into his feeble and indolent character, the vigorous and independent principle of action, which renders the laborious pursuit of glory essentially necessary to the happiness, and almost to the existence, of the hero. As soon as time and accident had removed those faithful counsellors from the throne, the emperor of the West insensibly descended to the level of his natural genius; abandoned the reins of government to the ambitious hands which were stretched forwards to grasp them ; and amused his leisure with the most frivolous gratifications. A public sale of favour and injustice was instituted,

(Mem. de l'Academie des Inscriptions, tom. xv, p. 125-438). The poetical fame of Ausonius condemns the taste of his age.

[b] Ausonius was successively promoted to the pretorian prefecture of Italy, (A. D. 377), and of Gaul, (A. D. 378) ; and was at length invested with the consulship, (A. D. 379). He expressed his gratitude in a servile and insipid piece of flattery, (Actio Gratiarum, p. 699-736), which has survived more worthy production.

both in the court, and in the provinces, by the
worthless delegates of his power, whose merit
it was made *sacrilege* to question.[c] The conscience of the credulous prince was directed by
saints and bishops;[d] who procured an imperial
edict to punish, as a capital offence, the violation, the neglect, or even the ignorance of the
divine law.[e] Among the various arts which
had exercised the youth of Gratian, he had applied himself, with singular inclination and success, to manage the horse, to draw the bow, and
to dart the javelin; and these qualifications,
which might be useful to a soldier, were prostituted to the viler purposes of hunting. Large
parks were inclosed for the imperial pleasures,
and plentifully stocked with every species of
wild beasts ; and Gratian neglected the duties,
and even the dignity, of his rank, to consume
whole days in the vain display of his dexterity
and boldness in the chace. The pride and wish
of the Roman emperor to excel in an art, in
which he might be surpassed by the meanest
of his slaves, reminded the numerous spectators of the examples of Nero and Commodus:

[c] Disputare de principali judicio non opórtet.   Sacrilegii enim instar
est dubitare, an is dignus sit, quem elegerit imperator.   Codex Justinian. l. ix, tit. xxix, leg. 3.   This convenient law was revived and promulgated, after the death of Gratian, by the feeble court of Milan.

[d] Ambrose composed, for his instruction, a theological treatise on
the faith of the Trinity : and Tillemont (Hist. des Empereurs, tom. v,
p. 158, 169) ascribes to the archbishop the merit of Gratian's intolerant laws.

[e] Qui divinæ legis sanctitatem nesciendo omittunt, aut negligendo
violant, et offendunt, sacrilegium committunt.   Codex Justinian. l. ix,
tit. xxix, leg. 1.   Theodosius indeed may claim his share in the merit
of this comprehensive law.

but the chaste and temperate Gratian was a stranger to their monstrous vices; and his hands were stained only with the blood of animals.[f]

The behaviour of Gratian, which degraded his character in the eyes of mankind, could not have disturbed the security of his reign, if the army had not been provoked to resent their peculiar injuries. As long as the young emperor was guided by the instructions of his masters, he professed himself the friend and pupil of the soldiers; many of his hours were spent in the familiar conversation of the camp, and the health, the comforts, the rewards, the honours, of his faithful troops, appeared to be the object of his attentive concern. But, after Gratian more freely indulged his prevailing taste for hunting and shooting, he naturally connected himself with the most dexterous ministers of his favourite amusement. A body of the Alani was received into the military and domestic service of the palace; and the admirable skill, which they were accustomed to display in the unbounded plains of Scythia, was exercised on a more narrow theatre, in the parks and inclosures of Gaul. Gratian admired the talents and customs of these favourite guards, to whom alone he intrusted the defence of his person: and, as if he meant to insult the public opinion, he frequently shewed himself to the soldiers

[f] Ammianus (xxxi, 10) and the younger Victor acknowledge the virtues of Gratian; and accuse, or rather lament, his degenerate taste. The odious parallel of Commodus is saved by "licit incruentus;" and perhaps Philostorgius (l. x, c. 10, and Godefroy, p. 432) had guarded, with some similar reserve, the comparison of Nero.

and people, with the dress and arms, the long bow, the sounding quiver, and the fur garments, of a Scythian warrior. The unworthy spectacle of a Roman prince, who had renounced the dress and manners of his country, filled the minds of the legions with grief and indignation.[5] Even the Germans, so strong and formidable in the armies of the empire, affected to disdain the strange and horrid appearance of the savages of the North, who, in the space of a few years, had wandered from the banks of the Volga to those of the Seine. A loud and licentious murmur was echoed through the camps and garrisons of the West; and as the mild indolence of Gratian neglected to extinguish the first symptoms of discontent, the want of love and respect was not supplied by the influence of fear. But the subversion of an established government is always a work of some real, and of much apparent, difficulty; and the throne of Gratian was protected by the sanctions of custom, law, religion, and the nice balance of the civil and military powers, which had been established by the policy of Constantine. It is not very important to inquire from what causes the revolt of Britain was produced. Accident is commonly the parent of disorder; the seeds of rebellion happened to fall on a soil which was supposed to be more fruitful than any other

[5] Zosimus (l. iv, p. 247) and the younger Victor ascribe the revolution to the favour of the Alani, and the discontent of the Roman troops. Dum exercitum negligeret, et paucos ex Alanis, quos ingenti auro ad se transtulerat, anteferret veteri ac Romano militi.

in tyrants and usurpers;[a] the legions of that sequestered island had long been famous for a spirit of presumption and arrogance;[i] and the name of Maximus was proclaimed by the tumultuary, but unanimous voice, both of the soldiers and of the provincials. The emperor, or the rebel, for his title was not yet ascertained by fortune, was a native of Spain, the countryman, the fellow-soldier, and the rival of Theodosius, whose elevation he had not seen without some emotions of envy and resentment: the events of his life had long since fixed him in Britain; and I should not be unwilling to find some evidence for the marriage, which he is said to have contracted with the daughter of a wealthy lord in Caernarvonshire.[k] But this provincial rank might justly be considered as a state of exile and obscurity; and if Maximus had obtained any civil or military office, he was not invested with the authority either of governor or general.[l] His abilities, and even his

CHAP.
XXVII.

Revolt of
Maximus
in Britain.

[a] Britannia fertilis provincia tyrannorum, is a memorable expression, used by Jerom in the Pelagian controversy, and variously tortured in the disputes of our national antiquaries. The revolutions of the last age appeared to justify the images of the sublime Bossuet, " cette isle plus orageuse que les mers qui l'environnent."

[i] Zosimus says of the British soldiers, των αλλων απαντων πλιον αυθαδι φ και θυμω τικομινους.

[k] Helena the daughter of Eudda. Her chapel may still be seen at Caerfegot, now Caer-narvon, (Carte's Hist. of England, vol. i, p. 186, from Rowland's Mona Antiqua). The prudent reader may not perhaps be satisfied with such Welsh evidence.

[l] Cambden (vol. i, introduct. p. ci) appoints him governor of Britain; and the father of our antiquities is followed, as usual, by his blind progeny. Pacatus and Zosimus had taken some pains to prevent this error, or fable; and I shall protect myself by their decisive testimonies. Regali habitû *exulem* suum, illi exules orbis induerunt, (in Panegyr. Vet. xii, 23), and the Greek historian, still less equivocally, αυτος (Maximus) δε ωδι τις αρχον αντιμαν ετυχε προσλθον, (l. iv, p. 248).

CHAP.
XXVII.

Flight and
death of
Gratian.

integrity, are acknowledged by the partial writers of the age; and the merit must indeed have been conspicuous, that could extort such a confession in favour of the vanquished enemy of Theodosius. The discontent of Maximus might incline him to censure the conduct of his sovereign, and to encourage, perhaps without any views of ambition, the murmurs of the troops. But in the midst of the tumult, he artfully, or modestly, refused to ascend the throne; and some credit appears to have been given to his own positive declaration, that he was compelled to accept the dangerous present of the imperial purple.[m]

But there was danger likewise in refusing the empire; and from the moment that Maximus had violated his allegiance to his lawful sovereign, he could not hope to reign, or even to live, if he confined his moderate ambition within the narrow limits of Britain. He boldly and wisely resolved to prevent the designs of Gratian; the youth of the island crowded to his standard, and he invaded Gaul with a fleet and army, which were long afterwards remembered, as the emigration of a considerable part of the British nation.[a] The emperor, in his peaceful resi-

[m] Sulpicius Severus, Dialog. ii, 7. Orosius, l. vii. 34, p. 556. They both acknowledge (Sulpicius had been his subject) his innocence and merit. It is singular enough, that Maximus should be less favourably treated by Zosimus, the partial adversary of his rival.

[a] Archbishop Usher (Antiquitat. Britan. Eccles. p. 107, 108) has diligently collected the legends of the island and the continent. The whole emigration consisted of 30,000 soldiers, and 100,000 plebeians, who

dence of Paris, was alarmed by their hostile
approach; and the darts which he idly wasted
on lions and bears, might have been employed
more honourably against the rebels. But his
feeble efforts announced his degenerate spirit
and desperate situation; and deprived him of
the resources, which he still might have found,
in the support of his subjects and allies. The
armies of Gaul, instead of opposing the march
of Maximus, received him with joyful and loyal
acclamations; and the shame of the desertion
was transferred from the people to the prince.
The troops, whose station more immediately
attached them to the service of the palace,
abandoned the standard of Gratian the first
time that it was displayed in the neighbourhood
of Paris. The emperor of the West fled towards Lyons, with a train of only three hundred horse; and, in the cities along the road,
where he hoped to find a refuge, or at least a
passage, he was taught, by cruel experience,
that every gate is shut against the unfortunate.
Yet he might still have reached, in safety, the
dominions of his brother; and soon have returned with the forces of Italy and the East; if he
had not suffered himself to be fatally deceived
by the perfidious governor of the Lyonnese
province. Gratian was amused by protesta-
tions of doubtful fidelity, and the hopes of a

who settled in Bretagne. Their destined brides, St. Ursula with 11,000
noble, and 60,000 plebeian, virgins, mistook their way; landed at Co-
logne, and were all most cruelly murdered by the Huns. But the plebeian sisters have been defrauded of their equal honours; and, what is
still harder, John Trithemius presumes to mention the *children* of these
British *virgins.*

CHAP. XXVII.

support, which could not be effectual; till the arrival of Andragathius, the general of the cavalry of Maximus, put an end to his suspense. That resolute officer executed, without remorse, the orders, or the intentions, of the usurper. Gratian, as he rose from supper, was delivered into the hands of the assassin; and his body was denied to the pious and pressing entreaties of his brother Valentinian.[o] The death of the emperor was followed by that of his powerful general Mellobaudes, the king of the Franks; who maintained, to the last moment of his life, the ambiguous reputation, which is the just recompence of obscure and subtle policy.[p] These executions might be necessary to the public safety: but the successful usurper, whose power was acknowledged by all the provinces of the West, had the merit, and satisfaction, of boasting, that except those who had perished by the chance of war, his triumph was not stained with the blood of the Romans.[q]

A. D. 383. Aug. 25.

[o] Zosimus (l. iv, p. 248, 249) has transported the death of Gratian from Lugdunum in Gaul (Lyons) to Singidunum in Mœsia. Some hints may be extracted from the Chronicles; some lies may be detected in Sozomen, (l. vii. c. 13), and Socrates, (l. v, c. 11). Ambrose is our most authentic evidence, (tom. i, Enarrat. in Psalm lxi, p. 961; tom. ii, epist. xxiv, p. 888, &c. and de Obitû Valentinian. Consolat. No. 28, p. 1182).

[p] Pacatus (xii, 28) celebrates his fidelity; while his treachery is marked in Prosper's Chronicle, as the cause of the ruin of Gratian. Ambrose, who has occasion to exculpate himself, only condemns the death of Vallio, a faithful servant of Gratian, (tom. ii, epist. xxiv, p. 891, edit. Benedict.)

[q] He protested, nullum ex adversariis nisi in acie occubuisse. Sulp. Severus in Vit. B. Martin. c. 23. The orator of Theodosius bestows reluctant, and therefore weighty, praise on his clemency. Si cui ille, pro ceteris sceleribus suis, *minus crudelis* fuisse videtur. (Panegyr. Vet. xii, 28.

The events of this revolution had passed in such rapid succession, that it would have been impossible for Theodosius to march to the relief of his benefactor, before he received the intelligence of his defeat and death. During the season of sincere grief, or ostentatious mourning, the Eastern emperor was interrupted by the arrival of the principal chamberlain of Maximus; and the choice of a venerable old man, for an office which was usually exercised by eunuchs, announced to the court of Constantinople the gravity and temperance of the British usurper. The ambassador condescended to justify, or excuse, the conduct of his master; and to protest, in specious language, that the murder of Gratian had been perpetrated without his knowledge or consent, by the precipitate zeal of the soldiers. But he proceeded, in a firm and equal tone, to offer Theodosius the alternative of peace or war. The speech of the ambassador concluded with a spirited declamation, that although Maximus, as a Roman, and as the father of his people, would choose rather to employ his forces in the common defence of the republic, he was armed and prepared, if his friendship should be rejected, to dispute in a field of battle, the empire of the world. An immediate and peremptory answer was required; but it was extremely difficult for Theodosius to satisfy, on this important occasion, either the feelings of his own mind, or the expectations of the public. The imperious voice of honour and gratitude called aloud for revenge. From the liberality of Gra-

CHAP.
XXVII.
~~~~~~~~
Treaty of
peace be-
tween
Maximus
and Theo-
dosius,
A. D. 382.
387.

tian, he had received the imperial diadem: his
patience would encourage the odious suspicion,
that he was more deeply sensible of former
injuries, than of recent obligations; and if he
accepted the friendship, he must seem to share
the guilt, of the assassin.   Even the principles
of justice, and the interest of society, would receive a fatal blow from the impunity of Maximus: and the example of successful usurpation
would tend to dissolve the artificial fabric of
government, and once more to replunge the
empire in the crimes and calamities of the preceding age.   But, as the sentiments of gratitude
and honour should invariably regulate the conduct of an individual, they may be overbalanced
in the mind of a sovereign, by the sense of superior duties : and the maxims both of justice
and humanity must permit the escape of an
atrocious criminal, if an innocent people would
be involved in the consequences of his punishment.   The assassin of Gratian had usurped,
but he actually possessed, the most warlike
provinces of the empire : the East was exhausted by the misfortunes, and even by the success,
of the Gothic war ; and it was seriously to be
apprehended, that, after the vital strength of
the republic had been wasted in a doubtful and
destructive contest, the feeble conqueror would
remain an easy prey to the barbarians of the
North.   These weighty considerations engaged
Theodosius to dissemble his resentment, and to
accept the alliance of the tyrant.   But he stipulated, that Maximus should content himself

with the possession of the countries beyond the
Alps. The brother of Gratian was confirmed
and secured in the sovereignty of Italy, Africa,
and the Western Illyricum; and some honourable conditions were inserted in the treaty, to
protect the memory, and the laws, of the deceased emperor.[r] According to the custom of
the age, the images of the three imperial colleagues were exhibited to the veneration of the
people: nor should it be lightly supposed, that,
in the moment of a solemn reconciliation, Theodosius secretly cherished the intention of perfidy and revenge.[s]

The contempt of Gratian for the Roman soldiers had exposed him to the fatal effects
of their resentment. His profound veneration
for the Christian clergy was rewarded by the
applause and gratitude of a powerful order,
which has claimed, in every age, the privilege
of dispensing honours, both on earth and in heaven.[t] The orthodox bishops bewailed his death,
and their own irreparable loss; but they were
soon comforted by the discovery, that Gratian
had committed the sceptre of the East to the
hands of a prince, whose humble faith, and fervent zeal, were supported by the spirit and abilities of a more vigorous character. Among the

CHAP.
XXVII.

Baptism
and orthodox edicts
of Theodosius,
A. D. 380,
Feb. 28.

---

[r] Ambrose mentions the laws of Gratian, quas non abrogavit hostis,
(tom. ii, epist. xvii, p. 827).

[s] Zosimus, l. iv, p. 251, 252. We may disclaim his odious suspicions;
but we cannot reject the treaty of peace which the friends of Theodosius have absolutely forgotten, or slightly mentioned.

[t] Their oracle, the archbishop of Milan, assigns to his pupil Gratian
an high and respectable place in heaven, (tom. ii, de Obit. Val. Consol.
p. 1198).

CHAP.
XXVII.
~~~~~~~

benefactors of the church, the fame of Constantine has been rivalled by the glory of Theodosius. If Constantine had the advantage of erecting the standard of the cross, the emulation of his successor assumed the merit of subduing the Arian heresy, and of abolishing the worship of idols in the Roman world. Theodosius was the first of the emperors baptised in the true faith of the Trinity. Although he was born of a Christian family, the maxims, or at least the practice of the age, encouraged him to delay the ceremony of his initiation; till he was admonished of the danger of delay, by the serious illness which threatened his life, towards the end of the first year of his reign. Before he again took the field against the Goths, he received the sacrament of baptism[u] from Acholius, the orthodox bishop of Thessalonica;[x] and, as the emperor ascended from the holy font, still glowing with the warm feelings of regeneration, he dictated a solemn edict, which proclaimed his own faith, and prescribed the religion of his subjects. " It is our pleasure (such is the imperial style) " that all the nations, which are governed by our " clemency and moderation, should stedfastly " adhere to the religion which was taught by St.

---

[u] For the baptism of Theodosius see Sozomen, (l. vii, c. 4); Socrates, (l. v, c. 6), and Tillemont, (Hist. des Empereurs, tom. v, p. 728.

[x] Ascolius, or Acholius, was honoured by the friendship, and the praises, of Ambrose; who styles him, murus fidei atque sanctitatis, (tom. ii, epist. xv, p. 820); and afterwards celebrates his speed and diligence in running to Constantinople, Italy, &c. (epist, xvi, p. 822); a virtue which does not appertain either to a *wall*, or a *bishop*.

" Peter to the Romans; which faithful tradition
" has preserved; and which is now professed by
" the pontiff Damasus, and by Peter, bishop of
" Alexandria, a man of apostolic holiness. Ac-
" cording to the discipline of the apostles, and
" the doctrine of the gospel, let us believe the
" sole deity of the Father, the Son, and the
" Holy Ghost; under an equal majesty, and a
" pious Trinity. We authorise the followers of
" this doctrine to assume the title of Catholic
" Christians; and as we judge, that all others are
" extravagant madmen, we brand them with the
" infamous name of Heretics; and declare, that
" their conventicles shall no longer usurp the
" respectable appellation of churches. Besides
" the condemnation of Divine justice, they must
" expect to suffer the severe penalties, which our
" authority, guided by heavenly wisdom, shall
" think proper to inflict upon them."[y] The faith
of a soldier is commonly the fruit of instruction,
rather than of inquiry; but as the emperor always
fixed his eyes on the visible land-marks of orthodoxy, which he had so prudently constituted,
his religious opinions were never affected by the
specious texts, the subtle arguments, and the
ambiguous creeds of the Arian doctors. Once
indeed he expressed a faint inclination to converse
with the eloquent and learned Eunomius, who
lived in retirement at a small distance from Con-

[y] Codex. Theodos. l. xvi, tit. i, leg. 2, with Godefroy's Commentary, tom. vi, p. 5-9. Such an edict deserved the warmest praises
of Baronius, auream sanctionem, edictum pium et salutare.—Sic itur
ad astra.

stantinople. But the dangerous interview was prevented by the prayers of the empress Flaccilla, who trembled for the salvation of her husband; and the mind of Theodosius was confirmed by a theological argument, adapted to the rudest capacity. He had lately bestowed, on his eldest son, Arcadius, the name and honours of Augustus; and the two princes were seated on a stately throne to receive the homage of their subjects. A bishop, Amphilochius of Iconium, approached the throne, and after saluting, with due reverence, the person of his sovereign, he accosted the royal youth with the same familiar tenderness, which he might have used towards a plebeian child. Provoked by this insolent behaviour, the monarch gave orders, that the rustic priest should be instantly driven from his presence. But while the guards were forcing him to the door, the dexterous polemic had time to execute his design, by exclaiming, with a loud voice,—" Such is the treatment, O Emperor! " which the King of Heaven has prepared for " those impious men, who affect to worship the " Father, but refuse to acknowledge the equal " majesty of his divine Son." Theodosius immediately embraced the bishop of Iconium; and never forgot the important lesson, which he had received from this dramatic parable.[a]

---

[a] Sozomen, l. vii, c. 6; Theodoret, l. v, c. 16. Tillemont is dis, ed (Mem. Eccles. tom. vi, p. 627, 628) with the terms of " rustic . shop," " obscure city." Yet I must take leave to think, that both Amphilochius and Iconium were objects of inconsiderable magnitude in the Roman empire.

Constantinople was the principal seat and for- tress of Arianism; and, in a long interval of forty years,[a] the faith of the princes and prelates, who reigned in the capital of the East, was rejected in the purer schools of Rome and Alexandria. The archiepiscopal throne of Macedonius, which had been *polluted with so much Christian blood,* was successively filled by Eudoxus and Damophilus. Their diocese enjoyed a free importation of vice and error from every province of the empire; the eager pursuit of religious controversy afforded a new occupation to the busy idleness of the metropolis; and we may credit the assertion of an intelligent observer, who describes, with some pleasantry, the effects of their loquacious zeal. " This city," says he, " is full of mechanics and " slaves, who are all of them profound theolo- " gians; and preach in the shops, and in the " streets. If you desire a man to change a piece " of silver, he informs you, wherein the Son " differs from the Father: if you ask the price " of a loaf, you are told, by way of reply, that " the Son is inferior to the Father; and if you " inquire whether the bath is ready, the answer " is, that the Son was made out of nothing "[b]

---

[a] Sozomen, l. vii, c. 5. Socrates, l. v, c. 7. Marcellin. in Chron. The account of forty years must be dated from the election or intrusion of Eusebius; who wisely exchanged the bishopric of Nicomedia for the throne of Constantinople.

[b] See Jortin's Remarks on Ecclesiastical History, vol. iv, p. 71. Thirty-third Oration of Gregory Nazianzen affords indeed some similar ideas, even some still more ridiculous; but I have not yet found the *words* of this remarkable passage, which I allege on the faith of a correct and liberal scholar.

The heretics, of various denominations, subsisted in peace under the protection of the Arians of Constantinople; who endeavoured to secure the attachment of those obscure sectaries; while they abused, with unrelenting severity, the victory which they had obtained over the followers of the council of Nice. During the partial reigns of Constantius and Valens, the feeble remnant of the Homoousians was deprived of the public and private exercise of their religion; and it has been observed, in pathetic language, that the scattered flock was left without a shepherd to wander on the mountains, or to be devoured by rapacious wolves.[c] But, as their zeal, instead of being subdued, derived strength and vigour from oppression, they seized the first moments of imperfect freedom, which they acquired by the death of Valens, to form themselves into a regular congregation, under the conduct of an episcopal pastor.

Gregory Nazianzen.
Two natives of Cappadocia, Basil, and Gregory Nazianzen,[d] were distinguished above all their contemporaries,[e] by the rare union of profane eloquence

[c] See the thirty-second Oration of Gregory Nazianzen, and the account of his own life, which he has composed in 1800 iambics. Yet every physician is prone to exaggerate the inveterate nature of the disease which he has cured.

[d] I confess myself deeply indebted to the *two* lives of Gregory Nazianzen, composed, with very different views, by Tillemont, (Mem. Eccles. tom. ix, p. 305-560, 692-731), and Le Clerc, (Bibliotheque Universelle, tom. xviii, p. 1-128).

[e] Unless Gregory Nazianzen mistook thirty years in his own age, he was born, as well as his friend Basil, about the year 329. The preposterous chronology of Suidas has been graciously received; because it removes the scandal of Gregory's father, a saint likewise, begetting children, after he became a bishop. (Tillemont, Mem. Eccles. tom. ix, p. 693-697).

and of orthodox piety. These orators, who might sometimes be compared, by themselves, and by the public, to the most celebrated of the ancient Greeks, were united by the ties of the strictest friendship. They had cultivated, with equal ardour, the same liberal studies in the schools of Athens; they had retired, with equal devotion, to the same solitude in the deserts of Pontus; and every spark of emulation, or envy, appeared to be totally extinguished in the holy and ingenuous breasts of Gregory and Basil. But the exaltation of Basil, from a private life to the archiepiscopal throne of Cæsarea, discovered to the world, and perhaps to himself, the pride of his character; and the first favour which he condescended to bestow on his friend was received, and perhaps was intended, as a cruel insult.[f] Instead of employing the superior talents of Gregory in some useful and conspicuous station, the haughty prelate selected, among the fifty bishoprics of his extensive province, the wretched village

[f] Gregory's Poem on his own life contains some beautiful lines, (tom. ii, p. 8), which burst from the heart, and speak the pangs of injured and lost friendship.—

.... ποτοι κοινοι λογων,
Ομοςεγος τε και συνεςιος βιος,
Νυς ἱις εν αμφοιν ....
Διεσκιδασαι παντα, ερριπται χαμαι,
Αυραι φερουσι τας παλαιας ελπιδας.

In the Midsummer Night's Dream, Helenia addresses the same pathetic complaint to her friend Hermia.—

Is all the counsel that we two have shared,
The sister's vows, &c.

Shakespeare had never read the poems of Gregory Nazianzen; he was ignorant of the Greek language; but his mother-tongue, the language of nature, is the same in Cappadocia and in Britain.

of Sasima,[s] without water, without verdure, without society, situate at the junction of three highways, and frequented only by the incessant passage of rude and clamorous waggoners. Gregory submitted with reluctance to this humiliating exile: he was ordained bishop of Sasima; but he solemnly protests, that he never consummated his spiritual marriage with this disgusting bride. He afterwards consented to undertake the government of his native church of Nazianzus,[h] of which his father had been bishop above five and forty years. But as he was still conscious, that he deserved another

Accepts
the mis-
sion of
Constanti-
nople,
A. D. 378,
November
audience, and another theatre, he accepted, with no unworthy ambition, the honourable invitation, which was addressed to him from the orthodox party of Constantinople. On his arrival in the capital, Gregory was entertained in the house of a pious and charitable kinsman; the most spacious room was consecrated to the uses of religious worship; and the name of *Anastasia* was chosen to express the resurrection of the Nicene faith. This private conventicle was afterwards converted into a magnificent church; and the credulity of the succeeding age

---

[s] This unfavourable portrait of Sasima is drawn by Gregory Nazianzen, (tom. ii, de Vitâ suâ, p. 7, 8). Its precise situation forty-nine miles from Archilais, and thirty-two from Tyana, is fixed in the Itinerary of Antoninus, (p. 144, edit. Wesseling).

[h] The name of Nazianzus has been immortalized by Gregory; but his native town, under the Greek or Roman title of Diocæsarea, (Tillemont, Mem. Eccles. tom. ix, p. 692), is mentioned by Pliny, (vi, 3), Ptolemy, and Hierocles, (Itinerar. Wesseling, p. 709). It appears to have been situate on the edge of Isauria.

was prepared to believe the miracles and visions,
which attested the presence, or at least the protection, of the Mother of God.[l] The pulpit of the Anastasia was the scene of the labours and triumphs of Gregory Nazianzen; and, in the space of two years, he experienced all the spiritual adventures which constitute the prosperous or adverse fortunes of a missionary.[k] The Arians, who were provoked by the boldness of his enterprise, represented his doctrine, as if he had preached three distinct and equal Deities; and the devout populace was excited to suppress, by violence and tumult, the irregular assemblies of the Anthanasian heretics. From the cathedral of St. Sophia, there issued a motley crowd " of common beggars, who had for- " feited their claim to pity; of monks, who had " the appearance of goats or satyrs; and of " women, more terrible than so many Jezebels." The doors of the Anastasia were broke open; much mischief was perpetrated, or attempted, with sticks, stones, and firebrands; and as a man lost his life in the affray, Gregory, who was summoned the next morning before the magistrate, had the satisfaction of supposing, that he publicly confessed the name of Christ. After he was delivered from the fear and danger of a foreign enemy, his infant church was

[l] See Ducange, Constant. Christiana, l. iv, p. 141, 142. The δυναμις of Sozomen (l. vii, c. 5) is interpreted to mean the Virgin Mary.

[k] Tillemont (Mem. Eccles. tom. ix, p. 432, &c.) diligently collects, enlarges, and explains, the oratorical and poetical hints of Gregory himself.

disgraced and distracted by intestine faction. A stranger, who assumed the name of Maximus,[1] and the cloak of a Cynic philosopher, insinuated himself into the confidence of Gregory; deceived and abused his favourable opinion; and forming a secret connection with some bishops of Egypt, attempted, by a clandestine ordination, to supplant his patron in the episcopal seat of Constantinople. These mortifications might sometimes tempt the Cappadocian missionary to regret his obscure solitude. But his fatigues were rewarded by the daily increase of his fame and his congregation; and he enjoyed the pleasure of observing, that the greater part of his numerous audience retired from his sermons, satisfied with the eloquence of the preacher,[m] or dissatisfied with the manifold imperfections of their faith and practice.[n]

Ruin of
Arianism
at Constantinople,
A. D. 380,
Nov. 26.
The Catholics of Constantinople were animated with joyful confidence by the baptism and edict of Theodosius; and they impatiently waited the effects of his gracious promise. Their hopes were speedily accomplished; and the emperor, as soon as he had finished the operations of the campaign, made his public

[1] He pronounced an oration (tom. i, orat. xxiii, p. 409) in his praise; but after their quarrel, the name of Maximus was changed into that of Heron, (see Jerom. tom. i, in Catalog. Script. Eccles. p. 301). I touch slightly on these obscure and personal squabbles.

[m] Under the modest emblem of a dream, Gregory (tom. ii, carmen ix, p. 78) describes his own success with some human complacency. Yet it should seem, from his familiar conversation with his auditor St. Jerom. (tom. i, Epist. ad Nepotian. p. 14), that the preacher understood the true value of popular applause.

[n] Lachrymæ auditorum laudes tuæ sint, is the lively and judicious advice of St. Jerom.

entry into the capital at the head of a victorious army. The next day after his arrival, he
summoned Damophilus to his presence; and
offered that Arian prelate the hard alternative
of subscribing the Nicene creed, or of instantly
resigning, to the orthodox believers, the use and
possession of the episcopal palace, the cathedral of St. Sophia, and all the churches of Constantinople. The zeal of Damophilus, which
in a catholic saint would have been justly applauded, embraced, without hesitation, a life of
poverty and exile,° and his removal was immediately followed by the purification of the imperial city. The Arians might complain, with
some appearance of justice, that an inconsiderable congregation of sectaries should usurp the
hundred churches, which they were insufficient
to fill; whilst the far greater part of the people
was cruelly excluded from every place of religious worship. Theodosius was still inexorable; but as the angels who protected the catholic cause, were only visible to the eyes of faith,
he prudently reinforced those heavenly legions,
with the more effectual aid of temporal and carnal weapons: and the church of St. Sophia was
occupied by a large body of the imperial guards.
If the mind of Gregory was susceptible of
pride, he must have felt a very lively satisfaction, when the emperor conducted him through
the streets in solemn triumph; and, with his

° Socrates (l. v, c. 7), and Sozomen, (l. viis c. 5), relate the evange-
lical words and actions of Damophilus without a word of approbation.
He considered, says Socrates, that it is difficult to *resist* the powerful t
but it was easy, and would have been profitable, to *submit*.

C 4

own hand, respectfully placed him on the archiepiscopal throne of Constantinople. But the saint (who had not subdued the imperfections of human virtue) was deeply affected by the mortifying consideration, that his entrance into the fold was that of a wolf, rather than of a shepherd: that the glittering arms, which surrounded his person, were necessary for his safety; and that he alone was the object of the imprecations of a great party, whom, as men and citizens, it was impossible for him to despise. He beheld the innumerable multitude of either sex, and of every age, who crowded the streets, the windows, and the roofs of the houses; he heard the tumultuous voice of rage, grief, astonishment, and despair; and Gregory fairly confesses, that on the memorable day of his installation, the capital of the East wore the appearance of a city taken by storm, and in the hands of a barbarian conqueror.[p] About six weeks afterwards, Theodosius declared his resolution of expelling from all the churches of his dominions, the bishops and their clergy, who should obstinately refuse to believe, or at least to profess, the doctrine of the council of Nice. His lieutenant Sapor was armed with the ample powers of a general law, a special commission, and a military force;[q] and this ec-

In the
East,
A. D. 381,
Jan. 10.

---

[p] See Gregory Nazianzen, tom. ii, de Vitâ suâ, p. 21, 22. For the sake of posterity, the bishop of Constantinople records a stupendous prodigy. In the month of November, it was a cloudy morning, but the sun broke forth, when the procession entered the church.

[q] Of the three ecclesiastical historians, Theodoret alone (l. v, c. 2), has mentioned this important commission of Sapor, which Tillemont (Hist. des Empereurs, tom. v, p. 728) judiciously removes from the reign of Gratian, to that of Theodosius.

clesiastical revolution was conducted with so
much discretion and vigour, that the religion of
the emperor was established, without tumult or
bloodshed, in all the provinces of the East. The
writings of the Arians, if they had been permitted to exist, would perhaps contain the la-
mentable story of the persecution, which afflicted the church under the reign of the impious
Theodosius ; and the sufferings of *their* holy
confessors might claim the pity of the disinterested reader. Yet there is reason to imagine,
that the violence of zeal and revenge was, in some
measure, eluded by the want of resistence; and
that, in their adversity, the Arians displayed
much less firmness, than had been exerted by the
orthodox party under the reign of Constantius
and Valens. The moral character and conduct
of the hostile sects appear to have been governed by the same common principles of nature and
religion : but a very material circumstance may
be discovered, which tended to distinguish the
degrees of their theological faith. Both parties,
in the schools, as well as in the temples, acknowledged and worshipped the divine majesty
of Christ ; and, as we are always prone to im-
pute our own sentiments and passions to the
Deity, it would be deemed more prudent and
respectful to exaggerate, than to circumscribe,
the adorable perfections of the Son of God. The
disciple of Athanasius exulted in the proud confidence, that he had entitled himself to the divine

I do not reckon Philostorgius, though he mentions (l. ix, c. 19) the
expulsion of Damophilus. The Eunomian historian has been carefully
strained through an orthodox sieve.

favour; while the follower of Arius must have
been tormented, by the secret apprehension, that
he was guilty, perhaps of an unpardonable
offence, by the scanty praise, and parsimonious
honours, which he bestowed on the Judge of the
World. The opinions of Arianism might satisfy
a cold and speculative mind; but the doctrine of
the Nicene Creed, most powerfully recommended by the merits of faith and devotion, was
much better adapted to become popular and
successful in a believing age.

The coun-
cil of Con-
stantino-
ple,
A. D. 381,
May.
The hope that truth and wisdom would be
found in the assemblies of the orthodox clergy,
induced the emperor to convene, at Constantinople, a synod of one hundred and fifty bishops,
who proceeded, without much difficulty or delay, to complete the theological system which
had been established in the council of Nice.
The vehement disputes of the fourth century
had been chiefly employed on the nature of the
Son of God; and the various opinions, which
were embraced concerning the *Second*, were extended and transferred, by a natural analogy, to
the *Third*, person of the Trinity.[*] Yet it was
found, or it was thought, necessary, by the victorious adversaries of Arianism, to explain the

---

[*] Le Clerc has given a curious extract (Bibliotheque Universelle,
tom. xviii, p. 91-105) of the theological sermons which Gregory
Nazianzen pronounced at Constantinople against the Arians, Eunomians, Macedonians, &c. He tells the Macedonians, who deified the
Father and the Son, without the Holy Ghost, that they might as
well be styled *Tritheists* as *Ditheists*. Gregory himself was almost a
Tritheist; and his monarchy of heaven resembles a well-regulated
aristocracy.

ambiguous language of some respectable doctors; to confirm the faith of the catholics; and to condemn an unpopular and inconsistent sect of Macedonians; who freely admitted that the Son was consubstantial to the Father, while they were fearful of seeming to acknowledge the existence of *Three* Gods. A final and unanimous sentence was pronounced to ratify the equal Deity of the Holy Ghost; the mysterious doctrine has been received by all the nations, and all the churches, of the Christian world; and their grateful reverence has assigned to the bishops of Theodosius, the second rank among the general councils.' Their knowledge of religious truth may have been preserved by tradition, or it may have been communicated by inspiration; but the sober evidence of history will not allow much weight to the personal authority of the Fathers of Constantinople. In an age, when the ecclesiastics had scandalously degenerated from the model of apostolical purity, the most worthless and corrupt were always the most eager to frequent, and disturb, the episcopal assemblies. The conflict and fermentation of so many opposite interests and tempers inflamed the passions of the bishops: and their ruling passions were, the love of gold, and the love of dispute. Many of the same prelates who now applauded the orthodox piety of Theodosius, had repeatedly changed, with pru-

---

' The first general council of Constantinople now triumphs in the Vatican; but the popes had long hesitated, and their hesitation perplexes, and almost staggers, the humble Tillemont (Mem. Eccles. tom. ix, p 499, 500).

dent flexibility, their creeds and opinions; and in the various revolutions of the church and state, the religion of their sovereign was the rule of their obsequious faith. When the emperor suspended his prevailing influence, the turbulent synod was blindly impelled, by the absurd or selfish motives of pride, hatred, and resentment. The death of Meletius, which happened at the council of Constantinople, presented the most favourable opportunity of terminating the schism of Antioch, by suffering his aged rival, Paulinus, peaceably to end his days in the episcopal chair. The faith and virtues of Paulinus were unblemished. But his cause was supported by the Western churches; and the bishops of the synod resolved to perpetuate the mischiefs of discord, by the hasty ordination of a perjured candidate,[u] rather than to betray the imagined dignity of the East, which had been illustrated by the birth and death of the Son of God. Such unjust and disorderly proceedings forced the gravest members of the assembly to dissent and to secede; and the clamorous majority, which remained masters of the field of battle, could be compared only to wasps or magpies, to a flight of cranes or to a flock of geese.[x]

[u] Before the death of Maletius, six or eight of his most popular ecclesiastics, among whom was Flavian, had *abjured*, for the sake of peace, the bishopric of Antioch, (Sozomen, l. vii, c. 3, 11; Socrates, l. v, c. 5). Tillemont thinks it his duty to disbelieve the story; but he owns that there are many circumstances in the life of Flavian, which *seem* inconsistent with the praises of Chrysostom, and the character of a saint, (Mem. Eccles. tom. x, p. 541).

[x] Consult Gregory Nazianzen, de Vitâ suâ, tom. ii, p 25-28. His general and particular opinion of the clergy and their assemblies may be
seen

A suspicion may possibly arise, that so unfavourable a picture of ecclesiastical synods has
been drawn by the partial hand of some obstinate heretic, or some malicious infidel. But
the name of the sincere historian, who has con-
veyed this instructive lesson to the knowledge
of posterity, must silence the impotent murmurs
of superstition and bigotry. He was one of the
most pious and eloquent bishops of the age ; a
saint and a doctor of the church ; the scourge
of Arianism, and the pillar of the orthodox faith ;
a distinguished member of the council of Constantinople, in which, after the death of Meletius, he exercised the functions of president : in
a word—Gregory Nazianzen himself. The
harsh and ungenerous treatment which he experienced,[y] instead of derogating from the truth
of his evidence, affords an additional proof of
the spirit which actuated the deliberations of
the synod. Their unanimous suffrage had confirmed the pretensions which the bishop of Constantinople derived from the choice of the
people, and the approbation of the emperor.
But Gregory soon became the victim of malice
and envy. The bishops of the East, his strenuous adherents, provoked by his moderation

seen in verse and prose, (tom. i, orat. i, p. 33, epist. iv, p. 814 ; tom.
ii, carmen x, p. 81). Such passages are faintly marked by Tillemont
and fairly produced by Le Clerc.

[y] See Gregory, tom. ii, de Vitâ suâ, p. 28-31. The fourteenth,
twenty-seventh, and thirty-second orations were pronounced in the
several stages of this business. The peroration of the last, (tom. i,
p. 528), in which he takes a solemn leave of men and angels, the city
and the emperor, the East and the West, &c. is pathetic, and almost
sublime.

in the affairs of Antioch, abandoned him, without support, to the adverse faction of the Egyptians; who disputed the validity of his election, and rigorously asserted the obsolete canon, that prohibited the licentious practice of episcopal translations. The pride, or the humility, of Gregory, prompted him to decline a contest which might have been imputed to ambition and avarice; and he publicly offered, not without some mixture of indignation, to renounce the government of a church, which had been restored, and almost created, by his labours. His resignation was accepted by the synod, and by the emperor, with more readiness than he seems to have expected. At the time when he might have hoped to enjoy the fruits of his victory, his episcopal throne was filled by the senator Nectarius; and the new archbishop, accidentally recommended by his easy temper and venerable aspect, was obliged to delay the ceremony of his consecration, till he had previously dispatched the rites of his baptism.* After this remarkable experience of the ingratitude of princes and prelates, Gregory retired once more to his obscure solitude of Cappadocia; where he employed the remainder of his life, about eight years, in the exercises of poetry and devotion. The title of saint has been added to

---

* The whimsical ordination of Nectarius is attested by Sozomen, (l. vii, c. 8); but Tillemont observes, (Mem. Eccles. tom. ix, p. 719), Après tout, ce narré de Sozomene est si honteux pour tous ceux qu'il y mele, et surtout pour Theodose, qu'il vaut mieux travailler à le detruire, qu'à le soutenir; an admirable canon of criticism.

his name; but the tenderness of his heart,[a] and the elegance of his genius, reflect a more pleasing lustre on the memory of Gregory Nazianzen.

It was not enough that Theodosius had suppressed the insolent reign of Arianism, or that he had abundantly revenged the injuries which the catholics sustained from the zeal of Constantius and Valens. The orthodox emperor considered every heretic as a rebel against the supreme powers of heaven, and of earth; and each of those powers might exercise their peculiar jurisdiction over the soul and body of the guilty. The decrees of the council of Constantinople had ascertained the true standard of the faith; and the ecclesiastics, who governed the conscience of Theodosius, suggested the most effectual methods of persecution. In the space of fifteen years, he promulgated at least fifteen severe edicts against the heretics;[b] more especially against those who rejected the doctrine of the Trinity; and to deprive them of every hope of escape, he sternly enacted, that if any laws, or rescripts, should be alleged in their favour, the judges should consider them as the illegal productions either, of fraud, or forgery. The penal statutes were directed against the ministers, the assemblies, and the persons, of the heretics; and the passion of the legislator were expressed

[a] I can only be understood to mean, that such was his natural temper; when it was not hardened, or influenced, by religious zeal. From his retirement, he exhorts Nectarius to prosecute the heretics of Constantinople.

[b] See the Theodosian Code, l. xvi, tit. v, leg. 6-23, with Godefroy's Commentary, on each law, and his general summary, on *Paratitlon,* tom vi, p. 104-110

in the language of declamation and invective.
I. The heretical teachers, who usurped the sacred titles of Bishops, or Presbyters, were not
only excluded from the privileges and emoluments so liberally granted to the orthodox clergy, but they were exposed to the heavy penalties of exile and confiscation, if they presumed
to preach the doctrine, or to practise the rites,
of their *accursed* sects. A fine of ten pounds of
gold (above four hundred pounds sterling) was
imposed on every person who should dare to
confer, or receive, or promote, an heretical ordination: and it was reasonably expected, that if
the race of pastors could be extinguished, their
helpless flocks would be compelled, by ignorance and hunger, to return within the pale of the
catholic church. II. The rigorous prohibition
of conventicles was carefully extended to every
possible circumstance, in which the heretics
could assemble with the intention of worship-
ping God and Christ according to the dictates
of their conscience. Their religious meetings,
whether public or secret, by day, or by night, in
cities or in the country, were equally prescribed
by the edicts of Theodosius; and the building
or ground, which had been used for that illegal
purpose, was forfeited to the imperial domain.
III. It was supposed, that the error of the heretics could proceed only from the obstinate temper of their minds; and that such a temper was
a fit object of censure and punishment. The ana-
themas of the church were fortified by a sort of
civil excommunication; which separated them
from their fellow-citizens, by a peculiar brand of

infamy; and this declaration of the supreme magistrate tended to justify, or at least to excuse,
the insults of a fanatic populace. The sectaries
were gradually disqualified for the possession
of honourable, or lucrative, employments; and
Theodosius was satisfied with his own justice,
when he decreed, that as the Eunomians distinguished the nature of the son from that of the
father, they should be incapable of making their
wills, or of receiving any advantage from testa-
mentary donations. The guilt of the Manichæan heresy was esteemed of such magnitude,
that it could be expiated only by the death
of the offender; and the same capital punishment was inflicted on the Audians, or *Quarto-
decimans*,[c] who should dare to perpetrate the
atrocious crime, of celebrating, on an improper
day, the festival of Easter. Every Roman might
exercise the right of public accusation; but the
office of *Inquisitors* of the Faith, a name so deservedly abhorred, was first instituted under
the reign of Theodosius. Yet we are assured
that the execution of his penal edicts was seldom enforced; and that the pious emperor appeared less desirous to punish, than to reclaim,
or terrify, his refractory subjects.[d]

The theory of persecution was established by
Theodosius, whose justice and piety have been
applauded by the saints; but the practice of it,

[c] They always kept their Easter, like the Jewish Passover, on the
fourteenth day of the first moon after the vernal equinox; and thus per-
tinaciously opposed the Roman church and Nicene synod, which had
fixed Easter to a Sunday. Bingham's Antiquities, l. xx, c, 5, vol. ii,
p. 309, fol. edit.

[d] Sozomen, l. vii, c. 12.

in the fullest extent, was reserved for his rival and colleague, Maximus, the first among the Christian princes, who shed the blood of his Christian subjects, on account of their religious opinions. The cause of the Priscillianists,[e] a recent sect of heretics, who disturbed the provinces of Spain, was transferred, by appeal, from the synod of Bourdeaux to the imperial consistory of Treves; and by the sentence of the pretorian prefect, seven persons were tortured, condemned, and executed. The first of these was Priscillian[f] himself, bishop of Avila,[g] in Spain; who adorned the advantages of birth and fortune, by the accomplishments of eloquence and learning. Two presbyters, and two deacons, accompanied their beloved master in his death, which they esteemed as a glorious martyrdom; and the number of religious victims was completed by the execution of Latronian, a poet, who rivalled the fame of the ancients; and of Euchrocia, a noble matron of Bourdeaux, the widow of the orator Delphi-

---

[e] See the Sacred History of Sulpicius Severus, (l. ii, p. 437-452, edit. Lugd. Bat. 1647), a correct and original writer. Dr. Lardner (Credibility, &c. part ii, vol. ix, p. 256-350) has laboured this article, with pure learning, good sense, and moderation. Tillemont, (Mem. Eccles. tom. viii, p. 491-527) has raked together all the dirt of the fathers : an useful scavenger !

[f] Severus Sulpicius mentions the arch-heretic with esteem and pity. Fœlix profecto, si non pravo studio corrumpisset optimum ingenium : prorsus multa in eo animi et corporis bona cerneres, (Hist, Sacra. l. ii, p. 439). Even Jerom (tom. i, in Script. Eccles. p. 302) speaks with temper of Priscillian and Latronian.

[g] The bishopric (in old Castile) is now worth 20,000 ducats a year. (Busching's Geography, vol. ii, p. 308); and is, therefore, much less likely to produce the author of a new heresy.

dius.[h] Two bishops, who had embraced the sentiments of Priscillian, were condemned to a distant and dreary exile;[i] and some indulgence was shewn to the meaner criminals, who assumed the merit of an early repentance. If any credit could be allowed to confessions extorted by fear or pain, and to vague reports, the offspring of malice and credulity, the heresy of the Priscillianists would be found to include the various abominations of magic, of impiety, and of lewdness.[k] Priscillian, who wandered about the world in the company of his spiritual sisters, was accused of praying stark-naked in the midst of the congregation; and it was confidently asserted, that the effects of his criminal intercourse with the daughter of Euchrocia, had been suppressed, by means still more odious and criminal. But an accurate, or rather a candid, inquiry, will discover, that if the Priscillianists violated the laws of nature, it was not by the licentiousness, but by the austerity, of their lives. They absolutely condemned the use of the marriage-bed; and the peace of families was often disturbed by indiscreet separations. They enjoined, or recommended, a total abstinence

---

[h] Exprobabatur mulieri viduæ nimia religio, et diligentius cula divinitas, (Pacat. in Panegyr. Vet. xii, 29). Such was the idea of a human, though ignorant, Polytheist.

[i] One of them was sent in Syllinam insulam quæ ultra Britanniam est. What must have been the ancient condition of the rocks of Sicily? (Camden's Britannia, vol. ii, p. 1519).

[k] The scandalous calumnies of Augustin, Pope Leo, &c. which Tillemont swallows like a child, and Lardner refutes like a man, may suggest some candid suspicions in favour of the older Gnostics.

CHAP.
XXVII.

from all animal food ; and their continual prayers, fasts, and vigils, inculcated a rule of strict
and perfect devotion. The speculative tenets
of the sect, concerning the person of Christ, and
the nature of the human soul, were derived from
the Gnostic and Manichæan system ; and this
vain philosophy, which had been transported
from Egypt to Spain, was ill adapted to the
grosser spirits of the West. The obscure dis-
ciples of Priscillian suffered, languished, and
gradually disappeared : his tenets were rejected by the clergy and people ; but his death wa
the subject of a long and vehement controver
sy ; while some arraigned, and others applauded, the justice of his sentence. It is with pleasure that we can observe the humane inconsis-
tency of the most illustrious saints and bishops,
Ambrose of Milan,[1] and Martin of Tours ;[m] who,
on this occasion, asserted the cause of toleration. They pitied the unhappy man, who had
been executed at Treves ; they refused to hold
communication with their episcopal murderers ;
and if Martin deviated from that generous resolution, his motives were laudable, and his
repentance was exemplary. The bishops of
Tours and Milan pronounced, without hesitation, the eternal damnation of heretics ; but
they were surprised, and shocked, by the bloody
image of their temporal death, and the honest

[1] Ambros. tom. ii, epist. xxiv, p. 891.
[m] In the sacred History, and the life of St. Martin, Sulpicius Severus
uses some caution ; but he declares himself more freely in the Dialogues, (iii, 15). Martin was reproved, however, by his own conscience,
and by an angel ; nor could he afterwards perform miracles with so
much ease.

feelings of nature resisted the artificial prejudices of theology. The humanity of Ambrose
and Martin was confirmed by the scandalous
irregularity of the proceedings against Priscillian, and his adherents. The civil and ecclesiastical ministers had transgressed the limits
of their respective provinces. The secular
judge had presumed to receive an appeal, and
to pronounce a definitive sentence, in a matter
of faith and episcopal jurisdiction. The bishops
had disgraced themselves, by exercising the
function of accusers in a criminal prosecution.
The cruelty of Ithacius,[*] who beheld the tortures, and solicited the death, of the heretics,
provoked the just indignation of mankind ; and
the vices of that profligate bishop were admitted
as a proof, that his zeal was instigated by the
sordid motives of interest. Since the death of
Priscillian, the rude attempts of persecution
have been refined and methodised in the holy
office, which assigns their distinct parts to the
ecclesiastical and secular powers. The devoted
victim is regularly delivered by the priest to
the magistrate, and by the magistrate to the
executioner : and the inexorable sentence of the
church, which declares the spiritual guilt of the
offender, is expressed in the mild language of
pity and intercession.

Among the ecclesiastics, who illustrated the
reign of Theodosius, Gregory Nazianzen was
distinguished by the talents of an eloquent

[*] The catholic presbyter, (Sulp. Sever. l. ii, p. 448), and the pagan
orator, (Pacat. in Panegyr. Vet. xii, 29), reprobate with equal indignation, the character and conduct of Ithacius.

preacher; the reputation of miraculous gifts added weight and dignity to the monastic virtues of Martin of Tours;[o] but the palm of episcopal vigour and ability was justly claimed by the intrepid Ambrose.[p] He was descended from a noble family of Romans; his father had exercised the important office of pretorian prefect of Gaul; and the son, after passing through the studies of a liberal education, attained, in the regular gradation of civil honours, the station of consular of Liguria, a province which included the imperial residence of Milan. At the age of thirty-four, and before he had received the sacrament of baptism, Ambrose, to his own surprise, and to that of the world, was suddenly transformed from a governor to an archbishop Without the least mixture, as it is said, of art or intrigue, the whole body of the people unanimously saluted him with the episcopal title; the concord and perseverance of their acclamations were ascribed to a preternatural impulse; and the reluctant magistrate was compelled to undertake a spiritual office, for which he was not prepared by the habits and occupations of his former life. But the active force of his genius

---

[o] The life of St. Martin, and the Dialogues concerning his miracles, contain facts adapted to the grossest barbarism, in a style not unworthy of the Augustan age. So natural is the alliance between good taste and good sense, that I am always astonished by this contrast.

[p] The short and superficial life of St. Ambrose, by his deacon Paulinus, (Appendix ad edict. Benedict. p. i-xv), has the merit of original evidence. Tillemont, (Mem. Eccles. tom. x, p. 78-306), and the Benedictine editors, (p. xxxi-lxiii), have laboured with their usual diligence.

soon qualified him to exercise, with zeal and prudence, the duties of his ecclesiastical jurisdiction; and, while he cheerfully renounced the vain and splendid trappings of temporal greatness, he condescended, for the good of the church, to direct the conscience of the emperors, and to controul the administration of the empire. Gratian loved and revered him as a father; and the elaborate treatise on the faith of the Trinity, was designed for the instruction of the young prince. After his tragic death, at a time when the empress Justina trembled for her own safety, and for that of her son Valentinian, the archbishop of Milan was despatched, on two different embassies, to the court of Treves. He exercised, with equal firmness and dexterity, the powers of his spiritual and political characters; and perhaps contributed, by his authority and eloquence, to check the ambition of Maximus, and to protect the peace of Italy.[q] Ambrose had devoted his life, and his abilities, to the service of the church. Wealth was the object of his contempt; he had renounced his private patrimony; and he sold, without hesitation, the consecrated plate, for the redemption of captives. The clergy and people of Milan were attached to their archbishop; and he deserved the esteem, without soliciting the favour, or apprehending the displeasure, of his feeble sovereigns.

The government of Italy, and of the young emperor, naturally devolved to his mother Justina,

[q] Ambrose himself (tom. ii, epist. xxiv, p. 888-891) gives the emperor a very spirited account of his own embassy.

CHAP.
XXVII.
~~~~~~~~~
His suc-
cessful op-
position
to the em-
press Jus-
tina,
A. D. 385,
April 3-10
a woman of beauty and spirit, but who, in the midst of an orthodox people, had the misfortune of professing the Arian heresy, which she endeavoured to instil into the mind of her son. Justina was persuaded, that a Roman emperor might claim, in his own dominions, the public exercise of his religion; and she proposed to the archbishop, as a moderate and reasonable concession, that he should resign the use of a single church, either in the city or suburbs of Milan. But the conduct of Ambrose was governed by very different principles.[r] The palaces of the earth might indeed belong to Cæsar; but the churches were the houses of God; and, within the limits of his diocese, he himself, as the lawful successor of the apostles, was the only minister of God. The privileges of Christianity, temporal as well as spiritual, were confined to the true believers; and the mind of Ambrose was satisfied, that his own theological opinions were the standard of truth and orthodoxy. The archbishop, who refused to hold any conference, or negotiation, with the instruments of Satan, declared, with modest firmness, his resolution to die a martyr, rather than to yield to the impious sacrilege; and Justina, who resented the refusal as an act of insolence and rebellion, hastily determined to exert the imperial prerogative of her son. As she desired to perform her public

---

[r] His own representation of his principles and conduct, (tom. ii, epist. xx, xxi, xxii, p. 852-880), is one of the curious monuments of ecclesiastical antiquity. It contains two letters to his sister Marcellina, with a petition to Valentinian, and the sermon *de Basilicis non tradendis.*

devotions on the approaching festival of Easter, Ambrose was ordered to appear before the council. He obeyed the summons with the respect of a faithful subject; but he was followed, without his consent, by an innumerable people: they pressed, with impetuous zeal, against the gates of the palace; and the affrighted ministers of Valentinian, instead of pronouncing a sentence of exile on the archbishop of Milan, humbly requested that he would interpose his authority, to protect the person of the emperor, and to restore the tranquillity of the capital. But the promises which Ambrose received and communicated, were soon violated by a perfidious court; and, during six of the most solemn days, which Christian piety has set apart for the exercise of religion, the city was agitated by the irregular convulsions of tumult and fanaticism. The officers of the household were directed to prepare, first, the Portian, and afterwards, the new, *Basilica*, for the immediate reception of the emperor, and his mother. The splendid canopy and hangings of the royal seat were arranged in the customary manner; but it was found necessary to defend them, by a strong guard, from the insults of the populace. The Arian ecclesiastics, who ventured to shew themselves in the streets, were exposed to the most imminent danger of their lives; and Ambrose enjoyed the merit and reputation of rescuing his personal enemies from the hands of the enraged multitude.

But while he laboured to restrain the effects of their zeal, the pathetic vehemence of his ser-

mons continually inflamed the angry and seditious temper of the people of Milan.   The characters of Eve, of the wife of Job, of Jezebel, of
Herodias, were indecently applied to the mother of the emperor; and her desire to obtain a
church for the Arians, was compared to the
most cruel persecutions which Christianity had
endured under the reign of paganism.   The
measures of the court served only to expose the
magnitude of the evil.   A fine of two hundred
pounds of gold was imposed on the corporate
body of merchants and manufacturers: an order was signified, in the name of the emperor,
to all the officers, and inferior servants, of the
courts of justice, that, during the continuance
of the public disorders, they should strictly
confine themselves to their houses: and the
ministers of Valentinian imprudently confessed,
that the most respectable part of the citizens of
Milan was attached to the cause of their archbishop. He was again solicited to restore peace
to his country, by a timely compliance with the
will of his sovereign.   The reply of Ambrose
was couched in the most humble and respectful terms, which might, however, be interpreted
as a serious declaration of civil war.   " His
" life and fortune were in the hands of the em-
" peror; but he would never betray the church
" of Christ, or degrade the dignity of the epi-
" scopal character.   In such a cause, he was
" prepared to suffer whatever the malice of the
" demon could inflict; and he only wished to
" die in the presence of his faithful flock, and
" at the foot of the altar: *he* had not contribut-

" ed to excite, but it was in the power of God
" alone to appease the rage of the people : he
" deprecated the scenes of blood and confusion,
" which were likely to ensue ; and it was his
" fervent prayer, that he might not survive to
" behold the ruin of a flourishing city, and per-
" haps the desolation of all Italy."[*] The obstinate bigotry of Justina would have endanger-
ed the empire of her son, if, in this contest with
the church and people of Milan, she could have
depended on the active obedience of the troops
of the palace. A large body of Goths had
marched to occupy the *Basilica*, which was the
object of the dispute: and it might be expected
from the Arian principles, and barbarous manners, of these foreign mercenaries, that they
would not entertain any scruples in the execution of the most sanguinary orders. They were
encountered, on the sacred threshold, by the
archbishop, who, thundering against them a
sentence of excommunication, asked them, in
the tone of a father and a master, Whether it
was to invade the house of God, that they had
implored the hospitable protection of the republic ? The suspense of the barbarians allowed
some hours for a more effectual negotiation ;
and the empress was persuaded, by the advice
of her wisest counsellors, to leave the catholics
in possession of all the churches of Milan ; and
to dissemble, till a more convenient season, her

[*] Retz had a similar message from the queen, to request that he would appease the tumult of Paris. It was no longer in his power, &c. A quoi j'ajoutai tout ce que vous pouvez vous imaginer de respect, de douleur, de regret, et de soumission, &c. (Memoires, tom. i, p. 140). Certain-ly I do not compare either the causes, or the men ; yet the coadjutor himself had some idea (p. 84) of imitating St. Ambrose.

intentions of revenge. The mother of Valentinian could never forgive the triumph of Ambrose; and the royal youth uttered a passionate exclamation, that his own servants were ready to betray him into the hands of an insolent priest.

The laws of the empire, some of which were inscribed with the name of Valentinian, still condemned the Arian heresy, and seems to excuse the resistance of the catholics. By the influence of Justin, an edict of toleration was promulgated in all the provinces which were subject to the court of Milan; the free exercise of their religion was granted to those who professed the faith of Rimini; and the emperor declared, that all persons who should infringe this sacred and salutary constitution, should be capitally punished, as the enemies of the public peace.[t] The character and language of the archbishop of Milan may justify the suspicion, that his conduct soon afforded a reasonable ground, or at least a specious pretence, to the Arian ministers, who watched the opportunity of surprising him in some act of disobedience to a law, which he strangely represents as a law of blood and tyranny. A sentence of easy and honourable banishment was pronounced, which enjoined Ambrose to depart from Milan without delay; whilst it permitted him to choose the place of his exile, and the number of his companions. But the authority of the saints, who have preached and practised the maxims of passive loyalty,

A.D. 386.

---

[t] Sozomen alone (l. vii. c. 13) throws this luminous fact into a dark and perplexed narrative.

appeared to Ambrose of less moment than the extreme and pressing danger of the church. He boldly refused to obey; and his refusal was supported by the unanimous consent of his faithful people." They guarded by turns the person of their archbishop; the gates of the cathedral and the episcopal palace were strongly secured; and the imperial troops, who had formed the blockade, were unwilling to risk the attack, of that impregnable fortress. The numerous poor, who had been relieved by the liberality of Ambrose, embraced the fair occasion of signalizing their zeal and gratitude; and as the patience of the multitude might have been exhausted by the length and uniformity of nocturnal vigils, he rudently introduced into the church of Milan the useful institution of a loud and regular psalmody. While he maintained this arduous contest, he was instructed, by a dream, to open the earth in a place where the remains of two martyrs, Gervasius and Protasius,[x] had been deposited above three hundred years. Immediately under the pavement of the church two perfect skeletons were found,[y] with the heads separated from their bodies, and a plentiful ef-

---

" Excubabat pia plebs in ecclesiâ mori parata cum episcopo suo... Nos adhuc frigidi excitabamur tamen civitate attonitâ atque turbatâ Augustin. Confession. l. ix, c. 7.

[x] Tillemont, Mem. Eccles. tom. ii, p. 78, 498. Many churches in Italy, Gaul, &c. were dedicated to these unknown martyrs, of whom St. Gervase seems to have been more fortunate than his companion.

[y] Invenimus miræ magnitudinis viros duos, ut prisca ætas ferebat, tom. ii, epist. xxii, p. 875. The size of these skeletons was fortunately, or skilfully, suited to the popular prejudice of the gradual decrease

of

fusion of blood. The holy relics were presented, in solemn pomp, to the veneration of the people; and every circumstance of this fortunate
discovery was admirably adapted to promote
the designs of Ambrose. The bones of the martyrs, their blood, their garments, were supposed
to contain a healing power; and their preternatural influence was communicated to the most
distant objects, without losing any part of it
original virtue. The extraordinary cure of a
blind man, and the reluctant confessions of several demoniacs, appeared to justify the faith
and sanctity of Ambrose; and the truth of those
miracles is attested by Ambrose himself, by his
secretary Paulinus, and by his proselyte, the celebrated Augustin, who, at that time, professed
the art of rhetoric, in Milan. The reason of the
present age may possibly approve the incredu-
lity of Justina and her Arian court; who derid-
ed the theatrical representations, which were
exhibited by the contrivance, and at the expence,
of the archbishop. Their effect, however, on
the minds of the people was rapid and irresistible; and the feeble sovereign of Italy found
himself unable to contend with the favourite of

of the human stature; which has prevailed in every age since the time
of Homer.

Grandiaque effossis mirabitur ossa sepulchris.

Ambros. tom. ii, epist. xxii, p. 875. Augustin. Confes. l. ix, c. 7.
Dei Civitat. Dei, l. xxii, c. 8. Paulin. in Vitâ St. Ambros. c. 14, in
Append. Benedict. p. 4. The blind man's name was Severus; he
touched the holy garment, recovered his sight, and devoted the rest of
his life (at least twenty-five years) to the service of the church. I should
recommend this miracle to our divines, if it did not prove the worship
of relics, as well as the Nicene creed.

Paulin. in Vit. St. Ambros. c. 5, in Append. Benedict. p. 5.

heaven. The powers likewise of the earth interposed in the defence of Ambrose; the disinterested advice of Theodosius was the genuine result of pity and friendship; and the mask of religious zeal concealed the hostile and ambitious designs of the tyrant of Gaul.[h]

The reign of Maximus might have ended in peace and prosperity, could he have contented himself with the possession of three ample countries, which now constitute the three most flourishing kingdoms of modern Europe. But the aspiring usurper, whose sordid ambition was not dignified by the love of glory and of arms, considered his actual forces as the instruments only of his future greatness, and his success was the immediate cause of his destruction. The wealth which he extorted[c] from the oppressed provinces of Gaul, Spain, and Britain, was employed in levying and maintaining a formidable army of barbarians, collected, for the most part, from the fiercest nations of Germany. The conquest of Italy was the object of his hopes and preparations; and he secretly meditated the ruin of an innocent youth, whose government was abhorred and despised by his catholic subjects. But as Maximus wished to occupy, without resistance, the passes of the Alps, he received, with perfidious smiles, Domninus of

Maximus
invades
Italy,
A. D. 387,
August.

[h] Tillemont, Mem. Eccles. tom. x, p. 190, 750. He partially allows the mediation of Theodosius; and capriciously rejects that of Maximus, though it is attested by Prosper, Sozomen, and Theodoret.

[c] The modest censure of Sulpicius (Dialog. iii, 15) inflicts a much deeper wound than the feeble declamation of Pacatus, (xii, 25, 36).

CHAP.
XXVII.

Syria, the ambassador of Valentinian, and pres
sed him to accept the aid of a considerable body
of troops for the service of a Pannonian war.
The penetration of Ambrose had discovered
the snares of an enemy under the professions of
friendship;[4] but the Syrian Domninus was corrupted, or deceived, by the liberal favour of the
court of Treves; and the council of Milan obstinately rejected the suspicion of danger, with
a blind confidence, which was the effect, not of
courage, but of fear. The march of the auxiliaries was guided by the ambassador; and they
were admitted, without distrust, into the fortresses of the Alps. But the crafty tyrant followed, with hasty and silent footsteps, in the
rear; and, as he diligently intercepted all intelligence of his motions, the gleam of armour,
and the dust excited by the troops of cavalry, first announced the hostile approach of a
stranger to the gates of Milan. In this extremity, Justina and her son might accuse their own
imprudence, and the perfidious arts of Maximus; but they wanted time, and force, and resolution, to stand against the Gauls and Germans, either in the field, or within the walls of a
large and disaffected city. Flight was their
only hope, Aquileia their only refuge; and
as Maximus now displayed his genuine character, the brother of Gratian might expect the
same fate from the hands of the same assassin.

---

[4] Est tutior adversus hominem, pacis involucro tegentem, was the
wise caution of Ambrose, (tom. ii, p. 891), after his return from his
second embassy.

Maximus entered Milan in triumph; and if the wise archbishop refused a dangerous and criminal connection with the usurper, he might indirectly contribute to the success of his arms, by inculcating, from the pulpit, the duty of resignation, rather than that of resistance.[*] The unfortunate Justina reached Aquileia in safety; but she distrusted the strength of the fortifications; she dreaded the event of a siege; and she resolved to implore the protection of the great Theodosius, whose power and virtue were celebrated in all the countries of the West. A vessel was secretly provided to transport the imperial family; they embarked with precipitation in one of the obscure harbours of Venetia, or Istria; traversed the whole extent of the Hadriatic and Ionian seas; turned the extreme promontory of Peloponnesus; and, after a long, but successful, navigation, reposed themselves in the port of Thessalonica. All the subjects of Valentinian deserted the cause of a prince, who, by his abdication, had absolved them from the duty of allegiance; and if the little city of Æmona, on the verge of Italy, had not presumed to stop the career of his inglorious victory, Maximus would have obtained, without a struggle, the sole possession of the western empire.

Flight of Valentinian.

Instead of inviting his royal guests to the palace of Constantinople, Theodosius had some unknown reasons to fix their residence at Thessa-

* Baronius (A. D. 387, No. 63) applies to this season of public distress some of the penitential sermons of the archbishop.

VOL. V. E

CHAP.
XXVII.

Theodosi-
us takes
arms in
the cause
of Valen-
tinian,
A. D. 387.

lonica; but these reasons did not proceed from contempt or indifference, as he speedily made a visit to that city, accompanied by the greatest part of his court and senate. After the first tender expressions of friendship and sympathy, the pious emperor of the East gently admonished Justina, that the guilt of heresy was sometimes punished in this world, as well as in the next; and that the public profession of the Nicene faith would be the most efficacious step to promote the restoration of her son, by the satisfaction which it must occasion both on earth and in heaven. The momentous question of peace or war was referred, by Theodosius, to the deliberation of his council; and the arguments which might be alledged on the side o. honour and justice, had acquired, since the death of Gratian, a considerable degree of additional weight. The persecution of the imperial family, to which Theodosius himself had been indebted for his fortune, was now aggravated by recent and repeated injuries. Neither oaths nor treaties could restrain the boundless ambition of Maximus; and the delay of vigorous and decisive measures, instead of prolonging the blessings of peace, would expose the eastern empire to the danger of an hostile invasion. The barbarians, who had passed the Danube, had lately assumed the character of soldiers and subjects, but their native fierceness was yet untamed; and the operations of a war, which would exercise their valour, and diminish their numbers, might tend to relieve the provinces from an intolerable oppression. Notwithstanding these specious and solid reasons, which were approved by a majority of the council, Theodosius still hesitated, whether he should draw the sword in a contest, which could no longer admit any terms of reconciliation; and his magnanimous character was not disgraced by the apprehensions which he felt for the safety of his infant sons, and the welfare of his exhausted people. In this moment of anxious doubt, while the fate of the Roman world depended on the resolution of a single man, the charms of the princess Galla most powerfully pleaded the cause of her brother Valentinian.[f] The heart of Theodosius was softened by the tears of beauty; his affections were insensibly engaged by the graces of youth and innocence; the art of Justina managed and directed the impulse of passion; and the celebration of the royal nuptials was the assurance and signal of the civil war. The unfeeling critics, who consider every amorous weakness as an indelible stain on the memory of a great and orthodox emperor, are inclined, on this occasion, to dispute the suspicious evidence of the historian Zosimus. For my own part, I shall frankly confess, that I am willing to find, or even to seek, in the revolutions of the world, some traces of the mild and tender sentiments of domestic life; and,

[f] The flight of Valentinian, and the love of Theodosius for his sister, are related by Zosimus (l. iv, p. 263, 264). Tillemont produces some weak and ambiguous evidence to antedate the second marriage of Theodosius, (Hist. des Empereurs, tom. v, p. 740), and consequently to refute ces contes de Zosime, qui seroient trop contraires à la piété de Theodose.

amidst the crowd of fierce and ambitious conquerors, I can distinguish, with peculiar complacency, a gentle hero, who may be supposed to receive his armour from the hands of love. The alliance of the Persian king was secured by the faith of treaties; the martial barbarians were persuaded to follow the standard, or to respect the frontiers, of an active and liberal monarch; and the dominions of Theodosius, from the Euphrates to the Hadriatic, resounded with the preparations of war both by land and sea. The skilful disposition of the forces of the East seemed to multiply their numbers, and distracted the attention of Maximus. He had reason to fear, that a chosen body of troops, under the command of the intrepid Arbogastes, would direct their march along the banks of the Danube, and boldly penetrate through the Rhætian provinces into the centre of Gaul. A powerful fleet was equipped in the harbours of Greece and Epirus, with an apparent design, that as soon as a passage had been opened by a naval victory, Valentinian, and his mother, should land in Italy, proceed, without delay, to Rome, and occupy the majestic seat of religion and empire. In the meanwhile, Theodosius himself advanced at the head of a brave and disciplined army, to encounter his unworthy rival, who, after the siege of Æmona, had fixed his camp in the neighbourhood of Siscia, a city of Pannonia, strongly fortified by the broad and rapid stream of the Save.

The veterans, who still remembered the long resistance, and successive resources, of the tyrant Magnentius, might prepare themselves for the la-

bours of three bloody campaigns. But the contest with his successor, who, like him, had
usurped the throne of the West, was easily decided in the term of two months,[s] and within the
space of two hundred miles. The superior genius of the emperor of the East might prevail
over the feeble Maximus; who, in this important
crisis, shewed himself destitute of military skill,
or personal courage; but the abilities of Theodosius were seconded by the advantage which
he possessed of a numerous and active cavalry.
The Huns, Alani, and, after their example, the
Goths themselves, were formed into squadrons
of archers; who fought on horseback, and confounded the steady valour of the Gauls and Germans, by the rapid motions of a Tartar war.
After the fatigue of a long march, in the heat of
summer, they spurred their foaming horses into
the waters of the Save, swam the river in the
presence of the enemy, and instantly charged
and routed the troops who guarded the high
ground on the opposite side. Marcellinus, the
tyrant's brother, advanced to support them with
the select cohorts, which were considered as the
hope and strength of the army. The action,
which had been interrupted by the approach of
night, was renewed in the morning; and after
a sharp conflict, the surviving remnant of the
bravest soldiers of Maximus threw down their
arms at the feet of the conqueror. Without suspending his march, to receive the loyal acclamations of the citizens of Æmona, Theodosius

[s] See Godefroy's Chronology of the Laws, Cod. Theodos. tom. i, p. 119.

CHAP.
XXVII.

pressed forwards, to terminate the war by the death or captivity of his rival, who fled before him with the diligence of fear. From the summit of the Julian Alps, he descended with such incredible speed into the plain of Italy, that he reached Aquileia on the evening of the first day; and Maximus, who found himself encompassed on all sides, had scarcely time to shut the gates of the city. But the gates could not long resist the effort of a victorious enemy; and the despair, the disaffection, the indifference of the soldiers and people, hastened the downfal of the wretched Maximus. He was dragged from his throne, rudely stripped of the imperial ornaments, the robe, the diadem, and the purple slippers; and conducted, like a malefactor, to the camp and presence of Theodosius, at a place about three miles from Aquileia. The behaviour of the emperor was not intended to insult, and he shewed some disposition to pity and forgive, the tyrant of the West, who had never been his personal enemy, and was now become the object of his contempt. Our sympathy is the most forcibly excited by the misfortunes to which we are exposed; and the spectacle of a proud competitor, now prostrate at his feet, could not fail of producing very serious and solemn thoughts in the mind of the victorious emperor. But the feeble emotion of involuntary pity was checked by his regard for public justice, and the memory of Gratian; and he abandoned the victim to the pious zeal of the soldiers, who drew him out of the imperial presence, and instantly separated his head from his body. The intelligence of his defeat and death was received with sincere, or well-dissembled, joy : his son Victor, on whom he had conferred the title of Augustus, died by the order, perhaps by the hand, of the bold Arbogastes ; and all the military plans of Theodosius were successfully executed. When he had thus terminated the civil war, with less difficulty and bloodshed than he might naturally expect, he employed the winter months of his residence at Milan, to restore the state of the afflicted provinces ; and early in the spring he made, after the example of Constantine and Constantius, his triumphal entry into the ancient capital of the Roman empire.[h]

The orator, who may be silent without danger, may praise without difficulty, and without reluctance ;[i] and posterity will confess, that the character of Theodosius[k] might furnish the subject of a sincere and ample panegyric. The wisdom of his laws, and the success of his arms,

Virtues of Theodosius.

[h] Besides the hints which may be gathered from chronicles and ecclesiastical history, Zosimus, (l. iv, p. 259-267), Orosius, (l. vii, c. 35), and Pacatus (in Panegyr. Vet. xii, 30-47), supply the loose and scanty materials of this civil war. Ambrose (tom. ii, epist. xl, p. 952, 953), darkly alludes to the well-known events of a magazine surprised, an action at Petovio, a Sicilian, perhaps a naval, victory, &c. Ausonius (p. 256, edit. Toll.) applauds the peculiar merit, and good fortune, of Aquileia.

[i] Quam promptum laudare principem, tam tutum siluisse de principe, (Pacat. in Panegyr. Vet. xii, 2). Latinus Pacatus Drepanius, a native of Gaul, pronounced this oration at Rome, (A. D. 388). He was afterwards proconsul of Africa ; and his friend Ausonius praises him as a poet, second only to Virgil. See Tillemont, Hist. des Empereurs, tom. v, p. 303.

[k] See the fair portrait of Theodosius, by the younger Victor ; the strokes are distinct, and the colours are mixed. The praise of Pacatus is too vague ; and Claudian always seems afraid of exalting the father above the son

rendered his administration respectable in the eyes both of his subjects, and of his enemies. He loved and practised the virtues of domestic life, which seldom hold their residence in the palaces of kings. Theodosius was chaste and temperate; he enjoyed, without excess, the sensual and social pleasures of the table; and the warmth of his amorous passions was never diverted from their lawful objects. The proud titles of imperial greatness were adorned by the tender names of a faithful husband, an indulgent father; his uncle was raised, by his affectionate esteem, to the rank of a second parent: Theodosius embraced, as his own, the children of his brother and sister; and the expressions of his regard were extended to the most distant and obscure branches of his numerous kindred. His familiar friends were judiciously selected from among those persons, who, in the equal intercourse of private life, had appeared before his eyes without a mask: the consciousness of personal and superior merit enabled him to despise the accidental distinction of the purple; and he proved by his conduct, that he had forgotten all the injuries, while he most gratefully remembered all the favours and services, which he had received before he ascended the throne of the Roman empire. The serious, or lively, tone of his conversation, was adapted to the age, the rank, or the character, of his subjects whom he admitted into his society; and the affability of his manners displayed the image of his mind. Theodosius respected the simplicity of the good and virtuous; every art, every talent, of an useful, or even of an innocent, nature, was rewarded by his judicious liberality; and, except the heretics, whom he persecuted with implacable hatred, the diffusive circle of his benevolence was circumscribed only by the limits of the human race. The government of a mighty empire may assuredly suffice to occupy the time, and the abilities, of a mortal: yet the diligent prince, without aspiring to the unsuitable reputation of profound learning, always reserved some moments of his leisure for the instructive amusement of reading. History, which enlarged his experience, was his favourite study. The annals of Rome, in the long period of eleven hundred years, presented him with a various and splendid picture of human life; and it has been particularly observed, that whenever he perused the cruel acts of Cinna, of Marius, or of Sylla, he warmly expressed his generous detestation of those enemies of humanity and freedom. His disinterested opinion of past events was usefully applied as the rule of his own actions; and Theodosius has deserved the singular commendation, that his virtues always seemed to expand with his fortune: the season of his prosperity was that of his moderation; and his clemency appeared the most conspicuous after the danger and success of the civil war. The Moorish guards of the tyrant had been massacred in the first heat of the victory; and a small number of the most obnoxious criminals suffered the punishment of the law. But the emperor shewed himself much more attentive to relieve the innocent, than to chastise the guilty. The oppressed subjects of the West, who would have deemed themselves happy in the restoration of their lands, were astonished to receive a sum of money equivalent to their losses; and the liberality of the conqueror supported the aged mother, and educated the orphan daughters, of Maximus.[l] A character thus accomplished, might almost excuse the extravagant supposition of the orator Pacatus; that, if the elder Brutus could be permitted to revisit the earth, the stern republican would abjure, at the feet of Theodosius, his hatred of kings; and ingenuously confess, that such a monarch was the most faithful guardian of the happiness and dignity of the Roman people.[m]

Faults of Theodosius.

Yet the piercing eye of the founder of the republic must have discerned two essential imperfections, which might, perhaps, have abated his recent love of despotism. The virtuous mind of Theodosius was often relaxed by indolence,[n] and it was sometimes inflamed by passion.[o] In the pursuit of an important object, his active cou-

[l] Ambros. tom. ii, epist. xl, p. 955. Pacatus, from the want of skill, or of courage, omits this glorious circumstance.

[m] Pacat. in Panegyr. Vet. xii, 20.

[n] Zosimus, l. iv, p. 271, 272. His partial evidence is marked by an air of candour and truth. He observes these vicissitudes of sloth and activity, not as a vice, but as a singularity, in the character of Theodosius.

[o] This choleric temper is acknowledged, and excused, by Victor. Sed habes (says Ambrose, in decent and manly language, to his sovereign) naturæ impetum, quem si quis lenire velit, cito vertes ad misericordiam: si quis stimulet, in magis exsuscitas, ut eum revocare vix possis, (tom. ii, epist. li, p. 998). Theodosius (Claud. in iv. Cons. Hon. 266, &c.) exhorts his son to moderate his anger.

rage was capable of the most vigorous exertions;
but as soon as the design was accomplished, or
the danger was surmounted, the hero sunk into
inglorious repose; and, forgetful that the time of
a prince is the property of his people, resigned,
himself to the enjoyment of the innocent, but trifling, pleasures of a luxurious court. The natural disposition of Theodosius was hasty and
choleric; and, in a station where none could resist, and few would dissuade, the fatal consequence of his resentment, the humane monarch
was justly alarmed by the consciousness of his
infirmity, and of his power. It was the constant
study of his life to suppress, or regulate, the intemperate sallies of passion; and the success of
his efforts enhanced the merit of his clemency.
But the painful virtue which claims the merit of
victory, is exposed to the danger of defeat; and
the reign of a wise and merciful prince was polluted by an act of cruelty, which would stain
the annals of Nero or Domitian. Within the
space of three years, the inconsistent historian
of Theodosius must relate the generous pardon
of the citizens of Antioch, and the inhuman massacre of the people of Thessalonica.

The lively impatience of the inhabitants of
Antioch was never satisfied with their own situation, or with the character, and conduct, of
their successive sovereigns. The Arian subjects
of Theodosius deplored the loss of their churches:
and, as three rival bishops disputed the throne
of Antioch, the sentence which decided their pretensions excited the murmurs of the two unsuc-

cessful congregations. The exigencies of the Gothic war, and the inevitable expence that accompanied the conclusion of the peace, had constrained the emperor to aggravate the weight of the public impositions; and the provinces of Asia, as they had not been involved in the distress, were the less inclined to contribute to the relief of Europe. The auspicious period now approached of the tenth year of his reign; a festival more grateful to the soldiers, who received a liberal donative, than to the subjects, whose voluntary offerings had been long since converted into an extraordinary and oppressive burden. The edicts of taxation interrupted the repose, and pleasures, of Antioch; and the tribunal of the magistrate was besieged by a suppliant crowd; who, in pathetic, but, at first, in respectful language, solicited the redress of their grievances. They were gradually incensed by the pride of their haughty rulers, who treated their complaints as a criminal resistance; their satirical wit degenerated into sharp and angry invectives; and, from the subordinate powers of government, the invectives of the people insensibly rose to attack the sacred character

Feb. 26. of the emperor himself. Their fury, provoked by a feeble opposition, discharged itself on the images of the imperial family, which were erected as objects of public veneration, in the most conspicuous places of the city. The statues of Theodosius, of his father, of his wife Flaccilla, of his two sons, Arcadius and Honorius, were

insolently thrown down from their pedestals,
broken in pieces, or dragged with contempt
through the streets : and the indignities which
were offered to the representations of imperial
majesty sufficiently declared the impious and
treasonable wishes of the populace. The tumult
was almost immediately suppressed by the arrival of a body of archers; and Antioch had leisure
to reflect on the nature and consequences of her
crime.[p] According to the duty of his office, the
governor of the province dispatched a faithful
narrative of the whole transaction ; while the
trembling citizens intrusted the confession of
their crime, and the assurance of their repentance, to the zeal of Flavian their bishop, and to
the eloquence of the senator Hilarius, the friend,
and, most probably, the disciple, of Libanius ;
whose genius, on this melancholy occasion, was
not useless to his country.[q] But the two capitals, Antioch and Constantinople, were separated by the distance of eight hundred miles ; and,
notwithstanding the diligence of the imperial
posts, the guilty city was severely punished by
a long and dreadful interval of suspense. Every
rumour agitated the hopes and fears of the Antiochians, and they heard with terror, that their

---

[p] The Christians and pagans agreed in believing, that the sedition
of Antioch was excited by the demons. A gigantic woman (says
Sozomen, l. vii, c. 23) paraded the streets with a scourge in her hand.
An old man (says Libanius, Orat. xii, p. 396) transformed himself into
a youth, then a boy, &c.

[q] Zosimus, in his short and disingenuous account, l. iv, p. 258, 259),
is certainly mistaken in sending Libanius himself to Constantinople.
His own orations fix him at Antioch.

sovereign, exasperated by the insult which had been offered to his own statues, and, more especially, to those of his beloved wife, had resolved to level with the ground the offending city; and to massacre, without distinction of age or sex, the criminal inhabitants;[r] many of whom were actually driven, by their apprehensions, to seek a refuge in the mountains of Syria, and the adjacent desert.

March 22.

At length, twenty-four days after the sedition, the general Hellebicus, and Cæsarius, master of the offices, declared the will of the emperor, and the sentence of Antioch. That proud capital was degraded from the rank of a city; and the metropolis of the East, stripped of its lands, its privileges, and its revenues, was subjected, under the humiliating denomination of a village, to the jurisdiction of Laodicea.[s] The baths, the circus, and the theatres, were shut: and, that every source of plenty and pleasure might at the same time be intercepted, the distribution of corn was abolished, by the severe instructions of Theodosius. His commissioners then proceeded to inquire into the guilt of individuals; of those who had perpetrated, and of those who had not prevented, the destruction of the sacred statues. The tribunal of Hellebicus and Cæsa-

[r] Libanius (Orat. i, p. 6, edit. Venet.) declares, that, under such a reign, the fear of a massacre was groundless and absurd, especially in the emperor's absence; for his presence, according to the eloquent slave, might have given a sanction to the most bloody acts.

[s] Laodicea, on the sea-coast, sixty-five miles from Antioch, (see Noris, Epoch. Syro-Maced. Dissert. iii, p. 230). The Antiochians were offended, that the dependent city of Seleucia should presume to intercede for them.

rius, encompassed with armed soldiers, was
erected in the midst of the Forum. The noblest, and most wealthy, of the citizens of Antioch, appeared before them in chains; the
examination was assisted by the use of torture,
and their sentence was pronounced or suspended, according to the judgment of these extraordinary magistrates. The houses of the criminals were exposed to sale, their wives and
children were suddenly reduced, from affluence
and luxury, to the most abject distress ; and a
bloody execution was expected to conclude the
horrors of a day,[t] which the preacher of Antioch, the eloquent Chrysostom, has represented
as a lively image of the last and universal judgment of the world. But the ministers of Theodosius performed, with reluctance, the cruel task
which had been assigned them ; they dropped a
gentle tear over the calamities of the people ;
and they listened with reverence to the pressing
solicitations of the monks and hermits, who descended in swarms from the mountains.[u] Hellebicus and Cæsarius were persuaded to suspend
the execution of their sentence; and it was a-
greed, that the former should remain at Antioch, while the latter returned, with all possible speed, to Constantinople ; and presumed
once more to consult the will of his sovereign.

[t] As the days of the tumult depend on the *moveable* festival of Easter,
they can only be determined by the previous determination of the year.
The year 387 has been preferred, after a laborious inquiry, by Tillemont, (Hist. des Emp. tom. v, p. 741-744,) and Montfaucon, (Chrysostom. xiii, p. 105-110).

[u] Chrysostom opposes *their* courage, which was not attended with
much risk, to the cowardly flight of the Cynics.

Clemency
of Theo-
dosius.

The resentment of Theodosius had already subsided; the deputies of the people, both the bishop
and the orator, had obtained a favourable audience; and the reproaches of the emperor were
the complaints of injured friendship, rather
than the stern menaces of pride and power. A
free and general pardon was granted to the
city and citizens of Antioch; the prison-doors
were thrown open; and senators, who des-
paired of their lives, recovered the possession
of their houses and estates; and the capital of
the East was restored to the enjoyment of her
ancient dignity and splendour. Theodosius
condescended to praise the senate of Constantinople, who had generously interceded for their
distressed brethren: he rewarded the eloquence
of Hilarius with the government of Palestine;
and dismissed the bishop of Antioch with the
warmest expressions of his respect and grati-

April 25.

tude. A thousand new statues arose to the
clemency of Theodosius; the applause of his
subjects was ratified by the approbation of his
own heart; and the emperor confessed, that, if
the exercise of justice is the most important
duty, the indulgence of mercy is the most exquisite pleasure, of a sovereign.[x]

The sedition of Thessalonica is ascribed to a
more shameful cause, and was productive of

---

[x] The sedition of Antioch is represented in a lively, and almost
dramatic, manner, by two orators, who had their respective shares
of interest and merit. See Libanius (Orat. xiv, xv, p. 389-420, edit.
Morel. Orat. i, p. 1-14, Venet. 1754), and the twenty orations of St.
John Chrysostom, *de Statuis*, (tom. ii, p. 1-225, edit. Montfaucon). I
do not pretend to *much* personal acquaintance with Chrysostom; but
Tillemont, (Hist. des Empereurs, tom. v, p. 263-283), and Hermant,
(Vie de St. Chrysostom. tom. i, p. 137-224), had read him with pious
curiosity and diligence.

much more dreadful consequences. That great city, the metropolis of all the Illyrian provinces, had been protected from the dangers of the Gothic war by strong fortifications, and a numerous garrison. Botheric, the general of those troops, and, as it should seem from his name, a barbarian, had among his slaves a beautiful boy, who excited the impure desires of one of the charioteers of the Circus. The insolent and brutal lover was thrown into prison by the order of Botheric; and he sternly rejected the importunate clamours of the multitude, who, on the day of the public games, lamented the absence of their favourite; and considered the skill of a charioteer as an object of more importance than his virtue. The resentment of the people was embittered by some previous disputes; and, as the strength of the garrison had been drawn away for the service of the Italian war, the feeble remnant, whose numbers were reduced by desertion, could not save the unhappy general from their licentious fury. Botheric, and several of his principal officers, were inhumanly murdered: their mangled bodies were dragged about the streets; and the emperor, who then resided at Milan, was surprised by the intelligence of the audacious and wanton cruelty of the people of Thessalonica. The sentence of a dispassionate judge would have inflicted a severe punishment on the authors of the crime; and the merit of Botheric might contribute to exasperate the grief and indignation of his master. The fiery and choleric temper of Theodosius was impatient of the dilatory forms of a judicial inquiry; and he hastily resolved, that the blood of his lieutenant should be expiated by the blood of the guilty people. Yet his mind still fluctuated between the counsels of clemency and of revenge; the zeal of the bishops had almost extorted from the reluctant emperor the promise of a general pardon; his passion was again inflamed by the flattering suggestions of his minister, Rufinus; and, after Theodosius had dispatched the messengers of death, he attempted, when it was too late, to prevent the execution of his orders. The punishment of a Roman city was blindly committed to the undistinguishing sword of the barbarians; and the hostile preparations were concerted with the dark and perfidious artifice of an illegal conspiracy. The people of Thessalonica were treacherously invited, in the name of their sovereign, to the games of the Circus; and such was their insatiate avidity for those amusements, that every consideration of fear, or suspicion, was disregarded by the numerous spectators. As soon as the assembly was complete, the soldiers, who had secretly been posted round the Circus, received the signal, not of the races, but of a general massacre. The promiscuous carnage continued three hours, without discrimination of strangers or natives, of age or sect, of innocence or guilt; the most moderate accounts state the number of the slain at seven thousand; and it is affirmed by some writers, that more than fifteen thousand victims were sacrificed to the manes of Botheric. A foreign merchant, who had probably no concern in his murder, offered his own life, and all his wealth, to supply the place of *one* of his two sons ; but, while the father hesitated with equal tenderness, while he was doubtful to choose, and unwilling to condemn, the soldiers determined his suspense, by plunging their daggers at the same moment into the breasts of the defenceless youths. The apology of the assassins, that they were obliged *to* produce the prescribed number of heads, serves only to increase, by an appearance of order and design, the horrors of the massacre, which was executed by the commands of Theodosius. The guilt of the emperor is aggravated by his long and frequent residence at Thessalonica. The situation of the unfortunate city, the aspect of the streets and buildings, the dress and faces of the inhabitants, were familiar, and even present, to his imagination ; and Theodosius possessed a quick and lively sense of the existence of the people whom he destroyed.[7]

The respectful attachment of the emperor for the orthodox clergy, had disposed him to love and admire the character of Ambrose ; who united all the episcopal virtues in the most eminent degree. The friends and ministers of Theodosius

Influence and conduct of Ambrose, A. D. 388,

[7] The original evidence of Ambrose (tom. ii, epist. xl, p. 998) ; Augustin, (de Civitat. Dei, v, 26), and Paulinus, (in Vit. Ambros. c. 24), is delivered in vague expressions of horror and pity. It is illustrated by the subsequent and unequal testimonies of Sozomen (l. vii c. 25) ; Theodoret, (l. v, c. 17) ; Theophanes (Chronographu p. 62) ; Cedrenus, (p. 317), and Zonaras, (tom. ii, l. xiii, p. 34). Zosimus *alone,* the partial enemy of Theodosius, most unaccountably passes over in silence the worst of his actions.

imitated the example of their sovereign; and he observed, with more surprise than displeasure, that all his secret counsels were immediately communicated to the archbishop; who acted from the laudable persuasion, that every measure of civil government may have some connection with the glory of God, and the interest of the true religion. The monks and populace of Callinicum, an obscure town on the frontier of Persia, excited by their own fanaticism, and by that of their bishop, had tumultuously burnt a conventicle of the Valentinians, and a synagogue of the Jews. The seditious prelate was condemned, by the magistrate of the province, either to rebuild the synagogue, or to repay the damage; and this moderate sentence was confirmed by the emperor. But it was not confirmed by the archbishop of Milan.[a] He dictated an epistle of censure and reproach, more suitable, perhaps, if the emperor had received the mark of circumcision, and renounced the faith of his baptism. Ambrose considers the toleration of the Jewish, as the persecution of the Christian, religion; boldly declares, that he himself, and every true believer, would eagerly dispute with the bishop of Callinicum the merit of the deed, and the crown of martyrdom; and laments, in the most pathetic terms, that the execution of the sentence would be fatal to the fame and salvation of Theodosius. As this private admonition did not produce an immediate effect, the archbishop, from his pul-

[a] See the whole transaction in Ambrose, (tom. ii., epist. xl, xli, p. 946-956), and his biographer Paulinus, (c. 23). Bayle and Barbeyrac (Morales de Pères, c. xvii, p. 325, &c.) have justly condemned the archbishop.

pit,[a] publicly addressed the emperor on his throne;[b] nor would he consent to offer the oblation of the altar, till he had obtained from Theodosius a solemn and positive declaration, which secured the impunity of the bishops and monks of Callinicum. The recantation of Theodosius was sincere;[c] and, during the term of his residence at Milan, his affection for Ambrose was continually increased by the habits of pious and familiar conversation.

When Ambrose was informed of the massacre of Thessalonica, his mind was filled with horror and anguish. He retired into the country to indulge his grief, and to avoid the presence of Theodosius. But as the archbishop was satisfied that a timid silence would render him the accomplice of his guilt, he represented, in a private letter, the enormity of the crime; which could only be effaced by the tears of penitence. The episcopal vigour of Ambrose was tempered by prudence; and he contented himself with signifying[d] an indirect sort of excommunica-

CHAP.
XXVII.

Penance
of Theodosius,
A. D. 390,

[a] His sermon is a strange allegory of Jeremiah's rod, of an almond-tree, of the woman who washed and anointed the feet of Christ. But the peroration is direct and personal

[b] Hodie, Episcope, de me proposuisti. Ambrose modestly confessed it: but he sternly reprimanded Timasius, general of the horse and foot, who had presumed to say, that the monks of Callinicum deserved punishment.

[c] Yet, five years afterwards, when Theodosius was absent from his spiritual guide, he tolerated the Jews, and condemned the destruction of their synagogue. Cod. Theodos. l. xvi. tit. viii, leg. 9, with Godefroy's Commentary, tom. vi, p. 225.

[d] Ambros. tom. ii, epist. li, p. 997. 1001. His Epistle is a miserable rhapsody on a noble subject. Ambrose could act better than he could write. His compositions are destitute of taste, or genius; without the spirit of Tertullian, the copious elegance of Lactantius, the lively wit of Jerom, or the grave energy of Augustin.

tion, by assurance, that he had been warned in
a vision, not to offer the oblation in the name, or
in the presence of, Theodosius; and by the advice, that he would confine himself to the use
of prayer, without presuming to approach the
altar of Christ, or to receive the holy eucharist
with those hands that were still polluted with
the blood of an innocent people.   The emperor
was deeply affected by his own reproaches, and
by those of his spiritual father; and, after he
had bewailed the mischievous and irreparable
consequences of his rash fury, he proceeded, in
the accustomed manner, to perform his devotions
in the great church of Milan.   He was stopped
in the porch by the archbishop; who, in the tone
and language of an ambassador of Heaven, declared to his sovereign, that private contrition
was not sufficient to atone for a public fault, or
to appease the justice of the offended Deity.
Theodosius humbly represented, that if he had
contracted the guilt of homicide, David, the man
after God's own heart, had been guilty, not only
of murder, but of adultery.   " You have imitat-
" ed David in his crime, imitate then his repent-
" ance," was the reply of the undaunted Ambrose.   The rigorous conditions of peace and
pardon were accepted; and the public penance of
the emperor Theodosius has been recorded as
one of the most honourable events in the annals
of the church.   According to the mildest rules
of ecclesiastical discipline, which were estab
lished in the fourth century, the crime of homicide was expiated by the penitence of twenty

years ;[*] and it was impossible, in the period of human life, to purge the accumulated guilt of the massacre of Thessalonica, the murderer should have been excluded from the holy communion till the hour of his death. But the archbishop, consulting the maxims of religious policy, granted some indulgence to the rank of his illustrious penitent, who humbled in the dust the pride of the diadem; and the public edification might be admitted as a weighty reason to abridge the duration of his punishment. It was sufficient, that the emperor of the Romans, stripped of the ensigns of royalty, should appear in a mournful and suppliant posture; and that, in the midst of the church of Milan, he should humbly solicit, with sighs and tears, the pardon of his sins.[f] In this spiritual cure, Ambrose employed the various methods of mildness and severity. After a delay of about eight months, Theodosius was restored to the communion of the faithful; and the edict, which interposes a salutary interval of thirty days between the sentence and the execution, may be accepted as the worthy fruits of his

[*] According to the discipline of St. Basil, (Canon. lvi), the voluntary homicide was *four* years a mourner; *five* an hearer; *seven* in a prostrate state; and *four* in a standing posture. I have the original (Beveridge, Pandect. tom. ii, p. 47-151), and a translation, (Chardon, Hist. des Sacremens, tom. iv, p. 219-277), of the Canonical Epistles of St. Basil.

[f] The penance of Theodosius is authenticated by Ambrose, tom. vi, de Obit. Theodos. c. 34, p. 1207; Augustin, de (Civitat. Dei, v, 26), and Paulinus, (in Vit. Ambros. c. 24). Socrates is ignorant; Sozomen (l. vii, c. 25) concise; and the copious narrative of Theodoret (l. v, c. 18) must be used with precaution.

CHAP.
XXVII.
repentance.[g] Posterity has applauded the virtuous firmness of the archbishop: and the example of Theodosius may prove the beneficial influence of those principles, which could force a monarch, exalted above the apprehension of human punishment, to respect the laws, and ministers, of an invisible Judge. "The prince," says Montesquieu, "who is actuated by the "hopes and fears of religion, may be compared "to a lion, docile only to the voice, and tract-"able to the hand, of his keeper."[b] The motions of the royal animal will therefore depend on the inclination, and interest, of the man who has acquired such dangerous authority over him; and the priest, who holds in his hand the conscience of a king, may inflame, or moderate, his sanguinary passions. The cause of humanity, and that of persecution, have been asserted by the same Ambrose, with equal energy, and with equal success.

Generosity
of Theo-
dosius,
A. D. 388-
391.
After the defeat and death of the tyrant of Gaul, the Roman world was in the possession of Theodosius. He derived from the choice of Gratian his honourable title to the provinces of the East: he had acquired the West by the right of conquest; and the three years which he spent in Italy, were usefully employed to restore the

---

[g] Codex. Theodos. l. ix, tit. xl, leg. 13. The date and circumstances of this law are perplexed with difficulties; but I feel myself inclined to favour the honest efforts of Tillemont, (Hist. des Emp. tom. v, p. 721), and Pagi, (Critica, tom. i, p. 578).

[b] Un prince qui aime la religion, et qui la craint, est un lion qui cède à la main qui le flatte, ou à la voix qui l'appaise. Esprit des Loix, l. xxiv, c. 2.

authority of the laws; and to correct the abuses, which had prevailed with impunity under the usurpation of Maximus, and the minority of Valentinian. The name of Valentinian was regularly inserted in the public acts: but the tender age, and doubtful faith, of the son of Justina, appeared to require the prudent care of an orthodox guardian; and his specious ambition might have excluded the unfortunate youth, without a struggle, and almost without a murmur, from the administration, and even from the inheritance, of the empire. If Theodosius had consulted the rigid maxims of interest and policy, his conduct would have been justified by his friends; but the generosity of his behaviour on this memorable occasion has extorted the applause of his most inveterate enemies. He seated Valentinian on the throne of Milan; and, without stipulating any present or future advantages, restored him to the absolute dominion of all the provinces from which he had been driven by the arms of Maximus. To the restitution of his ample patrimony, Theodosius added the free and generous gift of the countries beyond the Alps, which his successful valour had recovered from the assassin of Gratian.[1] Satisfied with the glory which he had acquired, by revenging the death of his benefactor, and delivering the West from the yoke of tyranny, the emperor returned from

[1] Τυτο περι της ενεργετας καθακον ιδεξιν ειναι, is the niggard praise of Zosimus himself, (l. iv, p. 267). Augustin says, with some happiness of expression, Valentinianum.......misericordissimâ veneratione restituit.

CHAP.
XXVII.

Milan to Constantinople; and, in the peaceful possession of the East, insensibly relapsed into his former habits of luxury and indolence. Theodosius discharged his obligation to the brother, he indulged his conjugal tenderness to the sister, of Valentinian : and posterity, which admires the pure and singular glory of his elevation, must applaud his unrivalled generosity in the use of victory.

Character
of Valentinian,
A. D. 391.

The empress Justina did not long survive her return to Italy; and, though she beheld the triumph of Theodosius, she was not allowed to influence the government of her son.[k] The pernicious attachment to the Arian sect, which Valentinian had imbibed from her example and instructions, were soon erased by the lessons of a more orthodox education. His growing zeal for the faith of Nice, and his filial reverence for the character and authority of Ambrose, disposed the catholics to entertain the most favourable opinion of the virtues of the young emperor of the West.[l] They applauded his chastity and temperance, his contempt of pleasure, his application to business, and his tender affection for his two sisters; which could not, however, seduce his impartial equity to pronounce an unjust sentence against the meanest of his subjects. But this amiable youth, before he had accomplished the twentieth year of his age, was

[k] Sozomen, l. vii, c. 14. His chronology is very irregular.
[l] See Ambrose, (tom. ii, de Obit. Valentinian, c. 15, &c. p. 1178; c. 36, &c. p. 1184). When the young emperor gave an entertainment, he fasted himself; he refused to see an handsome actress, &c. Since he ordered his wild beasts to be killed, it is ungenerous in Philostorgius, (l. xi, c. 1) to reproach him with the love of that amusement.

oppressed by domestic treason ; and the empire
was again involved in the horrors of a civil war. Arbogastes,[m] a gallant soldier of the nation of the Franks, held the second rank in the service of Gratian. On the death of his master, he joined the standard of Theodosius ; contributed, by his valour and military conduct, to the destruction of the tyrant; and was appointed, after the victory, master-general of the armies of Gaul. His real merit, and apparent fidelity, had gained the confidence both of the prince and people; his boundless liberality corrupted the allegiance of the troops ; and, whilst he was universally esteemed as the pillar of the state, the bold and crafty barbarian was secretly determined, either to rule, or to ruin, the empire of the West. The important commands of the army were distributed among the Franks ; the creatures of Arbogastes were promoted to all the honours and offices of the civil government; the progress of the conspiracy removed every faithful servant from the presence of Valentinian; and the emperor, without power, and without intelligence, insensibly sunk into the precarious and dependant condition of a captive.[n] The indignation which he expressed, though it might arise only from the rash and impatient temper of youth, may be candidly ascribed to the generous spirit of a prince, who

[m] Zosimus (l. iv, p. 275) praises the enemy of Theodosius. But he is detested by Socrates, (l. v, c. 25), and Orosius, (l. vii, c. 35).

[n] Gregory of Tours (l. ii, c. 9, p. 165, in the second volume of the Historians of France) has preserved a curious fragment of Sulpicius Alexander, an historian far more valuable than himself.

felt that he was not unworthy to reign. He secretly invited the archbishop of Milan to undertake the office of a mediator; as the pledge of his sincerity, and the guardian of his safety. He contrived to apprise the emperor of the East of his helpless situation; and he declared, that, unless Theodosius could speedily march to his assistance, he must attempt to escape from the palace, or rather prison, of Vienna in Gaul, where he had imprudently fixed his residence in the midst of the hostile faction. But the hopes of relief were distant and doubtful; and, as every day furnished some new provocation, the emperor, without strength or counsel, too hastily resolved to risk an immediate contest with his powerful general. He received Arbogastes on the throne; and, as the count approached with some appearance of respect, delivered to him a paper, which dismissed him from all his employments. " My authority," replied Arbogastes, with insulting coolness, " does not de-" pend on the smile, or the frown, of a monarch;" and he contemptuously threw the paper on the ground. The indignant monarch snatched at the sword of one of the guards, which he struggled to draw from its scabbard; and it was not without some degree of violence that he was prevented from using the deadly weapon against his enemy, or against himself. A few days after

His death
A. D 392.
May 15.
this extraordinary quarrel, in which he had exposed his resentment and his weakness, the unfortunate Valentinian was found strangled in his apartment; and some pains were employed to

disguise the manifest guilt of Arbogastes, and to persuade the world that the death of the young emperor had been the voluntary effect of his own despair.[o] His body was conducted with decent pomp to the sepulchre of Milan; and the archbishop pronounced a funeral oration to commemorate his virtue, and his misfortunes.[p] On this occasion the humanity of Ambrose tempted him to make a singular breach in his theological system; and to comfort the weeping sisters of Valentinian, by the firm assurance, that their pious brother, though he had not received the sacrament of baptism, was introduced, without difficulty, into the mansions of eternal bliss.[q]

The prudence of Arbogastes had prepared the success of his ambitious designs: and the provincials, in whose breasts every sentiment of patriotism or loyalty were extinguished, expected, with tame resignation, the unknown master, whom the choice of a Frank might place on the imperial throne. But some remains of pride and prejudice still opposed the elevation of Arbogastes himself; and the judicious barbarian thought it

Usurpation of Eugenius, A. D. 392-394.

---

[o] Godefroy (Dissertat. ad Philostorg. p. 429-434) has diligently collected all the circumstances of the death of Valentinian II. The variations, and the ignorance, of contemporary writers, prove that it was secret.

[p] De Obitû Valentinian. tom. ii, p. 1173-1196. He is forced to speak a discreet and obscure language: yet he is much bolder than any layman, or perhaps, any other ecclesiastic, would have dared to be.

[q] See c. 51, p. 1188: c. 75, p. 1193. Don Chardon (Hist. des Sacremens, tom. i, p. 86), who owns that St. Ambrose most strenuously maintains the indispensable necessity of baptism, labours to reconcile the contradiction.

more advisable to reign under the name of some dependent Roman. He bestowed the purple on the rhetorician Eugenius;[r] whom he had already raised from the place of his domestic secretary, to the rank of master of the offices. In the course both of his private and public service, the count had always approved the attachment and abilities of Eugenius; his learning and eloquence, supported by the gravity of his manners, recommended him to the esteem of the people; and the reluctance, with which he seemed to ascend the throne, may inspire a favourable prejudice of his virtue and moderation. The ambassadors of the new emperor were immediately despatched to the court of Theodosius, to communicate, with affected grief, the unfortunate accident of the death of Valentinian; and, without mentioning the name of Arbogastes, to request that the monarch of the East would embrace, as his lawful colleague, the respectable citizen, who had obtained the unanimous suffrage of the armies and provinces of the West.[s] Theodosius was justly provoked, that the perfidy of a barbarian should have destroyed, in a moment, the labours, and the fruit, of his former victory; and he was excited by the

[r] Quem sibi Germanus famulum delegerat exul, is the contemptuous expression of Claudian, (iv Cons. Hon. 74). Eugenius professed Christianity; but his secret attachment to paganism (Sozomen, l. vii, c. 22. Philostorg. l. xi, c. 2) is probable in a grammarian, and would secure the friendship of Zosimus, (l. iv, p. 276, 277).

[s] Zosimus (l. iv, p. 278) mentions this embassy; but he is diverted by another story from relating the events.

tears of his beloved wife,[t] to revenge the fate of her unhappy brother, and once more to assert by arms the violated majesty of the throne. But as the second conquest of the West was a task of difficulty and danger, he dismissed, with splendid presents, and an ambiguous answer, the ambassadors of Eugenius ; and almost two years were consumed in the preparations of the civil war. Before he formed any decisive resolution, the pious emperor was anxious to discover the will of Heaven ; and as the progress of Christianity had silenced the oracles of Delphi and Dodona, he consulted an Egyptian monk, who possessed, in the opinion of the age, the gift of miracles, and the knowledge of futurity. Eutropius, one of the favourite eunuchs of the palace of Constantinople, embarked for Alexandria, from whence he sailed up the Nile as far as the city of Lycopolis, or of Wolves, in the remote province of Thebais.[u] In the neighbourhood of that city, and on the summit of a lofty mountain, the holy John[x] had constructed with his own hands, an humble cell, in

Theodosius prepares for war.

---

[t] Σνιστυραξεν η τυτυ γαμεττε Γαλλα τα βασιλεια τον αδελφον ελοφυρομενη. Zosim. l. iv, p. 277. He afterwards says (p. 280), that Galla died in childbed ; and intimates, that the affliction of her husband was extreme, but short.

[u] Lycopolis is the modern Siut, or Osiot, a town of Said, about the size of St. Denys, which drives a profitable trade with the kingdom of Sennaar, and has a very convenient fountain, " cujus potu signa virginitatis eripiuntur." See d'Anville, Description de l'Egypte, p. 181 ; Abulfeda, Descrip. Ægypt. p. 14, and the curious Annotations, p. 25, 92, of his editor Michaelis.

[x] The life of John of Lycopolis is described by his two friends, Rufinus, (l. ii, c. i, p. 449), and Palladius, (Hist. Lauaiac. c. 33, p. 738), in
Roswyde's

which he had dwelt above fifty years, without opening his door, without seeing the face of a woman, and without tasting any food that had been prepared by fire, or any human art. Five days of the week he spent in prayer and meditation; but on Saturday and Sundays he regularly opened a small window, and gave audience to the crowd of suppliants, who successively flowed from every part of the Christian world. The eunuch of Theodosius approached the window with respectful steps, proposed his questions concerning the event of the civil war, and soon returned with a favourable oracle, which animated the courage of the emperor by the assurance of a bloody, but infallible victory.[v] The accomplishment of the prediction was forwarded by all the means that human prudence could supply. The industry of the two master-generals, Stilicho and Timasius, was directed to recruit the numbers, and to revive the discipline, of the Roman legions. The formidable troops of barbarians marched under the ensigns of their national chieftains. The Iberian, the Arab, and the Goth, who gazed on each other with mutual astonishment, were inlisted in the service of the same prince; and the renowned Alaric acquired, in the school of Theodosius, the knowledge of the art of war, which he after-

Roswyde's great Collection of the Vitæ Patrum. Tillemont, (Mem. Eccles. tom x, p. 718, 720) has settled the chronology.

[v] Sozomen, l. vii, c. 22. Claudian (in Eutrop. l. i, 312) mentions the eunuch's journey; but he most contemptuously derides the Egyptian dreams, and the oracles of the Nile.

wards so fatally exerted for the destruction of
Rome.[z]

The emperor of the West, or, to speak more properly, his general Arbogastes, was instructed by the misconduct and misfortune of Maximus, how dangerous it might prove to extend the line of defence against a skilful antagonist, who was free to press, or to suspend, to contract, or to multiply, his various methods of attack.[a] Arbogastes fixed his station on the confines of Italy: the troops of Theodosius were permitted to occupy, without resistance, the provinces of Pannonia, as far as the foot of the Julian Alps; and even the passages of the mountains were negligently, or perhaps artfully, abandoned, to the bold invader. He descended from the hills, and beheld, with some astonishment, the formidable camp of the Gauls and Germans, that covered with arms and tents the open country, which extends to the walls of Aquileia, and the banks of

[z] Zosimus, l. iv, p. 280. Socrates, l. vii, 10. Alaric himself (de Bell. Getico, 524) dwells with more complacency on his early exploits against the Romans.
. . . . . . Tot Augustus Hebro qui teste fugavi.
Yet his vanity could scarcely have proved this *plurality* of flying emperors.

[a] Claudian (in iv Cons. Honor. 77, &c.) contrasts the military plans of the two usurpers.—
. . . . . . Novitas audere priorem
Suadebat ; cautumque dabant exempla sequentem.
Hic nova moilri præceps : hic quærere tutus
Providus. Hic fusis ; collectis viribus ille.
Hic vagus excurrens ; his intra claustra reductus
Dissimiles ; sed morte pares. . . . . .

the Frigidus,[b] or Cold River.[c] This narrow theatre of the war, circumscribed by the Alps and the Hadriatic, did not allow much room for the operations of military skill; the spirit of Arbogastes would have disdained a pardon; his guilt extinguished the hope of a negotiation: and Theodosius was impatient to satisfy his glory and revenge, by the chastisement of the assassins of Valentinian. Without weighing the natural and artificial obstacles that opposed his efforts, the emperor of the East immediately attacked the fortifications of his rivals, assigned the post of honourable danger to the Goths, and cherished a secret wish, that the bloody conflict might diminish the pride and numbers of the conquerors. Ten thousand of those auxiliaries, and Bacurius, general of the Iberians, died bravely on the field of battle. But the victory was not purchased by their blood: the Gauls maintained their advantage; and the approach of night protected the disorderly flight, or retreat, of the troops of Theodosius. The emperor retired to the adjacent hills; where he passed a disconsolate night, without sleep, without provisions, and without

[b] The Frigidus, a small, though memorable, stream in the country of Goretz, now called the Vipao, falls into the Sontius, or Lisonzo, above Aquileia, some miles from the Hadriatic. See d'Anville's Ancient and Modern Maps, and the Italia Antiqua of Cluverius, (tom. i, p. 188).

[c] Claudian's wit is intolerable: the snow was dyed red; the cold river smoaked; and the channel must have been choaked with carcasses, if the current had not been swelled with blood

hopes;[a] except that strong assurance, which,
under the most desperate circumstances, the independent mind may derive from the contempt of fortune and of life. The triumph of Eugenius was celebrated by the insolent and dissolute joy of his camp; whilst the active and vigilant Arbogastes secretly detached a considerable body of troops to occupy the passes of the mountains, and to encompass the rear of the eastern army. The dawn of day discovered to the eyes of Theodosius the extent and the extremity of his danger: but his apprehensions were soon dispelled, by a friendly message from the leaders of those troops, who expressed their inclination to desert the standard of the tyrant. The honourable and lucrative rewards, which they stipulated as the price of their perfidy, were granted without hesitation; and as ink and paper could not easily be procured, the emperor subscribed, on his own tablets, the ratification of the treaty. The spirit of his soldiers was revived by this seasonable reinforcement: and they again marched, with confidence, to surprise the camp of a tyrant, whose principal officers appeared to distrust, either the justice, or the success, of his arms. In the heat of the battle, a violent tempest,[b] such as is often felt

[a] Theodoret affirms, that St. John, and St. Philip, appeared to the waking, or sleeping, emperor, on horseback, &c. This is the first instance of apostolic chivalry, which afterwards became so popular in Spain, and in the Crusades.

[b] Te propter, gelidis Aquilo de monte procellis
Obruit adversas acies; revolutaque tela
Vertit in auctores, et turbine reppulit hastas.
O nimium dilecte Deo, cui fundit ab antris

Æolus

among the Alps, suddenly arose from the east. The army of Theodosius was sheltered by their position from the impetuosity of the wind, which blew a cloud of dust in the faces of the enemy, disordered their ranks, wrested their weapons from their hands, and diverted, or repelled, their ineffectual javelins. This accidental advantage was skilfully improved; the violence of the storm was magnified by the superstitious terrors of the Gauls; and they yielded without shame to the invisible powers of heaven, who seemed to militate on the side of the pious emperor. His victory was decisive; and the deaths of his two rivals were distinguished only by the difference of their characters. The rhetorician Eugenius, who had almost acquired the dominion of the world, was reduced to implore the mercy of the conqueror; and the unrelenting soldiers separated his head from his body, as he lay prostrate at the feet of Theodosius. Arbogastes, after the loss of a battle, in which he had discharged the duties of a soldier and a general, wandered several days among the mountains. But when he was convinced, that his cause was desperate, and his escape impracticable, the intrepid barbarian imitated the ex-

---

Æolus armatas hyemes; cui militat Æther,
Et conjurati veniunt ad classica venti.

These famous lines of Claudian (in iii Cons. Honor. 93, &c. A. D. 396) are alleged by his contemporaries, Augustin and Orosius; who suppress the pagan deity of Æolus; and add some circumstances from the information of eye-witnesses. Within four months after the victory, it was compared by Ambrose to the miraculous victories of Moses and Joshua.

ample of the ancient Romans, and turned his sword against his own breast. The fate of the empire was determined in a narrow corner of Italy; and the legitimate successor of the house of Valentinian embraced the archbishop of Milan, and graciously received the submission of the provinces of the West. Those provinces were involved in the guilt of rebellion; while the inflexible courage of Ambrose alone had resisted the claims of successful usurpation. With a manly freedom, which might have been fatal to any other subject, the archbishop rejected the gifts of Eugenius, declined his correspondence, and withdrew himself from Milan, to avoid the odious presence of a tyrant; whose downfal he predicted in discreet and ambiguous language. The merit of Ambrose was applauded by the conqueror, who secured the attachment of the people by his alliance with the church: and the clemency of Theodosius is ascribed to the humane intercession of the archbishop of Milan.[f]

After the defeat of Eugenius, the merit, as well as the authority, of Theodosius, was cheerfully acknowledged by all the inhabitants of the Roman world. The experience of his past conduct encouraged the most pleasing expectations of his future reign; and the age of the emperor, which did not exceed fifty years, seemed to

Death of Theodosius, A. D. 395 Jan. 17.

[f] The events of this civil war are gathered from Ambrose, (tom. ii, epist. lxii, p. 1022); Paulinus, (in Vit. Ambros. c. 26-34); Augustin, (de Civitat. Dei, v, 26); Orosius, (l. vii, c. 35); Sozomen (l. vii. c. 24); Theodoret, (l. v, c. 24); Zosimus, (l. iv, p. 281-282); Claudian, (in iii Cons. Hon. 63-105, in iv Cons. Hon. 70-177), and the Chronicles published by Scaliger.

CHAP.
XXVII.
extend the prospect of the public felicity. His death, only four months after his victory, was considered by the people as an unforeseen and fatal event, which destroyed, in a moment, the hopes of the rising generation. But the indulgence of ease and luxury had secretly nourished the principles of disease.[g] The strength of Theodosius was unable to support the sudden and violent transition from the palace to the camp; and the increasing symptoms of a dropsy announced the speedy dissolution of the emperor. The opinion, and perhaps the interest, of the public had confirmed the division of the eastern and western empires; and the two royal youths, Arcadius and Honorius, who had already obtained, from the tenderness of their father, the title of Augustus, were destined to fill the thrones of Constantinople and of Rome. Those princes were not permitted to share the danger and glory of the civil war;[h] but as soon as Theodosius had triumphed over his unworthy rivals, he called his younger son, Honorius, to enjoy the fruits of the victory, and to receive the sceptre of the West from the hands of his dying father. The arrival of Honorius at Milan was welcomed by a splendid exhibition of the games of the Circus; and the em-

---

[g] This disease, ascribed by Socrates (l. v, c. 26) to the fatigues of war, is represented by Philostorgius, (l. xi, c. 2), as the effect of sloth and intemperance; for which Photius calls him an impudent liar, (Godefroy, Dissert. p. 438).

[h] Zosimus supposes, that the boy Honorius accompanied his father, (l. iv, p. 280). Yet the quanto flagrabant pectora voto, is all that flattery would allow to a contemporary poet; who clearly describes the emperor's refusal, and the journey of Honorius, *after* the victory, (Claudian in iii Cons. 78-125).

peror, though he was oppressed by the weight of his disorder, contributed by his presence to the public joy. But the remains of his strength were exhausted by the painful effort, which he made, to assist at the spectacles of the morning. Honorius supplied, during the rest of the day, the place of his father; and the great Theodosius expired in the ensuing night. Notwithstanding the recent animosities of a civil war, his death was universally lamented. The barbarians, whom he had vanquished, and the churchmen, by whom he had been subdued, celebrated, with loud and sincere applause, the qualities of the deceased emperor, which appeared the most valuable in their eyes. The Romans were terrified by the impending dangers of a feeble and divided administration; and every disgraceful moment of the unfortunate reigns of Arcadius and Honorius revived the memory of their irreparable loss.

In the faithful picture of the virtues of Theo- dosius, his imperfections have not been dissembled; the act of cruelty, and the habits of indolence, which tarnished the glory of one of the greatest of the Roman princes. An historian, perpetually adverse to the fame of Theodosius, has exaggerated his vices, and their pernicious effects; he boldly asserts, that every rank of subjects imitated the effeminate manners of their sovereign; that every species of corruption polluted the course of public and private life; and that the feeble restraints of order and decency were insufficient to resist the progress of that degenerate spirit, which sacrifices, without a blush, the consideration of duty and interest to the base indulgence of sloth and appetite.[1] The complaints of contemporary writers, who deplore the increase of luxury, and depravation of manners, are commonly expressive of their peculiar temper and situation. There are few observers, who possess a clear and comprehensive view of the revolutions of society; and who are capable of discovering the nice and secret springs of action, which impel, in the same uniform direction, the blind and capricious passions of a multitude of individuals. If it can be affirmed, with any degree of truth, that the luxury of the Romans was more shameless and dissolute in the reign of Theodosius than in the age of Constantine, perhaps, or of Augustus, the alteration cannot be ascribed to any beneficial improvements, which had gradually increased the stock of national riches. A long period of calamity or decay must have checked the industry, and diminished the wealth, of the people; and their profuse luxury must have been the result of that indolent despair, which enjoys the present hour, and declines the thoughts of futurity. The uncertain condition of their property discouraged the subjects of Theodosius from engaging in those useful and laborious undertakings which require an immediate expence, and promise a slow and distant advantage. The frequent examples of ruin and desolation tempted them not to spare the remains of a patrimony, which

[1] Zosimus, l iv. p. 244.

might, every hour, become the prey of the rapacious Goth. And the mad prodigality which
prevails in the confusion of a shipwreck, or a
siege, may serve to explain the progress of luxury amidst the misfortunes and terrors of a
sinking nation.

The effeminate luxury, which infected the
manners of courts and cities, had instilled a
secret and destructive poison into the camps of
the legions: and their degeneracy has been
marked by the pen of a military writer, who
had accurately studied the genuine and ancient
principles of Roman discipline. It is the just
and important observation of Vegetius, that the
infantry was invariably covered with defensive
armour, from the foundation of the city, to the
reign of the emperor Gratian. The relaxation
of discipline, and the disuse of exercise, rendered the soldiers less able, and less willing, to
support the fatigues of the service; they complained of the weight of the armour, which they
seldom wore; and they successively obtained
the permission of laying aside both their cuirasses and their helmets. The heavy weapons
of their ancestors, the short sword, and the formidable *pilum*, which had subdued the world,
insensibly dropped from their feeble hands. As
the use of the shield is incompatible with that
of the bow, they reluctantly marched into the
field; condemned to suffer, either the pain of
wounds, or the ignominy of flight, and always
disposed to prefer the more shameful alternative. The cavalry of the Goths, the Huns, and
the Alani, had felt the benefits, and ado ted the

use of defensive armour ; and, as they excelled in the management of missile weapons,
they easily overwhelmed the naked and trembling legions, whose heads and breasts were
exposed, without defence, to the arrows of the
barbarians. The loss of armies, the destruction of cities, and the dishonour of the Roman
name, ineffectually solicited the successors of
Gratian to restore the helmets and cuirasses of
the infantry. The enervated soldiers abandoned their own, and the public, defence ; and
their pusillanimous indolence may be considered as the immediate cause of the downfal of the
empire.[k]

[k] Vegetius, de Re Militari, l. i, c. 10. The series of calamities, which
he marks, compel us to believe, that the *Hero*, to whom he dedicates
his book, is the last and most inglorious of the Valentinians

CHAP. XXVIII.

Final destruction of paganism—Introduction of the worship of saints, and relics, among the Christians.

THE ruin of paganism, in the age of Theodosius, is perhaps the only example of the total extirpation of any ancient and popular superstition; and may, therefore, deserve to be considered, as a singular event in the history of the human mind. The christians, more especially the clergy, had impatiently supported the prudent delays of Constantine, and the equal toleration of the elder Valentinian; nor could they deem their conquest perfect or secure, as long as their adversaries were permitted to exist. The influence, which Ambrose and his brethren had acquired over the youth of Gratian, and the piety of Theodosius, was employed to infuse the maxims of persecution into the breasts of their imperial proselytes. Two specious principles of religious jurisprudence were established, from whence they deduced a direct and rigorous conclusion, against the subjects of the empire, who still adhered to the ceremonies of their ancestors: *that* the magistrate is, in some measure, guilty of the crimes which he neglects to prohibit, or to punish; and *that* the idolatrous worship of fabulous deities, and real demons, is the most abominable crime against the supreme majesty of the Creator. The laws of Moses, and the examples of Jewish history,[a] were hastily, perhaps erroneously, applied, by the clergy, to the mild and universal reign of Christianity.[b] The zeal of the emperors was excited to vindicate their own honour, and that of the Deity: and the temples of the Roman world were subverted, about sixty years after the conversion of Constantine.

State of
paganism
at Rome.
From the age of Numa, to the reign of Gratian, the Romans preserved the regular succession of the several colleges of the sacerdotal order.[c] Fifteen PONTIFFS exercised their supreme jurisdiction over all things, and persons, that were consecrated to the service of the gods; and the various questions which perpetually arose in a loose and traditionary system, were submitted to the judgment of their holy tribunal. Fifteen grave and learned AUGURS observed the face of the heavens, and prescribed the actions of heroes, according to the flight of birds. Fifteen keepers of the Sybilline books

[a] St. Ambrose, (tom. ii, de Obit. Theodos. p. 1208) expressly praises and recommends the zeal of Josiah in the destruction of idolatry. The language of Julius Firmicus Maternus on the same subject (de Errore Profan. Relig. p. 467, edit. Gronov.) is piously inhuman. Nic filio jubet (the Mosaic Law) parci, nec fratri, et per amatam conjugem gladium vindicem ducit, &c.

[b] Bayle (tom. ii, p. 406, in his Commentaire Philosophique) justifies, and limits, these intolerant laws by the temporal reign of Jehovah over the Jews. The attempt is laudable.

[c] See the outlines of the Roman hierarchy in Cicero, (de Legibus, ii, 7, 8); Livy, (i, 20); Dionysius Harlicarnassensis, (l. ii, p. 119-129, edit. Hudson); Beaufort, (Republique Romaine, tom. i, p. 1-90), and Moyle, (vol. i, p. 10-55). The last is the work of an English whig, as well as of a Roman antiquary.

(their name of QUINDECEMVIRS was derived from their number) occasionally consulted the history of future, and, as it should seem, of contingent, events.. Six VESTALS devoted their virginity to the guard of the sacred fire, and of the unknown pledges of the duration of Rome; which no mortal had been suffered to behold with impunity.[d] Seven EPULOS prepared the table of the gods, conducted the solemn procession, and regulated the ceremonies of the annual festival. The three FLAMENS of Jupiter, of Mars, and of Quirinus, were considered as the peculiar ministers of the three most powerful deities, who watched over the fate of Rome and of the universe. The KING of the SACRIFICES represented the person of Numa, and of his successors, in the religious functions, which could be performed only by royal hands. The confraternities of the SALIANS, the LUPERCALE, &c. practised such rites as might extort a smile of contempt from every reasonable man, with a lively confidence of recommending themselves to the favour of the immortal gods. The authority, which the Roman priests had formerly obtained in the councils of the republic, was gradually abolished by the establishment of monarchy, and the removal of

[d] These mystic, and perhaps imaginary, symbols have given birth to various fables and conjectures. It seems probable, that the Palladium was a small statue (three cubits and a half high) of Minerva, with a lance and distaff; that it was usually inclosed in a *seria*, or barrel; and that a similar barrel was placed by its side, to disconcert curiosity, or sacrilege. See Mezeriac, (Comment. sur les Epitres d'Ovide, tom. i, p 60-66), and Lipsius, (tom. iii, p. 610, de Vestâ, &c. c. 10).

the seat of empire. But the dignity of their sacred character was still protected by the laws and manners of their country; and they still continued, more especially the college of pontiffs, to exercise in the capital, and sometimes in the provinces, the rites of their ecclesiastical and civil jurisdiction. Their robes of purple, chariots of state, and sumptuous entertainments, attracted the admiration of the people; and they received, from the consecrated lands, and the public revenue, an ample stipend, which liberally supported the splendour of the priesthood, and all the expences of the religious worship of the state. As the service of the altar was not incompatible with the command of armies, the Romans, after their consulships and triumphs, aspired to the place of pontiff, or of augur; the seats of Cicero* and Pompey were filled, in the fourth century, by the most illustrious members of the senate; and the dignity of their birth reflected additional splendour on their sacerdotal character. The fifteen priests, who composed the college of pontiffs, enjoyed a more distinguished rank as the companions of their sovereign; and the Christian emperors condescended to accept the robe and ensigns, which were appropriated to the office of supreme pontiff. But when Gratian ascended the throne, more scrupulous, or more enlightened,

---

* Cicero frankly, (ad Atticum, l. ii, epist. 5), or indirectly, (ad Familiar l. xv, epist. 4), confesses, that the *augurate* is the supreme object of his wishes. Pliny is proud to tread in the footsteps of Cicero, (l. iv, epist. 8), and the chain of tradition might be continued from history and marbles.

he sternly rejected those profane symbols ;[f] applied to the service of the state, or of the church,
the revenues of the priests or vestals ; abolished
their honours and immunities ; and dissolved the
ancient fabric of Roman superstition, which was
supported by the opinions, and habits, of eleven
hundred years. Paganism was still the consti-
tutional religion of the senate. The hall or
temple, in which they assembled, was adorned
by the statue and altar of Victory ;[s] a majestic
female standing on a globe, with flowing garments, expanded wings, and a crown of laurel
in her out-stretched hand.[h] The senators were
sworn on the altar of the goddess, to observe the
laws of the emperor and of the empire ; and a
solemn offering of wine and incense was the
ordinary prelude of their public deliberations.[i]
The removal of this ancient monument was the
only injury which Constantius had offered to
the superstition of the Romans. The altar of
Victory was again restored by Julian, tolerated
by Valentinian, and once more banished from
the senate by the zeal of Gratian.[k] But the

[f] Zosimus, l. iv, p. 249, 250. I have suppressed the foolish pun
about *Pontifex* and *Maximus*.

[s] This statue was transported from Tarentum to Rome, placed in
the *Curia Julia* by Cæsar, and decorated by Augustus with the spoils
of Egypt.

[h] Prudentius (l. ii, in initio) has drawn a very awkward portrait of
Victory ; but the curious reader will obtain more satisfaction from
Montfaucon's Antiquities, (tom. i, p. 341).

[i] See Suetonius, (in August. c. 35), and the Exordium of Pliny's
Panegyric.

[k] These facts are mutually allowed by the two advocates, Symmachus and Ambrose.

emperor yet spared the statues of the gods which were exposed to the public veneration; four hundred and twenty-four temples, or chapels, still remained to satisfy the devotion of the people; and in every quarter of Rome the delicacy of the Christians was offended by the fumes of idolatrous sacrifice.[1]

Petition
of the se-
nate for
the altar
of Vic-
tory,
A. D. 384.
But the Christians formed the least numerous party in the senate of Rome;[m] and it was only by their absence, that they could express their dissent from the legal, though profane, acts of a pagan majority. In that assembly, the dying embers of freedom were, for a moment, revived and inflamed by the breath of fanaticism. Four respectable deputations were successively voted to the imperial court,[n] to represent the grievances of the priesthood and the senate; and to solicit the restoration of the altar of Victory. The conduct of this important business was intrusted to the eloquent Symmachus,[o] a wealthy and

[1] The *Notitia Urbis*, more recent than Constantine, does not find one Christian church worthy to be named among the edifices of the city. Ambrose (tom. ii, epist. xvii, p. 825) deplores the public scandals of Rome, which continually offended the eyes, the ears, and the nostrils of the faithful.

[m] Ambrose repeatedly affirms, in contradiction to common sense, (Moyle's Works, vol. ii, p. 147), that the Christians had a majority in the senate.

[n] The *first* (A. D. 382) to Gratian, who refused them audience. The *second* (A. D. 384) to Valentinian, when the field was disputed by Symmachus and Ambrose. The *third* (A. D. 388) to Theodosius; and the *fourth* (A. D. 392) to Valentinian. Lardner (Heathen Testimonies, vol. iv, p. 372-399) fairly represents the whole transaction.

[o] Symmachus, who was invested with all the civil and sacerdotal honours, represented the emperor under the two characters of *Pontifex Maximus*

noble senator, who united the sacred characters of pontiff and augur, with the civil dignities of proconsul of Africa, and prefect of the city. The breast of Symmachus was animated by the warmest zeal for the cause of expiring paganism; and his religious antagonists lamented the abuse of his genius, and the inefficacy of his moral virtues.[p] The orator, whose petition is extant to the emperor Valentinian, was conscious of the difficulty and danger of the office which he had assumed. He cautiously avoids every topic which might appear to reflect on the religion of his sovereign; humbly declares, that prayers and entreaties are his only arms; and artfully draws his arguments from the schools of rhetoric, rather than from those of philosophy. Symmachus endeavours to seduce the imagination of a young prince, by displaying the attributes of the goddess of Victory; he insinuates, that the confiscation of the revenues, which were consecrated to the service of the gods, was a measure unworthy of his liberal and disinterested character; and he maintains, that the Roman sacrifices would be deprived of their force and energy, if they were no longer celebrated at the expence, as well as in the name, of the republic. Even scepticism is made to supply an apology for superstition. The great and in-

---

Maximus, and *Princeps Senatus.* See the proud inscription at the head of his work.

[p] As if any one, says Prudentius (in Symmach. i, 639), should dig in the mud with an instrument of gold and ivory. Even saints, and polemic saints, treat this adversary with respect and civility.

comprehensible *secret* of the universe eludes the inquiry of man. Where reason cannot instruct, custom may be permitted to guide; and every nation seems to consult the dictates of prudence, by a faithful attachment to those rights, and opinions, which have received the sanction of ages. If those ages have been crowned with glory and prosperity, if the devout people have frequently obtained the blessings which they have solicited at the altars of the gods, it must appear still more advisable to persist in the same salutary practice; and not to risk the unknown perils that may attend any rash innovations. The test of antiquity and success was applied with singular advantage to the religion of Numa; and ROME herself, the celestial genius that presided over the fates of the city, is introduced by the orator to plead her own cause before the tribunal of the emperors. " Most ex-" cellent princes," says the venerable matron, " fathers of your country! pity and respect my " age, which has hitherto flowed in an uninter-" rupted course of piety. Since I do not repent, " permit me to continue in the practice of my " ancient rites. Since I am born free, allow me " to enjoy my domestic institutions. This reli-" gion has reduced the world under my laws. " These rites have repelled Hannibal from the " city, and the Gauls from the capitol. Were " my gray hairs reserved for such intolerable dis-" grace? I am ignorant of the new system, that " I am required to adopt; but I am well assured, " that the correction of old age is always an

ungrateful and ignominious office."[q] The CHAP. XXVIII.
fears of the people supplied what the discretion
of the orator had suppressed; and the calamities, which afflicted, or threatened, the declining
empire, were unanimously imputed, by the pagans, to the new religion of Christ and of Constantine.

But the hopes of Symmachus were repeatedly Conversion of
Rome,
A. D. 388,
&c. baffled by the firm and dexterous opposition of
the archbishop of Milan; who fortified the emperors against the fallacious eloquence of the
advocate of Rome. In this controversy, Ambrose condescends to speak the language of a
philosopher, and to ask, with some contempt,
why it should be thought necessary to introduce an imaginary and invisible power, as the
cause of those victories, which were sufficiently
explained by the valour and discipline of the
legions. He justly derides the absurd reverence for antiquity, which could only tend to
discourage the improvements of art, and to replunge the human race into their original barbarism. From thence gradually rising to a more
lofty and theological tone, he pronounces, that
Christianity alone is the doctrine of truth and
salvation; and that every mode of polytheism
conducts its deluded votaries through the paths

[q] See the fifty-fourth epistle of the tenth book of Symmachus. In
the form and disposition of his ten books of epistles, he imitated the
younger Pliny; whose rich and florid style he was supposed, by his
friends, to equal or excel, (Macrob. Saturnal. l. v, c. 1) But the
luxuriancy of Symmachus consists of barren leaves, without fruits,
and even without flowers. Few facts, and few sentiments, can be extracted from his verbose correspondence.

CHAP.
XXVIII.
of error, to the abyss of eternal perdition.[r] Arguments like these, when they were suggested by a favourite bishop, had power to prevent the restoration of the altar of Victory; but the same arguments fell, with much more energy and effect, from the mouth of a conqueror; and the gods of antiquity were dragged in triumph at the chariot-wheels of Theodosius.[s] In a full meeting of the senate, the emperor proposed, according to the forms of the republic, the important question, Whether the worship of Jupiter, or that of Christ, should be the religion of the Romans? The liberty of suffrages, which he affected to allow, was destroyed by the hopes and fears that his presence inspired; and the arbitrary exile of Symmachus was a recent admonition, that it might be dangerous to oppose the wishes of the monarch. On a regular division of the senate, Jupiter was condemned and degraded by the sense of a very large majority; and it is rather surprising, that any members should be found bold enough to declare, by their

[r] See Ambrose, (tom. ii, epist. xxvii, xviii, p. 825-833). The former of these epistles is a short caution; the latter is a formal reply to the petition or *libel* of Symmachus. The same ideas are more copiously expressed in the poetry, if it may deserve that name, of Prudentius; who composed his two books against Symmachus, (A. D. 404), while that senator was still alive. It is whimsical enough, that Montesquieu (Considerations, &c. c. xix, tom. iii, p. 487) should overlook the two professed antagonists of Symmachus; and amuse himself with descanting on the more remote and indirect confutations of Orosius, St. Augustin, and Salvian.

[s] See Prudentius, in Symmach. l. i, 545, &c.) The Christian agrees with the pagan Zosimus, (l. iv, p. 283), in placing this visit of Theodosius after the *second* civil war, gemini bis victor cæde Tyranni, (l. i, 410). But the time and circumstances are better suited to his *first* triumph.

speeches and votes, that they were still attached to the interest of an abdicated deity.[t] The hasty conversion of the senate must be attributed, either to supernatural or to sordid motives; and many of these reluctant proselytes betrayed, on every favourable occasion, their secret disposition to throw aside the mask of odious dissimulation. But they were gradually fixed in the new religion, as the cause of the ancient became more hopeless ; they yielded to the authority of the emperor, to the fashion of the times, and to the entreaties of their wives and children,[u] who were instigated and governed by the clergy of Rome and the monks of the East. The edifying example of the Anician family was soon imitated by the rest of the nobility: the Bassi, the Paullini, the Gracchi, embraced the Christian religion ; and " the luminaries of the world, the venerable assembly " of Catos, (such are the high-flown expressions " of Prudentius,) were impatient to strip themselves of their pontifical garment ; to cast the " skin of the old serpent ; to assume the snowy

[t] Prudentius, after proving that the sense of the senate is declared by a legal majority, proceeds to says, (609, &c.)

Adspice quam pleno subsellia nostra Senatû
Decernant infame Jovis pulvinar, et omne
Idolium longe purgatâ ab urbe fugandum.
Qua vocat egregii sententiâ Principis, illuc
Libera, cum pedibus, tum corde, frequentia transit.

Zosimus ascribes to the conscript fathers an heathenish courage, which few of them are found to possess.

[u] Jerom specifies the pontiff Albinus, who was surrounded with such a believing family of children and grandchildren, as would have been sufficient to convert even Jupiter himself; an extraordinary proselyte ! (tom. i, ad Lætam, p. 54).

H 3

CHAP.
XXVIII.

" robes of baptismal innocence; and to humble
" the pride of the consular fasces before the
" tombs of the martyrs."[x] The citizens, who
subsisted by their own industry, and the populace, who were supported by the public
liberality, filled the churches of the Lateran,
and Vatican, with an incessant throng of devout proselytes. The decrees of the senate,
which proscribed the worship of idols, were
ratified by the general consent of the Romans:[y]
the splendour of the capitol was defaced, and
the solitary temples were abandoned to ruin
and contempt.[z] Rome submitted to the yoke
of the gospel; and the vanquished provinces
had not yet lost their reverence for the name
and authority of Rome..

Destruc-
tion of the
temples in
the pro-
vinces,
A. D. 381,
&c.

The filial piety of the emperors themselves engaged them to proceed, with some caution and
tenderness, in the reformation of the eternal city.
Those absolute monarchs acted with less regard
to the prejudices of the provincials. The pious
labour which had been suspended near twenty
years since the death of Constantius,[a] was vi-

[x] Exultare Patres videas, pulcherrima mundi
  Lumina; Conciliumque senûm gestire Catonum
  Candidiore togâ niveum pietatis amictum
  Sumere; et exuvias deponere pontificales.
The fancy of Prudentius is warmed and elevated by victory.
  [y] Prudentius, after he has described the conversion of the senate and
people, asks, with some truth and confidence,
        Et dubitamus adhuc Romam, tibi, Christe, dicatam
        In leges transisse tuas?
  [z] Jerom exults in the desolation of the capitol, and the other temple
of Rome, (tom. i, p. 54; tom. ii, p. 95).
  [a] Libanius (Orat. pro Templis, p. 10, Grenev. 1634, published by
James Godefroy, and now extremely scarce) accuses Valentinian and
                                                    Valens

gorously resumed, and finally accomplished, by CHAP.
the zeal of Theodosius. Whilst that warlike XXVIII.
prince yet struggled with the Goths, not for the
glory, but for the safety of the republic; he ventured to offend a considerable party of his subjects, by some acts which might perhaps secure
the protection of Heaven, but which must seem
rash and unseasonable in the eye of human prudence. The success of his first experiments
against the pagans, encouraged the pious emperor to reiterate and enforce his edicts of proscription; the same laws which had been originally
published in the provinces of the East, were
applied, after the defeat of Maximus, to the
whole extent of the Roman empire; and every
victory of the orthodox Theodosius contributed
to the triumph of the Christian and Catholic
faith.[b] He attacked superstition in her most
vital part, by prohibiting the use of sacrifices,
which he declared to be criminal as well as infamous; and if the terms of his edicts more
strictly condemned the impious curiosity which
examined the entrails of the victims,[c] every
subsequent explanation tended to involve,

Valens of prohibiting sacrifices. Some partial order may have been
issued by the eastern emperor; but the idea of any general law is con-
tradicted by the silence of the Code, and the evidence of ecclesiastical
history.

[b] See his laws in the Theodosian Code, l. xvi, tit. x, leg. 7-11.

[c] Homer's sacrifices are not accompanied with any inquisition of
entrails, (see Feithius, Antiquitat. Homer. l. i, c. 10, 16). The Tuscans, who produced the first *Haruspices*, subdued both the Greeks and
the Romans, (Cicero de Divinatione, ii, 23).

CHAP.
XXVIII.
in the same guilt, the general practice of *immo-lation*, which essentially constituted the religion of the pagans. As the temples had been erected for the purpose of sacrifice, it was the duty of a benevolent prince to remove from his subjects the dangerous temptation, of offending against the laws which he had enacted. A special commission was granted to Cynegius, the pretorian prefect of the East, and afterwards to the counts Jovius and Gaudentius, two officers of distinguished rank in the West; by which they were directed to shut the temples, to seize or destroy the instruments of idolatry, to abolish the privileges of the priests, and to confiscate the consecrated property for the benefit of the emperor, of the church, or of the army.[4] Here the desolation might have stopped : and the naked edifices, which were no longer employed in the service of idolatry, might have been protected from the destructive rage of fanaticism. Many of those temples were the most splendid and beautiful monuments of Grecian architecture : and the emperor himself was interested not to deface the splendour of his own cities, or to diminish the value of his own possessions. Those stately edifices might be suffered to remain as so many lasting trophies of the victory of Christ. In the decline of the arts, they might be usefully converted into magazines, manufac-

[4] Zosimus, l. iv, p. 245, 249. Theodoret, l. v, c. 21, Idatius in Chron. Prosper. Aquitan. l. iii, c. 38, apud Baronium, Annal. Eccles. A. D. 389, No. 52. Libanius (pro Templis, p. 10) labours to prove that the commands of Theodosius were not direct and positive.

tures, or places of public assembly: and perhaps, when the walls of the temple had been sufficiently purified by holy rites, the worship of the true Diety might be allowed to expiate the ancient guilt of idolatry. But as long as they subsisted, the pagans fondly cherished the secret hope, that an auspicious revolution, a second Julian, might again restore the altars of the gods ; and the earnestness with which they addressed their unavailing prayers to the throne,[e] increased the zeal of the Christian reformers to extirpate, without mercy, the root of superstition. The laws of the emperors exhibit some symptoms of a milder disposition :[f] but their cold and languid efforts were insufficient to stem the torrent of enthusiasm and rapine, which was conducted, or rather impelled, by the spiritual rulers of the church. In Gaul, the holy Martin, bishop of Tours,[g] marched, at the head of his faithful monks, to destroy the idols, the temples, and the consecrated trees of his extensive diocese ; and, in the execution of this arduous task, the prudent reader will judge whether Martin was supported by the aid of miraculous

---

[e] Cod. Theodos. l. xvi, tit. x, leg. 8, 18. There is room to believe, that this temple of Edessa, which Theodosius wished to save for civil uses, was soon afterwards a heap of ruins, (Libanius pro Templis, p. 26, 27, and Godefroy's notes, p. 59).

[f] See this curious oration of Libanius pro Templis, pronounced, or rather composed, about the year 390. I have consulted, with advantage, Dr. Lardner's version and remarks, (Heathen Testimonies, vol. iv, p. 135-163).

[g] See the life of Martin, by Sulpicius Severus, c. 9-14. The saint once mistook (as Don Quixote might have done) an harmless funeral for an idolatrous procession, and imprudently committed a miracle.

CHAP. XXVIII.

powers, or of carnal weapons. In Syria, the divine and excellent Marcellus,[b] as he is styled by Theodoret, a bishop animated with apostolic fervour, resolved to level with the ground the stately temples within the diocese of Apamea. His attack was resisted, by the skill and solidity, with which the temple of Jupiter had been constructed. The building was seated on an eminence: on each of the four sides, the lofty roof was supported by fifteen massy columns, sixteen feet in circumference; and the large stones, of which they were composed, were firmly cemented with lead and iron. The force of the strongest and sharpest tools had been tried without effect. It was found necessary to undermine the foundations of the columns, which fell down as soon as the temporary wooden props had been consumed with fire; and the difficulties of the enterprise are described under the allegory of a black demon, who retarded, though he could not defeat, the operations of the Christian engineers. Elated with victory, Marcellus took the field in person against the powers of darkness; a numerous troop of soldiers and gladiators marched under the episcopal banner, and he successively attacked the villages and country temples of the diocese of Apamea. Whenever any resistance or danger was apprehended, the champion of the faith, whose lameness would not allow him either to fight or fly,

---

[b] Compare Sozomen, (l. vii, c. 15) with Theodoret (l. v, c. 21). Between them, they relate the crusade and death of Marcellus.

placed himself at a convenient distance, beyond the reach of darts. But this prudence was the occasion of his death: he was surprised and slain by a body of exasperated rustics: and the synod of the province pronounced, without hesitation, that the holy Marcellus had sacrificed his life in the cause of God. In the support of this cause, the monks, who rushed with tumultuous fury, from the desert, distinguished themselves by their zeal and diligence. They deserved the enmity of the pagans ; and some of them might deserve the reproaches of avarice and intemperance ; of avarice, which they gratified with holy plunder, and of intemperance, which they indulged at the expence of the people, who foolishly admired their tattered garments, loud psalmody, and artificial paleness.[i] A small number of temples was protected by the fears, the venality, the taste, or the prudence, of the civil and ecclesiastical governors. The temple of the celestial Venus at Carthage, whose sacred precincts formed a circumference of two miles, was judiciously converted into a Christian church ;[k] and a similar consecration has preserved inviolate the majestic dome of the Pantheon of Rome.[l] But in almost every province

[i] Libanius, pro Templis, p. 10-13. He rails at these black-garbled men, the Christian monks, who eat more than elephants. Poor elephants ! they are temperate animals.

[k] Prosper Aquitan. l. iii, c. 38, apud Baronium ; Annal. Eccles. A. D. 389, No. 58, &c. The temple had been shut some time, and the access to it was overgrown with brambles.

[l] Donatus, Roma Antiqua et Nova, l. iv, c. iv, p. 468. This consecration was performed by Pope Boniface IV. I am ignorant of the favourable circumstances which had preserved the Pantheon above two hundred years after the reign of Theodosius.

of the Roman world, an army of fanatics, without authority, and without discipline, invaded the peaceful inhabitants; and the ruin of the fairest structures of antiquity still displays the ravages of *those* barbarians, who alone had time and inclination to execute such laborious destruction. ·

The temple of Serapis at Alexandria.

In this wide and various prospect of devastation, the spectator may distinguish the ruins of the temple of Serapis, at Alexandria.[m] Serapis does not appear to have been one of the native gods, or monsters, who sprung from the fruitful soil of superstitious Egypt.[n] The first of the Ptolemies had been commanded, by a dream, to import the mysterious stranger from the coast of Pontus, where he had been long adored by the inhabitants of Sinope; but his attributes and his reign were so imperfectly understood, that it became a subject of dispute, whether he represented the bright orb of day, or the gloomy monarch of the subterraneous regions.[o] The Egyptians, who were obstinately devoted to the religion of their fathers, refused to admit this foreign deity within the walls of their

[m] Sophronius composed a recent and separate history, (Jerom, in Script. Eccles tom. i, p. 303), which had furnished materials to Socrates, (l. v, c. 16), Theodoret, (l. v, c. 22), and Rufinus, (l. ii, c. 22). Yet the last, who had been at Alexandria before and after the event, may deserve the credit of an original witness.

[n] General Vossius (Opera, tom. v, p. 80, and de Idololatrio, l. i, c. 29) strives to support the strange notion of the fathers; that the patriarch Joseph was adored in Egypt, as the bull Apis, and the god Serapis.

[o] Origo dei nondum nostris celebrata. Ægyptiorum antistites sic memorant, &c. Tacit Hist. iv, 88. The Greeks, who had travelled into Egypt were alike ignorant of this new deity.

cities.[p] But the obsequious priests, who were seduced by the liberality of the Ptolemies, submitted, without resistance, to the power of the god of Pontus : an honourable and domestic genealogy was provided ; and this fortunate usurper was introduced into the throne and bed of Osiris,[q] the husband of Isis, and the celestial monarch of Egypt. Alexandria, which claimed his peculiar protection, gloried in the name of the city of Serapis. His temple,[r] which rivalled the pride and magnificence of the capitol, was erected on the spacious summit of an artificial mount, raised one hundred steps above the level of the adjacent parts of the city ; and the interior cavity was strongly supported by arches, and distributed into vaults and subterraneous apartments. The consecrated buildings were surrounded by a quandrangular portico ; the stately halls, and exquisite statues, displayed the triumph of the arts; and the treasures of ancient learning were preserved in the famous Alexandrian library, which had arisen with new splendour from its ashes.[s] After the edicts of

[p] Macrobius, Saturnal. l. i, c. 7. Such a living fact decisively proves his foreign extraction.

[q] At Rome, Isis and Serapis were united in the same temple. The precedency which the queen assumed, may seem to betray her unequal alliance with the stranger of Pontus. But the superiority of the female sex was established in Egypt as a civil and religious institution, (Diodor. Sicul. tom. i, l. i, p. 31, edit. Wesseling); and the same order is observed in Plutarch's Treatise of Isis and Osiris, whom he identifies with Serapis.

[r] Ammianus (xxii, 16). The Expositio totius Mundi (p. 8, in Hudson's Geograph. Minor. tom. iii), and Rufinus, (l. ii, c. 22), celebrate the Serapeum, as one of the wonders of the world.

[s] See Memoires de l'Acad. des Inscriptions, tom. ix, p. 397–416.

The

Theodosius had severely prohibited the sacrifices of pagans, they were still tolerated in the city and temple of Serapis; and this singular indulgence was imprudently ascribed to the superstitious terrors of the Christians themselves; as if they had feared to abolish those ancient rites, which could alone secure the inundations of the Nile, the harvests of Egypt, and the subsistence of Constantinople.[t]

Its final
destruction,
A. D. 389.
At that time,[u] the archiepiscopal throne of Alexandria was filled by Theophilus,[x] the perpetual enemy of peace and virtue; a bold, bad man, whose hands were alternately polluted with gold, and with blood. His pious indignation was excited by the honours of Serapis; and the insults which he offered to an ancient chapel of Bacchus, convinced the pagans that he meditated a more important and dangerous enterprise. In the tumultuous capital of Egypt, the slightest provocation was sufficient to inflame a civil war. The votaries of Serapis, whose strength and numbers were much inferior to those of their antagonists, rose in arms at the instigation of the philo-

The *old* library of the Ptolemies was *totally* consumed in Cæsar's Alexandrian war. Marc Antony gave the whole collection of Pergamus (200,000 volumes) to Cleopatra, as the foundation of the *new* library of Alexandria.

[t] Libanius (pro Templis, p. 21) indiscreetly provokes his Christian masters by this insulting remark.

[u] We may choose between the date of Marcellinus, (A. D. 389), or that of Prosper, (A. D. 391). Tillemont (Hist. des Emp. tom. v, p. 310, 756) prefers the former, and Pagi the latter.

[x] Tillemont, Mem. Eccles. tom. xi, p. 441-500. The ambiguous situation of Theophilus, a *saint*, as the friend of Jerom; a *devil*, as the enemy of Chrysostom; produce a sort of impartiality: yet, upon the whole the balance is justly inclined against him.

sopher Olympius,[y] who exhorted them to die in
the defence of the altars of the gods. The pagan fanatics fortified themselves in the temple, or
rather fortress, of Serapis; repelled the besiegers
by daring sallies, and a resolute defence; and,
by the inhuman cruelties which they exercised
on their Christian prisoners, obtained the last
consolation of despair. The efforts of the prudent magistrate were usefully exerted for the
establishment of a truce, till the answer of Theodosius should determine the fate of Serapis.
The two parties assembled, without arms, in
the principal square; and the imperial rescript
was publicly read. But when a sentence of
destruction against the idols of Alexandria was
pronounced, the Christians set up a shout of
joy and exultation; whilst the unfortunate pagans, whose fury had given way to consternation, retired with hasty and silent steps, and
eluded, by their flight or obscurity, the resentment of their enemies. Theophilus proceeded
to demolish the temple of Serapis, without any
other difficulties, than those which he found in
the weight and solidity of the materials; but
these obstacles proved so insuperable, that he
was obliged to leave the foundations; and to
content himself with reducing the edifice itself
to a heap of rubbish, a part of which was soon
afterwards cleared away to make room for a
church erected in honour of the Christian mar-

[y] Lardner (Heathen Testimonies, vol. iv, p. 411) has alleged a beautiful passage from Suidas, or rather from Damascus, which shews the
devout and virtuous Olympius, not in the light of a warrior, but of a
prophet.

tyrs. The valuable library of Alexandria was pillaged or destroyed ; and, near twenty years afterwards. the appearance of the empty shelves excited the regret and indignation of every spectator, whose mind was not totally darkened by religious prejudice.[a] The compositions of ancient genius, so many of which have irretrievably perished, might surely have been excepted from the wreck of idolatry, for the amusement and instruction of succeeding ages ; and either the zeal or the avarice of the archbishop,[b] might have been satiated with the rich spoils, which were the reward of his victory. While the images and vases of gold and silver were carefully melted, and those of a less valuable metal were contemptuously broken, and cast into the streets. Theophilus laboured to expose the frauds and vices of the ministers of the idols ; their dexterity in the management of the loadstone ; their secret methods of introducing an human actor into a hollow statue ; and their scandalous abuse of the confidence of devout husbands, and unsuspecting females.[c] Charges like these may

[a] Nos vidimus armaria librorum, quibus direptis, exinanita ea a nostris hominibus, nostris temporibus memorant. Orosius, l. vi, c. 15, p. 421, edit. Havercamp. Though a bigot, and a controversial writer, Orosius seems to blush.

[b] Eunapius, in the lives of Antoninus and Ædesius, execrates the sacrilegious rapine of Theophilus. Tillemont (Mem. Eccles. tom. xiii, p. 453) quotes an epistle of Isidore of Pelusium, which reproaches the primate with the idolatrous worship of gold, the auri sacra fames.

[c] Rufinus names the priest of Saturn, who, in the character of the god, familiarly conversed with many pious ladies of quality ; till
he

seem to deserve some degree of credit, as they are not repugnant to the crafty and interested spirit of superstition. But the same spirit is equally prone to the base practice of insulting and calumniating a fallen enemy; and our belief is naturally checked by the reflection, that it is much less difficult to invent a fictitious story, than to support a practical fraud. The colossal statue of Serapis[c] was involved in the ruin of his temple and religion. A great number of plates of different metals, artificially joined together, composed the majestic figure of the deity, who touched on either side the walls of the sanctuary. The aspect of Serapis, his sitting posture, and the sceptre, which he bore in his left hand, were extremely similar to the ordinary representations of Jupiter. He was distinguished from Jupiter by the basket, or bushel, which was placed on his head; and by the emblematic monster, which he held in his right hand; the head and body of a serpent branching into three tails, which were again terminated by the triple heads of a dog, a lion, and a wolf. It was confidently affirmed, that if any impious hand should dare to violate the majesty of the god, the heavens and the earth would in-

---

he betrayed himself in a moment of transport, when he could not disguise the tone of his voice. The authentic and impartial narrative of Æschines, (see Bayle, Dictionnaire Critique, SCAMANDRE), and the adventure of Mundus, (Joseph. Antiquitat. Judaic. l. xviii, c. 3, p. 877, edit. Havercamp.) may prove that such amorous frauds have been practised with success.

[c] See the images of Serapis, in Montfaucon, (tom. ii, p. 297): but the description of Macrobius (Saturnal. l. i, c. 20) is much more picturesque and satisfactory.

stantly return to their original chaos.   An intrepid soldier, animated by zeal, and armed
with a weighty battle-axe, ascended the ladder;
and even the Christian multitude expected, with
some anxiety, the event of the combat.[4] He
aimed a vigorous stroke against the cheek of
Serapis ; the cheek fell to the ground; the thunder was still silent, and both the heavens and
the earth continued to preserve their accustomed order and tranquillity.   The victorious soldier repeated his blows : the huge idol was overthrown, and broken in pieces ; and the limbs of
Serapis were ignominiously dragged through
the streets of Alexandria.   His mangled car-
case was burnt in the amphitheatre, amidst the
shouts of the populace; and many persons attributed their conversion to this discovery of
the impotence of their tutelar deity.   The popular modes of religion, that propose any visible and material objects of worship, have the
advantage of adapting and familiarizing themselves to the senses of mankind : but this advantage is counterbalanced by the various and inevitable accidents to which the faith of the ido-
later is exposed.   It is scarcely possible, that,
in every disposition of mind, he should preserve

[4] Sed fortes tremuere manus, montique verendâ
  Majestate loci, si robora sacra ferirent
  In sua credebant redituras membra secures.
(Lucan. iii, 429).   " Is it true, (said Augustus to a veteran of Italy,
" at whose honse he supped), that, the man, who gave the first blow to
" the golden statue at Anaitis, was instantly deprived of his eyes, and
" of his life?"   " I was that man, (replied the clear-sighted veteran),
" and you now sup on one of the legs of the goddess." (Plin. Hist.
Natur. xxxiii, 24).

his implicit reverence for the idols, or the relics, which the naked eye, and the profane hand, are unable to distinguish from the most common productions of art, or nature; and if, in the hour of danger, their secret and miraculous virtue does not operate for their own preservation, he scorns the vain apologies of his priests, and justly derides the object, and the folly, of his superstitious attachment.[e] After the fall of Serapis, some hopes were still entertained by the pagans, that the Nile would refuse his annual supply to the impious masters of Egypt; and the extraordinary delay of the inundation seemed to announce the displeasure of the rival-god. But this delay was soon compensated by the rapid swell of the waters. They suddenly rose to such an unusual height, as to comfort the discontented party with the pleasing expectation of a deluge; till the peaceful river again subsided to the well-known and fertilizing level of sixteen cubits, or about thirty English feet.[f]

The temples of the Roman empire were deserted, or destroyed; but the ingenious superstition of the pagans still attempted to elude the laws of Theodosius, by which all sacrifices had

The pagan religion is prohibited, A. D. 390,

---

[e] The History of the Reformation affords frequent examples of the sudden change from superstition to contempt.

[f] Sozomen, l. vii, c. 20. I have supplied the measure. The same standard of the inundation, and consequently of the cubit, has uniformly subsisted since the time of Herodotus. See Freret, in the Mem. de l'Academie des Inscriptions, tom. xvi. p. 344-353. Greaves's Miscellaneous Works, vol. i, p. 233. The Egyptian cubit is about twenty-two inches of the English measure.

been severely prohibited. The inhabitants of the
country, whose conduct was less exposed to the
eye of malicious curiosity, disguised their *religious*, under the appearance of *convivial*, meetings.
On the days of solemn festivals, they assembled
in great numbers under the spreading shade of
some consecrated trees; sheep and oxen were
slaughtered and roasted; and this rural entertainment was sanctified by the use of incense,
and by the hymns, which were sung in honour
of the gods. But it was alledged, that, as
no part of the animal was made a burnt-
offering, as no altar was provided to receive
the blood, and as the previous oblation of
salt cakes, and the concluding ceremony of
libations, were carefully omitted, these festal
meetings did not involve the guests in the guilt,
or penalty, of an illegal sacrifice.[g] Whatever
might be the truth of the facts, or the merit of
the distinction,[h] these vain pretences were swept
away by the last edict of Theodosius; which inflicted a deadly wound on the superstition of the
pagans.[i] This prohibitory law is expressed in

[g] Libanius (pro Templis, p. 15, 16, 17) pleads their cause with gentle and insinuating rhetoric. From the earliest age, such feasts had
enlivened the country; and those of Bacchus (Georgic. ii, 380) had
produced the theatre of Athens. See Godefroy, ad loc. Liban. and
Codex Theodos. tom. vi, p. 284.

[h] Honorius tolerated these rustic festivals, (A. D. 399). "Absque
"ullo sacrificio, atque ulla superstitione damnabili." But nine years
afterwards he found it necessary to reiterate and enforce the same
proviso, (Codex Theodos. l. xvi, tit. x, leg. 17, 19).

[i] Cod. Theodos. l. xvi, tit. x, leg. 12. Jortin (Remarks on Eccles.
History, vol. iv, p. 134) censures, with becoming asperity, the style
and sentiments of this intolerant law.

the most absolute and comprehensive terms.
" It is our will and pleasure," says the emperor,
" that none of our subjects, whether magistrates
" or private citizens, however exalted or how-
" ever humble may be their rank and condition,
" shall presume, in any city, or in any place, to
" worship an inanimate idol, by the sacrifice of
" a guiltless victim." The act of sacrificing, and
the practice of divination by the entrails of the
victim, are declared (without any regard to the
object of the inquiry) a crime of high treason
against the state; which can be expiated only by
the death of the guilty. The rites of pagan
superstition, which might seem less bloody and
atrocious, are abolished, as highly injurious to
the truth and honour of religion; luminaries,
garlands, frankincense, and libations of wine,
are specially enumerated and condemned; and
the harmless claims of the domestic genius, of
the household gods, are included in this rigorous
proscription. The use of any of these profane
and illegal ceremonies, subjects the offender to
the forfeiture of the house, or estate, where they
have been performed; and if he has artfully
chosen the property of another for the scene of
his impiety, he is compelled to discharge, without delay, a heavy fine of twenty-five pounds of
gold, or more than one thousand pounds sterling.
A fine not less considerable, is imposed on the
connivance of the secret enemies of religion, who
shall neglect the duty of their respective stations, either to reveal or to punish, the guilt of
idolatry. Such was the persecuting spirit of

the laws of Theodosius, which were repeatedly enforced by his sons and grandsons, with the loud and unanimous applause of the Christian world.[k]

oppressed, In the cruel reigns of Decius and Diocletian, Christianity had been proscribed, as a revolt from the ancient and hereditary religion of the empire; and the unjust suspicions which were entertained of a dark and dangerous faction, were, in some measure, countenanced by the inseparable union, and rapid conquests, of the catholic church. But the same excuses of fear and ignorance cannot be applied to the Christian emperors, who violated the precepts of humanity and of the gospel. The experience of ages had betrayed the weakness, as well as folly, of paganism; the light of reason and of faith had already exposed, to the greatest part of mankind, the vanity of idols; and the declining sect, which still adhered to their worship, might have been permitted to enjoy, in peace and obscurity, the religious customs of their ancestors. Had the pagans been animated by the undaunted zeal, which possessed the minds of the primitive believers, the triumph of the church must have been stained with blood; and the martyrs of Jupiter and Apollo might have em-

[k] Such a charge should not be lightly made; but it may surely be justified by the authority of St. Augustin, who thus addressed the Donatists.—" Quis nostrûm, quis vestrûm non laudat leges ab impera-" toribus datas adversus sacrificia paganorum? Et certe longe ibi " pœna severior constituta est; illius quippe impietatis capitale suppli-" cium est." Epist. xciii, No. 10, quoted by Le Clerc, (Bibliotheque Choisie, tom. viii, p. 277), who adds some judicious reflections on the intolerance of the victorious Christians.

braced the glorious opportunity of devoting their lives and fortunes at the foot of their altars. But such obstinate zeal was not congenial to the loose and careless temper of polytheism. The violent and repeated strokes of the orthodox princes, were broken by the soft and yielding substance against which they were directed; and the ready obedience of the pagans protected them from the pains and penalties of the Theodosian code.[1] Instead of asserting, that the authority of the gods was superior to that of the emperor, they desisted, with a plaintive murmur, from the use of those sacred rites which their sovereign had condemned. If they were sometimes tempted, by a sally of passion, or by the hopes of concealment, to indulge their favourite superstition; their humble repentance disarmed the severity of the Christian magistrate, and they seldom refused to atone for their rashness, by submitting, with some secret reluctance, to the yoke of the gospel. The churches were filled with the increasing multitude of these unworthy proselytes, who had conformed, from temporal motives, to the reigning religion; and whilst they devoutly imitated the postures, and recited the prayers, of the faithful, they satisfied their conscience by the silent and sincere invocation of the gods of antiquity.[m] If the pagans wanted

---

[1] Orosius, l. vii, c. 28, p. 537. Augustin (Enarrat. in Psalm cxl apud Lardner, Heathen Testimonies, vol. iv, p. 458) insults their cowardice. "Quis eorum comprehensus est in sacrificio (cum his legibus ista prohiberentur) et non negavit?"

[m] Libanius (pro Templis, p. 17, 18) mentions, without censure, the occasional conformity, and as it were theatrical play, of these hypocrites.

....
patience to suffer, they wanted spirit to resist;
and the scattered myriads, who deplored the
ruin of the temples, yielded, without a contest,
to the fortune of their adversaries. The disorderly opposition[a] of the peasants of Syria, and
the populace of Alexandria, to the rage of private fanaticism, was silenced by the name and
authority of the emperor. The pagans of the
West, without contributing to the elevation of
Eugenius, disgraced, by their partial attachment, the cause and character of the usurper.
The clergy vehemently exclaimed, that he aggravated the crime of rebellion by the guilt of
apostacy; that, by his permission, the altar of
Victory was again restored; and that the idolatrous symbols of Jupiter and Hercules were
displayed in the field, against the invincible
standard of the cross. But the vain hopes of
the pagans were soon annihilated by the defeat
of Eugenius; and they were left exposed to the
resentment of the conqueror, who laboured to
deserve the favour of heaven by the extirpation
of idolatry.[b]

and final-
ly extin-
guished.
A. D. 390-
420, &c.
A nation of slaves is always prepared to applaud the clemency of their master, who, in the
abuse of absolute power, does not proceed to
the last extremes of injustice and oppression.
Theodosius might undoubtedly have proposed
to his pagan subjects the alternative of baptism

---

[a] Libanius concludes his apology, (p. 32), by declaring to the emperor, that unless he expressly warrants the destruction of the temples,
ωσθι τας των αγρων δεσποτας, και αυτοις, και τω νομω βοηθησοντας, the proprietors will defend themselves and the laws.

[b] Paulinus, in Vit. Ambros. c. 26.   Augustin de Civitat. Dei, l. v, c.
26.   Theodoret, l. v, c. 24.

or of death; and the eloquent Libanius has praised the moderation of a prince, who never enacted, by any positive law, that all his subjects should immediately embrace and practise the religion of their sovereign.[p] The profession of Christianity, was not made an essential qualification for the enjoyment of the civil rights of society, nor were any peculiar hardships imposed on the sectaries, who credulously received the fables of Ovid, and obstinately rejected the miracles of the gospel. The palace, the schools, the army, and the senate, were filled with declared and devout pagans; they obtained, without distinction, the civil and military honours of the empire. Theodosius distinguished his liberal regard for virtue and genius, by the consular dignity which he bestowed on Symmachus;[q] and by the personal friendship which he expressed to Libanius;[r] and the two eloquent apologists of paganism were never required either to change, or to dissemble, their religious opinions. The pagans were indulged in the most licentious freedom of speech and writing;

[p] Libanius suggests the form of a persecuting edict, which Theodosius might enact, (pro Templis, p. 32); a rash joke, and a dangerous experiment. Some princes would have taken his advice.

[q] Denique pro meritis terrestribus æque rependens
Munera, sacricolis summos impertit honores.
*   *   *   *   *   *   *   *   *
Ipse magistratum tibi consulis, ipse tribunal
Contulit.
Prudent. in Symmach. i, 617, &c.

[r] Libanius (pro Templis, p. 32) is proud that Theodosius should thus distinguish a man, who even in his *presence* would swear by Jupiter. Yet this presence seems to be no more than a figure of rhetoric.

CHAP.
XXVIII.

the historical and philosophical remains of Eu napius, Zosimus,[a] and the fanatic teachers of the school of Plato, betray the most furious animosity, and contain the sharpest invectives, against the sentiments and conduct of their victorious adversaries. If these audacious libels were publicly known, we must applaud the good sense of the Christian princes, who viewed, with a smile of contempt, the last struggles of superstition and despair.[b] But the imperial laws, which prohibited the sacrifices and ceremonies of paganism, were rigidly executed; and every hour contributed to destroy the influence of a religion, which was supported by custom, rather than by argument. The devotion of the poet, or the philosopher, may be secretly nourished by prayer, meditation, and study; but the exercise of public worship appears to be the only solid foundation of the religious sentiments of the people, which derive their force from imitation and habit. The interruption of that public exercise may consummate, in the period of a few years, the important work of a national revolution. The memory of theological opinions cannot long be preserved, without the artificial helps of priests, of

[a] Zosimus, who styles himself Count and Ex-advocate of the Treasury, reviles, with partial and indecent bigotry, the Christian princes, and even the father of his sovereign. His work must have been privately circulated, since it escaped the invectives of the ecclesiastical historians prior to Evagrius, (l. iii, c. 40-42), who lived towards the end of the sixth century.

[b] Yet the pagans of Africa complained, that the times would not allow them to answer with freedom the city of God : nor does St. Augustin (v. 26) deny the charge.

temples, and of books." The ignorant vulgar, whose minds are still agitated by the blind hopes and terrors of superstition, will be soon persuaded by their superiors, to direct their vows to the reigning deities of the age; and will insensibly imbibe an ardent zeal for the support and propagation of the new doctrine, which spiritual hunger at first compelled them to accept. The generation that arose in the world after the promulgation of the imperial laws, was attracted within the pale of the catholic church: and so rapid, yet so gentle, was the fall of paganism, that only twenty-eight years after the death of Theodosius, the faint and minute vestiges were no longer visible to the eye of the legislator.ˣ

The ruin of the pagan religion is described by the sophists, as a dreadful and amazing prodigy, which covered the earth with darkness, and restored the ancient dominion of chaos and of night. They relate, in solemn and pathetic strains, that the temples were converted into sepulchres; and that the holy places, which had been adorned by the statues of the gods, were basely polluted by the relics of Christian martyrs. " The monks" (a race of filthy animals, to whom Eunapius is tempted to refuse

---

* The Moors of Spain, who secretly preserved the Mahometan religion, above a century, under the tyranny of the Inquisition, possessed the Koran, with the peculiar use of the Arabic tongue. See the curious and honest story of their expulsion in Geddes, (Miscellanies, vol. i, p. 1-198).

ˣ Paganos qui supersunt, quanquam jam nullos esse credamus, &c. Cod. Theodos. l. xvi, tit. x, leg. 22, A. D. 423. The younger Theodosius was afterwards satisfied, that his judgment had been somewhat premature.

the name of men) " are the authors of the new
" worship, which, in the place of those deities,
" who are conceived by the understanding, has
" substituted the meanest and most contemp-
" tible slaves. The heads, salted and pickled,
" of those infamous malefactors, who, for the
" multitude of their crimes, have suffered a just
" and ignominious death; their bodies, still
" marked by the impression of the lash, and
" the scars of those tortures which were inflict-
" ed by the sentence of the magistrate; such"
(continues Eunapius) " are the gods which the
" earth produces in our days; such are the
" martyrs, the supreme arbitrators of our pray-
" ers and petitions to the Deity, whose tombs
" are now consecrated as the objects of the ve-
" neration of the people."[y] Without approving
the malice, it is natural enough to share the surprise, of the sophist, the spectator of a revolution, which raised those obscure victims of the
laws of Rome, to the rank of celestial and invisible protectors of the Roman empire. The
grateful respect of the Christians for the martyrs of the faith, was exalted, by time and victory, into religious adoration; and the most illustrious of the saints and prophets, were deservedly associated to the honours of the martyrs. One hundred and fifty years after the
glorious deaths of St. Peter and St. Paul, the
Vatican and the Ostian road were distinguished
by the tombs, or rather by the trophies, of those

[y] See Eunapius, in his life of the sophist Ædesius; in that of Eusta-
thius he foretels the ruin of paganism, καὶ τι μυθῶδες, καὶ αειδες σκότος
τυραννησει τα επι γης καλλιςα.

spiritual heroes.[a] In the age which followed the conversion of Constantine, the emperors, the consuls, and the generals of armies, devoutly visited the sepulchres of a tent-maker and a fisherman;[a] and their venerable bones were deposited under the altars of Christ, on which the bishops of the royal city continually offered the unbloody sacrifice.[b] The new capital of the eastern world, unable to produce any ancient and domestic trophies, was enriched by the spoils of dependant provinces. The bodies of St. Andrew, St. Luke, and St. Timothy, had reposed, near three hundred years, in the obscure graves, from whence they were transported, in solemn pomp, to the church of the apostles, which the magnificence of Constantine had founded on the banks of the Thracian Bosphorus.[c] About fifty years afterwards, the same banks were honoured by the presence of Samuel, the judge and prophet of

[a] Caius, (apud Euseb. Hist. Eccles. l. ii, c. 25), a Roman presbyter, who lived in the time of Zephyrinus, (A. D. 202-219), is an early witness of this superstitious practice.

[a] Chrysostom. Quod Christus sit Deus. Tom. i, nov. edit. No. 9. I am indebted for this quotation to Benedict the XIVth's pastoral letter on the jubilee of the year 1750. See the curious and entertaining letters of M. Chais, tom. iii.

[b] Male facit ergo Romanus episcopus? qui, super mortuorum hominum, Petri and Pauli, secundum nos, ossa veneranda . . . . offert Domino sacrificia, et tumulos eorum, Christi arbitratur altaria. Jerom. tom. ii, advers. Vigilant. p. 153.

[c] Jerom (tom. ii, p. 122) bears witness to these translations, which are neglected by the ecclesiastical historians. The passion of St. Andrew at Patræ, is described in an epistle from the clergy of Achaia, which Baronius (Annal. Eccles. A. D. 60, No. 34) wishes to believe, and Tillemont is forced to reject. St. Andrew was adopted as the spiritual founder of Constantinople, (Mem. Eccles. tom. i, p. 317-323, 588-591).

CHAP.
XXVIII.
~~~~~~~~~~

the people of Israel.   His ashes, deposited in a golden vase, and covered with a silken veil, were delivered by the bishops into each other's hands. The relics of Samuel were received by the people, with the same joy and reverence which they would have shewn to the living prophet; the highways, from Palestine to the gates of Constantinople, were filled with an uninterrupted procession; and the emperor Arcadius himself, at the head of the most illustrious members of the clergy and senate, advanced to meet his extraordinary guest, who had always deserved and claimed the homage of kings.[d]   The example of Rome and Constantinople confirmed the faith and discipline of the catholic world.   The honours of the saints and martyrs, after a feeble and ineffectual murmur of profane reason,[e] were universally established; and in the age of Ambrose and Jerom, something was still deemed wanting to the sanctity of a Christian church, till it had been consecrated by some portion of holy relics, which fixed and inflamed the devotion of the faithful.

General
reflections

In the long period of twelve hundred years, which elapsed between the reign of Constantine and the reformation of Luther, the worship of

[d] Jerom. (tom. ii, p. 122) pompously describes the translation of Samuel, which is noticed in all the chronicles of the times.

[e] The presbyter Vigilantius, the protestant of his age, firmly, though ineffectually withstood the superstition of monks, relics, saints, fasts, &c. for which Jerom compares him to the Hydra, Cerberus, the Centaurs, &c. and considers him only as the organ of the demon, (tom ii, p. 120-126).   Whoever will peruse the controversy of St. Jerom and Vigilantius, and St. Augustin's account of the miracles of St. Stephen, may speedily gain some idea of the spirit of the fathers.

saints and relics corrupted the pure and perfect simplicity of the Christian model; and some symptoms of degeneracy may be observed even in the first generations which adopted and cherished this pernicious innovation.

I. The satisfactory experience, that the relics of saints were more valuable than gold or precious stones,[f] stimulated the clergy to multiply the treasures of the church. Without much regard for truth or probability, they invented names for skeletons, and actions for names. The fame of the apostles, and of the holy men who had imitated their virtues, was darkened by religious fiction. To the invincible band of genuine and primitive martyrs, they added myriads of imaginary heroes, who had never existed, except in the fancy of crafty or credulous legendaries; and there is reason to suspect, that Tours might not be the only diocese in which the bones of a malefactor were adored, instead of those of a Saint.[g] A superstitious practice, which tended to increase the temptations of fraud, and credulity, insensibly extinguished the light of history, and of reason, in the Chris tian world.

II. But the progress of superstition would have been much less rapid and victorious, if the faith

---

[f] M. de Beausobre (Hist. du Manicheisme. tom. ii, p. 648) had applied a worldly sense to the pious observation of the clergy of Smyrna, who carefully preserved the relics of St. Polycarp the martyr.

[g] Martin of Tours (see his Life c. 8, by Sulpicius Severus) extorted this confession from the mouth of the dead man. The error is allowed to be natural; the discovery is supposed to be miraculous. Which of the two was likely to happen most frequently?

of the people had not been assisted by the seasonable aid of visions and miracles, to ascertain the authenticity and virtue of the most suspicious relics. In the reign of the younger Theodosius, Lucian,[b] a presbyter of Jerusalem, and the ecclesiastical minister of the village of Caphargamala, about twenty miles from the city, related a very singular dream, which, to remove his doubts, had been repeated on three successive Saturdays. A venerable figure stood before him, in the silence of the night, with a long beard, a white robe, and a gold rod; announced himself by the name of Gamaliel, and revealed to the astonished presbyter, that his own corpse, with the bodies of his son Abibas, his friend Nicodemus, and the illustrious Stephen, the first martyr of the Christian faith, were secretly buried in the adjacent field. He added, with some impatience, that it was time to release himself, and his companions, from their obscure prison; that their appearance would be salutary to a distressed world; and that they had made choice of Lucian to inform the bishop of Jerusalem of their situation, and their wishes. The doubts and difficulties which still retarded this important discovery, were successively re-

---

[b] Lucian composed in Greek his original narrative, which has been translated by Avitus, and published by Baronius, (Annal. Eccles. A. D. 415, No. 7-16). The Benedictine editors of St. Augustin have given (at the end of the work de Civitate Dei) two several copies, with many various readings. It is the character of falsehood to be loose and inconsistent. The most incredible parts of the legend are smoothed and softened by Tillemont. (Mem. Eccles. tom. ii, p. 9 &c.)

moved by new visions: and the ground was opened by the bishop, in the presence of an innumerable multitude. The coffins of Gamaliel, of his son, and of his friend, were found in regular order; but when the fourth coffin, which contained the remains of Stephen, was shown to the light, the earth trembled, and an odour, such as that of paradise, was smelt, which instantly cured the various diseases of seventy-three of the assistants. The companions of Stephen were left in their peaceful residence of Caphargamala; but the relics of the first martyr were transported, in solemn procession, to a church constructed in their honour on Mount Sion; and the minute particles of those relics, a drop of blood,[l] or the scrapings of a bone, were acknowledged, in almost every province of the Roman world, to possess a divine and miraculous virtue. The grave and learned Augustin,[k] whose understanding scarcely admits the excuse of credulity, has attested the innumerable prodigies which were performed in Africa by the relics of St. Stephen; and this marvellous narrative is inserted in the elaborate work of the City of God, which the bishop of Hippo designed as a solid and immortal proof of the truth of

[l] A phial of St. Stephen's blood was annually liquified at Naples, till he was superseded by St. Januarius, (Ruinart. Hist. Persecut. Vandal. p, 529).

[k] Augustin composed the two and twenty books de Civitate Dei in the space of thirteen years. A. D. 413-426. (Tillemont, Mem. Eccles. tom. xiv, p. 608, &c.) His learning is too often borrowed, and his arguments are two often his own; but the whole work claims the merit of a magnificent design, vigorously, and not unskilfully, executed.

Christianity.   Augustin solemnly declares, that
he had selected those miracles only which were
publicly certified by the persons who were either the objects, or the spectators, of the power
of the martyr.   Many prodigies were omitted,
or forgotten; and Hippo had been less favourably treated than the other cities of the province.   And yet the bishop enumerates above
seventy miracles, of which three were resurrec-
tions from the dead, in the space of two years,
and within the limits of his own diocese.[1]   If
we enlarge our view to all the dioceses, and all
the saints, of the Christian world, it will not be
easy to calculate the fables, and the errors,
which issued from this inexhaustible source.
But we may surely be allowed to observe, that
a miracle, in that age of superstition and credulity, lost its name and its merit, since it
could scarcely be considered as a deviation
from the ordinary, and established, laws of nature.

III. Revi-
val of po-
lytheism.
III.   The innumerable miracles, of which the
tombs of the martyrs were the perpetual theatre,
revealed to the pious believer the actual state and
constitution of the invisible world ; and his religious speculations appeared to be founded on
the firm basis of fact and experience.   Whatever
might be the condition of vulgar souls, in the
long interval between the dissolution and the

---

[1] See Augustin. de Civitat. Dei, l. xxii, c. 22, and the Appendix,
which contains two books of St. Stephen's miracles by Evodius, bishop
of Uzalis.   Freculphus (apud Basnage, Hist. des Juifs, tom. viii, p.
349) has preserved a Gallic or Spanish proverb, " Whoever pretends
to have read all the miracles of St. Stephen, he lies."

resurrection of their bodies, it was evident the
superior spirits of the saints and martyrs did
not consume that portion of their existence in
silent and inglorious sleep.[m] It was evident,
(without presuming to determine the place of
their habitation, or the nature of their felicity),
that they enjoyed the lively and active consciousness of their happiness, their virtue, and
their powers; and that they had already secured the possession of their eternal reward.
The enlargement of their intellectual faculties
surpassed the measure of the human imagination; since it was proved by *experience*, that
they were capable of hearing and understanding the various petitions of their numerous votaries; who, in the same moment of time, but in
the most distant parts of the world, invoked
the name and assistance of Stephen or of Martin.[a] The confidence of their petitioners was
founded on the persuasion that the saints, who
reigned with Christ, cast an eye of pity upon
earth; that they were warmly interested in the
prosperity of the catholic church; and that the

[m] Burnet (de Statû Mortuorum, p. 56-84) collects the opinions of
the Fathers, as far as they assert the sleep, or repose, of human souls,
till the day of judgment. He afterwards exposes (p. 91, &c.) the in-
conveniencies which must arise, if they possessed a more active and
sensible existence.

[a] Vigilantius placed the souls of the prophets and martyrs, either in
the bosom of Abraham (in loco refrigerii), or else under the altar of
God. Nec posse suis tumulis et ubi voluerunt adesse præsentes. But
Jerom (tom. ii, p. 122) sternly refutes this *blasphemy*. Tu Deo leges
pones? Tu apostolis vincula injicies, ut usque ad diem judicii
teneantur custodiâ, nec sint cum Domino suo; de quibus scriptum est,
Sequuntur Agnum quocunque vadit. St. Agnus ubique, ergo, et hi qui
cum Agno sunt, ubique esse credendi sunt. Et cum diabolus et dæmo-
nes toto vagentur in orbe, &c.

K 2

CHAP.
XXVIII.

individuals, who imitated the example of their faith and piety, were the peculiar and favourite objects of their most tender regard. Sometimes, indeed, their friendship might be influenced by considerations of a less exalted kind : they viewed, with partial affection, the places which had been consecrated by their birth, their residence, their death, their burial, or the possession of their relics. The meaner passions of pride, avarice, and revenge, may be deemed unworthy of a celestial breast ; yet the saints themselves condescended to testify their grateful approbation of the liberality of their votaries ; and the sharpest bolts of punishment were hurled against those impious wretches, who violated their magnificent shrines, or disbelieved their supernatural power.° Atrocious, indeed, must have been the guilt, and strange would have been the scepticism, of those men, if they had obstinately resisted the proofs of a divine agency, which the elements, the whole range of the animal creation, and even the subtle and invisible operations of the human mind, were compelled to obey.ᵖ The immediate, and almost instantaneous, effects, that were supposed to follow the prayer, or the offence, satisfied the Christians, of the ample measure of favour and authority, which the saints enjoyed in the presence of the Supreme God ; and it seemed al-

° Fleury, Discours sur l'Hist. Ecclesiastique, iii, p. 80.

ᵖ At Minorca, the relics of St. Stephen converted, in eight days, 540 Jews ; with the help, indeed, of some wholesome severities, such as burning the synagogue, driving the obstinate infidels to starve among the rocks, &c. See the original letter of Severus bishop of Minorca, (ad calcem St. Augustin. de Civ. Dei), and the judicious remark of Basnage, (tom. viii, p. 245-251).

most superfluous to inquire, whether they were
continually obliged to intercede before the
throne of grace ; or whether they might not be
permitted to exercise, according to the dictates
of their benevolence and justice, the delegated
powers of their subordinate ministry. The imagination, which had been raised by a painful
effort to the contemplation and worship of the
Universal Cause, eagerly embraced such inferior objects of adoration, as were more proportioned to its gross conceptions and imperfect
faculties. The sublime and simple theology of
the primitive Christians was gradually corrupted ; and the MONARCHY of heaven, already
clouded by metaphysical subtleties, was degraded by the introduction of a popular mytho-
logy, which tended to restore the reign of polytheism. [q]

IV. As the objects of religion were gradually
reduced to the standard of the imagination, the
rites and ceremonies were introduced that seemed most powerfully to affect the senses of the
vulgar. If, in the beginning of the fifth century.[r]
Tertullian, or Lactantius,[s] had been suddenly
raised from the dead, to assist at the festival of

---

[q] Mr. Hume (Essays, vol. ii, p. 434) observes, like a philosopher, the
natural flux and reflux of polytheism and theism.

[r] D'Aubigné (see his own Memoires, p. 156-160) frankly offered, with
the consent of the Huguenot ministers, to allow the first 400 years as
the rule of faith. The Cardinal du Perron haggled for forty years
more, which were indiscreetly given. Yet neither party would have
found their account in this foolish bargain.

[s] The worship practised and inculcated by Tertullian, Lactantius,
Arnobius, &c. is so *extremely* pure and spiritual, that their declamations
against the pagan, sometimes glance against the Jewish, ceremonies.

CHAP.
XXVIII.

some popular saint, or martyr;[*] they would have gazed with astonishment, and indignation, on the profane spectacle, which had succeeded to the pure and spiritual worship of a Christian congregation. As soon as the doors of the church were thrown open, they must have been offended by the smoke of incense, the perfume of flowers, and the glare of lamps and tapers, which diffused, at noon-day, a gawdy, superfluous, and in their opinion, a sacrilegious light. If they approached the balustrade of the altar, they made their way through the prostrate crowd, consisting, for the most part of strangers and pilgrims, who resorted to the city on the vigil of the feast; and who already felt the strong intoxication of fanaticism, and, perhaps, of wine. Their devout kisses were imprinted on the walls and pavement of the sacred edifice; and their fervent prayers were directed, whatever might be the language of their church, to the bones, the blood, or the ashes of the saint, which were usually concealed, by a linen or silken veil, from the eyes of the vulgar. The Christians frequented the tombs of the martyrs, in the hope of obtaining, from their powerful intercession, every sort of spiritual, but more especially of temporal, blessings. They implored the preservation of their health, or the cure of their infirmities;

---

[*] Faustus the Manichæan accuses the catholics of idolatry. Vertitis idola in martyres . . . . quos votis similibus colitis. M. de Beausobre, (Hist. Critique du Manicheisme, tom. ii, p. 629-700), a protestant, but a philosopher, has represented, with candour and learning, the introduction of *Christian idolatry* in the fourth and fifth centuries.

the fruitfulness of their barren wives, or the safety and happiness of their children. Whenever
they undertook any distant or dangerous journey, they requested, that the holy martyrs
would be their guides and protectors on the
road ; and if they returned, without having experienced any misfortune, they again hastened
to the tombs of the martyrs, to celebrate, with
grateful thanksgivings, their obligations to the
memory and relics of those heavenly patrons.
The walls were hung round with symbols of the
favours which they had received ; eyes, and
hands, and feet, of gold and silver ; and edifying pictures, which could not long escape the
abuse of indiscreet or idolatrous devotion, represented the image, the attributes, and the
miracles of the tutelar saint. The same uniform original spirit of superstition might suggest, in the most distant ages and countries, the
same methods of deceiving the credulity, and of
affecting the senses, of mankind:" but it must
ingenuously be confessed, that the ministers of
the catholic church imitated the profane model,
which they were impatient to destroy. The
most respectable bishops had persuaded themselves, that the ignorant rustics would more
cheerfully renounce the superstitions of paganism, if they found some resemblance, some

---

" The resemblance of superstition, which could not be imitated,
might be traced from Japan to Mexico. Warburton has seized this
idea, which he distorts, by rendering it too general and absolute
(Divine Legation, vol. iv, p. 126, &c.)

compensation in the bosom of Christianity. The religion of Constantine achieved, in less than a century, the final conquest of the Roman empire: but the victors themselves were insensibly subdued by the arts of their vanquished rivals.[x]

---

[x] The imitation of paganism is the subject of Dr. Middleton's agreeable letter from Rome. Warburton's animadversions obliged him to connect (vol. iii, p. 120-132) the history of the two religions; and to prove the antiquity of the Christian copy.

CHAP. XXIX.

Final division of the Roman empire between the sons of Theodosius—Reign of Arcadius and Honorius——Administration of Rufinus and Stilicho—Revolt and defeat of Gildo in Africa.

THE genius of Rome expired with Theodosius; the last of the successors of Augustus and Constantine, who appeared in the field at the head of their armies, and whose authority was universally acknowledged throughout the whole extent of the empire. The memory of his virtues still continued, however, to protect the feeble and inexperienced youth of his two sons. After the death of their father, Arcadius and Honorius were saluted, by the unanimous consent of mankind, as the lawful emperors of the East, and of the West; and the oath of fidelity was eagerly taken by every order of the state; the senates of old and new Rome, the clergy, the magistrates, the soldiers, and the people. Arcadius, who was then about eighteen years of age, was born in Spain, in the humble habitation of a private family. But he received a princely education in the palace of Constantinople; and his inglorious life was spent in that peaceful and splendid seat of royalty, from whence he appeared to reign over the provinces of Thrace, Asia Minor, Syria, and Egypt, from the Lower Danube to the confines of Persia and Ethiopia. His younger brother,

CHAP. XXIX.

Division of the empire between Arcadius and Honorius, A. D. 295, Jan. 17.

Honorius, assumed, in the eleventh year of his age, the nominal government of Italy, Africa, Gaul, Spain, and Britain; and the troops, which guarded the frontiers of his kingdom, where opposed, on one side, to the Caledonians, and on the other to the Moors. The great and martial prefecture of Illyricum was divided between the two princes; the defence and possession of the provinces of Noricum, Pannonia, and Dalmatia, still belonged to the western empire; but the two large dioceses of Dacia and Macedonia, which Gratian had intrusted to the valour of Theodosius, were for ever united to the empire of the East. The boundary in Europe was not very different from the line which now separates the Germans and the Turks; and the respective advantages of territory, riches, populousness, and military strength, where fairly balanced and compensated, in this final and permanent division of the Roman empire. The hereditary sceptre of the sons of Theodosius appeared to be the gift of nature, and of their father; the generals and ministers had been accustomed to adore the majesty of the royal infants; and the army and people were not admonished of their rights, and of their power, by the dangerous example of a recent election. The gradual discovery of the weakness of Arcadius and Honorius, and the repeated calamities of their reign, were not sufficient to obliterate the deep and early impressions of loyalty. The subjects of Rome, who still reverenced the persons, or rather the names, of their sovereigns, beheld, with equal abhorrence, the rebels who opposed, and the ministers who abused, the authority of the throne.

Theodosius had tarnished the glory of his reign by the elevation of Rufinus; an odious favourite, who, in an age of civil and religious faction, has deserved, from every party, the imputation of every crime. The strong impulse of ambition and avarice[a] had urged Rufinus to abandon his native country, an obscure corner of Gaul,[b] to advance his fortune in the capital of the East: the talent of bold and ready elocution[c] qualified him to succeed in the lucrative profession of the law; and his success in that profession was a regular step to the most honourable and important employments of the state. He was raised, by just degrees, to the station of master of the offices. In the exercise of his various functions, so essentially connected with the whole system of civil government, he acquired the confidence of a monarch, who soon discovered his diligence and capacity in business, and who long remained ignorant of the pride, the malice, and the covetousness, of his disposition. These vices were concealed beneath the mask of profound dissimulation;[d]

Character
and admi-
nistration
of Rufi-
nus,
A. D. 386-
395.

[a] Alecto, envious of the public felicity, convenes an infernal synod. Magæra recommends her pupil Rufinus, and excites him to deeds of mischief, &c. But there is as much difference between Claudian's fury and that of Virgil, as between the characters of Turnus and Rufinus.

[b] It is evident, (Tillemont, Hist. des Emp. tom. v, p. 770), though de Marca is ashamed of his countrymen, that Rufinus was born at Elusa, the metropolis of Novempopulania, now a small village of Gascony, (d'Anville, Notice de l'Ancienne Gaule, p. 289).

[c] Philostorgius, l. xi, c. 3, with Godefroy's Dissert. p. 440.

[d] A passage of Suidas is expressive of his profound dissimulation; Βαθυγνωμων ανθρωπος και κρυψινος

his passions were subservient only to the passions of his master; yet, in the horrid massacre of Thessalonica, the cruel Rufinus inflamed the fury, without imitating the repentance, of Theodosius. The minister, who viewed with proud indifference the rest of mankind, never forgave the appearance of an injury; and his personal enemies had forfeited, in his opinion, the merit of all public services. Promotus, the master-general of the infantry, had saved the empire from the invasion of the Ostrogoths; but he indignantly supported the pre-eminence of a rival, whose character and profession he despised; and, in the midst of a public council, the impatient soldier was provoked to chastise with a blow the indecent pride of the favourite. This act of violence was represented to the emperor as an insult, which it was incumbent on *his* dignity to resent. The disgrace and exile of Promotus were signified by a peremptory order, to repair, without delay, to a military station on the banks of the Danube; and the death of that general (though he was slain in a skirmish with the barbarians) was imputed to the perfidious arts of Rufinus.[e] The sacrifice of an hero gratified his revenge; the honours of the consulship elated his vanity; but his power was still imperfect and precarious, as long as the important posts of prefect of the East, and of prefect of Constantinople, were filled by Tatian,[f]

[e] Zosimus, l. iv, p 272, 273.
[f] Zosimus, who describes the fall of Tatian and his son, (l. iv, p. 273, 274), asserts their innocence: and even *his* testimony may outweigh the charges of their enemies, (Cod. Theodos. tom. iv, p. 489), who accuse

and his son Proculus; whose united authority balanced, for some time, the ambition and favour of the master of the offices. The two prefects were accused of rapine and corruption in the administration of the laws and finances. For the trial of these illustrious offenders, the emperor constituted a special commission; several judges were named to share the guilt and reproach of injustice; but the right of pronouncing sentence was reserved to the president alone, and that president was Rufinus himself. The father, stripped of the prefecture of the East, was thrown into a dungeon; but the son, conscious that few ministers can be found innocent, where an enemy is their judge, had secretly escaped; and Rufinus must have been satisfied with the least obnoxious victim, if despotism had not condescended to employ the basest and most ungenerous artifice. The prosecution was conducted with an appearance of equity and moderation, which flattered Tatian with the hope of a favourable event; his confidence was fortified by the solemn assurances, and perfidious oaths, of the president, who presumed to interpose the sacred name of Theodosius himself; and the unhappy father was at last persuaded to recal, by a private letter, the fugitive Proculus. He was instantly seized, examined, condemned, and beheaded, in one of the suburbs of Constantinople, with a precipi-

accuse them of oppressing the *Curiæ*. The connection of Tatian with the Arians, while he was prefect of Egypt, (A. D. 363), inclines Tillemont to believe that he was guilty of every crime, (Hist. des Emp. tom. v, p. 360. Mem. Eccles. tom vi, p. 589).

tation which disappointed the clemency of the emperor. Without respecting the misfortunes of a consular senator, the cruel judges of Tatian compelled him to behold the execution of his son: the fatal cord was fastened round his own neck; but in the moment when he expected, and perhaps desired, the relief of a speedy death, he was permitted to consume the miserable remnant of his old age in poverty and exile.[g] The punishment of the two prefects might, perhaps, be excused by the exceptionable parts of their own conduct; the enmity of Rufinus might be palliated by the jealous and unsociable nature of ambition. But he indulged a spirit of revenge, equally repugnant to prudence and to justice, when he degraded their native country of Lycia, from the rank of Roman provinces; stigmatized a guiltless people with a mark of ignominy; and declared that the countrymen of Tatian and Proculus should ever remain incapable of holding any employment of honour or advantage, under the imperial government.[h] The new prefect of the East

---

[g] ————Juvenum torantia colla
Ante patrum vultus strictâ cecidere securi.
Ibat grandævus nato moriente superstes
Post tiabens exsul.   In Rufin. i, 248.
The *facts* of Zosimus explain the *allusions* of Claudian; but his classic interpreters were ignorant of the fourth century. The *fatal cord*, I found, with the help of Tillemont, in a sermon of St. Asterius of Amasea.

[h] This odious law is recited, and repealed, by Arcadius, (A. D. 396), in the Theodosian Code, l. ix, tit. xxxviii, leg. 9. The sense, as it is explained by Claudian, (in Rufin. i, 234), and Godefroy, (tom. iii, p 279), is perfectly clear.
— —Exscindere cives
Funditus; et nomen gentis delere laborat.

(for Rufinus instantly succeeded to the vacant honours of his adversary) was not diverted, however, by the most criminal pursuits, from the performance of the religious duties, which in that age were considered as the most essential to salvation. In the suburb of Chalcedon, surnamed the *Oak,* he had built a magnificent villa; to which he devoutly added a stately church, consecrated to the apostles St. Peter and St. Paul, and continually sanctified by the prayers, and penance, of a regular society of monks. A numerous, and almost general, synod of the bishops of the eastern empire was summoned to celebrate, at the same time, the dedication of the church, and the baptism of he founder. This double ceremony was performed with extraordinary pomp; and when Rufinus was purified, in the holy font, from all the sins that he had hitherto committed, a venerable hermit of Egypt rashly proposed himself as the sponsor of a proud and ambitious statesman.[1]

The character of Theodosius imposed on his minister the task of hypocrisy, which disguised, and sometimes restrained, the abuse of power; and Rufinus was apprehensive of disturbing the indolent slumber of a prince, still capable of exerting the abilities, and the virtue, which had

---

The scruples of Pagi and Tillemont can arise only from their zeal for the glory of Theodosius.

[1] Ammonius . . . . Rufinum propriis manibus suscepit sacro fonte mundatum. See Rosweyde's Vitæ Patrum, p. 947. Sozomen, l. viii, c. 17) mentions the church and monastery; and Tillemont (Mem. Eccles. tom. ix, p. 593) records this synod, in which St. Gregory of Nyssa performed a conspicuous part.

raised him to the throne.[k] But the absence, and soon afterwards, the death, of the emperor, confirmed the absolute authority of Rufinus over the person and dominions of Arcadius; a feeble youth, whom the imperious prefect considered as his pupil, rather than his sovereign. Regardless of the public opinion, he indulged his passions without remorse, and without resistance; and his malignant and rapacious spirit rejected every passion that might have contributed to his own glory, or the happines of the people. His avarice,[l] which seems to have prevailed in his corrupt mind, over every other sentiment, attracted the wealth of the East, by the various arts of partial, and general, extortion; oppressive taxes, scandalous bribery, immoderate fines, unjust confiscations, forced or fictitious testaments, by which the tyrant despoiled of their lawful inheritance the children of strangers, or enemies; and the public sale of justice, as well as of favour, which he instituted in the palace of Constantinople. The ambitious

[k] Montesquieu (Esprit des Loix, l. xii, c. 12) praises one of the laws of Theodosius addressed to the prefect Rufinus, (l. ix, tit. iv, leg. unic.) to discourage the prosecution of treasonable, or sacrilegious, words. A tyrannical statue always proves the existence of tyranny; but a laudable edict may only contain the specious professions, or ineffectual wishes, of the prince, or his ministers. This, I am afraid, is a just, though mortifying, canon of criticism.

———fluctibus auri
Expleri ille calor nequit———
     *   *   *   *   *
Congestæ cumulantur opes; orbisque rapinas
Accipit una domus.———

This character (Claudian. in Rufin. 1, 184-220) is confirmed by Jerom, a disinterested witness, (dedecus insatiabilis avaritiæ, tom. i, ad Heliodor. p. 26). by Zosimus, (l. v, p. 286), and by Suidas, who copied the history of Eunapius.

candidate eagerly solicited, at the expence of
the fairest part of his patrimony, the honours
and emoluments of some provincial government;
the lives and fortunes of the unhappy people
were abandoned to the most liberal purchaser;
and the public discontent was sometimes appeased by the sacrifice of an unpopular criminal, whose punishment was profitable only to
the prefect of the East, his accomplice and his
judge. If avarice were not the blindest of the
human passions, the motives of Rufinus might
excite our curiosity; and we might be tempted
to inquire, with what view he violated every
principle of humanity and justice, to accumu-
late those immense treasures, which he could
not spend without folly, nor possess without
danger. Perhaps he vainly imagined, that he
laboured for the interest of an only daughter,
on whom he intended to bestow his royal pupil,
and the august rank of empress of the East.
Perhaps he deceived himself by the opinion,
that his avarice was the instrument of his ambition. He aspired to place his fortune on a
secure and independent basis, which should no
longer depend on the caprice of the young emperor; yet he neglected to conciliate the hearts
of the soldiers and people, by the liberal distribution of those riches, which he had acquired with so much toil, and with so much
guilt. The extreme parsimony of Rufinus left
him only the reproach, and envy, of ill-gotten
wealth; his dependants served him without attachment; the universal hatred of mankind was

repressed only by the influence of servile fear. The fate of Lucian proclaimed to the East, that the prefect, whose industry was much abated in the despatch of ordinary business, was active and indefatigable in the pursuit of revenge. Lucian, the son of the prefect Florentius, the oppressor of Gaul, and the enemy of Julian, had employed a considerable part of his inheritance, the fruit of rapine and corruption, to purchase the friendship of Rufinus, and the high office of count of the East. But the new magistrate imprudently departed from the maxims of the court, and of the times; disgraced his benefactor, by the contrast of a virtuous and temperate administration; and presumed to refuse an act of injustice, which might have tended to the profit of the emperor's uncle. Arcadius was easily persuaded to resent the supposed insult; and the prefect of the East resolved to execute in person the cruel vengeance which he meditated against this ungrateful delegate of his power. He performed with incessant speed the journey of seven or eight hundred miles, from Constantinople to Antioch, entered the capital of Syria at the dead of night, and spread universal consternation among a people, ignorant of his design, but not ignorant of his character. The count of the fifteen provinces of the East was dragged, like the vilest malefactor, before the arbitrary tribunal of Rufinus. Notwithstanding the clearest evidence of his integrity, which was not impeached even by the voice of an accuser, Lucian was condemned, almost without a trial, to suffer a cruel and ignominious punishment. The ministers of the tyrant, by the order, and in the presence, of their master, beat him on the neck with leather thongs, armed at the extremities with lead; and when he fainted under the violence of the pain, he was removed in a close litter, to conceal his dying agonies from the eyes of the indignant city. No sooner had Rufinus perpetrated this inhuman act, the sole object of his expedition, than he returned, amidst the deep, and silent, curses of a trembling people, from Antioch to Constantinople; and his diligence was accelerated, by the hope of accomplishing, without delay, the nuptials of his daughter with the emperor of the East.[m]

But Rufinus soon experienced, that a prudent minister should constantly secure his royal captive by the strong, though invisible, chain of habit; and that the merit, and much more easily the favour, of the absent, are obliterated in a short time from the mind of a weak and capricious sovereign. While the prefect satiated his revenge at Antioch, a secret conspiracy of the favourite eunuchs, directed by the great chamberlain Eutropius, undermined his power in the palace of Constantinople. They discovered that Arcadius was not inclined to love the daughter of Rufinus, who had been chosen, without his consent, for his bride; and they contrived to substitute in her place the fair Eudoxia,

He is disappointed by the marriage of Arcadius, A. D. 395, April 27.

[m] ———Cætera segnis;
  Ad facinus velox: penitus regione remotas
  Impiger ire vias.
This allusion of Claudian (in Rufin. i, 241) is again explained by the circumstantial narrative of Zosimus, (l. v, p. 288, 289).

the daughter of Bauto,[a] a general of the Franks
in the service of Rome; and who was educated,
since the death of her father, in the family of
the sons of Promotus. The young emperor,
whose chastity had been strictly guarded by
the pious care of his tutor Arsenius,[b] eagerly
listened to the artful and flattering descriptions
of the charms of Eudoxia: he gazed with impatient ardour on her picture, and he understood the necessity of concealing his amorous
designs from the knowledge of a minister, who
was so deeply interested to oppose the consummation of his happiness. Soon after the return
of Rufinus, the approaching ceremony of the
royal nuptials was announced to the people of
Constantinople, who prepared to celebrate, with
false and hollow acclamations, the fortune of
his daughter. A splendid train of eunuchs and
officers issued, in hymeneal pomp, from the
gates of the palace; bearing aloft the diadem,
the robes, and the inestimable ornaments, of the
future empress. The solemn procession passed
through the streets of the city, which were
adorned with garlands, and filled with spectators; but, when it reached the house of the sons
of Promotus, the principal eunuch respectfully
entered the mansion, invested the fair Eudoxia
with the imperial robes, and conducted her in

[a] Zosimus (l. iv, p. 243) praises the valour, prudence, and integrity
of Bauto the Frank. See Tillemont, Hist. des Empereurs, tom. v, p.
771.

[b] Arsenius escaped from the palace of Constantinople, and passed
fifty-five years in rigid penance in the monasteries of Egypt. See Tillemont, Mem. Eccles. tom. xiv, p. 676-722; and Fleury, Hist. Eccles.
tom. v, p. 1, &c. but the latter, for the want of authentic materials, has
given too much credit to the legend of Metaphrastes.

triumph to the palace and bed of Arcadius.[p] The secrecy, and success, with which this conspiracy against Rufinus had been conducted, imprinted a mark of indelible ridicule on the character of a minister, who had suffered himself to be deceived, in a post where the arts of deceit and dissimulation constitute the most distinguished merit. He considered, with a mixture of indignation and fear, the victory of an aspiring eunuch, who had secretly captivated the favour of his sovereign; and the disgrace of his daughter, whose interest was inseparably connected with his own, wounded the tenderness, or, at least, the pride, of Rufinus. At the moment when he flattered himself that he should become the father of a line of kings, a foreign maid, who had been educated in the house of his implacable enemies, was introduced into the imperial bed; and Eudoxia soon displayed a superiority of sense and spirit, to improve the ascendant which her beauty must acquire over the mind of a fond and youthful husband. The emperor would soon be instructed to hate, to fear, and to destroy, the powerful subject, whom he had injured; and the consciousness of guilt deprived Rufinus of every hope, either of safety or comfort, in the retirement of a private life. But he still possessed the most effectual means of defending his dignity, and perhaps of oppressing his enemies. The prefect still exer-

[p] This story (Zosimus, l. v, p. 290) proves that the hymeneal rites of antiquity were still practised, without idolatry, by the Christians of the East; and the bride was *forcibly* conducted from the house of her parents to that of her husband. Our form of marriage requires, with less delicacy, the express and public consent of a virgin.

cised an uncontrouled authority over the civil and military government of the East : and his treasures, if he could resolve to use them, might be employed to procure proper instruments, for the execution of the blackest designs, that pride, ambition, and revenge, could suggest to a desperate statesman. The character of Rufinus seemed to justify the accusations, that he conspired against the person of his sovereign, to seat himself on the vacant throne ; and that he had secretly invited the Huns, and the Goths, to invade the provinces of the empire, and to increase the public confusion. The subtle prefect, whose life had been spent in the intrigues of the palace, opposed, with equal arms, the artful measures of the eunuch·Eutropius; but the timid soul of Rufinus was astonished by the hostile approach of a more formidable rival, of the great Stilicho, the general, or rather the master, of the empire of the West.[q]

Character of Stilicho, the minister, and general, of the western empire. The celestial gift which Achilles obtained, and Alexander envied, of a poet worthy to celebrate the actions of heroes, has been enjoyed by Stilicho, in a much higher degree than might have been expected from the declining state of genius, and of art. The muse of Claudian,[r] devoted to his service, was always prepared to stigmatize his adversaries, Rufinus, or Eutropius, with eternal infamy ; or to paint, in the

[q] Zosimus, (l. v, p. 290) ; Orosius, (l. vii, c. 37), and the Chronicle of Marcellinus. Claudian (in Rufin. ii, 7-100) paints, in lively colours, the distress and guilt of the prefect.

[r] Stilicho, directly or indirectly, is the perpetual theme of Claudian The youth, and private life, of the hero, are vaguely expressed in the poem on his first consulship. 35-140.

most splendid colours, the victories and virtues, of a powerful benefactor. In the review of a period indifferently supplied with authentic materials, we cannot refuse to illustrate the annals of Honorius, from the invectives, or the panegyrics, of a contemporary writer: but as Claudian appears to have indulged the most ample privilege of a poet and a courtier, some criticism will be requisite to translate the language of fiction, or exaggeration, into the truth and simplicity of historic prose. His silence concerning the family of Stilicho may be admitted as a proof, that his patron was neither able, nor desirous, to boast of a long series of illustrious progenitors; and the slight mention of his father, an officer of barbarian cavalry, in the service of Valens, seems to countenance the assertion, that the general, who so long commanded the armies of Rome, was descended from the savage and perfidious race of the Vandals.* If Stilicho had not possessed the external advantages of strength and stature, the most flattering bard, in the presence of so many thousand spectators, would have hesitated to affirm, that he surpassed the measure of the demi-gods of antiquity; and, that whenever he moved, with lofty steps, through the streets of the capital, the astonished crowd made room for the stranger, who displayed, in a private condition, the awful majesty of a hero. From his earliest youth he embraced the profession of

* Vandalorum, imbellis, avaræ, perfidæ, et dolosæ, gentis, genere editus. Orosius, l. vii, c. 38. Jerom tom. i, and Gerontiam, p. 93, calls him a semi-barbarian.

arms; his prudence and valour were soon distinguished in the field; the horsemen and archers of the East admired his superior dexterity; and in each degree of his military promotions, the public judgment always prevented and approved the choice of the sovereign. He was named by Theodosius, to ratify a solemn treaty with the monarch of Persia: he supported, during that important embassy, the dignity of the Roman name; and after his return to Constantinople, his merit was rewarded by an intimate and honourable alliance with the imperial family. Theodosius had been prompted, by a pious motive of fraternal affection, to adopt, for his own, the daughter of his brother Honorius; the beauty and accomplishments of Serena[t] were universally admired by the obsequious court; and Stilicho obtained the preference over a crowd of rivals, who ambitiously disputed the hand of the princess, and the favour of her adoptive father.[u] The assurance that the husband of Serena would be faithful to the throne, which he was permitted to approach, engaged the emperor to exalt the fortunes, and to employ the abilities, of the sagacious and intrepid Stilicho. He rose through the successive steps of master of the horse, and

His military command

count of the domestics, to the supreme rank of master-general of all the cavalry and infantry of

[t] Claudian, in an imperfect poem, has drawn a fair, perhaps a flattering, portrait of Serena. That favourite niece of Theodosius was born, as well as her sister Thermantia, in Spain; from whence, in their earliest youth, they were honourably conducted to the palace of Constantinople.

[u] Some doubt may be entertained, whether this adoption was legal or only metaphorical, (see Ducange, Fam. Byzant. p. 75). An old inscription gives Stilicho the singular title of *Pro gener Divi Theodosii.*

the Roman, or at least of the western, empire;[x] and his enemies confessed, that he invariably disdained to barter for gold the rewards of merit, or to defraud the soldiers of the pay and gratifications, which they deserved, or claimed, from the liberality of the state.[y] The valour and conduct which he afterwards displayed, in the defence of Italy, against the arms of Alaric and Radagaisus, may justify the fame of his early achievements; and in an age less attentive to the laws of honour, or of pride, the Roman generals might yield the pre-eminence of rank, to the ascendant of superior genius.[z] He lamented, and revenged, the murder of Promotus, his rival and his friend; and the massacre of many thousands of the flying Bastarnæ is represented by the poet, as a bloody sacrifice, which the Roman Achilles offered to the manes of another Patroclus. The virtues and victories of Stilicho deserved the hatred of Rufinus: and the arts of

---

[x] Claudian (Laus Serenæ, 190, 193), expresses in poetic language, the " dilectus equorum," and the " gemino mox idem culmine duxit " agmina." The inscription adds, " count of the domestics," an important command, which Stilicho, in the height of his grandeur, might prudently retain.

[y] The beautiful lines of Claudian (in i Cons. Stilich. ii, 113) display *his* genius: but the integrity of Stilicho (in the military administration) is much more firmly established by the unwilling evidence of Zosimus, (l. v, p. 345).

[z] —— Si bellica moles
   Ingrueret, qnamvis annis et jure minori,
   Cedere grandævos equitum peditumque magistros
   Adspiceres.——   Claudian, Laus Seren. p. 196, &c.
A modern general would deem their submission, either heroic patriotism, or abject servility.

calumny might have been successful, if the tender and vigilant Serena had not protected her husband against his domestic foes, whilst he vanquished in the field the enemies of the empire.[a] Theodosius continued to support an unworthy minister, to whose diligence he delegated the government of the palace, and of the East; but when he marched against the tyrant Eugenius, he associated his faithful general to the labours and glories of the civil war; and, in the last moments of his life, the dying monarch recommended to Stilicho the care of his sons, and of the republic.[b] The ambition and the abilities of Stilicho were not unequal to the important trust; and he claimed the guardianship of the two empires, during the minority of Arcadius and Honorius.[c] The first measure of his administration, or rather of his reign, displayed to the nations the vigour and activity of a spirit worthy to command. He passed the Alps in the depth of winter; descended the stream of

[a] Compare the poem on the first consulship, (i, 95-115), with the *Laus Seneræ*, (227-237, where it unfortunately breaks off). We may perceive the deep inveterate malice of Rufinus.

[b] ————Quem *fratribus* ipse
Discedens, clypeumque defensoremque dedisti.
Yet the nomination (iv Cons. Hon. 432) was private, (iii Cons. Hon. 142) cunctos discedere . . . jubet; and may, therefore, be suspected. Zosimus, and Suidas, apply to Stilicho, and Rufinus, the same equal title of Εππτροποι, guardians, or procurators.

[c] The Roman law distinguishes two sorts of *minority*, which expired at the age of fourteen and of twenty-five. The one was subject to the *tutor*, or guardian, of the person; the other to the *curator*, or trustee, of the estate, (Heineccius, Antiquitat. Rom. ad Jurisprudent, pertinent. l. i, tit. xxii, xxiii, p. 218-232). But these legal ideas were never accurately transferred into the constitution of an elective monarchy.

the Rhine, from the fortress of Basil to the marches of Batavia; reviewed the state of the garrisons; repressed the enterprises of the Germans; and, after establishing along the banks a firm and honourable peace, returned with incredible speed to the palace of Milan.[d] The person and court of Honorius were subject to the master-general of the West; and the armies and provinces of Europe obeyed, without hesitation, a regular authority, which was exercised in the name of their young sovereign. Two rivals only remained to dispute the claims, and to provoke the vengeance, of Stilicho. Within the limits of Africa, Gildo, the Moor, maintained a proud and dangerous independence; and the minister of Constantinople asserted his equal reign over the emperor, and the empire, of the East.

The impartiality which Stilicho affected, as the common guardian of the royal brothers, engaged him to regulate the equal division of the arms, the jewels, and the magnificent wardrobe and furniture of the deceased emperor.[e] But the most important object of the inheritance consisted of the numerous legions, cohorts, and squadrons of Romans, or barbarians, whom the event of the civil war had united under the standard of Theodosius. The various multi-

---

[d] See Claudian (i Cons. Stilich. i, 188-242); but he must allow more than fifteen days for the journey and return between Milan and Leyden.

[e] I Cons. Stilich. ii, 88-94. Not only the robes and diadems of the deceased emperor, but even the helmets, sword-hilts, belts, cuirasses, &c. were enriched with pearls, emeralds, and diamonds.

tudes of Europe and Asia, exasperated by recent animosities, were overawed by the authority of a single man'; and the rigid discipline of
Stilicho protected the lands of the citizen from
the rapine of the licentious soldier.[f]   Anxious,
however, and impatient, to relieve Italy from
the presence of this formidable host, which
could be useful only on the frontiers of the empire, he listened to the just requisition of the
minister of Arcadius, declared his intention of
re-conducting in person the troops of the East;
and dexterously employed the rumour of a Gothic tumult, to conceal his private designs of
ambition and revenge.[g]   The guilty soul of Rufinus was alarmed by the approach of a warrior
and a rival, whose enmity he deserved; he computed, with increasing terror, the narrow space
of his life and greatness; and, as the last hope
of safety, he interposed the authority of the emperor Arcadius.   Stilicho, who appears to have
directed his march along the sea-coast of the
Hadriatic, was not far distant from the city of
Thessalonica, when he received a peremptory
message, to recal the troops of the East, and to
declare, that *his* nearer approach would be con-

―――Tantoque remoto
Principe, mutatas orbis non sensit habenas.
This high commendation (i Cons. Stil. i, 149) may be justified by the
fears of the dying emperor, (de Bell. Gildon. 292-301); and the
peace and good order which were enjoyed after his death, (i Cons.
Stil. i, 150-168).

[g] Stilicho's march, and the death of Rufinus, are described by Claudian, (in Rufin. l. ii, 101-453; Zosimus, (l. v, p. 296, 297); Sozomen,
(l. viii, c. 1); Socrates, (l. vi, c. 1); Philostorgius, (l. xi, c. 3, with
Godefroy, p. 441), and the Chronicle of Marcellinus.

sidered, by the Byzantine court, as an act of
hostility. The prompt and unexpected obedience of the general of the West, convinced the
vulgar of his loyalty and moderation ; and, as
he had already engaged the affection of the eastern troops, he recommended to their zeal the
execution of his bloody design, which might be
accomplished in his absence, with less danger
perhaps, and with less reproach. Stilicho left
the command of the troops of the East to Gainas, the Goth, on whose fidelity he firmly relied ; with an assurance, at least, that the hardy
barbarian would never be diverted from his purpose by any consideration of fear or remorse.
The soldiers were easily persuaded to punish
the enemy of Stilicho, and of Rome ; and such
was the general hatred which Rufinus had excited, that the fatal secret, communicated to
thousands, was faithfully preserved during the
long march from Thessalonica to the gates of
Constantinople. As soon as they had resolved
his death, they condescended to flatter his
pride ; the ambitious prefect was seduced to
believe, that those powerful auxiliaries might be
tempted to place the diadem on his head ; and
the treasures which he distributed, with a tardy
and reluctant hand, were accepted by the indignant multitude, as an insult, rather than as a
gift. At the distance of a mile from the capital, in the field of Mars, before the palace of
Hebdomon, the troops halted : and the emperor,
as well as his minister, advanced, according to
ancient custom, respectfully to salute the power
which supported their throne. As Rufinus

CHAP. passed along the ranks, and disguised, **with**
XXIX. studied courtesy, his innate haughtiness, the
wings insensibly wheeled from the right and
left, and inclosed the devoted victim within the
circle of their arms.   Before he could reflect on
the danger of his situation, Gainas gave the signal of death; a daring and forward soldier
plunged his sword into the breast of the guilty
prefect, and Rufinus fell, groaned, and expired,
at the feet of the affrighted emperor.   If the
agonies of a moment could expiate the crimes
of a whole life, or if the outrages inflicted on a
breathless corpse could be the object of pity,
our humanity might perhaps be affected by the
horrid circumstances which accompanied the
murder of Rufinus.   His mangled body was
abandoned to the brutal fury of the populace
of either sex, who hastened in crowds, from
every quarter of the city, to trample on the remains of the haughty minister, at whose frown
they had so lately trembled.   His right hand
was cut off, and carried through the streets of
Constantinople, in cruel mockery, to extort
contributions for the avaricious tyrant, whose
head was publicly exposed, borne aloft on the
point of a long lance.[h]   According to the savage maxims of the Greek republics, his innocent family would have shared the punishment
of his crimes.   The wife and daughter of Rufinus were indebted for their safety to the
influence of religion.   *Her* sanctuary protected

[h] The *dissection* of Rufinus, which Claudian performs with the savage coolness of an anatomist, (in Rufin. ii, 405-415), is likewise speci-
fied by Zosimus and Jerom, (tom. i, p. 26).

them from the raging madness of the people;
and they were permitted to spend the remainder
of their lives in the exercises of Christian devotion, in the peaceful retirement of Jerusalem.[j]

The servile poet of Stilicho applauds, with
ferocious joy, this horrid deed, which, in the
execution, perhaps, of justice, violated every
law of nature and society, profaned the majesty
of the prince, and renewed the dangerous examples of military licence. The contemplation of
the universal order and harmony had satisfied
Claudian of the existence of the Deity; but the
prosperous impunity of vice appeared to con-
tradict his moral attributes; and the fate of
Rufinus was the only event which could dispel
the religious doubts of the poet.[k] Such an act
might vindicate the honour of Providence; but
it did not much contribute to the happiness of
the people. In less than three months they
were informed of the maxims of the new administration, by a singular edict, which established the exclusive right of the treasury over the
spoils of Rufinus; and silenced, under heavy
penalties, the presumptuous claims of the subjects of the eastern empire, who had been in-

[j] The pagan Zosimus mentions their sanctuary and pilgrimage. The sister of Rufinus, Sylvania, who passed her life at Jerusalem, is famous in monastic history. 1. The studious virgin had diligently, and even repeatedly, perused the commentators on the bible, Origen, Gregory, Basil, &c. to the amount of five millions of lines. 2. At the age of threescore, she could boast, that she had never washed her hands, face, or any part of her whole body, except the tips of her fingers, to receive the communion. See the Vitæ Patrum, p. 779, 977.

[k] See the beautiful exordium of his invective against Rufinus, which is curiously discussed by the sceptic Bayle, Dictionnaire Critique, Rufin. Not. E.

jured by his rapacious tyranny.[1]   Even Stilicho did not derive from the murder of his rival, the fruit which he had proposed; and though he gratified his revenge, his ambition was disappointed.   Under the name of a favourite, the weakness of Arcadius required a master; but he naturally preferred the obsequious arts of the eunuch Eutropius, who had obtained his domestic confidence; and the emperor contemplated, with terror and aversion, the stern genius of a foreign warrior.   Till they were divided by the jealousy of power, the sword of Gainas, and the charms of Eudoxia, supported the favour of the great chamberlain of the palace: the perfidious Goth, who was appointed master-general of the East, betrayed, without scruple, the interest of his benefactor; and the same troops, who had so lately massacred the enemy of Stilicho, were engaged to support, against him, the independence of the throne of Constantinople.   The favourites of Arcadius fomented a secret and irreconcileable war against a formidable hero, who aspired to govern, and to defend, the two empires of Rome, and the two sons of Theodosius.   They incessantly laboured, by dark and treacherous machinations, to deprive him of the esteem of the prince, the respect of the people, and the friendship of the barbarians.   The life of Stilicho was repeatedly attempted by the dagger of hired assassins; and a decree was obtained, from the senate of Con-

[1] See the Theodosian Code, l. ix, tit. xlii, leg. 14, 16   The new ministers attempted, with inconsistent avarice, to seize the spoils of their predecessor, and to provide for their own future security.

stantinople, to declare him an enemy of the republic, and to confiscate his ample possessions in the provinces of the East. At a time when the only hope of delaying the ruin of the Roman name, depended on the firm union, and reciprocal aid, of all the nations to whom it had been gradually communicated, the subjects of Arcadius and Honorius were instructed, by their respective masters, to view each other in a foreign, and even hostile, light; to rejoice in their mutual calamities, and to embrace, as their faithful allies, the barbarians, whom they excited to invade the territories of their countrymen.[m] The natives of Italy affected to despise the servile and effeminate Greeks of Byzantium, who presumed to imitate the dress, and to usurp the dignity, of Roman senators;[n] and the Greeks had not yet forgot the sentiments of hatred and contempt, which their polished ancestors had so long entertained for the rude inhabitants of the West. The distinction of two governments, which soon produced the separation of two nations, will justify my design of suspending the series of the Byzantine history, to prosecute, without interruption,

---

[m] See Claudian, (i Cons. Stilich. l. i, 275, 292, 296; l. ii, 83), and Zosimus, l. v, p. 302).

[n] Claudian turns the consulship of the eunuch Eutropius into a national reflection, (l. ii, 134).
———Plaudentem cerne senatum
Et Byzantinos proceres, *Graiosque* Quirites :
O patribus plebes, O digni consule patres.
It is curious to observe the first symptoms of jealousy and schism between old and new Rome, between the Greeks and Latins.

CHAP.
XXIX.
~~~~~~~~~ the disgraceful, but memorable, reign of Honorious.

Revolt of
Gildo in
Africa,
A. D. 386-
398. The prudent Stilicho, instead of persisting to force the inclinations of a prince, and people, who rejected his government, wisely abandoned Arcadius to his unworthy favourites; and his reluctance to involve the two empires in a civil war, displayed the moderation of a minister, who had so often signalized his military spirit and abilities. But if Stilicho had any longer endured the revolt of Africa, he would have betrayed the security of the capital, and the majesty of the western emperor, to the capricious insolence of a Moorish rebel. Gildo,° the brother of the tyrant Firmus, had preserved, and obtained, as the reward of his apparent fidelity, the immense patrimony which was forfeited by treason; long and meritorious service, in the armies of Rome, raised him to the dignity of a military count; the narrow policy of the court of Theodosius had adopted the mischievous expedient of supporting a legal government by the interest of a powerful family; and the brother of Firmus was invested with the command of Africa. His ambition soon usurped the administration of justice, and of the finances, without account, and without controul; and he maintained, during a reign of twelve years, the possession of an office from which it was impossible to remove him, without the danger of a civil

---

° Claudian may have exaggerated the vices of Gildo; but his Moorish extraction, his notorious actions, and the complaints of St. Augustin, may justify the poet's's invectives. Baronius (Annal. Eccles. A. D. 398, No. 35-56) has treated the African rebellion with skill and learning.

war. During those twelve years, the province of Africa groaned under the dominion of a tyrant, who seemed to unite the unfeeling temper of a stranger, with the partial resentments of domestic faction. The forms of law were often superseded by the use of poison; and if the trembling guests, who were invited to the table of Gildo, presumed to express their fears, the insolent suspicion served only to excite his fury, and he loudly summoned the ministers of death. Gildo alternately indulged the passions of avarice and lust;[p] and if his *days* were terrible to the rich, his *nights* were not less dreadful to husbands and parents. The fairest of their wives and daughters were prostituted to the embraces of the tyrant; and afterwards abandoned to a ferocious troop of barbarians and assassins, the black, or swarthy natives of the desert; whom Gildo considered as the only guardians of his throne. In the civil war between Theodosius and Eugenius, the count, or rather the sovereign, of Africa, maintained a haughty and suspicious neutrality; refused to assist either of the contending parties with troops or vessels, expected the declaration of fortune, and reserved for the

---

[p] Instat terribilis vivis, morientibus hæres
Virginibus raptor, thalamis obscænus adulter.
Nulla quies : oritur prædâ cessante libido,
Divitibusque dies, et nox metuenda maritis.
————Mauris clarissima quæque
Fastidita datur.————
Baronius condemns, still more severely, the licentiousness of Gildo; as his wife, his daughter, and his sister, were examples of perfect chastity. The adulteries of the African soldiers are checked by one of the imperial laws.

N 2

CHAP.
XXIX. conqueror, the vain professions of his allegiance. Such professions would not have satisfied the master of the Roman world; but the death of Theodosius, and the weakness and discord of his sons, confirmed the power of the Moor; who condescended, as a proof of his moderation, to abstain from the use of the diadem, and to supply Rome with the customary tribute, or rather subsidy, of corn. In every division of the empire, the five provinces of Africa were invariably assigned to the West; and Gildo had consented to govern that extensive country in the name of Honorius; but his knowledge of the character and designs of Stilicho, soon engaged him to address his homage to a more distant and feeble sovereign. The ministers of Arcadius embraced the cause of a perfidious rebel; and the delusive hope of adding the numerous cities of Africa to the empire of the East, tempted them to assert a claim, which they were incapable of supporting, either by reason, or by arms.[q]

He is condemned by the Roman senate,
A. D. 397. When Stilicho had given a firm and decisive answer to the pretensions of the Byzantine court, he solemnly accused the tyrant of Africa before the tribunal, which had formerly judged the kings and nations of the earth; and the image of the republic was revived, after a long interval, under the reign of Honorius. The emperor transmitted an accurate and ample detail of the complaints

[q] Inque tuam sortem numerosas transtulit urbes. Claudian (de Bell. Gildonico, 230—224) has touched, with political delicacy, the intrigues of the Byzantine court, which are likewise mentioned by Zosimus, (l. v, p. 302).

of the provincials, and the crimes of Gildo, to the Roman senate; and the members of that venerable assembly were required to pronounce the condemnation of the rebel. Their unanimous suffrage declared him the enemy of the republic; and the decree of the senate added a sacred and legitimate sanction to the Roman arms.[r] A people, who still remembered, that their ancestors had been the masters of the world, would have applauded, with conscious pride, the representation of ancient freedom; if they had not long since been accustomed to prefer the solid assurance of bread, to the unsubstantial visions of liberty and greatness. The subsistence of Rome depended on the harvests of Africa; and it was evident, that a declaration of war would be the signal of famine. The prefect Symmachus, who presided in the deliberations of the senate, admonished the minister of his just apprehension, that as soon as the revengeful Moor should prohibit the exportation of corn, the tranquillity, and perhaps the safety, of the capital, would be threatened by the hungry rage of a turbulent multitude.[s] The prudence of Stilicho conceived, and executed, without delay, the most effectual measure for the relief of the Roman people. A large and seasonable supply of corn, collected in the inland provinces of

[r] Symmachus (l. iv, epist. 4) expresses the judicial forms of the senate; and Claudian (i Cons. Stilich. l. i, 325, &c.) seems to feel the spirit of a Roman.

[s] Claudian finely displays these complaints of Symmachus, in a speech of the goddess of Rome, before the throne of Jupiter, (de Bell. Gildon. 28-128).

Gaul, was embarked on the rapid stream of the
Rhone, and transported, by an easy navigation,
from the Rhone to the Tiber. During the whole
term of the African war, the granaries of Rome
were continually filled, her dignity was vindicated from the humiliating dependence, and the
minds of an immense people were quieted by
the calm confidence of peace and plenty.[t]

The cause of Rome, and the conduct of the
African war, were intrusted by Stilicho, to a
general, active and ardent to revenge his private
injuries on the head of the tyrant. The spirit of
discord, which prevailed in the house of Nabal,
had excited a deadly quarrel between two of his
sons, Gildo and Mascezel.[u] The usurper pursued, with implacable rage, the life of his younger
brother, whose courage and abilities he feared;
and Mascezel, oppressed by superior power,
took refuge in the court of Milan; where he soon
received the cruel intelligence, that his two innocent and helpless children had been murdered
by their inhuman uncle. The affliction of the
father was suspended only by the desire of revenge. The vigilant Stilicho already prepared
to collect the naval and military forces of the
western empire; and he had resolved, if the tyrant should be able to wage an equal and doubtful war, to march against him in person. But

---

[t] See Claudian, in (Eutrop. l. i, 401, &c; i Cons. Stil. l. i, 306, &c.
ii Cons. Stilich. 91, &c.)

[u] He was of a mature age; since he had formerly (A. D. 373) served
against his brother Firmus, (Ammian. xxix, 5). Claudian, who understood the court of Milan, dwells on the injuries, rather than the merits,
of Mascezel, (de Bell. Gild. 389–414). The Moorish war was not wor
thy of Honorius, or Stilicho, &c.

as Italy required his presence, and as it might
be dangerous to weaken the defence of the frontier, he judged it more advisable, that Mascezel
should attempt this arduous adventure, at the
head of a chosen body of Gallic veterans, who
had lately served under the standard of Eugenius. These troops, who were exhorted to con-
vince the world that they could subvert, as well
as defend, the throne of an usurper, consisted
of the *Jovian*, the *Herculian*, and the *Augustan*,
legions; of the *Nervian* auxiliaries; of the soldiers, who displayed in their banners the sym-
bol of a *lion*, and of the troops which were distinguished by the auspicious names of *Fortunate*,
and *Invincible*. Yet such was the smallness of
their establishments, or the difficulty of recruit-
ing, that these *seven* bands,[x] of high dignity and
reputation in the service of Rome, amounted to
no more than five thousand effective men.[y] The
fleet of galleys and transports sailed in tempes-
tuous weather from the port of Pisa, in Tuscany, and steered their course to the little island
of Capraria; which had borrowed that name
from the wild goats, its original inhabitants,
whose place was now occupied by a new colony
of a strange and savage appearance. " The

---

[x] Claudian, Bell. Gild. 415-423. The change of discipline allowed
him to use indifferently the names of *Legio, Cohors, Manipulus*. See the
Notitia Imperii, S. 38, 40.

[y] Orosius, (l. vii, c. 36, p. 565) qualifies this account with an expression of doubt, (ut aiunt); and it scarcely coincides with the
δυναμεις αδρας of Zosimus, (l. v, p. 303). Yet Claudian, after some declamation about Cadmus's soldiers, frankly owns, that Stilicho sent a
small army; lest the rebel should fly, ne timeare times, (i Cons. Stilich.
l. i, 314, &c.

" whole island (says an ingenious traveller of
" those times) is filled, or rather defiled, by
" men, who fly from the light.   They call them-
" selves *Monks,* or solitaries, because they
" choose to live alone, without any witness of
" their actions.   They fear the gifts of fortune,
" from the apprehension of losing them ; and,
" lest they should be miserable, they embrace
" a life of voluntary wretchedness.   How ab-
" surd is their choice! how perverse their un-
" derstanding! to dread the evils, without being
" able to support the blessings, of the human
" condition.   Either this melancholy madness
" is the effect of disease, or else the conscious-
" ness of guilt urges these unhappy men to ex-
" ercise on their own bodies the tortures which
" are inflicted on fugitive slaves by the hand of
" justice."[a]   Such was the contempt of a profane magistrate for the monks of Capraria, who
were revered, by the pious Mascezel, as the
chosen servants of God.[b]   Some of them were
persuaded, by his entreaties, to embark on
board the fleet; and it is observed, to the praise
of the Roman general, that his days and nights
were employed in prayer, fasting, and the occupation of singing psalms.   The devout leader,

---

[a] Claud. Rutil. Numatian. Itinerar. i, 439-448. He afterwards (515-
526) mentions a religious madman on the isle of Gorgona. For such
profane remarks, Rutilius, and his accomplices, are styled, by his commentator, Barthius, rabiosi canes diaboli. Tillemont, (Mem. Eccles.
tom. xii, p. 471) more calmly observes, that the unbelieving poet
praises where he means to censure.

[b] Orosius, l. vii, c. 36, p. 564. Augustin commends two of these
savage saints of the isle of Goats, epist. lxxxi, apud Tillemont, Mem.
Eccles. tom. xiii, p. 317. and Baronius. Annal. Eccles. A. D. 398. No.
81).

who, with such a reinforcement, appeared confident of victory, avoided the dangerous rocks of Corsica, coasted along the eastern side of Sardinia, and secured his ships against the violence of the south wind, by casting anchor in the safe and capacious harbour of Cagliari, at the distance of one hundred and forty miles from the African shores.[b]

Gildo was prepared to resist the invasion with all the forces of Africa. By the liberality of his gifts and promises, he endeavoured to secure the doubtful allegiance of the Roman soldiers, whilst he attracted to his standard the distant tribes of. Gætulia and Æthiopia. He proudly reviewed an army of seventy thousand men, and boasted, with the rash presumption which is the forerunner of disgrace, that his numerous cavalry would trample under their horses feet the troops of Mascezel, and involve, in a cloud of burning sand, the natives of the cold regions of Gaul and Germany.[c] But the Moor, who commanded the legions of Honorius, was too well acquainted with the manners of his countrymen, to entertain any serious apprehension of a naked and disorderly host of barbarians; whose left arm, instead of a shield, was protected only by a mantle; who were totally disarmed as soon as they had darted their javelin from their right hand; and whose horses had never been taught

[b] Here the first book of the Gildonic war is terminated. The rest of Claudian's poem has been lost; and we are ignorant *how*, or *where*, the army made good their landing in Africa.

[c] Orosius must be responsible for the account. The presumption of Gildo, and his various train of barbarians, is celebrated by Claudian, (i Cons. Stil. l. i, 345-355).

to bear the controul, or to obey the guidance, of the bridle. He fixed his camp of five thousand veterans in the face of a superior enemy, and, after the delay of three days, gave the signal of a general engagement.[d] As Mascezel advanced before the front with fair offers of peace and pardon, he encountered one of the foremost standard-bearers of the Africans, and, on his refusal to yield, struck him on the arm with his sword. The arm, and the standard, sunk under the weight of the blow; and the imaginary act of submission was hastily repeated by all the standards of the line. At this signal, the disaffected cohorts proclaimed the name of their lawful sovereign; the barbarians, astonished by the defection of their Roman allies, dispersed, according to their custom, in tumultuary flight; and Mascezel obtained the honours of an easy, and almost bloodless victory.[e] The tyrant escaped from the field of battle to the sea-shore; and threw himself into a small vessel, with the hope of reaching in safety some friendly port of the empire of the East; but the obstinacy of the wind drove him back into the harbour of Tabraca[f] which had acknowledged, with the rest

---

[d] St. Ambrose, who had been dead about a year, revealed, in a vision, the time and place of the victory. Mascezel afterwards related his dream to Paulinus, the original biographer of the saint, from whom it might easily pass to Orosius.

[e] Zosimus, (l. v, p. 303) supposes an obstinate combat; but the narrative of Orosius appears to conceal a real fact, under the disguise of a miracle.

[f] Tabraca lay between the two Hippos, (Cellarius, tom. ii, p, ii, p. 112; d'Anville, tom. iii, p. 84). Orosius has distinctly named the field of battle, but our ignorance cannot define the precise situation.

of the province, the dominion of Honorius, and CHAP.
XXIX the authority of his lieutenant. The inhabitants, as a proof of their repentance and loyalty, seized and confined the person of Gildo in a dungeon; and his own despair saved him from the intolerable torture of supporting the presence of an injured, and victorious, brother.[e] The captives, and the spoils, of Africa, were laid at the feet of the emperor; but Stilicho, whose moderation appeared more conspicuous, and more sincere, in the midst of prosperity, still affected to consult the laws of the republic, and referred to the senate and people of Rome the judgment of the most illustrious criminals.[h] Their trial was public and solemn; but the judges, in the exercise of this obsolete and precarious jurisdiction, were impatient to punish the African magistrates, who had intercepted the subsistence of the Roman people. The rich and guilty province was oppressed by the imperial ministers, who had a visible interest to multiply the number of the accomplices of Gildo; and if an edict of Honorius seems to check the malicious industry of informers, a subsequent edict, at the distance of

[e] The death of Gildo is expressed by Claudian, (i Cons. Stil. l. 357), and his best interpreters, Zosimus and Orosius.

[h] Claudian (ii Cons. Stilich. 99-119) describes their trial, (tremuit quos Africa nuper, cernunt rostra reos), and applauds the restoration of the ancient constitution. It is here that he introduces the famous sentence, so familiar to the friends of despotism.—

———Nunquam libertas gratior exstat

Quam sub rege pio.———

But the freedom, which depends on royal piety scarcely deserves that appellation.

CHAP. XXIX.

ten years, continues and renews the prosecution of the offences which had been committed in the time of the general rebellion.[1] The adherents of the tyrant, who escaped the first fury of the soldiers, and the judges, might derive some consolation from the tragic fate of his brother, who could never obtain his pardon for the extraordinary services which he had performed. After he had finished an important war in the space of a single winter, Mascezel was received at the court of Milan with loud applause, affected gratitude, and secret jealousy;[k] and his death, which, perhaps, was the effect of accident, has been considered as the crime of Stilicho. In the passage of a bridge, the Moorish prince, who accompanied the master-general of the West, was suddenly thrown from his horse into the river; the officious haste of the attendants was restrained by a cruel and perfidious smile, which they observed on the countenance of Stilicho; and while they delayed the necessary assistance, the unfortunate Mascezel was irrecoverably drowned.[l]

Marriage, and character of Honorius, A. D. 398.

The joy of the African triumph was happily connected with the nuptials of the emperor Honorius, and of his cousin Maria, the daughter of Stilicho: and this equal and honourable alliance

[1] See the Theodosian Code, l. ix, tit. xxxix, leg. 3; tit. xl. leg. 19.
[k] Stilicho, who claimed an equal share in all the victories of Theodosius and his son, particularly asserts that Africa was recovered by the wisdom of his counsels, (see an inscription produced by Baronius).
[l] I have softened the narrative of Zosimus, which, in its crude simplicity, is almost incredible, (l. v, p. 303). Orosius damns the victorious general (p. 538) for violating the right of sanctuary.

seemed to invest the powerful minister with the
authority of a parent over his submissive pupil.
The muse of Claudian was not silent on this
propitious day :[m] he sung, in various and lively
strains, the happiness of the royal pair; and the
glory of the hero, who confirmed their union,
and supported their throne. The ancient fables
of Greece, which had almost ceased to be the
object of religious faith, were saved from oblivion by the genius of poetry. The picture of
the Cyprian grove, the seat of harmony and
love; the triumphant progress of Venus over her
native seas, and the mild influence which her
presence diffused in the palace of Milan, express to every age the natural sentiments of the
heart, in the just and pleasing language of al-
legorical fiction. But the amorous impatience,
which Claudian attributes to the young prince,[n]
must excite the smiles of the court; and his
beauteous spouse (if she deserved the praise
of beauty) had not much to fear or to hope
from the passions of her lover. Honorius was

[m] Claudian, as the poet laureat, composed a serious and elaborate
epithalamium of 340 lines; besides some gay Fescennines, which were
sung, in a more licentious tone, on the wedding night.

[n] —————Calet obvius ire
Jam princeps, tardumque cupit discedere solem.
Nobilis haud aliter *sonipes*
(de Nuptiis Honor. et Mariæ, 287), and more freely in the Fescennines,
(112-126).
Dices, *O quoties*, hoc mihi dulcius
Quam flavos *decies* vincere Sarmatas
— * * * * * * *.
Tum victor madido prosilias toro
Nocturni referens vulnera prælii.

CHAP.
XXIX.

only in the fourteenth year of his age; Serena, the mother of his bride, deferred, by art or persuasion, the consummation of the royal nuptials; Maria died a virgin, after she had been ten years a wife; and the chastity of the emperor was secured by the coldness, or, perhaps, the debility, of his constitution.[o] His subjects, who attentively studied the character of their young sovereign, discovered that Honorius was without passions, and consequently without talents; and that his feeble and languid disposition was alike incapable of discharging the duties of his rank, or of enjoying the pleasures of his age. In his early youth he made some progress in the exercises of riding and drawing the bow: but he soon relinquished these fatiguing occupations, and the amusement of feeding poultry became the serious and daily care of the monarch of the West,[p] who resigned the reigns of empire to the firm and skilful hand of his guardian Stilicho. The experience of history will countenance the suspicion, that a prince who was born in the purple, received a worse education than the meanest peasant of his dominions; and that the ambitious minister suffered him to attain the age of manhood, without attempting to excite his courage, or to enlighten his understanding.[q] The predecessors

[o] See Zosimus, l. v, p. 333.

[p] Procopius de Bell. Gothico, l. i, c. 2. I have borrowed the general practice of Honorius, without adopting the singular, and, indeed, improbable tale, which is related by the Greek historian.

[q] The lessons of Theodosius, or rather Claudian (iv Cons. Honor. 214-418), might compose a fine institution for the future prince of a great and free nation. It was far above Honorius, and his degenerate subjects.

of Honorius were accustomed to animate, by their example, or at least by their presence, the valour of the legions ; and the dates of their laws attest the perpetual activity of their motions through the provinces of the Roman world. But the son of Theodosius passed the slumber of his life, a captive in his palace, a stranger in his country, and the patient, almost the indifferent, spectator of the ruin of the western empire, which was repeatedly attacked, and finally subverted, by the arms of the barbarians. In the eventful history of a reign of twenty-eight years, it will seldom be necessary to mention the name of the emperor Honorius

CHAP. XXX.

Revolt of the Goths—They plunder Greece—Two great invasions of Italy by Alaric and Radagaisus—They are repulsed by Stilicho—The Germans overrun Gaul—Usurpation of Constantine in the West—Disgrace and death of Stilicho.

CHAP.
XXX.
‸‸‸‸‸‸‸
Revolt of
the Goths,
A. D. 396.

IF the subjects of Rome could be ignorant of their obligations to the great Theodosius, they were too soon convinced, how painfully the spirit and abilities of their deceased emperor had supported the frail and mouldering edifice of the republic. He died in the month of January, and before the end of the winter of the same year, the Gothic nation was in arms.[a] The barbarian auxiliaries erected their independent standard; and boldly avowed the hostile designs which they had long cherished in their ferocious minds. Their countrymen, who had been condemned, by the conditions of the last treaty, to a life of tranquillity and labour, deserted their farms at the first sound of the trumpet; and eagerly resumed the weapons which they had reluctantly laid down. The barriers of the Danube were thrown open; the savage warriors of Scythia issued from their forests; and the uncommon severity of the winter allowed the poet to remark, "that they rolled

[a] The revolt of the Goths, and the blockade of Constantinople, are distinctly mentioned by Claudian, (in Rufin. l. ii, 7-100); Zosimus, (l. v, p. 292), and Jornandes, (de Rebus Geticis, c. 29).

" their ponderous waggons over the broad and
" icy back of the indignant river."[b] The unhappy natives of the provinces to the south of
the Danube, submitted to the calamities, which,
in the course of twenty years, were almost grown
familiar to their imagination; and the various
troops of barbarians, who gloried in the Gothic
name, were irregularly spread from the woody
shores of Dalmatia, to the walls of Constantinople.[c] The interruption, or at least the dimu-
nition of the subsidy, which the Goths had received from the prudent liberality of Theodosius,
was the specious pretence of their revolt: the
affront was embittered by their contempt for
the unwarlike sons of Theodosius; and their
resentment was inflamed by the weakness, or
treachery, of the minister of Arcadius. The
frequent visits of Rufinus to the camp of the
barbarians, whose arms and apparel he affected
to imitate, were considered as a sufficient evidence of his guilty correspondence: and the
public enemy, from a motive either of gratitude
or of policy, was attentive, amidst the general
devastation, to spare the private estates of the
unpopular prefect. The Goths, instead of be-

[b] ——Alit per terga ferocis
Danubii solidata ruunt; expertaque remi
Frangunt stagna rotis.
Claudian and Ovid often amuse their fancy by interchanging the meta-
phors and properties of *liquid* water, and *solid* ice. Much false wit has
been expended in this easy exercise.

[c] Jerom, tom. i, p. 26. He endeavours to comfort his friend Helio-
dorus, bishop of Altinum, for the loss of his nephew Nepotian, by a
curious recapitulation of all the public and private misfortunes of the
times. See Tillemont, Mem. Eccles. tom. xii, p. 200, &c.

ing impelled by the blind and headstrong passions of their chiefs, were now directed by the bold and artful genius of Alaric. That renowned leader was descended from the noble race of the Balti;[d] which yielded only to the royal dignity of the Amali: he had solicited the command of the Roman armies; and the imperial court provoked him to demonstrate the folly of their refusal, and the importance of their loss. Whatever hopes might be entertained of the conquest of Constantinople, the judicious general soon abandoned an impracticable enterprise. In the midst of a divided court, and a discontented people, the emperor Arcadius was terrified by the aspect of the Gothic arms: but the want of wisdom and valour was supplied by the strength of the city; and the fortifications, both of the sea and land, might securely brave the impotent and random darts of the barbarians. Alaric disdained to trample any longer on the prostrate and ruined countries of Thrace and Dacia, and he resolved to seek a plentiful harvest of fame and riches in a province which had hitherto escaped the ravages of war.[e]

---

[d] *Baltha,* or *bold:* origo mirifica, says Jornandes, (c. 29). This illustrious race long continued to flourish in France, in the Gothic province of Septimania, of Languedoc; under the corrupted appellation of *Baux:* and a branch of that family afterwards settled in the kingdom of Naples, (Grotius in Prolegom. ad Hist. Gothic. p. 53). The lords of Baux, near Arles, and of seventy-nine subordinate places, were independent of the courts of Provence, (Longuerue, Description de la France, tom. i, p. 357).

[e] Zosimus (l. v, p. 293-295) is our best guide for the conquest of Greece: but the hints and allusion of Claudian are so many rays of historic light.

The character of the civil and military officers, on whom Rufinus had devolved the government of Greece, confirmed the public suspicion, that he had betrayed the ancient seat of freedom and learning to the Gothic invader. The proconsul Antiochus was the unworthy son of a respectable father; and Gerontius, who commanded the provincial troops, was much better qualified to execute the oppressive orders of a tyrant, than to defend, with courage and ability, a country most remarkably fortified by the hand of nature. Alaric had traversed, without resistance, the plains of Macedonia and Thessaly, as far as the foot of Mount Oeta, a steep and woody range of hills, almost impervious to his cavalry. They stretched from east to west, to the edge of the -shore; and left between the precipice and the Malian gulf, an interval of three hundred feet, which, in some places, was contracted to a road capable of admitting only a single carriage.[f] In this narrow pass of Thermopylæ, where Leonides and the three hundred Spartans had gloriously devoted their lives, the Goths might have been stopped, or destroyed, by a skilful general; and perhaps the view of that sacred spot might have kindled some sparks of military ardour in the breasts of the degenerate Greeks. The troops which had been posted to defend the streights of Thermopylæ, retired, as they were directed, without attempting

[f] Compare Herodotus, (l. vii, c. 176), and Livy, (xxxvi, 15). The narrow entrance of Greece was probably enlarged by each successive ravisher.

to disturb the secure and rapid passage of Alaric;[a] and the fertile fields of Phocis, and Bœotia, were instantly covered by a deluge of barbarians; who massacred the males of an age to bear arms, and drove away the beautiful females, with the spoil, and cattle, of the flaming villages. The travellers, who visited Greece several years afterwards, could easily discover the deep and bloody traces of the march of the Goths; and Thebes was less indebted for her preservation to the strength of her seven gates, than to the eager haste of Alaric, who advanced to occupy the city of Athens, and the important harbour of the Piræus. The same impatience urged him to prevent the delay and danger of a siege, by the offer of a capitulation; and as soon as the Athenians heard the voice of the Gothic herald, they were easily persuaded to deliver the greatest part of their wealth, as the ransom of the city of Minerva, and its inhabitants. The treaty was ratified by solemn oaths, and observed with mutual fidelity. The Gothic prince, with a small and select train, was admitted within the walls: he indulged himself in the refreshment of the bath, accepted a splendid banquet which was provided by the magistrate, and affected to shew that he was not ignorant of the manners of civilized nations.[b] But the

---

[a] He passed, says Ennapius, (in Vit. Philosoph. p. 93, edit. Commelin, 1596), through the streights, διὰ τῶν πυλῶν (of Thermopylæ) παρῆλθεν, ωσπερ διὰ ςαδιω, και ιππακρότυ πεδιω τρεχων.

[b] In obedience to Jerom, and Claudian, (in Rufin. l. ii, 191), I have mixed some darker colours in the mild representation of Zosimus, who wished to soften the calamities of Athens.

Nec

whole territory of Attica, from the promontory of Sunium to the town of Megara, was blasted by his baleful presence; and, if we may use the comparison of a contemporary philosopher, Athens itself resembled the bleeding and empty skin of a slaughtered victim. The distance between Megara and Corinth could not much exceed thirty miles; but the *bad road*, an expressive name, which it still bears among the Greeks, was, or might easily have been made, impassible for the march of an enemy. The thick and gloomy woods of Mount Cithæron covered the inland country; the Scironian rocks approached the water's edge, and hung over the narrow and winding path, which was confined above six miles along the sea-shore.[1] The passage of those rocks, so infamous in every age, was terminated by the isthmus of Corinth; and a small body of firm and intrepid soldiers might have successfully defended a temporary intrenchment of five or six miles from the Ionian to the Ægean sea. The confidence of the cities of Peloponnesus in their natural rampart, had

---

Nec fera Cecropias traxissent vincula matres.
Synesius (Epist. clvi, p. 272, edit. Petav.) observes, that Athens, whose sufferings he imputes to the proconsul's avarice, was at that time less famous for her schools of philosophy than for her trade of honey.

[1]   ——Vallata mari Scironia rupes,
Et duo continuo connectens æquora muro
Isthmos——
                        Claudian de Bell. Getico, 188.
The Scironian rocks are described by Pausanias, (l. i, c. 44, p. 197, edit. Kuhn), and our modern travellers, Wheeler (p. 436) and Chandler, (p. 298). Hadrian made the road passable for two carriages.

tempted them to neglect the care of their an-
tique walls; and the avarice of the Roman governors had exhausted and betrayed the unhappy province.[k]   Corinth, Argos, Sparta, yielded
without resistance to the arms of the Goths;
and the most fortunate of the inhabitants were
saved, by death, from beholding the slavery of
their families, and the conflagration of their
cities.[l]   The vases and statues were distributed
among the barbarians, with more regard to the
value of the materials, than to the elegance of
the workmanship; the female captives submitted to the laws of war; the enjoyment of beauty
was the reward of valour; and the Greeks
could not reasonably complain of an abuse,
which was justified by the example of the heroic times.[m]   The descendants of that extraordinary people, who had considered valour and
discipline as the walls of Sparta, no longer remembered the generous reply of their ancestors
to an invader more formidable than Alaric. " If
" thou art a god, thou wilt not hurt those who
" have never injured thee; if thou art a man,

---

[k] Claudian (in Rufin. l. ii, 186, and de Bello Getico, 611, &c) vaguely, though forcibly, delineates the scene of rapine and destruction.

[l] Τρις μακαρις Δαναοι και τετρακις, &c. These generous lines of Homer
(Odyss. l. v, 306) were transcribed by one of the captive youths of
Corinth: and the tears of Mummius may prove that the rude conque-
ror, though he was ignorant of the value of an original picture, posses-
sed the purest source of good taste, a benevolent heart, (Plutarch,
Symposiac. l. ix, tom. ii, p. 737, edit. Wechel).

[m] Homer perpetually describes the exemplary patience of those female
captives, who gave their charms, and even their hearts, to the murderers of their fathers, brothers, &c. Such a passion (of Eriphile for
Achilles) is touched with admirable delicacy by Racine.

" advance,—and thou wilt find men equal to
" thyself."ᵃ From Thermopylæ to Sparta, the
leader of the Goths pursued his victorious march
without encountering any mortal antagonists:
but one of the advocates of expiring paganism
has confidently asserted, that the walls of Athens
were guarded by the goddess Minerva, with her
formidable Ægis, and by the angry phantom of
Achilles;ᵇ and that the conqueror was dismayed
by the presence of the hostile deities of Greece.
In an age of miracles, it would perhaps be unjust to dispute the claim of the historian Zosimus to the common benefit; yet it cannot be
dissembled, that the mind of Alaric was ill prepared to receive, either in sleeping or waking
visions, the impressions of Greek superstition.
The songs of Homer, and the fame of Achilles,
had probably never reached the ear of the illiterate *barbarian;* and the *Christian* faith, which
he had devoutly embraced, taught him to despise the imaginary deities of Rome and Athens.
The invasion of the Goths, instead of vindicat-
ing the honour, contributed, at least accidentally, to extirpate the last remains of paganism;
and the mysteries of Ceres, which had subsist-

ᵃ Plutarch (in Pyrrho, tom. ii, p. 471, edit. Brian) gives the
genuine answer in the Laconic dialect. Pyrrhus attacked Sparta with
25,000 foot, 2,000 horse, and 24 elephants: and the defence of that
open town is a fine comment on the laws of Lycurgus, even in the last
stage of decay.

ᵇ Such, perhaps, as Homer (Iliad xx, 164) has so nobly painted
him.

ed eighteen hundred years, did not survive the destruction of Eleusis, and the calamities of Greece.[p]

The last hope of a people who could no longer depend on their arms, their gods, or their sovereign, was placed in the powerful assistance of the general of the West ; and Stilicho, who had not been permitted to repulse, advanced to chastise, the invaders of Greece.[q] A numerous fleet was equipped in the ports of Italy; and the troops, after a short and prosperous navigation over the Ionian sea, were safely disembarked on the isthmus, near the ruins of Corinth. The woody and mountainous country of Arcadia, the fabulous residence of Pan and the Dryads, became the scene of a long and doubtful conflict between two generals not unworthy of each other. The skill and perseverance of the Roman at length prevailed ; and the Goths, after sustaining a considerable loss from disease and desertion, gradually retreated to the lofty mountain of Pholoe, near the sources of the Peneus, and on the frontiers of Elis ; a sacred country, which had formerly been exempted from the calamities of war.[r] The camp of the barbarians

[p] Eunapius (in Vit. Philosoph. p. 90-93) intimates, that a troop of monks betrayed Greece, and followed the Gothic camp.

[q] For Stilicho's Greek war, compare the honest narrative of Zosimus, (l. v, p. 295, 296), with the curious circumstantial flattery of Claudian, (i Cons. Stilich. l. 172-186 ; iv Cons. Hon. 459-487). As the event was not glorious, it is artfully thrown into the shade.

[r] The troops who marched through Elis delivered up their arms. This security enriched the Eleans, who were lovers of a rural life. Riches begat pride ; they disdained their privilege, and they suffered. Polybius advises them to retire once more within their magic circle. See a
learned

was immediately besieged: the waters of the river[*] were diverted into another channel; and while they laboured under the intolerable pressure of thirst and hunger, a strong line of circumvallation was formed to prevent their escape. After these precautions, Stilicho, too confident of victory, retired to enjoy his triumph, in the theatrical games, and lascivious dances, of the Greeks; his soldiers, deserting their standards, spread themselves over the country of their allies, which they stripped of all that had been saved from the rapacious hands of the enemy. Alaric appears to have seized the favourable moment to execute one of those hardy enterprises, in which the abilities of a general are displayed with more genuine lustre, than in the tumult of a day of battle. To extricate himself from the prison of Peloponnesus, it was necessary that he should pierce the intrenchments which surrounded his camp; that he should perform a difficult and dangerous march of thirty miles, as far as the gulf of Corinth; and that he should transport his troops, his captives, and his spoil, over an arm of the sea, which, in the narrow interval between Rhium and the opposite shore, is at least half a

learned and judicious discourse on the Olympic games, which Mr. West has prefixed to his translation of Pindar.

[*] Claudian (in iv Cons. Hon. 480) alludes to the fact, without naming the river: perhaps the Alpheus, (i Cons. Stil. l. i, 185).

————Et Alpheus Geticis augustus acervis

Tardior ad Siculos etiamnum pergit amores.

Yet I should prefer the Peneus, a shallow stream in a wide and deep bed, which runs through Elis, and falls into the sea below Cylenne. It had been joined with the Alpheus, to cleanse the Augean stable, (Cellarius, tom. i, p. 760. Chandler's Travels, p. 286).

CHAP.
XXX.

Escapes
to Epirus.

mile in breadth.[t] The operations of Alaric must have been secret, prudent, and rapid; since the Roman general was confounded by the intelligence, that the Goths, who had eluded his efforts, were in full possession of the important province of Epirus. This unfortunate delay allowed Alaric sufficient time to conclude the treaty, which he secretly negotiated, with the ministers of Constantinople. The apprehension of a civil war compelled Stilicho to retire, at the haughty mandate of his rivals, from the dominions of Arcadius; and he respected, in the enemy of Rome, the honourable character of the ally and servant of the emperor of the East.

Alaric is
declared
master-
general of
the eastern
Illyricum,
A. D. 398.

A Grecian philosopher,[u] who visited Constantinople soon after the death of Theodosius, published his liberal opinions concerning the duties of kings, and the state of the Roman republic. Synesius observes, and deplores, the fatal abuse, which the imprudent bounty of the late emperor had introduced into the military service. The citizens, and subjects, had purchased an exemption from the indispensable duty of defending their country; which was supported by the arms of barbarian mercenaries. The fugitives of Scy-

[t] Strabo, l. viii, p. 517. Plin. Hist. Natur. iv, 3. Wheeler, p. 206. Chandler, p. 275. They measured, from different points, the distance between the two lands.

[u] Synesius passed three years (A. D. 397-400) at Constantinople, as deputy from Cyrene to the emperor Arcadius. He presented him with a crown of gold, and pronounced before him the instructive oration de Regno, (p. 1-32, edit. Petav. Paris, 1612). The philosopher was made bishop of Ptolemais, A. D. 410, and died about 430. See Tillemont, Mem. Eccles. tom. xii, p. 499, 554, 683-685.

thia were permitted to disgrace the illustrious
dignities of the empire; their ferocious youth,
who disdained the salutary restraint of laws,
were more anxious to acquire the riches, than
to imitate the arts, of a people, the object of
their contempt and hatred; and the power of
the Goths was the stone of Tantalus, perpetually suspended over the peace and safety of the
devoted state. The measures, which Synesius
recommends, are the dictates of a bold and generous patriot. He exhorts the emperor to revive the courage of his subjects, by the example
of manly virtue; to banish luxury from the court,
and from the camp; to substitute in the place
of the barbarian mercenaries, an army of men,
interested in the defence of their laws and of
their property; to force, in such a moment of
public danger, the mechanic from his shop, and
the philosopher from his school; to rouse the
indolent citizen from his dream of pleasure, and
to arm, for the protection of agriculture, the
hands of the laborious husbandman. At the
head of such troops, who might deserve the
name, and would display the spirit, of Romans,
he animates the son of Theodosius to encounter a race of barbarians, who were destitute of
any real courage; and never to lay down his
arms, till he had chased them far away into the
solitudes of Scythia; or had reduced them to
the state of ignominious servitude, which the
Lacedæmonians formerly imposed on the captive Helots.[x] The court of Arcadius indulged

[x] Synesius de Regno, p. 21-26.

the zeal, applauded the eloquence, and neglected the advice, of Synesius. Perhaps the philosopher, who addresses the emperor of the East, in the language of reason and virtue, which he might have used to a Spartan king, had not condescended to form a practicable scheme, consistent with the temper, and circumstances, of a degenerate age. Perhaps the pride of the ministers, whose business was seldom interrupted by reflection, might reject, as wild and visionary, every proposal, which exceeded the measure of their captivity, and deviated from the forms and precedents of office. While the oration of Synesius, and the downfal of the barbarians, were the topics of popular conversation, an edict was published at Constantinople, which declared the promotion of Alaric to the rank of master-general of the eastern Illyricum. The Roman provincials, and the allies, who had respected the faith of treaties, were justly indignant, that the ruin of Greece and Epirus should be so liberally rewarded. The Gothic conqueror was received as a lawful magistrate, in the cities which he had so lately besieged. The fathers, whose sons he had massacred, the husbands, whose wives he had violated, were subject to his authority : and the success of his rebellion encouraged the ambition of every leader of the foreign mercenaries. The use to which Alaric applied his new command, distinguishes the firm and judicious character of his policy. He issued his orders to the four magazines and manufacturers of offensive and defensive arms,

Margus, Ratiaria, Naissus, and Thessalonica, to provide his troops with an extraordinary supply of shields, helmets, swords, and spears: the unhappy provincials were compelled to forge the instruments of their own destruction; and the barbarians removed the only defect which had sometimes disappointed the efforts of their courage. The birth of Alaric, the glory of his past exploits, and the confidence in his future designs, insensibly united the body of the nation under his victorious standard; and with the unanimous consent of the barbarian chieftains, the master-general of Illyricum was elevated, according to ancient custom, on a shield, and solemnly proclaimed king of the Visigoths. Armed with this double power, seated on the verge of the two empires, he alternately sold his deceitful promises to the courts of Arcadius, and Honorius; till he declared, and executed, his resolution of invading the dominions of the West. The provinces of

and king of the Visigoths.

--------qui fœdera rumpit
Ditatur: qui servat, eget: vestator Achivæ
Gentis, et Epirum nuper populatus inultam
Præsidet Illyrico: jam, quos obsedit, amicos
Ingreditur muros; illis responsa daturus
Quorum conjugibus potitur, natosque peremit.
Claudian in Eutrop. l. ii, 212. Alaric applauds his own policy, (de Bell. Getic. 533-54?), in the use which he had made of this Illyrian jurisdiction.

ᶻ Jornandes, c. 29, p. 651. The Gothic historian adds, with unusual spirit, Cum suis deliberans suasit suo labore quærere regna, quam alienis per otium subjacere.

--------Discors odiisque anceps civibus Orbis
Non sua vis tutata diu, dum fœdera fallax
Ludit, et alternæ perjuria venditat aulæ.
Claudian de Bell. Get. 565.

Europe which belonged to the eastern emperor, were already exhausted; those of Asia were inaccessible; and the strength of Constantinople had resisted his attack. But he was tempted by the fame, the beauty, the wealth of Italy, which he had twice visited; and he secretly aspired to plant the Gothic standard on the walls of Rome, and to enrich his army with the accumulated spoils of three hundred triumphs.[b]

He invades Italy, A. D. 400-403.

The scarcity of facts,[c] and the uncertainty of dates[d] oppose our attempts to describe the circumstances of the first invasion of Italy by the arms of Alaric. His march, perhaps from Thessalonica, through the warlike and hostile country of Pannonia, as far as the foot of the Julian Alps; his passage of those mountains, which were strongly guarded by troops and intrenchments; the siege of Aquileia, and the conquest of the provinces of Istria and Venetia, appear to have employed a considerable time. Unless his operations were extremely cautious and slow,

[b] Alpibus Italiæ ruptis penetrabis ad *Urbem.* This authentic prediction was announced by Alaric, or at least by Claudian, (de Bell. Getico, 547), seven years before the event. But as it was not accomplished within the term which has been rashly fixed, the interpreters escaped through an ambiguous meaning.

[c] Our best materials are 970 verses of Claudian, in the poem on the Getic war, and the beginning of that which celebrates the sixth consulship of Honorius. Zosimus is totally silent; and we are reduced to such scraps, or rather crumbs, as we can pick from Orosius and the Chronicles.

[d] Notwithstanding the gross errors of Jornandes, who confounds the Italian wars of Alaric, (c. 29), his date of the consulship of Stilicho and Aurelian (A. D. 400) is firm and respectable. It is certain from Claudian, (Tillemont, Hist. des Emp. tom. v, p. 804), that the battle of Pollentia was fought A. D. 403; but we cannot easily fill the interval.

the length of the interval would suggest a probable suspicion, that the Gothic king retreated
towards the banks of the Danube; and reinforced his army with fresh swarms of barbarians,
before he again attempted to penetrate into the
heart of Italy. Since the public and important
events escape the diligence of the historian, he
may amuse himself with contemplating, for a
moment, the influence of the arms of Alaric on
the fortunes of two obscure individuals, a presbyter of Aquileia, and an husbandman of Verona. The learned Rufinus, who was summoned by his enemies to appear before a Roman synod,* wisely preferred the dangers of a
besieged city; and the barbarians, who furious-
ly shook the walls of Aquileia, might save him
from the cruel sentence of another heretic, who,
at the request of the same bishops, was severely whipped, and condemned to perpetual exile
on a desert island.' The *old man,*ᵉ who had
passed his simple and innocent life in the
neighbourhood of Verona, was a stranger to the

---

* Tantum Romanæ urbis judicium fugis, ut magis obsidionem bar-
baricam, quam *pacatæ* urbis judicium velis sustinere. Jerom. tom. ii,
p. 239.   Rufinus understood his own danger : the *peaceful* city was inflamed by the beldam Marcella, and the rest of Jerom's faction.

ᶠ Jovinian, the enemy of fasts and of celibacy, who was persecuted
and insulted by the furious Jerom, (Jortin's Remarks, vol. iv, p. 104,
&c.)   See the original edict of banishment in the Theodosian Code, l.
xvi, tit. v, leg. 43.

ᵍ This epigram (de Sene Veronensi qui suburbium nusquam egressus
est) is one of the earliest and most pleasing compositions of Claudian.
Cowley's imitation (Hurd's edition, vol. ii, p. 241) has some natural and
happy strokes ; but it is much inferior to the original portrait, which
is evidently drawn from the life.

quarrels both of kings and of bishops; *his* pleasures, his desires, his knowledge, were confined within the little circle of his paternal farm; and a staff supported his aged steps, on the same ground where he had sported in his infancy.   Yet even this humble and rustic felicity, (which Claudian describes with so much truth and feeling), was still exposed to the undistinguishing rage of war. His trees, his old *contemporary* trees,[h] must blaze in the conflagration of the whole country; a detachment of Gothic cavalry might sweep away his cottage and his family; and the power of Alaric could destroy this happiness, which he was not able either to taste, or to bestow. " Fame," says the poet, " encircling with ter-" ror or gloomy wings, proclaimed the march " of the barbarian army, and filled Italy with " consternation :" the apprehensions of each individual were increased in just proportion to the measure of his fortune ; and the most timid, who had already embarked their valuable effects, meditated their escape to the island of Sicily, or the African coast.   The public distress was aggravated by the fears and reproaches of superstition.[i] Every hour produced

---

*   Ingentem meminit parvo qui germine quercum
          Æquævumque videt consenuiste nemus.
     A neighbouring wood born with himself he sees
     And loves his old contemporary trees.
In this passage, Cowley is perhaps superior to his original ; and the English poet, who was a good botanist, has concealed the *oaks* under a more general expression.

[i] Claudian de Bell. Get. 192-266. He may seem prolix; but fear and superstition occupied as large a space in the minds of the Italians.

some horrid tale of strange and portentous accidents: the pagans deplored the neglect of omens,
and the interruption of sacrifices: but the
Christians still derived some comfort from the
powerful intercession of the saints and martyrs.[k]

The emperor Honorius was distinguished,
above his subjects, by the pre-eminence of fear,
as well as of rank. The pride and luxury in which
he was educated, had not allowed him to suspect,
that there existed on the earth any power presumptuous enough to invade the repose of the
successor of Augustus. The arts of flattery concealed the impending danger, till Alaric approached the palace of Milan. But when the
sound of war had awakened the young emperor,
instead of flying to arms with the spirit, or even
the rashness, of his age, he eagerly listened to
those timid counsellors, who proposed to convey
his sacred person, and his faithful attendants, to
some secure and distant station in the provinces
of Gaul. Stilicho alone[l] had courage and authority to resist this disgraceful measure, which
would have abandoned Rome and Italy to the
barbarians; but as the troops of the palace had
been lately detached to the Rhætian frontier,
and as the resource of new levies was slow and

---

[k] From the passages of Paulinus, which Baronius has produced,
(Annal. Eccles. A. D. 403, No. 51), it is manifest, that the general alarm
had pervaded all Italy, as far as Nola in Campania, where that famous
penitent had fixed his abode.

Solus erat Stilicho, &c. is the exclusive commendation which Claudian bestows, (de Bell. Get. 267), without condescending to except the
emperor. How insignificant must Honorius have appeared in his own
court!

precarious, the general of the West could only promise, that, if the court of Milan would maintain their ground during his absence, he would soon return with an army equal to the encounter of the Gothic king. Without losing a moment, (while each moment was so important to the public safety), Stilicho hastily embarked on the Larian lake, ascended the mountains of ice and snow, amidst the severity of an Alpine winter, and suddenly repressed, by his unexpected presence, the enemy, who had disturbed the tranquillity of Rhætia.[m] The barbarians, perhaps some tribes of the Alemanni, respected the firmness of a chief, who still assumed the language of command; and the choice which he condescended to make of a select number of their bravest youth, was considered as a mark of his esteem and favour. The cohorts, who were delivered from the neighbouring foe, diligently repaired to the imperial standard; and Stilicho issued his orders to the most remote troops of the West, to advance, by rapid marches, to the defence of Honorius and of Italy. The fortresses of the Rhine were abandoned; and the safety of Gaul was protected only by the faith of the Germans, and the ancient terror of the Roman name. Even the legion, which had been stationed to guard the wall of Britain against the Caledonians of the North, was hastily

---

[m] The face of the country, and the hardiness of Stilicho, are finely described, (de Bell. Get. 340-363)

recalled;" and a numerous body of the cavalry of the Alani was persuaded to engage in the service of the emperor, who anxiously expected the return of his general. The prudence and vigour of Stilicho were conspicuous on this occasion, which revealed, at the same time, the weakness of the falling empire. The legions of Rome, which had long since languished in the gradual decay of discipline and courage, were exterminated by the Gothic and civil wars; and it was found impossible, without exhausting and exposing the provinces, to assemble an army for the defence of Italy.

When Stilicho seemed to abandon his sovereign in the unguarded palace of Milan, he had probably calculated the term of his absence, the distance of the enemy, and the obstacles that might retard their march. He principally depended on the rivers of Italy, the Adige, the Mincius, the Oglio, and the Addua; which, in the winter or spring, by the fall of rains, or by the melting of the snows, are commonly swelled into broad and impetuous torrents." But the

He is pursued and besieged by the Goths.

" Venit et extremis legio praetenta Britannis
Quae Scoto dat frena truci.
De Bell. Get. 416.
Yet the most rapid march from Edinburgh, or Newcastle, to Milan, must have required a longer space of time than Claudian seems willing to allow for the duration of the Gothic war.

° Every traveller must recollect the face of Lombardy, (see Fontenelle, tom. v, p. 279), which is often tormented by the capricious and irregular abundance of waters. The Austrians, before Genoa, were encamped in the dry bed of the Polcevera. " Ne sarrebbe (says Muratori) " mai passato per mente a qué buoni Alemanni, che quel " picciolo torrente potesse, per cosi dire in un instante cangiarsi in un " terribil gigante." (Annal. d'Italia, tom. xvi, p. 443; Milan, 1752, 4vo. edit).

season happened to be remarkably dry; and the Goths could traverse, without impediment, the wide and stony beds, whose centre was faintly marked by the course of a shallow stream. The bridge and passage of the Addua were secured by a strong detachment of the Gothic army; and as Alaric approached the walls, or rather the suburbs, of Milan, he enjoyed the proud satisfaction of seeing the emperor of the Romans fly before him. Honorius, accompanied by a feeble train of statesmen and eunuchs, hastily retreated towards the Alps, with a design of securing his person in the city of Arles, which had often been the royal residence of his predecessors. But Honorius[p] had scarcely passed the Po, before he was overtaken by the speed of the Gothic cavalry;[q] since the urgency of the danger compelled him to seek a temporary shelter within the fortification of Asta, a town of Liguria or Piemont, situate on the banks of the Tanarus.[r] The siege of an obscure place, which contained so rich a prize, and seemed incapable of a long resistance, was instantly formed, and indefatigably pressed, by the king of the Goths; and the bold declaration, which the emperor

[p] Claudian does not clearly answer our question. Where was Honorius himself? Yet the flight is marked by the pursuit: and my idea of the Gothic war is justified by the Italian critics, Sigonius, (tom. i, P. ii, p. 369, de Imp. Occident. l. x), and Muratori, (Annali d'Italia, tom. iv, p. 45).

[q] One of the roads may be traced in the Itineraries, (p. 98, 288, 204, with Wesseling's Notes). Asta lay some miles on the right hand

[r] Asta, or Asti, a Roman colony, is now the capital of a pleasant county, which, in the sixteenth century, devolved to the Dukes of Savoy, (Leandro Alberti Descrizzione d'Italia, p. 382).

might afterwards make, that his breast had
never been susceptible of fear, did not probably obtain much credit, even in his own court.[*]
In the last, and almost hopeless extremity, after
the barbarians had already proposed the indig-
nity of a capitulation, the imperial captive was
suddenly relieved by the fame, the approach,
and at length the presence of the hero, whom
he had so long expected. At the head of a
chosen and intrepid vanguard, Stilicho swam
the stream of the Addua, to gain the time which
he must have lost in the attack of the bridge;
the passage of the Po was an enterprise of much
less hazard and difficulty; and the successful
action, in which he cut his way through the
Gothic camp under the walls of Asta, revived
the hopes, and vindicated the honour, of Rome.
Instead of grasping the fruit of his victory, the
barbarian was gradually invested, on every side,
by the troops of the West, who successively
issued through all the passes of the Alps; his
quarters were straitened; his convoys were intercepted; and the vigilance of the Romans prepared to form a chain of fortifications, and to
besiege the lines of the besiegers. A military
council was assembled of the long-haired chiefs
of the Gothic nation; of aged warriors, whose
bodies were wrapped in furs, and whose stern
countenances were marked with honourable
wounds. They weighed the glory of persisting

[*] Nec me timor impulit ullus. He might hold this proud language
the next year at Rome, five hundred miles from the scene of danger,
(vi Cons. Hon. 449).

CHAP.
XXX.

in their attempt against the advantage of securing their plunder; and they recommended the prudent measure of a seasonable retreat. In this important debate, Alaric displayed the spirit of the conqueror of Rome; and after he had reminded his countrymen of their achievements and of their designs, he concluded his animating speech, by the solemn and positive assurance, that he was resolved to find in Italy, either a kingdom, or a grave.[t]

Battle of
Pollentia
A. D. 403.
March 29.

The loose discipline of the barbarians always exposed them to the danger of a surprise; but, instead of choosing the dissolute hours of riot and intemperance, Stilicho resolved to attack the *Christian* Goths, whilst they were devoutly employed in celebrating the festival of Easter.[u] The execution of the stratagem, or, as it was termed by the clergy, of the sacrilege, was intrusted to Saul, a barbarian and a pagan, who had served, however, with distinguished reputation among the veteran generals of Theodosius. The camp of the Goths, which Alaric had pitched

[t] Hanc ego vel victor regno, vel morte tenebo
   Victus, humum———
The speeches (de Bell. Get. 479-549) of the Gothic Nestor, and Achilles, are strong, characteristic, adapted to the circumstances; and possibly not less genuine than those of Livy.

[u] Orosius, (l. vii, c 37) is shocked at the impiety of the Romans, who attacked, on Easter Sunday, such pious Christians. Yet, at the same time, public prayers were offered at the shrine of St. Thomas of Edessa, for the destruction of the Arian robber. See Tillemont, (Hist. des Emp. tom. v, p. 529), who quotes an homily, which has been erroneously ascribed to St. Chrysostom.

in the neighbourhood of Pollentia,[x] was thrown into confusion by the sudden and impetuous charge of the imperial cavalry; but, in a few moments, the undaunted genius of their leader gave them an order, and a field, of battle; and as soon as they had recovered from their astonishment, the pious confidence, that the God of the Christians would assert their cause, added new strength to their native valour. In this engagement, which was long maintained with equal courage and success, the chief of the Alani, whose diminutive and savage form concealed a magnanimous soul, approved his suspected loyalty, by the zeal with which he fought, and fell, in the service of the republic; and the fame of this gallant barbarian has been imperfectly preserved in the verses of Claudian, since the poet, who celebrates his virtue, has omitted the mention of his name. His death was followed by the flight and dismay of the squadrons which he commanded; and the defeat of the wing of cavalry might have decided the victory of Alaric, if Stilicho had not immediately led the Roman and barbarian infantry to the attack. The skill of the general, and the bravery of the soldiers, surmounted every obstacle. In the evening of the bloody day, the Goths retreated from the field of battle; the intrenchments of their camp were forced, and the scene of rapine and

---

[x] The vestiges of Pollentia are twenty-five miles to the south-east of Turin. *Urbs*, in the same neighbourhood, was a royal chase of the kings of Lombardy, and a small river, which excused the prediction, " penetrabis ad urbem." (Cluver. Ital. Antiq. tom. i, p. 83–85).

CHAP.
XXX.
slaughter made some atonement for the calami
ties which they had inflicted on the subjects of
the empire.[y]   The magnificent spoils of Corinth
and Argos enriched the veterans of the West;
the captive wife of Alaric, who had impatiently
claimed his promise of Roman jewels and patrician handmaids,[z] was reduced to implore the
mercy of the insulting foe; and many thousand
prisoners, released from the Gothic chains, dispersed through the provinces of Italy the praises
of their heroic deliverer. The triumph of Stilicho[a] was compared by the poet, and perhaps
by the public, to that of Marius; who, in the
same part of Italy, had encountered, and destroyed, another army of northern barbarians.
The huge bones, and the empty helmets, of the
Cimbri and of the Goths, would easily be confounded by succeeding generations; and posterity might erect a common trophy to the memory of the two most illustrious generals, who
had vanquished, on the same memorable ground,
the two most formidable enemies of Rome.[b]

---

[y] Orosius, wishes, in doubtful words, to insinuate the defeat of the
Romans. " Pugnantes vicimus, victores victi sumus."   Prosper (in
Chron.) makes it an equal and bloody battle; but the Gothic writers,
Cassiodorius (in Chron.) and Jornandes, (de Reb. Get. c. 29), claim a
decisive victory.

[z]   Demens Ausonidum gemmata monilia matrum,
        Romanasque altà famulas cervice petebat.
                                        De Bell. Get. 627.

[a] Claudian, (de Bell. Get. 580-647), and Prudentius, (in Symmach.
l. ii, 694-719), celebrate, without ambiguity, the Roman victory of
Pollentia.   They are poetical and party writers; yet some credit is
due to the most suspicious witnesses, who are checked by the recent
notoriety of facts.

[b] Claudian's peroration is strong and elegant; but the identity of the
Cimbric and Gothic fields, must be understood (like Virgil's Philippi,
                                        Georgic i.

CHAP.
XXX.
~~~~~~~

Boldness
and re-
treat of
Alaric.

The eloquence of Claudian[c] has celebrated, with lavish applause, the victory of Pollentia, one of the most glorious days in the life of his patron; but his reluctant and partial muse bestows more genuine praise on the character of the Gothic kind. His name is indeed branded with the reproachful epithets of pirate and robber, to which the conquerors of every age are so justly entitled; but the poet of Stilicho is compelled to acknowledge, that Alaric possessed the invincible temper of mind, which rises superior to every misfortune, and derives new resources from adversity. After the total defeat of his infantry, he escaped, or rather withdrew, from the field of battle, with the greatest part of his cavalry entire and unbroken. Without wasting a moment to lament the irreparable loss of so many brave companions, he left his victorious enemy to bind in chains the captive images of a Gothic king;[d] and boldly resolved to break through the unguarded passes of the Appenine, to spread desolation over the fruitful face of Tuscany, and to conquer or die before the gates of Rome. The capital was saved by the

Georgic i, 490) according to the loose geography of a poet. Vercellæ and Pollentia are sixty miles from each other; and the latitude is still greater, if the Cimbri were defeated in the wide and barren plain of Verona, (Maffei, Verona Illustrata, P. i, p. 54-62).

[c] Claudian and Prudentius must be strictly examined, to reduce the figures, and extort the historic sense, of those poets.

[d] Et gravant en airain ses fidèles avantages
  - De mes etats conquis enchainer les images.

The practice of exposing in triumph the images of kings and provinces was familiar to the Romans. The bust of Mithridates himself was 18 feet high, of massy gold, (Freinshem. Supplement Livian. ciii, 47).

active and incessant diligence of Stilicho: but he respected the despair of his enemy; and, instead of committing the fate of the republic to the chance of another battle, he proposed to purchase the absence of the barbarians. The spirit of Alaric would have rejected such terms, the permission of a retreat, and the offer of a pension, with contempt and indignation; but he exercised a limited and precarious authority over the independent chieftains, who had raised him, for *their* service, above the rank of his equals : they were still less disposed to follow an unsuccessful general, and many of them were tempted to consult their interest by a private negotiation with the minister of Honorius. The king submitted to the voice of his people, ratified the treaty with the empire of the West, and repassed the Po, with the remains of the flourishing army which he had led into Italy. A considerable part of the Roman forces still continued to attend his motions; and Stilicho, who maintained a secret correspondence with some of the barbarian chiefs, was punctually apprised of the designs that were formed in the camp and council of Alaric. The king of the Goths, ambitious to signalize his retreat by some splendid achievement, had resolved to occupy the important city of Verona, which commands the principal passage of the Rhætian Alps; and, directing his march through the territories of those German tribes, whose alliance would restore his exhausted strength, to invade, on the side of the Rhine, the wealthy and unsuspecting provinces of Gaul. Ignorant of the treason, which had already betrayed his bold and judicious enterprise, he advanced towards the passes of the mountains, already possessed by the imperial troops; where he was exposed, almost at the same instant, to a general attack in the front, on his flanks, and in the rear. In this bloody action, at a small distance from the walls of Verona, the loss of the Goths was not less heavy than that which they had sustained in the defeat of Pollentia; and their valiant king, who escaped by the swiftness of his horse, must either have been slain or made prisoner, if the hasty rashness of the Alani had not disappointed the measures of the Roman general. Alaric secured the remains of his army on the adjacent rocks; and prepared himself, with undaunted resolution, to maintain a siege against the superior numbers of the enemy, who invested him on all sides. But he could not oppose the destructive progress of hunger and disease; nor was it possible for him to check the continual desertion of his impatient and capricious barbarians. In this extremity, he still found resources in his own courage, or in the moderation of his adversary; and the retreat of the Gothic king was considered as the deliverance of Italy.[c] Yet the people, and even the clergy, incapable of forming any rational judgment of the business of peace and war, presumed to arraign the policy of Stilicho, who so often vanquished, so often surrounded,

[c] The Getic war and the sixth consulship of Honorius obscurely connect the events of Alaric's retreat and losses.

and so often dismissed the implacable enemy of the republic. The first moment of the public safety is devoted to gratitude and joy; but the second is diligently occupied by envy and calumny.[f]

The triumph of Honorius, at Rome, A. D. 404.

The citizens of Rome had been astonished by the approach of Alaric; and the diligence with which they laboured to restore the walls of the capital, confessed their own fears, and the decline of the empire. After the retreat of the barbarians, Honorius was directed to accept the dutiful invitation of the senate, and to celebrate, in the imperial city, the auspicious era of the Gothic victory, and of his sixth consulship.[s] The suburbs and the streets, from the Milvian bridge to the Palatine mount, were filled by the Roman people, who, in the space of an hundred years, had only thrice been honoured with the presence of their sovereigns. While their eyes were fixed on the chariot were Stilicho was deservedly seated by the side of his royal pupil, they applauded the pomp of a triumph, which was not stained, like that of Constantine, or of Theodosius, with civil blood. The procession passed under a lofty arch, which had been purposely erected: but in less than seven years, the Gothic conquerors of Rome might read, if they were able to read, the superb inscription of that monument, which attested the total defeat and

f Taceo de Alarico . . . sæpe victo, sæpe concluso, semperque dimisso. Orosius, l. vii, c. 37, p. 567. Claudian (vi Cons Hon. 320), drops the curtain with a fine image.

s The remainder of Claudian's poem on the sixth consulship of Honorius, describes the journey, the triumph, and the games, (330-660).

destruction of their nation.[a] The emperor re-sided several months in the capital, and every part of his behaviour was regulated with care to conciliate the affection of the clergy, the senate, and the people of Rome. The clergy was edi-fied by his frequent visits, and liberal gifts, to the shrines of the apostles. The senate, who, in the triumphal procession, had been excused from the humiliating ceremony of preceding on foot the imperial chariot, was treated with the decent reverence which Stilicho always affected for that assembly. The people was repeatedly gratified by the attention and courtesy of Ho-norius in the public games, which were celebrat-ed on that occasion with a magnificence not unworthy of the spectator. As soon as the ap-pointed number of chariot-races was concluded, the decoration of the circus was suddenly changed; the hunting of wild beasts afforded a various and splendid entertainment; and the chace was succeeded by a military dance, which seems, in the lively description of Claudian, to present the image of a modern tournament.

CHAP.
XXX.

In these games of Honorius, the inhuman combats of gladiators[i] polluted, for the last time, the amphitheatre of Rome. The first Christian emperor may claim the honour of the first edict, which condemned the art and amuse-

The gladi-ators abo-lished.

[a] See the inscription in Mascow's History of the Ancient Germans, viii, 12. The words are positive and indiscreet, Getarum natiopem in omne ævum domitam, &c.

[i] On the curious, though horrid, subject of the gladiators, consult the two books of the Saturnalia of Lipsius, who, as an *antiquarian*, is inclined to excuse the practice of *antiquity*, (tom. ii, p. 483-545).

CHAP.
XXX.
ment of shedding human blood ;[k] but this benevolent law expressed the wishes of the prince,
without reforming an inveterate abuse, which
degraded a civilized nation below the condition
of savage cannibals. Several hundred, perhaps
several thousand, victims were annually slaughtered in the great cities of the empire; and the
month of December, more peculiarly devoted
to the combats of gladiators, still exhibited, to
the eyes of the Roman people, a grateful spectacle of blood and cruelty. Amidst the general joy of the victory of Pollentia, a Christian
poet exhorted the emperor to extirpate, by his
authority, the horrid custom which had so long
resisted the voice of humanity and religion.[l]
The pathetic representations of Prudentius were
less effectual than the generous boldness of Te-
lemachus, an Asiatic monk, whose death was
more useful to mankind than his life.[m] The
Romans were provoked by the interruption of
their pleasures; and the rash monk, who had
descended into the arena, to separate the gladiators, was overwhelmed under a shower of
stones. But the madness of the people soon
subsided; they respected the memory of Tele-

---

[k] Cod. Theodos. l. xv, tit. xii, leg. 1.   The Commentary of Godefroy affords large materials (tom. v, p. 396) for the history of gladiators.

[l] See the peroration of Prudentius, (in Symmach. l. ii, 1121-1131),
who had doubtless read the eloquent invective of Lactantius, (Divin.
Institut. i. vi, c. 20).   The Christian apologists have not spared these
bloody games, which were introduced in the religious festivals of paganism.

[m] Theodoret, l. v, c. 26.   I wish to believe the story of St. Telema-
chus.   Yet no church has been dedicated, no altar has been erected,
to the only monk who died a martyr in the cause of humanity.

machus, who had deserved the honours of martyrdom; and they submitted, without a murmur,
to the laws of Honorius, which abolished for
ever the human sacrifices of the amphitheatre.
The citizens, who adhered to the manners of
their ancestors, might perhaps insinuate, that
the last remains of a martial spirit were preserved in this school of fortitude, which accustomed
the Romans to the sight of blood, and to the
contempt of death : a vain and cruel prejudice,
so nobly confuted by the valour of ancient
Greece, and of modern Europe.[a]

The recent danger, to which the person of the Honorius
fixes his
residence
at Ra-
venna,
A. D. 404.
emperor had been exposed in the defenceless palace of Milan, urged him to seek a retreat in some
inaccessible fortress of Italy, where he might
securely remain, while the open country was
covered by a deluge of barbarians. On the coast
of the Hadriatic, about ten or twelve miles from
the most southern of the seven mouths of the Po,
the Thessalians had founded the ancient colony
of RAVENNA,[c] which they afterwards resigned
to the natives of Umbria. Augustus, who had

[a] Crudele gladiatorum spectaculum et inhumanum *nonnullis* videri
solet, et *haud scio* an ita sit, ut nunc fit. Cicero Tusculan. ii, 17. He
faintly censures the *abuse*, and warmly defends the *use*, of these sports ;
oculis nulla poterat esse fortior contra dolorem et mortem disciplina.
Seneca (epist. vii) shews the feelings of a man.

[c] This account of Ravenna is drawn from Strabo, (l. v, p. 327);
Pliny, (iii, 20) ; Stephen of Byzantium, (sub voce *Ραβεννα*, p. 651, edit.
Berkel.) ; Claudian, (in vi Cons. Honor. 494, &c.); Sidonius Apollinaris, (l. i, epist. 5, 8) ; Jornandes, (de Reb. Get. c. 29); Procopius,
(de Bell. Gothic. L i, c. 1, p. 309, edit Louvre), and Cluverius, (Ital.
Antiq. tom. i, p. 301-307). Yet I still want a local antiquarian, and a
good topographical map.

observed the opportunity of the place, prepared, at the distance of three miles from the old town, a capacious harbour, for the reception of two hundred and fifty ships of war. This naval establishment, which included the arsenals and magazines, the barracks of the troops, and the houses of the artificers, derived its origin and name from the permanent station of the Roman fleet; the intermediate space was soon filled with buildings and inhabitants, and the three extensive and populous quarters of Ravenna gradually contributed to form one of the most important cities of Italy. The principal canal of Augustus poured a copious stream of the waters of the Po through the midst of the city, to the entrance of the harbour; the same waters were introduced into the profound ditches that encompassed the walls; they were distributed, by a thousand subordinate canals, into every part of the city, which they divided into a variety of small islands; the communication was maintained only by the use of boats and bridges; and the houses of Ravenna, whose appearance may be compared to that of Venice, were raised on the foundation of wooden piles. The adjacent country, to the distance of many miles, was a deep and impassable morass; and the artificial causeway, which connected Ravenna with the continent, might be easily guarded, or destroyed, on the approach of an hostile army. These morasses were interspersed, however, with vineyards; and though the soil was exhausted by four or five crops, the town enjoyed a more plentiful supply of wine than of fresh water.[p] The air instead of receiving the sickly, and almost pestilential, exhalations of low and marshy grounds, was distinguished, like the neighbourhood of Alexandria, as uncommonly pure and salubrious; and this singular advantage was ascribed to the regular tides of the Hadriatic, which swept the canals, interrupted the unwholesome stagnation of the waters, and floated, every day, the vessels of the adjacent country into the heart of Ravenna. The gradual retreat of the sea has left the modern city at the distance of four miles from the Hadriatic; and as early as the fifth or sixth century of the Christian era, the port of Augustus was converted into pleasant orchards; and a lonely grove of pines covered the ground where the Roman fleet once rode at anchor.[q] Even this alteration contributed to increase the natural strength of the place; and the shallowness of the water was a sufficient barrier against the large ships of the enemy. This advantageous situation was fortified by art and labour; and in the twentieth year of his age, the emperor of the

[p] Martial epigram iii, 56, 57) plays on the trick of the knave, who had sold him wine instead of water; but he seriously declares, that a cistern at Ravenna is more valuable than a vineyard. Sidonius complains that the town is destitute of fountains and aqueducts; and ranks the want of fresh water among the local evils, such as the croaking of frogs, the stinging of gnats, &c.

[q] The fable of Theodore and Honoria, which Dryden has so admirably transplanted from Bocaccio, (Giornata, iii, novell. viii) was acted in the wood of Chiassi, a corrupt word from Classis, the naval station, which, with the intermediate road or suburb, the Via Caesaris, constituted the triple city of Ravenna.

CHAP. West, anxious only for his personal safety, retir-
XXX. ed to the perpetual confinement of the walls and
morasses of Ravenna. The example of Honorius was imitated by his feeble successors, the
Gothic kings, and afterwards the exarchs, who
occupied the throne and palace of the emperors;
and, till the middle of the eighth century, Ravenna was considered as the seat of government,
and the capital of Italy.[r]

The revo-
lutions of
Scythia,
A. D. 400. The fears of Honorius were not without foundation, nor were his precautions without effect.
While Italy rejoiced in her deliverance from the
Goths, a furious tempest was excited among the
nations of Germany, who yielded to the irresistible impulse, that appears to have been gradually communicated from the eastern extremity of
the continent of Asia. The Chinese annals, as
they have been interpreted by the learned industry of the present age, may be usefully applied to reveal the secret and remote causes of
the fall of the Roman empire. The extensive
territory to the north of the great wall, was possessed, after the flight of the Huns, by the victorious Sienpi; who were sometimes broken
into independent tribes, and sometimes reunited
under a supreme chief; till at length styling
themselves *Topa*, or masters of the earth, they
acquired a more solid consistence, and a more
formidable power. The Topa soon compelled
the pastoral nations of the eastern desert to acknowledge the superiority of their arms; they

---

[r] From the year 404, the dates of the Theodosian Code become se
dentary at Constantinople and Ravenna. See Godefroy's Chronology
of the Laws, tom. i, p. 148, &c.

invaded China in a period of weakness and
intestine discord; and these fortunate Tar-
tars, adopting the laws and manners of the
vanquished people, founded an imperial dy-
nasty, which reigned near one hundred and
sixty years over the northern provinces of the
monarchy. Some generations before they ascended the throne of China, one of the Topa
princes had inlisted in his cavalry a slave of the
name of Moko, renowned for his valour; but
who was tempted, by the fear of punishment, to
desert his standard, and to range the desert at the
head of an hundred followers. This gang of robbers and outlaws swelled into a camp, a tribe, a
numerous people, distinguished by the appellation of *Geougen;* and their hereditary chieftains,
the posterity of Moko the slave, assumed their
rank among the Scythian monarchs. The youth
of Toulun, the greatest of his descendants, was
exercised by those misfortunes which are the
school of heroes. He bravely struggled with
adversity, broke the imperious yoke of the Topa,
and became the legislator of his nation, and the
conqueror of Tartary. His troops were distributed into regular bands of an hundred and of
a thousand men; cowards were stoned to death;
the most splendid honours were proposed as
the reward of valour; and Toulun, who had
knowledge enough to despise the learning of
China, adopted only such arts and institutions
as were favourable to the military spirit of his
government. His tents, which he removed in
the winter season to a more southern latitude,
were pitched, during the summer, on the fruit-

ful banks of the Selinga. His conquests stretched from Corea far beyond the river Irtish.. He
vanquished, in the country to the north of the
Caspian sea, the nation of the *Huns;* and the
new title of *Khan,* or *Cagan,* expressed the
fame and power which he derived from this
memorable victory.[a]

Emigra-
tion of the
northern
Germans,
A. D. 405.
The chain of events is interrupted, or rather
is concealed, as it passes from the Volga to the
Vistula, through the dark interval which separates the extreme limits of the Chinese, and of
the Roman geography.   Yet the temper of the
barbarians, and the experience of successive
emigrations, sufficiently declare, that the Huns,
who were oppressed by the arms of the Geougen, soon withdrew from the presence of an insulting victor. The countries towards the Euxine were already occupied by their kindred
tribes; and their hasty flight, which they soon
converted into a bold attack, would more naturally be directed towards the rich and level
plains, through which the Vistula gently flows
into the Baltic sea. The north must again have
been alarmed, and agitated, by the invasion of
the Huns; and the nations who retreated before them, must have pressed with incumbent
weight on the confines of Germany.[c] The inhabitants of those regions, which the ancients
have assigned to the Suevi, the Vandals, and

[a] See M. de Guignes, Hist. des Huns, tom. i, p. 179-189; tom. ii, p.
295, 334 338.
[c] Procopius (de Bell. Vandal. l. i, c. iii, p. 182) has observed an
emigration from the Palus Mæotis to the north of Germany, which he
ascribes to famine. But his views of ancient history are strangely
darkened by ignorance and error.

the Burgundians, might embrace the resolution
of abandoning to the fugitives of Sarmatia their
woods and morasses ; or at least of discharging
their superfluous numbers on the provinces of
the Roman empire." About four years after the
victorious Toulun had assumed the title of Khan
of the Geougen, another barbarian, the haughty
Rhodogast, or Radagaisus,ˣ marched from the
northern extremities of Germany almost to the
gates of Rome, and left the remains of his army
to achieve the destruction of the West. . The
Vandals, the Suevi, and the Burgundians, formed the strength of this mighty host; but the
Alani, who had found an hospitable reception
in their new seats, added their active cavalry to
the heavy infantry of the Germans; and the
Gothic adventurers crowded so eagerly to the
standard of Radagaisus, that, by some historians, he has been styled the king of the Goths.
Twelve thousand warriors, distinguished above
the vulgar by their noble birth, or their valiant
deeds, glittered in the van;ʸ and the whole
multitude, which was not less than two hundred thousand fighting men, might be increased

---

" Zosimus, (l. v, p. 331) uses the general description of the nations
beyond the Danube and the Rhine. Their situation, and consequently
their names, are manifestly shewn, even in the various epithets which
each ancient writer may have casually added.

ˣ The name of Rhadagast was that of a local deity of the Obotrites,
(in Mecklenburgh). A hero might naturally assume the appellation of
his tutelar god ; but it is not probable that the barbarians should worship an unsuccessful hero. See Mascou, Hist. of the Germans, viii, 14.

ʸ Olympiodorus (apud Photium, p. 180) uses the Greek word
Οπτιματοι; which does not convey any precise idea. I suspect that
they were the princes and nobles, with their faithful companions ; the
knights, with their squires, as they would have been styled some centuries afterwards.

CHAP.
XXX.

by the accession of women, of children, and of slaves, to the amount of four hundred thousand persons. This formidable emigration issued from the same coast of the Baltic, which had poured forth the myriads of the Cimbri and Teutones, to assault Rome and Italy in the vigour of the republic. After the departure of those barbarians, their native country, which was marked by the vestiges of their greatness, long ramparts, and gigantic moles,* remained, during some ages, a vast and dreary solitude; till the human species was renewed by the powers of generation, and the vacancy was filled by the influx of new inhabitants. The nations who now usurp an extent of land, which they are unable to cultivate, would soon be assisted by the industrious poverty of their neighbours, if the government of Europe did not protect the claims of dominion and property.

Radagaisus invades Italy,
A. D. 406.

The correspondence of nations was, in that age, so imperfect and precarious, that the revolutions of the north might escape the knowledge of the court of Ravenna; till the dark cloud, which was collected along the coast of the Baltic, burst in thunder upon the banks of the Upper Danube. The emperor of the West, if his ministers disturbed his amusements by the news of the impending danger, was satisfied with being the occasion, and the spectator of the war.ᵃ The

---

* Tacit. de Moribus Germanorum, c. 37.

a
——————Cujus agendi
Spectator vel causa fui.

Claudian, vi Cons. Hon. 439

is the modest language of Honorius, in speaking of the Gothic war, which he had seen somewhat nearer.

safety of Rome was intrusted to the counsels, and the sword, of Stilicho; but such was the feeble and exhausted state of the empire, that it was impossible to restore the fortifications of the Danube, or to prevent, by a vigorous effort, the invasion of the Germans.[b] The hopes of the vigilant ministers of Honorius were confined to the defence of Italy. He once more abandoned the provinces, recalled the troops, pressed the new levies, which were rigorously exacted, and pusillanimously eluded; employed the most efficacious means to arrest, or allure, the deserters; and offered the gift of freedom, and of two pieces of gold, to all the slaves who would inlist.[c] By these efforts, he painfully collected, from the subjects of a great empire, an army of thirty or forty thousand men, which, in the days of Scipio or Camillus, would have been instantly furnished by the free citizens of the territory of Rome.[d] The thirty legions of Stilicho were reinforced by a large body of barbarian auxiliaries; the faithful Alani

[b] Zosimus, (l. v, p. 331) transports the war, and the victory, of Stilicho, beyond the Danube. A strange error, which is awkwardly and imperfectly cured, by reading Αργον for Ιςρον, (Tillemont, Hist. des Emp. tom. v, p. 807). In good policy, we must use the service of Zosimus, without esteeming or trusting him.

[c] Codex Theodos. l. vii, tit. xiii, leg. 16. The date of this law (A. D. 406, May 18) satisfies me, as it had done Godefroy, (tom. ii, p. 387), of the true year of the invasion of Radagaisus. Tillemont, Pagi, and Muratori, prefer the preceding year; but they are bound by certain obligations of civility and respect, to St. Paulinus of Nola.

[d] Soon after Rome had been taken by the Gauls, the senate, on a sudden emergency, armed ten legions, 3,000 horse, and 42,000 foot; a force which the city could not have sent forth under Augustus, (Livy, vii, 25). This declaration may puzzle an antiquary, but it is clearly explained by Montesquieu.

were personally attached to his service; and the troops of Huns and of Goths who marched under the banners of their native princes, Huldid and Sarus, were animated by interest and resentment to oppose the ambition of Radagaisus. The king of the confederate Germans passed, without resistance, the Alps, the Po, and the Appenine; leaving on one hand the inaccessible palace of Honorius, securely buried among the marshes of Ravenna; and, on the other, the camp of Stilicho, who had fixed his head quarters at Ticinum, or Pavia, but who seems to have avoided a decisive battle, till he had assembled his distant forces. Many cities of Italy were pillaged, or destroyed; and the

Besieges Florence. siege of Florence,* by Radagaisus, is one of the earliest events in the history of that celebrated republic; whose firmness checked and delayed the unskilful fury of the barbarians. The senate and people trembled at their approach within an hundred and eighty miles of Rome; and anxiously compared the danger which they had escaped, with the new perils to which they were exposed. Alaric was a Christian and a soldier, the leader of a disciplined army; who understood the laws of war, who respected the sanctity of treaties, and who had familiarly con-

---

* Machiavel has explained, at least as a philosopher, the origin of Florence, which insensibly descended, for the benefit of trade, from the rock of Fæsulæ to the banks of the Arno, (Istoria Florentin. tom. i, l. ii, p. 36, Londra, 1747). The Triumvirs sent a colony to Florence, which, under Tiberius, (Tacit. Annal. i, 79), deserved the reputation and name of a *flourishing* city. See Cluver. Ital. Antiq. tom. i, p. 507, &c.

versed with the subjects of the empire in the same camps, and the same churches. The savage Radagaisus was a stranger to the manners, the religion, and even the language, of the civilized nations of the South. The fierceness of his temper was exasperated by cruel superstition; and it was universally believed, that he had bound himself, by a solemn vow, to reduce the city into a heap of stones and ashes, and to sacrifice the most illustrious of the Roman senators, on the altars of those gods, who were appeased by human blood. The public danger, which should have reconciled all domestic animosities, displayed the incurable madness of religious faction. The oppressed votaries of Jupiter and Mercury respected, in the implacable enemy of Rome, the character of a devout pagan; loudly declared, that they were more apprehensive of the sacrifices, than of the arms, of Radagaisus; and secretly rejoiced in the calamities of their country, which condemned the faith of their Christian adversaries.[f]

Florence was reduced to the last extremity; and the fainting courage of the citizens was supported only by the authority of St. Ambrose; who had communicated, in a dream, the promise of a speedy deliverance.[s] On a sudden, they

and threatens Rome

Defeat and destruction of his army by Stilicho, A. D. 406.

[f] Yet the Jupiter of Radagaisus, who worshipped Thor and Woden, was very different from the Olympic or Capitoline Jove. The accommodating temper of polytheism might unite those various and remote deities; but the genuine Romans abhorred the human sacrifices of Gaul and Germany.

[s] Paulinus (in Vit. Ambros. c. 50) relates this story, which he received from the mouth of Pansophia herself, a religious matron of Florence.

beheld, from their walls, the banners of Stilicho, who advanced, with his united force, to
the relief of the faithful city; and who soon
marked that fatal spot for the grave of the barbarian host.   The apparent contradictions of
those writers who variously relate the defeat of
Radagaisus, may be reconciled, without offering much violence to their respective testimonies.   Orosius and Augustin, who were intimately connected by friendship and religion,
ascribe this miraculous victory to the providence of God, rather than to the valour of man.[b]
They strictly exclude every idea of chance, or
even of bloodshed; and positively affirm, that
the Romans, whose camp was the scene of
plenty and idleness, enjoyed the distress of the
barbarians, slowly expiring on the sharp and
barren ridge of the hills of Fæsulæ, which rise
above the city of Florence.   Their extravagant
assertion, that not a single soldier of the Christian army was killed, or even wounded, may
be dismissed with silent contempt; but the rest
of the narrative of Augustin and Orosius is consistent with the state of the war, and the character of Stilicho.   Conscious that he commanded the *last* army of the republic, his prudence
would not expose it, in the open field, to the

rence.   Yet the archbishop soon ceased to take an active part in the
business of the world, and never became a popular saint.

   [b] **Augustin de Civitat. Dei, v. 23.   Orosius, l. vii, c. 37, p. 567-
571.** The two friends wrote in Africa, ten or twelve years after the
victory; and their authority is implicitly followed by Isidore of Seville,
(in Chron. p. 713, edit. Grot).   How many interesting facts might
Orosius have inserted in the vacant space which is devoted to pious
nonsense!

headstrong fury of the Germans. The method CHAP.
of surrounding the enemy with strong lines of XXX.
circumvallation, which he had twice employed
against the Gothic king, was repeated on a
larger scale, and with more considerable effect.
The examples of Cæsar must have been familiar to the most illiterate of the Roman warriors; and the fortifications of Dyrrachium, which
connected twenty-four castles, by a perpetual
ditch and rampart of fifteen miles, afforded the
model of an intrenchment which might confine,
and starve, the most numerous host of barbarians.[1] The Roman troops had less degenerated from the industry, than from the valour,
of their ancestors; and if the servile and laborious work offended the pride of the soldiers,
Tuscany could supply many thousand peasants,
who would labour, though, perhaps, they would
not fight, for the salvation of their native country. The imprisoned multitude of horses and
men[k] was gradually destroyed by famine, rather
than by the sword; but the Romans were exposed, during the progress of such an extensive
work, to the frequent attacks of an impatient
enemy. The despair of the hungry barbarians

---

[1] Franguntur montes, planumque per ardua Cæsar
  Ducit opus : pandit fossas, turritaque summis
  Disponit castella jugis, magnoque recessû
  Amplexux fines ; saltus nemorosaque tesqua
  Et silvas, vastâque feras indagine claudit.
Yet the simplicity of truth (Cæsar, de Bell. Civ. iii, 44) is far greater
than the amplifications of Lucan, (Pharsal. l. vi, 29-63).

[k] The rhetorical expressions of Orosius, " In arido et aspero montis
" jugo ;" " in unum ac parvum verticem ;" are not very suitable to
the encampment of a great army. But Fæsulæ, only three miles from
Florence, might afford space for the head-quarters of Radagaisus, and
would be comprehended within the circuit of the Roman lines.

would precipitate them against the fortifications
of Stilicho; the general might sometimes indulge the ardour of his brave auxiliaries, who
eagerly pressed to assault the camp of the Germans; and these various incidents might produce the sharp and bloody conflicts which dig-
nify the narrative of Zosimus, and the Chronicles of Prosper and Marcellinus.[1] A seasonable supply of men and provisions had been introduced into the walls of Florence; and the
famished host of Radagaisus was in its turn besieged. The proud monarch of so many warlike nations, after the loss of his bravest warriors, was reduced to confide either in the faith
of a capitulation, or in the clemency of Stilicho.[m] But the death of the royal captive, who
was ignominiously beheaded, disgraced the triumph of Rome and of Christianity; and the
short delay of his execution was sufficient to
brand the conqueror with the guilt of cool and
deliberate cruelty.[n] The famished Germans,
who escaped the fury of the auxiliaries, were
sold as slaves, at the contemptible price of as
many single pieces of gold: but the difference
of food and climate swept away great numbers
of those unhappy strangers; and it was observ-

[1] See Zosimus, l. v, p. 331, and the Chronicles of Prosper and Marcellinus.

[m] Olympiodorus (apud Photium, p. 180) uses an expression,
(προσηταιρισατο), which would denote a strict and friendly alliance, and
render Stilicho still more criminal. The paulisper detentus, deinde in-
terfectus, of Orosius, is sufficiently odious.

[n] Orosius, piously inhuman, sacrifices the king and people, Agag
and the Amalekites, without a symptom of compassion. The bloody
actor is less detestable than the cool unfeeling historian

ed that the inhuman purchasers, instead of reaping the fruits of their labour, were soon obliged to provide the expence of their interment. Stilicho informed the emperor and the senate of his success; and deserved, a second time, the glorious title of Deliverer of Italy.[o]

The fame of the victory, and more especially of the miracle, has encouraged a vain persuasion that the whole army, or rather nation, of Germans, who migrated from the shores of the Baltic, miserably perished under the walls of Florence. Such indeed was the fate of Radagaisus himself, of his brave and faithful companions, and of more than one-third of the various multitude of Sueves and Vandals, of Alani and Burgundians, who adhered to the standard of their general.[p] The union of such an army might excite our surprise, but the causes of separation are obvious and forcible; the pride of birth, the insolence of valour, the jealousy of command, the impatience of subordination, and the obstinate conflict of opinions, of interests, and of passions, among so many kings and warriors, who were untaught to yield, or to obey. After the defeat of Radagaisus, two parts of the German host, which must have exceeded the number of one hundred thousand men, still remained in

CHAP
XXX.

The remainder
of the
Germans
invade
Gaul,
A. D. 406,
Dec. 31.

[o] And Claudian's muse, was she asleep? had she been ill paid? Methinks the seventh consulship of Honorius (A. D. 407) would have furnished the subject of a noble poem. Before it was discovered that the state could no longer be saved, Stilicho (after Romulus, Camillus, and Marius) might have been worthily surnamed the fourth founder of Rome.

[p] A luminious passage of Prosper's Chronicle, " *In tres partes, per diversos principes, divisus exercitus,*" reduces the miracle of Florence, and connects the history of Italy Gaul, and Germany.

arms, between the Apennine and the Alps, or
between the Alps and the Danube. It is uncertain whether they attempted to revenge the
death of their general; but their irregular fury
was soon diverted by the prudence and firmness of Stilicho, who opposed their march, and
facilitated their retreat; who considered the
safety of Rome and Italy as the great object of
his care; and who sacrificed, with too much
indifference, the wealth and tranquillity of the
distant provinces.[q] The barbarians acquired,
from the junction of some Pannonian deserters,
the knowledge of the country, and of the roads;
and the invasion of Gaul, which Alaric had
designed, was executed by the remains of the
great army of Radagaisus.[r]

Yet if they expected to derive any assistance
from the tribes of Germany, who inhabited the
banks of the Rhine, their hopes were disappointed. The Alemanni preserved a state of inactive neutrality; and the Franks distinguished
their zeal and courage in the defence of the empire. In the rapid progress down the Rhine,
which was the first act of the administration of
Stilicho, he had applied himself, with peculiar

[q] Orosius and Jerom positively charge him with instigating the invasion. " Excitatæ a Stilichone gentes," &c. They must mean indirectly. He saved Italy at the expence of Gaul.

[r] The count de Buat is satisfied, that the Germans who invaded
Gaul were the *two-thirds* that yet remained of the army of Radagaisus.
See the Histoire Ancienne des Peuples de l'Europe, tom. vii, p. 87—
121; Paris, 1772; an elaborate work, which I had not the advantage of perusing till the year 1777. As early as 1771, I find the same
idea expressed in a rough draught of the present History. I have since
observed a similiar intimation in Mascou, (viii, 15). Such agreement,
without mutual communication, may add some weight to our common
sentiment.

attention, to secure the alliance of the warlike
Franks, and to remove the irreconcilable enemies of peace and of the republic. Marcomir, one of their kings, was publicly convicted, before the tribunal of the Roman magistrate, of violating the faith of treaties. He was sentenced to a mild, but distant, exile, in the province of Tuscany; and this degradation of the regal dignity was so far from exciting the resentment of his subjects, that they punished with death the turbulent Sunno, who attempted to revenge his brother; and maintained a dutiful allegiance to the princes, who were established on the throne by the choice of Stilicho.* When the limits of Gaul and Germany were shaken by the northern emigration, the Franks bravely encountered the single force of the Vandals; who, regardless of the lessons of adversity, had again separated their troops from the standard of their barbarian allies. They paid the penalty of their rashness; and twenty thousand Vandals, with their king Godigisclus, were slain in the field of battle. The whole people must have been extirpated, if the squadrons of the Alani, advancing to their relief had not trampled down the infantry of the Franks; who, after an honourable resistance, were compelled to relinquish the unequal con-

---

* —————Provincia missos
Expellet citius fasces, quam Francia reges
Quos dederis.
Claudian (i Cons. Stil. l. i, 235, &c.) is clear and satisfactory. These kings of France are unknown to Gregory of Tours; but the author of the Gesta Francorum mentions both Sunno and Marcomir, and names the latter as the father of Pharamond, (in tom. ii, p. 543). He seems to write from good materials, which he did not understand.

test. The victorious confederates pursued their march, and, on the last day of the year, in a season when the waters of the Rhine were most probably frozen, they entered, without opposition, the defenceless provinces of Gaul. This memorable passage of the Suevi, the Vandals, the Alani, and the Burgundians, who never afterwards retreated, may be considered as the fall of the Roman empire in the countries beyond the Alps ; and the barriers which had so long separated the savage and the civilized nations of the earth, were from that fatal moment levelled with the ground.[t]

Desolation of Gaul, A. D. 407, &c
While the peace of Germany was secured by the attachment of the Franks, and the neutrality of the Alemanni, the subjects of Rome, unconscious of their approaching calamities, enjoyed the state of quiet and prosperity, which had seldom blessed the frontiers of Gaul. Their flocks and herds were permitted to graze in the pastures of the barbarians; their huntsmen penetrated, without fear or danger, into the darkest recesses of the Hercynian wood.[u] The banks of the Rhine were crowned, like those of the

---

[t] See Zosimus, (l. vi, p. 373) ; Orosius, (l. vii, c. 40, p. 576), and the Chronicles. Gregory of Tours (l. ii, c. 9, p. 165, in the second volume of the Historians of France) has preserved a valuable fragment of Renatus Profuturus Frigeridus, whose three names denote a Christian, a Roman subject, and a semi-barbarian.

[u] Claudian (i Cons. Stil. l. i, 221, &c. ; l. ii, 186, describes the peace and prosperity of the Gallic frontiers. The Abbé Dubois (Hist. Critique, &c. tom. i, p. 174) would read *Alba*, (a nameless rivulet of the Ardennes), instead of *Albis* ; and expatiates on the danger of the Gallic cattle grazing beyond the *Elbe*. Foolish enough ! In poetical geography, the Elbe, and the Hercynian, signify any river, or any wood in Germany. Claudian is not prepared for the strict examination of our antiquaries.

Tiber, with elegant houses, and well cultivated farms; and if a poet descended the river, he might express his doubt, on which side was situated the territory, of the Romans.[x] This scene of peace and plenty was suddenly changed into a desert; and the prospect of the smoking ruins could alone distinguish the solitude of nature from the desolation of man. The flourishing city of Mentz was surprised and destroyed; and many thousand Christians were inhumanly massacred in the church. Worms perished after a long and obstinate siege; Strasburgh, Spires, Rheims, Tournay, Arras, Amiens, experienced the cruel oppression of the German yoke; and the consuming flames of war spread from the banks of the Rhine over the greatest part of the seventeen provinces of Gaul. That rich and extensive country, as far as the ocean, the Alps, and the Pyrenees, was delivered to the barbarians, who drove before them, in a promiscuous crowd, the bishop, the senator, and the virgin, laden with the spoils of their houses and altars.[y] The ecclesiastics, to whom we are indebted for this vague description of the public calamities, embraced the opportunity of exhorting the Christians to repent of the sins which had provoked the Divine Justice, and to renounce the perishable goods of a wretched and deceitful

[x] ————Geminasque viator
Cum videat ripas, quæ sit Romana requirat.
[y] Jerom. tom. i, p. 93.   See in the 1st vol. of the Historians of France, p. 777, 782, the proper extracts from the Carmen de Providentiâ Divinâ, and Salvian.   The anonymous poet was himself a captive, with his bishop and fellow-citizens.

world. But as the Pelagian controversy,[z] which attempts to sound the abyss of grace and predestination, soon became the serious employment of the Latin clergy; the Providence which had decreed, or foreseen, or permitted, such a train of moral and natural evils, was rashly weighed in the imperfect and fallacious balance of reason. The crimes, and the misfortunes, of the suffering people, were presumptuously compared with those of their ancestors; and they arraigned the Divine Justice, which did not exempt from the common destruction the feeble, the guiltless, the infant portion of the human species. These idle disputants overlooked the invariable laws of nature, which have connected peace with innocence, plenty with industry, and safety with valour. The timid and selfish policy of the court of Ravenna might recal the Palatine legions for the protection of Italy; the remains of the stationary troops might be unequal to the arduous task; and the barbarian auxiliaries might prefer the unbounded licence of spoil, to the benefits of a moderate and regular stipend. But the provinces of Gaul were filled with a numerous race of hardy and robust youth, who, in the defence of their houses, their families, and their altars, if they had dared to die, would have deserved to vanquish. The knowledge of their native country would have enabled them to op-

---

[z] The Pelagian doctrine, which was first agitated A. D. 405, was condemned, in the space of ten years, at Rome and Carthage. St. Augustin fought and conquered: but the Greek church was favourable to his adversaries; and (what is singular enough) the people did not take any part in a dispute which they could not understand.

pose continual and insuperable obstacles to the progress of an invader; and the deficiency of the barbarians, in arms as well as in discipline, removed the only pretence which excuses the submission of a populous country to the inferior numbers of a veteran army When France was invaded by Charles V, he inquired of a prisoner, How many *days* Paris might be distant from the frontier? " Perhaps *twelve*, but " they will be days of battle."[a] Such was the gallant answer which checked the arrogance of that ambitious prince. The subjects of Honorius, and those of Francis I, were animated by a very different spirit; and in less than two years, the divided troops of the savages of the Baltic, whose numbers, were they fairly stated, would appear contemptible, advanced, without a combat, to the foot of the Pyrenæan mountains.

In the early part of the reign of Honorius, the vigilance of Stilicho had successfully guarded the remote island of Britain from her incessant enemies of the ocean, the mountains, and the Irish coast.[b] But those restless barbarians

---

[a] See the Memoires de Guillaume du Bellay, l. vi. In French, the original reproof is less obvious, and more pointed, from the double sense of the word *journee*, which alike signifies, a day's travel, or a battle.

[b] Claudian (i Cons. Stil. l. ii, 250). It is supposed, that the Scots of Ireland invaded, by sea, the whole western coast of Britain : and some slight credit may be given even to Nennius and the Irish traditions, (Carte's Hist. of England, vol. i, p. 169. Whitaker's Genuine History of the Britons, p. 199). The sixty-six lives of St. Patrick, which were extant in the ninth century, must have contained as many thousand lies ; yet we may believe, that in one of these Irish inroads, the future apostle was led away captive, (Usher. Antiquit. Eccles. Britann

could not neglect the fair opportunity of the Gothic war, when the walls and stations of the province were stripped of the Roman troops. If any of the legionaries were permitted to return from the Italian expedition, their faithful report of the court and character of Honorius must have tended to dissolve the bonds of allegiance, and to exasperate the seditious temper of the British army.   The spirit of revolt, which had formerly disturbed the age of Gallienus, was revived by the capricious violence of the soldiers ; and the unfortunate, perhaps the ambitious, candidates, who were the objects of their choice, were the instruments, and at length the victims, of their passion.[c]   Marcus was the first whom they placed on the throne, as the lawful emperor of Britain, and of the West.   They violated, by the hasty murder of Marcus, the oath of fidelity which they had imposed on themselves ; and *their* disapprobation of his manners may seem to inscribe an honourable epitaph on his tomb.   Gratian was the next whom they adorned with the diadem and the purple ; and, at the end of four months, Gratian experienced the fate of his predecessor. The memory of the great Constantine, whom the British legions had given to the church and to the empire, suggested the singular motive of their third choice.   They discovered in the

tann, p. 431, and Tillemont, Mem. Eccles. tom. xvi, p. 456, 782, &c).

[c] The British usurpers are taken from Zosimus, (l. vi, p. 371-375); Orosius, (l. vii, c. 40, p. 576, 577) ; Olympiodorus, (apud Photium, p. 180, 181), the ecclesiastical historians, and the Chronicles. The Latins are ignorant of Marcus.

ranks a private soldier of the name of Constantine, and their impetuous levity had already seated him on the throne, before they perceived his incapacity to sustain the weight of that glorious appellation.[a] Yet the authority of Constantine was less precarious, and his government was more successful, than the transient reigns of Marcus and of Gratian. The danger of leaving his inactive troops in those camps, which had been twice polluted with blood and sedition, urged him to attempt the reduction of the western provinces. He landed at Boulogne with an inconsiderable force; and after he had reposed himself some days, he summoned the cities of Gaul, which had escaped the yoke of the barbarians, to acknowledge their lawful sovereign. They obeyed the summons without reluctance. The neglect of the court of Ravenna had absolved a deserted people from the duty of allegiance; their actual distress encouraged them to accept any circumstances of change, without apprehension, and, perhaps, with some degree of hope; and they might flatter themselves, that the troops, the authority, and even the name of a Roman emperor, who fixed his residence in Gaul, would protect the unhappy country from the rage of the barbarians. The first successes of Constantine against the detached parties of the Germans, were magnified by the voice of adulation into splendid

[a] Cum in Constantino *inconstantiam* . . . . . execrarentur, (Sidonius Apollinaris, l. v, epist. 9, p. 139, edit. secund. Sirmond). Yet Sidonius might be tempted, by so fair a pun, to stigmatize a prince who had disgraced his grandfather.

and decisive victories; which the reunion and insolence of the enemy soon reduced to their just value. His negotiations procured a short and precarious truce; and if some tribes of the barbarians were engaged, by the liberality of his gifts and promises, to undertake the defence of the Rhine, these expensive and uncertain treaties, instead of restoring the pristine vigour of the Gallic frontier, served only to disgrace the majesty of the prince, and to exhaust what yet remained of the treasures of the republic. Elated however with this imaginary triumph, the vain deliverer of Gaul advanced into the provinces of the South, to encounter a more pressing and personal danger. Sarus the Goth was ordered to lay the head of the rebel at the feet of the emperor Honorius; and the forces of Britain and Italy were unworthily consumed in this domestic quarrel. After the loss of his two bravest generals, Justinian and Nevigastes, the former of whom was slain in the field of battle, the latter in a peaceful but treacherous interview, Constantine fortified himself within the walls of Vienna. The place was ineffectually attacked seven days; and the imperial army supported, in a precipitate retreat, the ignominy of purchasing a secure passage from the freebooters and outlaws of the Alps.* Those mountains now separated the dominions of two rival monarchs: and the fortifications of the double

---

* *Bagaudæ* is the name which Zosimus applies to them; perhaps they deserved a less odious character, (see Dubois, Hist. Critique, tom. i, p. 203, and this History vol. ii, p. 121). We shall hear of them again.

frontier were guarded by the troops of the empire, whose arms would have been more usefully employed to maintain the Roman limits against the barbarians of Germany and Scythia.

On the side of the Pyrenees, the ambition of Constantine might be justified by the proximity of danger; but his throne was soon established by the conquest, or rather submission, of Spain; which yielded to the influence of regular and habitual subordination, and received the laws and magistrates of the Gallic prefecture. The only opposition which was made to the authority of Constantine, proceeded not so much from the powers of government, or the spirit of the people, as from the private zeal, and interest of the family of Theodosius. Four brothers[f] had obtained by the favour of their kinsman, the deceased emperor, an honourable rank, and ample possessions, in their native country: and the grateful youths resolved to risk those advantages in the service of his son. After an unsuccessful effort to maintain their ground at the head of the stationary troops of Lusitania, they retired to their estates; where they armed and levied, at their own expence, a considerable body of slaves and dependants, and boldly marched to occupy the strong posts of the Pyrenæan mountains. This domestic insurrection alarmed and perplexed the sovereign of Gaul and Britain; and he was compelled to negotiate with some troops of barbarian auxiliaries, for the ser-

He reduces Spain, A. D. 408.

[f] Verinianus, Didymus, Theodosius, and Lagodius, who, in modern courts, would be styled princes of the blood, were not distinguished by any rank or privileges above the rest of their fellow subjects.

vice of the Spanish war. They were distinguished by the title of *Honorians*,[s] a name which might have reminded them of their fidelity to their lawful sovereign; and if it should candidly be allowed that the *Scots* were influenced by any partial affection for a British prince, the *Moors* and the *Marcomanni* could be tempted only by the profuse liberality of the usurper, who distributed among the barbarians the military, and even the civil, honours of Spain. The nine bands of *Honorians*, which may be easily traced on the establishment of the western empire, could not exceed the number of five thousand men; yet this inconsiderable force was sufficient to terminate a war, which had threatened the power and safety of Constantine. The rustic army of the Theodosian family was surrounded and destroyed in the Pyrenees; two of the brothers had the good fortune to escape by sea to Italy, or the East; the other two, after an interval of suspense, were executed at Arles; and if Honorius could remain insensible of the public disgrace, he might perhaps be affected by the personal misfortunes of his generous kinsmen. Such were the feeble arms which decided the possession of the western provinces of Europe, from the walls of Antoninus to the columns of Hercules. The events of peace and war have undoubtedly been diminished by the

---

[s] These *Honoriani*, or *Honoriaci*, consisted of two bands of Scots, or Attacotti, two of Moors, two of Marcomanni, the Victores, the Ascarii, and the Gallicani, (Notitia Imperii, sect. xxxviii, edit. Lab). They were part of the sixty-five *Auxilia Palatina*, and are properly styled, ἡ τῶν αὐλῶν τάξις, by Zosimus, (l. vi, p. 374).

narrow and imperfect view of the historians of the times, who were equally ignorant of the causes, and of the effects, of the most important revolutions. But the total decay of the national strength had annihilated even the last resource of a despotic government; and the revenue of exhausted provinces could no longer purchase the military service of a discontented and pusillanimous people.

The poet, whose flattery has ascribed to the Roman eagle the victories of Pollentia and Verona, pursues the hasty retreat of Alaric, from the confines of Italy, with a horrid train of imaginary spectres, such as might hover over an army of barbarians, which was almost exterminated by war, famine, and disease.[b] In the course of this unfortunate expedition, the king of the Goths must indeed have sustained a considerable loss; and his harassed forces required an interval of repose to recruit their numbers, and revive their confidence. Adversity had exercised, and displayed, the genius of Alaric; and the fame of his valour invited to the Gothic standard the bravest of the barbarian warriors; who, from the Euxine to the Rhine, were agitated by the desire of rapine and conquest. He had deserved the esteem, and he soon accepted the friendship, of Stilicho himself. Renouncing the service of the emperor of the East,

Negotiation of Alaric and Stilicho, A. D. 404-408.

b ————Comitatur euntem
Pallor, et atra fames; et saucia lividus ora
Luctus; et inferni stridentes agmine morbi
Claudian in vi Cons. Hon. 321, &c.

CHAP.
XXX.
_____

Alaric concluded, with the court of Ravenna, a treaty of peace and alliance, by which he was declared master-general of the Roman armies throughout the prefecture of Illyricum; as it was claimed, according to the true and ancient limits, by the minister of Honorius.[1] The execution of the ambitious design, which was either stipulated, or implied, in the articles of the treaty, appears to have been suspended by the formidable irruption of Radagaisus; and the neutrality of the Gothic king may perhaps be compared to the indifference of Cæsar, who, in the conspiracy of Cataline, refused either to assist, or to oppose, the enemy of the republic. After the defeat of the Vandals, Stilicho resumed his pretensions to the provinces of the East, appointed civil magistrates for the administration of justice, and of the finances; and declared his impatience to lead to the gates of Constantinople, the united armies of the Romans and of the Goths. The prudence, however, of Stilicho, his aversion to civil war, and his perfect knowledge of the weakness of the state, may countenance the suspicion, that domestic peace, rather than foreign conquest, was the object of his policy; and that his principal care was to employ the forces of Alaric at a distance from Italy. This design could not long escape the penetration of the Gothic king, who continued to hold a doubtful, and perhaps a treacherous, correspondence with the rival courts; who pro-

[1] These dark transactions are investigated by the Count de Buat, (Hist. des Peuples de l'Europe, tom. vii, c. iii-viii, p. 69-200), whose laborious accuracy may sometimes fatigue a superficial reader.

tracted, like a dissatisfied mercenary, his languid operations in Thessaly and Epirus, and who soon returned to claim the extravagant reward of his ineffectual services. From his camp near Æmona,[k] on the confines of Italy, he transmitted, to the emperor of the West, a long account of promises, of expences, and of demands; called for immediate satisfaction, and clearly intimated the consequences of a refusal. Yet if his conduct was hostile, his language was decent and dutiful. He humbly professed himself the friend of Stilicho, and the soldier of Honorius; offered his person and his troops to march, without delay, against the usurper of Gaul; and solicited, as a permanent retreat for the Gothic nation, the possession of some vacant province of the western empire.

The political and secret transactions of two statesmen, who laboured to deceive each other and the world, must for ever have been concealed in the impenetrable darkness of the cabinet, if the debates of a popular assembly had not thrown some rays of light on the correspondence of Alaric and Stilicho. The necessity of finding some artificial support for a government, which, from a principle, not of moderation, but of weakness, was reduced to negotiate with its own subjects, had insensibly revived the authority of the Roman senate; and the minister of

---

[k] See Zosimus, l. v, p. 334, 335. He interrupts his scanty narrative, to relate the fable of Æmona, and of the ship Argo; which was drawn over land from that place to the Hadriatic. Sozomen, (l. viii, c. 25; l. ix, c. 4), and Socrates, (l. vii, c. 10), cast a pale and doubtful light; and Orosius (l. vii, c. 38, p. 571) is abominably partial.

Honorius respectfully consulted the legislative council of the republic. Stilicho assembled the senate in the palace of the Cæsars; represented, in a studied oration, the actual state of affairs; proposed the demands of the Gothic king, and submitted to their consideration the choice of peace or war. The senators, as if they had been suddenly awakened from a dream of four hundred years, appeared on this important occasion to be inspired by the courage, rather than by the wisdom, of their predecessors. They loudly declared, in regular speeches, or in tumultuary acclamations, that it was unworthy of the majesty of Rome, to purchase a precarious and disgraceful truce from a barbarian king; and that, in the judgment of a magnanimous people, the chance of ruin was always preferable to the certainty of dishonour. The minister, whose pacific intentions were seconded only by the voices of a few servile and venal followers, attempted to allay the general ferment, by an apology for his own conduct, and even for the demands of the Gothic prince. " The payment of a subsidy, which had excited " the indignation of the Romans, ought not " (such was the language of Stilicho) to be con- " sidered in the odious light, either of a tribute, " or of a ransom, extorted by the menaces of a " barbarian enemy. Alaric had faithfully as- " serted the just pretensions of the republic to " the provinces which were usurped by the " Greeks of Constantinople: he modestly re- " quired the fair and stipulated recompence of " his services; and if he had desisted from the

" prosecution of his enterprise, he had obeyed,
" in his retreat, the peremptory, though private,
" letters of the emperor himself. These contra-
" dictory orders (he would not dissemble the
" errors of his own family) had been procured
" by the intercession of Serena. The tender
" piety of his wife had been too deeply affected
" by the discord of the royal brothers, the sons
" of her adopted father; and the sentiments of
" nature had too easily prevailed over the stern
" dictates of the public welfare." These ostensible reasons, which faintly disguise the obscure intrigues of the palace of Ravenna, were supported by the authority of Stilicho; and obtained, after a warm debate, the reluctant approbation of the senate. The tumult of virtue and freedom subsided; and the sum of four thousand pounds of gold was granted, under the name of a subsidy, to secure the peace of Italy, and to conciliate the friendship of the king of the Goths. Lampadius alone, one of the most illustrious members of the assembly, still persisted in his dissent; exclaimed with a loud voice,—" This is not a treaty of peace, but of " servitude"[1] and escaped the danger of such bold opposition by immediately retiring to the sanctuary of a Christian church.

But the reign of Stilicho drew toward its end;
and the proud minister might perceive the symptoms of his approaching disgrace. The generous boldness of Lampadius had been applauded;

---

[1] Zosimus, l. v, p. 338, 339. He repeats the words of Lampadius, as they were spoke in Latin,—" Non est ista pax, sed pactio servitutis " and then translates them into Greek for the benefit of his readers.

and the senate, so patiently resigned to a long servitude, rejected with disdain the offer of invidious and imaginary freedom. The troops, who still assumed the name and prerogatives of the Roman legions, were exasperated by the partial affection of Stilicho for the barbarians : and the people imputed to the mischievous policy of the minister, the public misfortunes, which were the natural consequence of their own degeneracy. Yet Stilicho might have continued to brave the clamours of the people, and even of the soldiers, if he could have maintained his dominion over the feeble mind of his pupil. But the respectful attachment of Honorius was converted into fear, suspicion, and hatred. The crafty Olympius,[m] who concealed his vices under the mask of Christian piety, had secretly undermined the benefactor, by whose favour he was promoted to the honourable offices of the imperial palace. Olympius revealed to the unsuspecting emperor, who had attained the twenty-fifth year of his age, that he was without weight, or authority, in his own government ; and artfully alarmed his timid and indolent disposition by a lively picture of the designs of Stilicho, who already meditated the death of his sovereign, with the ambitious hope

[m] He came from the coast of the Euxine, and exercised a splendid office, λαμπρας δε σρα τειας εν τοις βασιλειοις αξιωμενος. His actions justify his character, which Zosimus (l. v. p. 340) exposes with visible satisfaction. Augustin revered the piety of Olympius, whom he styles a true son of the church, (Baronius, Annal. Eccles. A. D. 408, No. 19, &c. Tillemont, Mem. Eccles. tom. xiii, p. 467, 468). But these praises, which the African saint so unworthily bestows, might proceed, as well from ignorance, as from adulation.

of placing the diadem on the head of his son
Eucharius. The emperor was instigated, by his
new favourite, to assume the tone of independent
dignity; and the minister was astonished to find,
that secret resolutions were formed in the court
and council, which were repugnant to his interest, or to his intentions. Instead of residing
in the palace of Rome, Honorius declared, that
it was his pleasure to return to the secure fortress of Ravenna. On the first intelligence of
the death of his brother Arcadius, he prepared
to visit Constantinople, and to regulate, with
the authority of a guardian, the provinces of
the infant Theodosius.* The representation of
the difficulty and expence of such a distant expedition, checked this strange and sudden sally
of active diligence; but the dangerous project
of shewing the emperor to the camp of Pavia,
which was composed of the Roman troops, the
enemies of Stilicho, and his barbarian auxiliaries, remained fixed and unalterable. The minister was pressed, by the advice of his confident Justinian, a Roman advocate, of a lively
and penetrating genius, to oppose a journey so
prejudicial to his reputation and safety. His
strenuous, but ineffectual, efforts confirmed the
triumph of Olympius; and the prudent lawyer
withdrew himself from the impending ruin of
his patron.

In the passage of the emperor through Bo-

n Zosimus, l. v, p. 338, 339. Sozomen, l. ix, c. 4. Stilicho offered
to undertake the journey to Constantinople, that he might divert Honorius from the vain attempt. The eastern empire would not have
obeyed, and could not have been conquered.

CHAP.
XXX.

Disgrace
and death
of Stili-
cho,
A. D. 408,
Aug. 23.

logna, a mutiny of the guards was excited and appeased by the secret policy of Stilicho; who announced his instructions to decimate the guilty, and ascribed to his own intercession the merit of their pardon.   After this tumult, Honorius embraced, for the last time, the minister whom he now considered as a tyrant, and proceeded on his way to the camp of Pavia; where he was received by the loyal acclamations of the troops who were assembled for the service of the Gallic war.   On the morning of the fourth day, he pronounced, as he had been taught, a military oration in the presence of the soldiers, whom the charitable visits, and artful discourses, of Olympius had prepared to execute a dark and bloody conspiracy. At the first signal, they massacred the friends of Stilicho, the most illustrious officers of the empire; two pretorian prefects, of Gaul, and of Italy; two masters-general, of the cavalry, and infantry; the master of the offices; the questor, the treasurer, and the count of the domestics. Many lives were lost; many houses were plundered; the furious sedition continued to rage till the close of the evening; and the trembling emperor, who was seen in the streets of Pavia, without his robes or diadem, yielded to the persuasions of his favourite; condemned the memory of the slain; and solemnly approved the innocence and fidelity of their assassins.   The intelligence of the massacre of Pavia filled the mind of Stilicho with just and gloomy apprehensions; and he instantly summoned, in the camp of Bologna, a council of the confederate leaders, who were attached to his service, and would be involved in his ruin. The impetuous voice of the assembly called aloud for arms, and for revenge; to march, without a moment's delay, under the banners of a hero, whom they had so often followed to victory; to surprise, to oppress, to extirpate the guilty Olympius, and his degenerate Romans; and perhaps to fix the diadem on the head of their injured general. Instead of executing a resolution, which might have been justified by success, Stilicho hesitated till he was irrecoverably lost. He was still ignorant of the fate of the emperor; he distrusted the fidelity of his own party; and he viewed with horror the fatal consequences of arming a crowd of licentious barbarians, against the soldiers and people of Italy. The confederates, impatient of his timorous and doubtful delay, hastily retired, with fear and indignation. At the hour of midnight, Sarus, a Gothic warrior, renowned among the barbarians themselves for his strength and valour, suddenly invaded the camp of his benefactor, plundered the baggage, cut in pieces the faithful Huns, who guarded his person, and penetrated to the tent, where the minister, pensive and sleepless, meditated on the dangers of his situation. Stilicho escaped with difficulty from the sword of the Goths; and, after issuing a last and generous admonition to the cities of Italy, to shut their gates against the barbarians, his confidence, or his despair, urged him to throw himself into Ravenna, which was already in the absolute pos-

CHAP.
XXX.

session of his enemies. Olympius, who had assumed the dominion of Honorius, was speedily informed, that his rival had embraced, as a suppliant, the altar of the Christian church. The base and cruel disposition of the hypocrite was incapable of pity or remorse; but he piously affected to elude, rather than to violate, the privilege of the sanctuary. Count Heraclian, with a troop of soldiers, appeared, at the dawn of day, before the gates of the church of Ravenna. The bishop was satisfied, by a solemn oath, that the imperial mandate only directed them to secure the person of Stilicho: but, as soon as the unfortunate minister had been tempted beyond the holy threshold, he produced the warrant for his instant execution. Stilicho supported with calm resignation, the injurious names of traitor and parricide; repressed the unseasonable zeal of his followers, who were ready to attempt an ineffectual rescue; and, with a firmness not unworthy of the last of the Roman generals, submitted his neck to the sword of Heraclian.[o]

His memory persecuted.

The servile crowd of the palace, who had so long adored the fortune of Stilicho, affected to insult his fall; and the most distant connection with the master-general of the West, which had so lately been a title to wealth and honours, was studiously denied, and rigorously punish-

---

[o] Zosimus (l. v, p. 336345) has copiously, though not clearly related the disgrace and death of Stilicho. Olympiodorus, (apud Phot. p. 177); Orosius, (l. vii, c. 38, p. 571, 572); Sozomen, (l. ix, c. 4), and Philostorgius, (l. xi, c. 3; l. xiii, c. 2), afford supplemental hints.

ed. His family, united by a triple alliance with the family of Theodosius, might envy the condition of the meanest peasant. The flight of his son Eucherius was intercepted ; and the death of that innocent youth soon followed the divorce of Thermantia, who filled the place of her sister Maria ; and who, like Maria, had remained a virgin in the imperial bed.[p] The friends of Stilicho, who had escaped the massacre of Pavia, were persecuted by the implacable revenge of Olympius: and the most exquisite cruelty was employed to extort the confession of a treasonable and sacrilegious conspiracy. They died in silence : their firmness justified the choice,[q] and perhaps absolved the innocence of their patron ; and the despotic power, which could take his life without a trial, and stigmatize his memory without a proof, has no jurisdiction over the impartial suffrage of posterity.[r] The services of Stilicho are great and manifest ; his crimes, as they are vaguely stated in the language of flattery and hatred, are obscure, at least, and improbable. About four months after his death, an edict was published

[p] Zosimus, l. v, p. 333. The marriage of a Christian with two sisters, scandalizes Tillemont, (Hist. des Empereurs, tom. v, p. 557) ; who expects, in vain, that Pope Innocent I. should have done something in the way, either of censure, or of dispensation.

[q] Two of his friends are honourably mentioned, (Zosimus, l. v, p. 346) : Peter, chief of the school of notaries, and the great chamberlain Deuterius. Stilicho had secured the bed-chamber ; and it is surprising, that, under a feeble prince, the bed-chamber was not able to secure him.

[r] Orosius (l. vii, c. 38, p. 571, 572) seems to copy the false and furious manifestoes, which were dispersed through the provinces by the new administration.

in the name of Honorius, to restore the free
communication of the two empires, which had
been so long interrupted by the *public enemy.*'
The minister, whose fame and fortune depended on the prosperity of the state, was accused
of betraying Italy to the barbarians ; whom he
repeatedly vanquished at Pollentia, at Verona,
and before the walls of Florence.   His pretended design of placing the diadem on the head of
his son Eucherius, could not have been conducted without preparations or accomplices ;
and the ambitious father would not surely have
left the future emperor, till the twentieth year
of his age, in the humble station of tribune of
the notaries.   Even the religion of Stilicho was
arraigned by the malice of his rival.   The seasonable, and almost miraculous, deliverance
was devoutly celebrated by the applause of the
clergy ; who asserted, that the restoration of
idols, and the persecution of the church, would
have been the first measure of the reign of Eucherius.   The son of Stilicho, however, was
educated in the bosom of Christianity, which
his father had uniformly professed, and zealous-
ly supported.'   Serena had borrowed her magnificent necklace from the statue of Vesta," and
the pagans execrated the memory of the sacri-

' See the Theodosian Code, l. vii, tit. xvi, leg. 1 ; l. ix, tit. xlii, leg.
22.   Stilicho is branded with the name of *prædo publicus,* who employed his wealth, *ad omnem ditandam, inquietandamque barbariem.*

Augustin himself is satisfied with the effectual laws, which Stilicho
had enacted against heretics and idolaters ; and which are still extant
in the Code.   He only applies to Olympius for their confirmation, (Ba.
ronius, Annal. Eccles. A. D. 418, No. 19).

" Zosimus, l. v, p. 361.   We may observe the bad taste of the age,
in dressing their statues with such awkward finery.

legious minister, by whose order the Sybilline books, the oracles of Rome, had been committed to the flames.[x] The pride and power of Stilicho constituted his real guilt. An honour able reluctance to shed the blood of his countrymen, appears to have contributed to the success of his unworthy rival; and it is the last humiliation of the character of Honorius, that posterity has not condescended to reproach him with his base ingratitude to the guardian of his youth, and the support of his empire.

Among the train of dependants, whose wealth and dignity attracted the notice of their own times, *our* curiosity is excited by the celebrated name of the poet Claudian, who enjoyed the favour of Stilicho, and was overwhelmed in the ruin of his patron. The titular offices of tribune and notary fixed his rank in the imperial court: he was indebted to the powerful intercession of Serena for his marriage with a very rich heiress of the province of Africa;[y] and the statue of Claudian, erected in the forum of Trajan, was a monument of the taste, and liberality of the Roman senate.[z] After the praises

[x] See Rutilius Numatianus, (Itinerar. l. ii, 41—60), to whom religious enthusiasm has dictated some elegant and forcible lines. Stilicho likewise stripped the gold plates from the doors of the capitol, and read a prophetic sentence, which was engraven under them, (Zosimus, l. v, p. 352). These are foolish stories; yet the charge of *impiety* adds weight and credit to the praise which Zosimus reluctantly bestows, of his virtues.

[y] At the nuptials of Orpheus, (a modest comparison!), all the parts of animated nature contributed their various gifts; and the gods themselves enriched their favourite. Claudian had neither flocks, nor herds, nor vines, or olives. His wealthy bride was heiress to them all. But he carried to Africa, a recommendatory letter from Serena, his Juno, and was made happy, (Epist. ii, ad Serenam).

[z] Claudian feels the honour like a man who deserved it, (in præfat. Bell. Get). The original inscription, on marble, was found at Rome.

of Stilicho became offensive and criminal, Claudian was exposed to the enmity of a powerful and unforgiving courtier, whom he had provoked by the insolence of wit. He had compared, in a lively epigram, the opposite characters of two pretorian prefects of Italy; he contrasts the innocent repose of a philosopher, who sometimes resigned the hours of business to slumber, perhaps to study; with the interested diligence of a rapacious minister, indefatigable in the pursuit of unjust, or sacrilegious gain. " How happy," continues Claudian, " how " happy might it be for the people of Italy, if " Mallius could be constantly awake, and if " Hadrian would always sleep!"* The repose of Mallius was not disturbed by this friendly and gentle admonition; but the cruel vigilance of Hadrian watched the opportunity of revenge, and easily obtained, from the enemies of Stilicho, the trifling sacrifice of an obnoxious poet. The poet concealed himself, however, during the tumult of the revolution; and, consulting the dictates of prudence rather than of honour, he addressed, in the form of an epistle, a sup-

in the fifteenth century, in the house of Pomponius Lætus. The statue of a poet far superior to Claudian, should have been erected, during his lifetime, by the men of letters, his countrymen, and contemporaries. It was a noble design!

* See Epigram xxx.

> Mallius indulget somno noctesque diesque
> Insomnis *Pharius* sacra, pryfana, rapit.
> Omnibus, hoc, Italæ gentes, exposcite votis
> Mallius ut vigilet, dormiat ut Pharius.

Hadrian was a Pharian (of Alexandria). See his public life in Godefroy, Cod Theodos. tom. vi, p. 364. Mallius did not always sleep. He composed some elegant dialogues on the Greek systems of natural philosophy, (Claud. in Mall. Theodor. Cons. 61.112).

pliant and humble recantation to the offended
prefect. He deplores, in mournful strains, the
fatal indiscretion into which he had been hur-
ried by passion and folly; submits to the imitation of his adversary, the generous examples
of the clemency of gods, of heroes, and of lions;
and expresses his hope, that the magnanimity of
Hadrian will not trample on a defenceless and
contemptible foe, already humbled by disgrace
and poverty; and deeply wounded by the exile,
the tortures, and the death of his dearest
friends.[b] Whatever might be the success of his
prayer, or the accidents of his future life, the
period of a few years levelled in the grave the
minister and the poet : but the name of Hadrian is almost sunk in oblivion, while Claudian
is read with pleasure in every country which
has retained, or acquired, the knowledge of the
Latin language. If we fairly balance his merits
and his defects, we shall acknowledge, that
Claudian does not either satisfy, or silence, our
reason. It would not be easy to produce a passage that deserves the epithet of sublime or pathetic; to select a verse, that melts the heart, or
enlarges the imagination. We should vainly
seek, in the poems of Claudian, the happy invention, and artificial conduct, of an interesting
fable ; or the just and lively representation of
the characters and situations of real life. For
the service of his patron, he published occasional panegyrics and invectives : and the design
of these slavish compositions encouraged his
propensity to exceed the limits of truth and na-

[b] See Claudian's first Epistle. Yet, in some places, an air of irony
and indignation betrays his secret reluctance.

ture. These imperfections, however, are compensated in some degree by the poetical virtues of Claudian. He was endowed with the
rare and precious talent of raising the meanest,
of adorning the most barren, and of diversi-
fying the most similar, topics: his colouring,
more especially in descriptive poetry, is soft and
splendid; and he seldom fails to display, and
even to abuse, the advantages of a cultivated
understanding, a copious fancy, an easy, and
sometimes forcible, expression; and a perpetual flow of harmonious versification. To these
commendations, independent of any accidents of
time and place, we must add the peculiar merit
which Claudian derived from the unfavourable
circumstances of his birth. In the decline of arts,
and of empire, a native of Egypt,[c] who had received the education of a Greek, assumed, in a
mature age, the familiar use, and absolute command, of the Latin language;[d] soared above the
heads of his feeble contemporaries; and placed
himself, after an interval of three hundred years,
among the poets of ancient Rome.[e]

[c] National vanity has made him a Florentine, or a Spaniard. But
the first epistle of Claudian proves him a native of Alexandria, (Fabricius, Bibliot. Latin. tom. iii, p. 191-202, edit. Ernest).

[d] His first Latin verses were composed during the consulship of
Probinus, A. D. 895.

Romanos bibimus primum, te consule, fontes.
Et Latiæ cessit Graia Thalia togæ.

Besides some Greek epigrams, which are still extant, the Latin poet had
composed, in Greek, the Antiquities of Tarsus, Anazarbus, Berytus,
Nice, &c. It is more easy to supply the loss of good poetry than of
authentic history.

[e] Strada (Prolusion v, vi) allows him to contend with the five heroic
poets, Lucretius, Virgil, Ovid, Lucan, and Statius. His patron is the
accomplished courtier Balthazar Castiglione. His admirers are numerous and passionate. Yet the rigid critics reproach the exotic weeds,
or flowers, which spring too luxuriantly in his Latian soil.

CHAP. XXXI.

Invasion of Italy by Alaric—Manners of the Roman senate and people—Rome is thrice besieged, and at length pillaged by the Goths—Death of Alaric—The Goths evacuate Italy—Fall of Constantine—Gaul and Spain are occupied by the barbarians—Independence of Britain.

THE incapacity of a weak and distracted government may often assume the appearance, and produce the effects, of a treasonable correspondence with the public enemy. If Alaric himself had been introduced into the council of Ravenna, he would probably have advised the same measures which were actually pursued by the ministers of Honorius.[a] The king of the Goths would have conspired, perhaps with some reluctance, to destroy the formidable adversary, by whose arms, in Italy as well as in Greece, he had been twice overthrown. *Their* active and interested hatred laboriously accomplished the disgrace and ruin of the great Stilicho. The valour of Sarus, his fame in arms, and his personal, or hereditary, influence over the confederate barbarians, could recommend him only to the friends of their country, who despised, or detested, the worthless characters of Turpilio, Varanes, and Vigilantius. By the pressing

CHAP.
XXXI.

Weakness
of the
court of
Ravenna,
A. D. 408,
Sept.

[a] The series of events, from the death of Stilicho, to the arrival of Alaric before Rome, can only be found in Zosimus, l. v, p. 347-350.

instances of the new favourites, these generals, unworthy as they had shewn themselves of the name of soldiers,[b] were promoted to the command of the cavalry, of the infantry, and of the domestic troops. The Gothic prince would have subscribed with pleasure the edict which the fanaticism of Olympius dictated to the simple and devout emperor. Honorius excluded all persons, who were adverse to the catholic church, from holding any office in the state; obstinately rejected the service of all those who dissented from his religion; and rashly disqualified many of his bravest and most skilful officers, who adhered to the pagan worship, or who had imbibed the opinions of Arianism.[c] These measures, so advantageous to an enemy, Alaric would have approved, and might perhaps have suggested; but it may seem doubtful whether the barbarian would have promoted his interest at the expence of the inhuman and absurd cruelty, which was perpetrated by the direction, or at least with the connivance, of the imperial ministers. The foreign auxiliaries, who had been attached to the person of Stilicho, lamented his death; but the desire of revenge was checked by a natural apprehension for the safety of their wives and children; who were detained as hostages in the strong cities of Italy,

---

[b] The expression of Zosimus is strong and lively, καταφρονησιν εμποιησαι τοις πολεμιοις αρκουσας, sufficient to excite the contempt of the enemy.

[c] Eos qui catholicæ sectæ sunt inimici, intra palatium militare prohibemus. Nullus nobis sit aliquâ ratione conjunctus, qui a nobis fide et religione discordat. Cod. Theodos. l. xvi, tit. v, leg. 42, and Godefroy's Commentary, tom. vi, p. 164. This law was applied in the utmost latitude, and rigorously executed. Zosimus, l. v, p. 364.

where they had likewise deposited their most
valuable effects. At the same hour, and as if by
a common signal, the cities of Italy were polluted by the same horrid scenes of universal
massacre and pillage, which involved, in promiscuous destruction, the families and fortunes
of the barbarians. Exasperated by such an
injury, which might have awakened the tamest
and most servile spirit, they cast a look of indignation and hope towards the camp of Alaric, and unanimously swore to pursue, with just
and implacable war, the perfidious nation, that
had so basely violated the laws of hospitality.
By the imprudent conduct of the ministers of
Honorius, the republic lost the assistance, and
deserved the enmity, of thirty thousand of her
bravest soldiers; and the weight of that formidable army, which alone might have determined the event of the war, was transferred
from the scale of the Romans into that of the
Goths.

In the arts of negotiation, as well as in those
of war, the Gothic king maintained his superior
ascendant over an enemy, whose seeming changes
proceeded from the total want of counsel and
design. From his camp, on the confines of Italy,
Alaric attentively observed the revolutions of the
palace, watched the progress of faction and discontent, disguised the hostile aspect of a barbarian invader, and assumed the more popular appearance of the friend and ally of the great Stilicho; to whose virtues, when they were no longer formidable, he could pay a just tribute of

sincere praise and regret. The pressing invitation of the malcontents, who urged the king of the Goths to invade Italy, was enforced by a lively sense of his personal injuries; and he might speciously complain, that the imperial ministers still delayed and eluded the payment of the four thousand pounds of gold; which had been granted by the Roman senate, either to reward his services, or to appease his fury. His decent firmness was supported by an artful moderation, which contributed to the success of his designs. He required a fair and reasonable satisfaction; but he gave the strongest assurances, that as soon as he had obtained it, he would immediately retire. He refused to trust the faith of the Romans, unless Ætius and Jason, the sons of two great officers of state, were sent as hostages to his camp: but he offered to deliver, in exchange, several of the noblest youths of the Gothic nation. The modesty of Alaric was interpreted, by the ministers of Ravenna, as a sure evidence of his weakness and fear. They disdained either to negotiate a treaty, or to assemble an army; and, with a rash confidence, derived only from their ignorance of the extreme danger, irretrievably wasted the decisive moments of peace and war. While they expected, in sullen silence, that the barbarians should evacuate the confines of Italy, Alaric, with bold and rapid marches, passed the Alps and the Po; hastily pillaged the cities of Aquileia, Altinum, Concordia, and Cremona, which yielded to his arms; increased his

forces by the accession of thirty thousand auxiliaries; and, without meeting a single enemy in
the field, advanced as far as the edge of the
morass which protected the impregnable residence of the emperor of the West. Instead of
attempting the hopeless siege of Ravenna, the
prudent leader of the Goths proceeded to Rimini, stretched his ravages along the sea-coast
of the Hadriatic, and meditated the conquest of
the ancient mistress of the world. An Italian
hermit, whose zeal and sanctity were respected
by the barbarians themselves, encountered the
victorious monarch, and boldly denounced the
indignation of heaven against the oppressors of
the earth : but the saint himself was confounded by the solemn asseveration of Alaric, that
he felt a secret and preternatural impulse, which
directed, and even compelled, his march to the
gates of Rome. He felt, that his genius and
his fortune were equal to the most arduous enterprises; and the enthusiasm which he communicated to the Goths, insensibly removed the
popular, and almost superstitious, reverence of
the nations for the majesty of the Roman name.
His troops, animated by the hopes of spoil, followed the course of the Flaminian way, occupied the unguarded passes of the Apennine,[d]
descended into the rich plains of Umbria ; and,
as they lay encamped on the banks of the Cli-

[d] Addison (see his Works, vol. ii, p. 54, edit. Baskerville) has given
a very picturesque description of the road through the Apennine. The
Goths were not at leisure to observe the beauties of the prospect ; but
they were pleased to find that the Saxa Intercisa, a narrow passage
which Vespasian had cut through the rock, (Cluver. Italia Antiq. tom.
i, p. 618), was totally neglected.

CHAP.
XXXI.
‥‥‥‥

tumnus, might wantonly slaughter and devour
the milk-white oxen, which had been so long
reserved for the use of Roman triumphs.* A
lofty situation, and a seasonable tempest of
thunder and lightning, preserved the little city
of Narni; but the king of the Goths, despising
the ignoble prey, still advanced with unabated
vigour; and after he had passed through the
stately arches, adorned with the spoils of bar-
baric victories, he pitched his camp under the
walls of Rome.[f]

Hannibal
at the
gates of
Rome.

During a period of six hundred and nineteen
years, the seat of empire had never been violated
by the presence of a foreign enemy. The unsuccessful expedition of Hannibal,[g] served only to
display the character of the senate and people;
of a senate degraded, rather than ennobled, by
the comparison of an assembly of kings; and of
a people, to whom the ambassador of Pyrrhus
ascribed the inexhaustible resources of the Hydra.[h] Each of the senators, in the time of the
Punic war, had accomplished his term of mili-

* Hinc albi Clitumni greges, ex maxima Taurus
Victima; sæpe tuo perfusi flumine sacro
Romanos ad templa Deum duxere Triumphos.
Besides Virgil, most of the Latin poets, Propertius, Lucan, Silius,
Italicus, Claudian, &c. whose passages may be found in Cluverius and
Addison, have celebrated the triumphal victims of the Clitumnus.

[f] Some ideas of the march of Alaric are borrowed from the journey
of Honorius over the same ground, (see Claudian in vi Cons. Hon. 494.
522.) The measured distance between Ravenna and Rome was 254
Roman miles. Itenerar. Wesseling. p. 126.

[g] The march and retreat of Hannibal are described by Livy, l. xxvi,
c. 7, 8, 9, 10, 11; and the reader is made a spectator of the interesting
scene.

[h] These comparisons were used by Cyneas, the counsellor of Pyrrhus, after his return from his embassy, in which he had diligently
studied the discipline and manners of Rome._ See Plutarch in Pyrrho,
tom. ii, p. 459.

tary service, either in a subordinate or a superior station; and the decree, which invested with temporary command all those who had been consuls, or censors, or dictators, gave the republic the immediate assistance of many brave and experienced generals. In the beginning of the war, the Roman people consisted of two hundred and fifty thousand citizens of an age to bear arms.[1] Fifty thousand had already died in the defence of their country; and the twenty-three legions which were employed in the different camps of Italy, Greece, Sardinia, Sicily, and Spain, required about one hundred thousand men. But there still remained an equal number in Rome, and the adjacent territory, who were animated by the same intrepid courage; and every citizen was trained, from his earliest youth, in the discipline and exercises of a soldier. Hannibal was astonished by the constancy of the senate, who, without raising the siege of Capua, or recalling their scattered forces, expected his approach. He encamped on the banks of the Anio, at the distance of

[1] In the three census which were made of the Roman people, about the time of the second Punic war, the numbers stand as follows, (see Livy, Epitom. l. xx; Hist. l. xxvii, 36; xxix, 37), 270,213, 137,108, 214,000. The fall of the second, and the rise of the third, appears so enormous, that several critics, notwithstanding the unanimity of the mss. have suspected some corruption of the text of Livy. (See Drakenborch ad xxvii, 36, and Beaufort, Republique Romaine, tom. i, p. 325). They did not consider that the second census was taken only at Rome and that the numbers were diminished, not only by the death, but likewise by the absence, of many soldiers. In the third census, Livy expressly affirms, that the legions were mustered by the care of particular commissaries. From the numbers on the list, we must always deduct one-twelfth above threescore, and incapable of bearing arms. See Population de la France, p. 72.

three miles from the city : and he was soon informed, that the ground on which he had pitched his tent, was sold for an adequate price at a public auction ; and that a body of troops was dismissed by an opposite road, to reinforce the legions of Spain.[k] He led his Africans to the gates of Rome, where he found three armies in order of battle, prepared to receive him ; but Hannibal dreaded the event of a combat, from which he could not hope to escape, unless he destroyed the last of his enemies ; and his speedy retreat confessed the invincible courage of the Romans.

Genealogy of the senators.

From the time of the Punic war, the uninterrupted succession of senators had preserved the name and image of the republic; and the degenerate subjects of Honorius ambitiously derived their descent from the heroes who had repulsed the arms of Hannibal, and subdued the nations of the earth. The temporal honours, which the devout Paula[l] inherited and despised, are carefully recapitulated by Jerom, the guide of her conscience, and the historian of her life. The genealogy of her father, Rogatus, which ascended as high as Agamemnon, might seem to betray a Grecian origin ; but her mother, Blæ-

---

[k] Livy considers these two incidents as the effects only of chance and courage. I suspect that they were both managed by the admirable policy of the senate.

[l] See Jerom. tom. i, p. 169, 170, ad Eustochium ; he bestows on Paula the splendid titles of Gracchorum stirps, soboles Scipionum, Pauli hæres, cujus vocabulum trahit, Martiæ Papyriæ Matris Africani vera et germana propago. This particular description supposes a more solid title than the surname of Julius, which Texotius shared with a thousand families of the western provinces. See the Index of Tacitus, of Gruter's Inscriptions, &c.

silla, numbered the Scipios, Æmilius Paulus, and the Gracchi, in the list of her ancestors; and Toxotius, the husband of Paula, deduced his royal lineage from Æneas, the father of the Julian line. The vanity of the rich, who desired to be noble, was gratified by these lofty pretensions. Encouraged by the applause of their parasites, they easily imposed on the credulity of the vulgar; and were countenanced, in some measure, by the custom of adopting the name of their patron, which had always prevailed among the freedmen and clients of illustrious families. Most of those families, however, attacked by so many causes of external violence or internal decay, were gradually extirpated: and it would be more reasonable to seek for a lineal descent of twenty generations, among the mountains of the Alps, or in the peaceful solitude of Apulia, than on the theatre of Rome, the seat of fortune, of danger, and of perpetual revolutions. Under each successive reign, and from every province of the empire, a crowd of hardy adventurers, rising to eminence by their talents or their vices, usurped the wealth, the honours, and the palaces of Rome; and oppressed, or protected, the poor and humble remains of consular families; who were ignorant, perhaps, of the glory of their ancestors.[m]

In the time of Jerom and Claudian, the senators unanimously yielded the pre-eminence to The Anician family.

[m] Tacitus (Annal. iii, 55) affirms, that between the battle of Actium and the reign of Vespasian, the senate was gradually filled with new families from the Municipia and colonies of Italy.

CHAP.
XXXL.

the Anician line; and a slight view of *their* history will serve to appretiate the rank and antiquity of the noble families, which contended only for the second place.[a] During the five first ages of the city, the name of the Anicians was unknown; they appear to have derived their origin from Præneste; and the ambition of those new citizens was long satisfied with the plebeian honours of tribunes of the people.[a] One hundred and sixty-eight years before the Christian era, the family was ennobled by the pretorship of Anicius, who gloriously terminated the Illyrian war by the conquest of the nation, and the captivity of their king.[p] From the triumph of that general, three consulships, in distant periods, mark the succession of the Anician name.[q] From the reign of Diocletian

Nec quisquam Procerum tentet (licet ære vetusto
Floreat, et claro cingatur Roma senatû)
Se jactare parem; sed primâ sede relictâ
Aucheniis, de jure licet certâre secundo.

　　　　　　　　Claud. in Prob. et Olybrii Coss. 18.

Such a compliment paid to the obscure name of the Auchenii has amazed the critics; but they all agree, that whatever may be the true reading, the sense of Claudian can be applied only to the Anician family.

[a] The earliest date in the annals of Pighius, is that of M. Anicius Gallus. Trib. Pl. A. U. C. 506. Another tribute, Q. Anicius, A. U. C. 508, is distinguished by the epithet of Prænestinus. Livy (xiv, 43) places the Anicii below the great families of Rome.

[p] Livy, xliv, 30, 31; xlv, 3, 26, 43. He fairly appretiates the merit of Anicius, and justly observes, that his fame was clouded by the superior lustre of the Macedonian, which preceded the Illyrian, triumph.

[q] The dates of the three consulships are, A. U. C. 593, 818, 967: the two last under the reigns of Nero and Caracalla. The second of these consuls distinguished himself only by his infamous flattery, (Tacit. Annal. xv, 74): but even the evidence of crimes, if they bear the stamp of greatness and antiquity, is admitted without reluctance, to prove the genealogy of a noble house.

to the final extinction of the western empire, that name shone with a lustre which was not eclipsed in the public estimation, by the majesty of the imperial purple.[r] The several branches, to whom it was communicated, united, by marriage or inheritance, the wealth and titles of the Annian, the Petronian, and the Olybrian houses; and in each generation the number of consulships was multiplied by an hereditary claim.[s] The Anician family excelled in faith and in riches: they were the first of the Roman senate who embraced Christianity; and it is probable that Anicius Julian, who was afterwards consul and prefect of the city, atoned for his attachment to the party of Maxentius, by the readiness with which he accepted the religion of Constantine.[t] Their ample patrimony was increased by the industry of Probus, the chief of the Anician family, who shared with Gratian the honours of the consulship, and exercised, four times, the high office of pretorian prefect.[u] His immense

---

[r] In the sixth century, the nobility of the Anician name is mentioned, (Cassiodor. Variar. l. x, Ep. 10, 12), with a singular respect, by the ministers of a Gothic king of Italy.

[s] ————Fixus in omnes
Cognatos procedit honos; quencumque requiras
Hâc de stirpe virum, certum est de Consule nasci.
Per fasces numerantur Avi, semperque renatâ
Nobilitate virent, et prolem fata sequuntur.
Claudian in Prob. et Olyb. Consulat. 12, &c). The Annii, whose name seems to have merged in the Anician, mark the Fasti with many consulships, from the time of Vespasian to the fourth century.

[t] The title of first Christian senator may be justified by the authority of Prudentius, (in Symmach. i, 553), and the dislike of the pagans to the Anician family. See Tillemont, Hist. des Empereurs, tom. iv, p. 183; v, p. 44. Baron. Annal. A. D. 312, No. 78; A. D. 322, No. 2.

[u] Probus . . . . claritudine generis et potentiâ et opûm magnitudine

CHAP.
XXXI.

estates were scattered over the wide extent of the
Roman world; and though the public might suspect, or disapprove, the methods, by which they
had been acquired; the generosity and magnificence of that fortunate statesman deserved
he gratitude of his clients, and the admiration
of strangers.[x] Such was the respect entertained
for his memory, that the two sons of Probus, in
their earliest youth, and at the request of the
senate, were associated in the consular dignity :
a memorable distinction, without example in the
annals of Rome.[y]

Wealth of
the Ro-
man no-
bles.

" The marbles of the Anician palace," were
used as a proverbial expression of opulence and
splendour;[z] but the nobles and senators of Rome
aspired, in due gradation, to imitate that illustrious family. The accurate description of the
city, which was composed in the Theodosian
age, enumerates one thousand seven hundred
and eighty *houses*, the residence of wealthy and
honourable citizens.[a] Many of these stately
mansions might almost excuse the exaggeration

dine, cognitus Orbi Romano, per quem universum pœne patrimonia
sparsa possedit, juste an secus non judicioli est nostri. Ammian.
Marcellin. xxvii, 11. His children and widow erected for him a magnificent tomb in the Vatican, which was demolished in the time of Pope
Nicholas V, to make room for the new church of St. Peter. Baronius,
who laments the ruin of this Christian monument, has diligently preserved the inscriptions and basso-relievos. See Annal. Eccles. A. D.
395, No. 5-17.

[x] Two Persian satraps travelled to Milan and Rome, to hear St.
Ambrose, and to see Probus. (Paulin. in Vit. Ambros). Claudian
(in Cons. Probin. et Olybr, 30-60) seems at a loss how to express the
glory of Probus.

[y] See the poem which Claudian addressed to the two noble youths.

[z] Secundinus, the Manichæan, ap. Baron. Annal. Eccles. A. D. 390,
No. 34.

[a] See Nardini, Roma Antica, p. 89, 498, 500.

of the poet; that Rome contained a multitude of palaces, and that each palace was equal to a city: since it included within its own precincts, every thing which could be subservient either to use or luxury; markets, hippodromes, temples, fountains, baths, porticos, shady groves, and artificial aviaries.[b] The historian Olympiodorus, who represents the state of Rome when it was besieged by the Goths,[c] continues to observe, that several of the richest senators received from their estates an annual income of four thousand pounds of gold, above one hundred and sixty thousand pounds sterling; without computing the stated provision of corn and wine, which, had they been sold, might have equalled in value one third of the money. Compared to this immoderate wealth, an ordinary revenue of a thousand or fifteen hundred pounds of gold might be considered as no more than adequate to the dignity of the senatorial rank, which required many expences of a public and ostentatious kind. Several examples are recorded in the age of Honorius, of vain and popular nobles, who celebrated the year of their pretorship by a festival, which lasted seven days, and cost above one hundred thousand pounds sterling.[d]

---

[b]   Quid loquar inclusas inter laquearia sylvas,
    Vernula quæ vario carmine ludit avis.
               Claud. Rutil. Numatian Itinerar. ver. 111.
The poet lived at the time of the Gothic invasion. A moderate palace would have covered Cincinnatus's farm of four acres, (Val. Max. iv, 4). In laxitatem ruris excurrunt, says Seneca, Epist. 114. See a judicious note of Mr. Hume, Essays, vol. i, p. 562, last 8vo. edition.

[c] This curious account of Rome, in the reign of Honorius, is found in a fragment of the historian Olympiodorus, ap Photium, p. 197.

[d] The sons of Alypius, of Symmachus, and of Maximus, spent, dur-

The estates of the Roman senators, which so
far exceeded the proportion of modern wealth,
were not confined to the limits of Italy. Their
possessions extended far beyond the Ionian and
Ægean seas, to the most distant provinces ; the
city of Nicopolis, which Augustus had founded
as an eternal monument of the Actian victory,
was the property of the devout Paula;[*] and it is
observed by Seneca, that the rivers which had
divided hostile nations, now flowed through the
lands of private citizens.[f] According to their
temper and circumstances, the estates of the
Romans were either cultivated by the labour of
their slaves, or granted, for a certain and stipulated rent, to the industrious farmer. The

ing their respective pretorships, twelve, or twenty, or forty, *centenaries,*
(or hundred weight of gold). See Olympiodor. ap. Phot. p. 197.
This popular estimation allows some latitude ; but it is difficult to
explain a law in the Theodosian Code, (l. vi, leg. 5), which fixes the
expence of the first pretor at 25,000, of the second at 20,000, and of
the third at 15,000 *folles.* The name of *follis* (see Mem. de l'Academie
des Inscriptions, tom. xxviii, p. 727) was equally applied to a purse
of 125 pieces of silver, and to a small copper coin of the value of $\frac{1}{2625}$
part of that purse. In the former sense, the 25,000 folles would be
equal to 15,000l. in the latter to five or six pounds sterling. The one
appears extravagant, the other is ridiculous. There must have existed
some third, and middle value, which is here understood ; but ambiguity
is an inexcusable fault in the language of laws.

[*] Nicopolis . . . . in Actiaco littore sita possessionis vestræ nunc
pars vel maxima est. Jerom. in præfat. Comment. ad Epistol. ad
Titum, tom. ix. p. 243. M. de Tillemont supposes, strangely enough.
that it was part of Agamemnon's inheritance. Mem. Eccles. tom. xii,
p. 85.

[f] Seneca, Epist. lxxxix. His language is of the declamatory kind,
but declamation could scarcely exaggerate the avarice and luxury of
the Romans. The philosopher himself deserved some share of the reproach ; if it be true that his rigorous exaction of *Quadringenties,* above
three hundred thousand pounds, which he had lent at high interest
provoked a rebellion in Britain. Dion. Cassius, l. lxii, p. 1003). According to the conjecture of Gale, (Antoninus's Itinerary in Britain, p.
92), the same Faustinus possessed an estate near Bury, in Suffolk, and
another in the kingdom of Naples.

economical writers of antiquity strenuously recommend the former method, wherever it may
be practicable; but if the object should be removed by its distance or magnitude, from the
immediate eye of the master, they prefer the
active care of an old hereditary tenant, attached
to the soil, and interested in the produce, to the
mercenary administration of a negligent, perhaps
an unfaithful, steward.[s]

Their manners.

The opulent nobles of an immense capital,
who were never excited by the pursuit of military
glory, and seldom engaged in the occupations of
civil government, naturally resigned their leisure
to the business and amusements of private life.
At Rome, commerce was always held in contempt: but the senators, from the first age of
the republic, increased their patrimony, and
multiplied their clients, by the lucrative practice of usury; and the obsolete laws were eluded, or violated, by the mutual inclinations and
interest of both parties.[h] A considerable mass
of treasure must always have existed at Rome,
either in the current coin of the empire, or in
the form of gold and silver plate; and there
were many sideboards in the time of Pliny,
which contained more solid silver, than had

---

[s] Volusius, a wealthy senator, (Tacit. Annal. iii, 30), always preferred tenants born on the estate. Columella, who received this maxim
from him, argues very judiciously on the subject. De Re Rusticâ, l.
i, c. 7, p. 408, edit. Gesner, Leipsig, 1735.

[h] Valesius (ad Ammian. xiv, 6) has proved, from Chrysostom, and
Augustin, that the senators were not allowed to lend money at usury.
Yet it appears from the Theodosian Code, (see Godefroy ad l. ii, tit.
xxxiii, tom. i, p. 230-289), that they were permitted to take six per
cent. or one-half of the legal interest; and, what is more singular, this
permission was granted to the *young* senators.

been transported by Scipio from vanquished
Carthage.[l] The greater part of the nobles, who
dissipated their fortunes in profuse luxury,
found themselves poor in the midst of wealth;
and idle in a constant round of dissipation.
Their desires were continually gratified by the
labour of a thousand hands; of the numerous
train of their domestic slaves, who were actuated by the fear of punishment; and of the various professions of artificers and merchants,
who were more powerfully impelled by the
hopes of gain. The ancients were destitute of
many of the conveniences of life, which have
been invented or improved by the progress of
industry; and the plenty of glass and linen has
diffused more real comforts among the modern
nations of Europe, than the senators of Rome
could derive from all the refinements of pompous
or sensual luxury.[k] Their luxury, and their manners, have been the subject of minute and laborious disquisition: but as such inquiries would
divert me too long from the design of the present work, I shall produce an authentic state of
Rome and its inhabitants, which is more peculiarly applicable to the period of the Gothic invasion. Ammianus Marcellinus, who prudent-

[l] Plin. Hist. Natur. xxxiii, 50. He states the silver at only 4380
pounds, which is increased by Livy (xxx, 45) to 100,023: the former
seems too little for an opulent city, the latter two much for any private
sideboard.

[k] The learned Arbuthnot (Tables of Ancient Coins, &c. p. 153)
has observed, with humour, and I believe with truth, that Augustus,
had neither glass to his windows, nor a shirt to his back. Under the
lower empire, the use of linen and glass became somewhat more
common.

ly chose the capital of the empire, as the residence the best adapted to the historian of his
own times, has mixed with the narrative of public events, a lively representation of the scenes
with which he was familiarly conversant. The
judicious reader will not always approve the
asperity of censure, the choice of circumstances, or the style of expression: he will perhaps
detect the latent prejudices, and personal resentments, which soured the temper of Ammianus himself; but he will surely observe, with
philosophic curiosity, the interesting and original picture of the manners of Rome.[1]

CHAP.
XXXI.

"The greatness of Rome (such is the lan-
"guage of the historian) was founded on the
"rare, and almost incredible, alliance of virtue
"and of fortune. The long period of her in-
"fancy was employed in a laborious struggle
"against the tribes of Italy, the neighbours and
"enemies of the rising city. In the strength and
"ardour of youth, she sustained the storms of
"war; carried her victorious arms beyond the
"seas and the mountains; and brought home
"triumphant laurels from every country of the
"globe. At length, verging towards old age,
"and sometimes conquering by the terror only

Character
of the Ro-
man no-
bles, by
Ammianus
Marcelli-
nus.

[1] It is incumbent on me to explain the liberties which I have taken
with the text of Ammianus. 1. I have melted down into one piece the
sixth chapter of the fourteenth, and the fourth of the twenty-eighth
book. 2. I have given order and connection to the confused mass of
materials. 3. I have softened some extravagant hyperboles, and pared
away some superfluities of the original. 4. I have developed some
observations which were insinuated, rather than expressed. With these
allowances, my version will be found, not literal indeed, but faithful
and exact.

" of her name, she sought the blessings of ease
" and tranquillity. The VENERABLE CITY,
" which had trampled on the necks of the fiercest
" nations; and established a system of laws, the
" perpetual guardians of justice and freedom;
" was content, like a wise and wealthy parent,
" to devolve on the Cæsars, her favourite sons,
" the care of governing her ample patrimony."
" A secure and profound peace, such as had
" been once enjoyed in the reign of Numa, suc-
" ceeded to the tumults of a republic; while
" Rome was still adored as the queen of the
" earth; and the subject nations still reveren-
" ced the name of the people, and the majesty
" of the senate. But this native splendour (con-
" tinues Ammianus) is degraded, and sullied,
" by the conduct of some nobles; who, unmind-
" ful of their own dignity, and of that of their
" country, assume an unbounded licence of
" vice and folly. They contend with each
" other in the empty vanity of titles and sur-
" names; and curiously select, or invent, the
" most lofty and sonorous appellations, Rebur-
" rus, or Fabunius, Pagonius, or Tarrasius,"

---

[m] Claudian, who seems to have read the history of Ammianus,
speaks of this great revolution in a much less courtly style.—

Postquam jura ferox in se communia Cæsar
Transtulit; et lapsi mores; desuetaque priscis
Artibus, in gremium pacis servile recessi.
                                        De Bell. Gildonico, p. 49.

[n] The minute diligence of antiquarians has not been able to verify
these extraordinary names. I am of opinion that they were invented
by the historian himself, who was afraid of any personal satire or application. It is certain, however, that the simple denominations of the
Romans were gradually lengthened to the number of four, five, or even
seven, pompous surnames; as for instance, Marcus Mæcius Mæmmius
                                                          Furius

" which may impress the ears of the vulgar with
" astonishment and respect. From a vain am-
" bition of perpetuating their memory, they
" affect to multiply their likeness, in statues of
" bronze and marble; nor are they satisfied,
" unless those statues are covered with plates of
" gold; an honourable distinction, first granted
" to Acilius the consul, after he had subdued, by
" his arms and counsels, the power of king
" Antiochus. The ostentation of displaying, of
" magnifying, perhaps, the rent-roll of the estates
" which they possess in all the provinces, from
" the rising to the setting sun, provokes the just
" resentment of every man, who recollects, that
" their poor and invincible ancestors were not
" distinguished from the meanest of the soldiers,
" by the delicacy of their food, or the splendour
" of their apparel. But the modern nobles mea-
" sure their rank and consequence according to
" the loftiness of their chariots,° and the weighty
" magnificence of their dress. Their long robes
" of silk and purple float in the wind; and as
" they are agitated, by art or accident, they

Furius Balborius Cæcilianus Placidus. See Norris Cenotaph. Pisan.
Dissert. iv, p. 438.

° The *carrucæ*, or coaches of the Romans, were often of solid silver,
curiously carved and engraved; and the trappings of the mules, or
horses, were embossed with gold. This magnificence continued from
the reign of Nero to that of Honorius; and the Appian way was covered with the splendid equipages of the nobles, who came out to meet
St. Melania, when she returned to Rome, six years before the Gothic
siege, (Seneca, epist. lxxxvii; Plin. Hist. Natur. xxxiii, 49; Paulin.
Nolan. apud Baron. Annal. Eccles. A. D. 397, No. 5). Yet pomp is
well exchanged for convenience; and a plain modern coach that is hung
upon springs, is much preferable to the silver or gold *carts* of antiquity,
which rolled on the axle-tree, and were exposed, for the most part, to
the inclemency of the weather.

" occasionally discover the under garments, the
" rich tunics, embroidered with the figures of
" various animals.ᴾ Followed by a train of
" fifty servants, and tearing up the pavement,
" they move along the streets with the same
" impetuous speed as if they travelled with
" post-horses ; and the example of the senators
" is boldly imitated by the matrons and ladies,
" whose covered carriages are continually dri-
" ving round the immense space of the city and
" suburbs. Whenever these persons of high
" distinction condescend to visit the public
" baths, they assume, on their entrance, a tone
" of loud and insolent command, and appro-
" priate to their own use the conveniences which
" were designed for the Roman people. If, in
" these places of mixed and general resort, they
" meet any of the infamous ministers of their
" pleasures, they express their affection by a
" tender embrace ; while they proudly decline
" the salutations of their fellow-citizens, who
" are not permitted to aspire above the honour
" of kissing their hands, or their knees. As
" soon as they have indulged themselves in the
" refreshment of the bath, they resume their
" rings, and the other ensigns of their dignity ;
" select from their private wardrobe of the
" finest linen, such as might suffice for a dozen
" persons, the garments the most agreeable
" to their fancy, and maintain till their de-

ᴾ In a homily of Asterius, bishop of Amasia, M. de Valois has discovered, (ad Ammian. xiv, 6), that this was a new fashion ; that bears,
wolves, lions, and tigers, woods, hunting matches, &c. were represented in embroidery ; and that the more pious coxcombs, substituted the
figure or legend of some favourite saint.

" parture the same haughty demeanour; which
" perhaps might have been excused in the
" great Marcellus, after the conquest of Sy-
" racuse. Sometimes, indeed, these heroes
" undertake more arduous achievements; they
" visit their estates in Italy, and procure
" themselves, by the toil of servile hands,
" the amusements of the chase.�q If at any
" time, but more especially on a hot day, they
" have courage to sail, in their painted galleys,
" from the Lucrine lake,ʳ to their elegant villas
" on the sea-coast of Puteoli and Cayeta,ˢ they
" compare their own expeditions to the marches
" of Cæsar and Alexander. Yet should a fly
" presume to settle on the silken folds of their
" gilded umbrellas; should a sun-beam pene-
" trate through some unguarded and imper-
" ceptible chink, they deplore their intolerable
" hardships, and lament, in affected language,
" that they were not born in the land of the

�q See Pliny's Epistles, i, 6. Three large wild boars were allured,
and taken in the toils, without interrupting the studies of the philosophic sportsman.

ʳ The change from the inauspicious word *Avernus*, which stands
in the text, is immaterial. The two lakes, Avernus and Lucrinus,
communicated with each other, and were fashioned by the stupendous
moles of Agrippa into the Julian port, which opened, through a narrow entrance, into the gulf of Puteoli. Virgil, who resided on the
spot, has described (Géorgic ii, 161) this work at the moment of its
execution; and his commentators, especially Catrou, have derived
much light from Strabo, Suetonius, and Dion. Earthquakes and vol-
canos have changed the face of the country, and turned the Lucrine
lake, since the year 1538, into the Monte Nuovo. See Camillo Pelle-
grino Discorsi della Campania Felice, p. 239, 244, &c. Antonii San-
felicii Campania, p. 13, 88.

ˢ The regna Cumana et Puteolana; loca cæteroqui valde expetenda,
interpellantium autem multitudine pœne fugienda. Cicero ad Attic.
xvi, 17.

"Cimmerians,' the regions of eternal darkness.
" In these journeys into the country," the whole
" body of the household marches with their
" master. In the same manner as the cavalry and
" infantry, the heavy and the light armed troops,
" the advanced guard and the rear, are mar-
" shalled by the skill of their military leaders;
" so the domestic officers, who bear a rod, as an
" ensign of authority, distribute and arrange the
" numerous train of slaves and attendants. The
" baggage and wardrobe move in the front; and
" are immediately followed by a multitude of
" cooks, and inferior ministers, employed in the
" service of the kitchens, and of the table. The
" main body is composed of a promiscuous
" crowd of slaves, increased by the accidental
" concourse of idle or dependant plebeians.
" The rear is closed by the favourite band of
" eunuchs, distributed from age to youth, ac-
" cording to the order of seniority. Their num-
" bers, and their deformity, excite the horror
" of the indignant spectators, who are ready to

' The proverbial expression of *Cimmerian darkness* was originally
borrowed from the description of Homer, (in the eleventh book of the
Odyssey), which he applies to a remote, and fabulous country on the
shores of the ocean. See Erasmi Adagia, in his works, tom. i, p. 593,
the Leyden edition.

" We may learn from Seneca, epist. cxxiii, three curious circumstances relative to the journeys of the Romans. 1. They were preceded by a troop of Numidian light horse, who announced by a cloud of
dust, the approach of a great man. 2. Their baggage-mules transported not only the precious vases, but even the fragile vessels of chrystal
and *murra*, which last is almost proved, by the learned French transla-
tor of Seneca, (tom. iii, p. 402–422), to mean the porcelain of China
and Japan. 3. The beautiful faces of the young slaves were covered
with a medicated crust, or ointment, which secured them against the
effects of the sun and frost.

" execrate the memory of Semiramis, for the
" cruel art which she invented, of frustrating the
" purposes of nature, and of blasting in the bud
" the hopes of future generations. In the exer-
" cise of domestic jurisdiction, the nobles of
" Rome express an exquisite sensibility for any
" personal injury, and a contemptuous in-
" difference for the rest of the human species.
" When they have called for warm water, if a
" slave has been tardy in his obedience, he is
" instantly chastised with three hundred lashes:
" but should the same slave commit a wilful
" murder, the master will mildly observe, that
" he is a worthless fellow ; but that, if he re-
" peats the offence, he shall not escape punish-
" ment. Hospitality was formerly the virtue of
" the Romans ; and every stranger, who could
" plead either merit or misfortune, was relieved
" or rewarded, by their generosity. At present,
" if a foreigner, perhaps of no contemptible
" rank, is introduced to one of the proud and
" wealthy senators, he is welcomed indeed in the
" first audience, with such warm professions, and
" such kind inquiries, that he retires, enchanted
" with the affability of his illustrious friend, and
" full of regret that he had so long delayed his
" journey to Rome, the native seat of manners,
" as well as of empire. Secure of a favourable
" reception, he repeats his visit the ensuing day,
" and is mortified by the discovery, that his
" person, his name, and his country, are already
" forgotten. If he still has resolution to perse-
" vere, he is gradually numbered in the train of

" dependants, and obtains the permission to pay
" his assiduous and unprofitable court to a haugh-
" ty patron, incapable of gratitude or friendship;
" who scarcely deigns to remark his presence,
" his departure, or his return. Whenever the
" rich prepare a solemn and popular entertain-
" ment;[x] whenever they celebrate, with profuse
" and pernicious luxury, their private banquets;
" the choice of the guests is the subject of anxi-
" ous deliberation. The modest, the sober, and
" the learned, are seldom preferred; and the
" nomenclators, who are commonly swayed by
" interested motives, have the address to insert,
" in the list of invitations, the obscure names of
" the most worthless of mankind. But the fre-
" quent and familiar companions of the great,
" are those parasites, who practise the most use-
" ful of all arts, the art of flattery; who eagerly
" applaud each word, and every action, of their
" immortal patron; gaze with rapture on his
" marble columns, and variegated pavements;
" and strenuously praise the pomp and elegance,
" which he is taught to consider as a part of his
" personal merit. At the Roman tables, the

[x] Distributio solemnium sportularum. The *sportulæ,* or *sportellæ,*
were small baskets, supposed to contain a quantity of hot provisions,
of the value of 100 quadrantes, or twelvepence halfpenny, which were
ranged in order in the hall, and ostentatiously distributed to the hungry or servile crowd, who waited at the door. This indelicate custom
is very frequently mentioned in the epigrams of Martial, and the satires
of Juvenal. See likewise Suetonius, in Claud. c. 21; in Neron. c. 16;
in Domitian, c. 4, 7. These baskets of provisions were afterwards converted into large pieces of gold and silver coin, or plate, which were
mutually given and accepted even by the persons of the highest rank,
(See Symmach. epist iv, 55, ix, 124; and Miscell. p. 256), on solemn
occasions, of consulships marriages, &c.

" birds, the *squirrels*,[y] or the fish, which appear
" of an uncommon size, are contemplated with
" curious attention; a pair of scales is accurate-
" ly applied, to ascertain their real weight; and,
" while the more rational guests are disgusted
" by the vain and tedious repetition, notaries are
" summoned to attest, by an authentic record,
" the truth of such a marvellous event. Ano-
" ther method of introduction into the houses
" and society of the great, is derived from the
" profession of gaming, or, as it is more politely
" styled, of play. The confederates are united
" by a strict and indissoluble bond of friendship,
" or rather of conspiracy: a superior degree of
" skill in the *Tesserarian* art, (which may be in-
" terpreted the game of dice and tables),[z] is a

[y] The want of an English name obliges me to refer to the common genus of squirrels, the Latin *glis*, the French *loir*; a little animal, who inhabits the woods, and remains torpid in cold weather, (see Plin. Hist. Natur. vii, 82. Buffon, Hist. Naturelle, tom. viii, p. 158. Pennant's Synopsis of Quadrupeds, p. 289). The art of rearing and fattening great numbers of *glires* was practised in Roman villas, as a profitable article of rural economy, (Varro de Re Rusticâ, iii, 15). The excessive demand of them for luxurious tables, was increased by the foolish prohibitions of the Censors, and it is reported, that they are still esteemed in modern Rome, and are frequently sent as presents by the Collonna princes, (see Brotier, the last editor of Pliny, tom. ii, p. 458, apud Barbou, 1779).

[z] This game, which might be translated by the more familiar names of *trictrac*, or *backgammon*, was a favourite amusement of the gravest Romans; and old Mucius Scævola, the lawyer, had the reputation of a very skilful player. It was called *ludus duodecim scriptorum*, from the twelve *scripta*, or lines, which equally divided the *alveolus*, or table. On these, the two armies, the white and the black, each consisting of fifteen men, or *calculi*, were regularly placed, and alternately moved, according to the laws of the game; and the chances of the *tesseræ*, or dice. Dr. Hyde, who diligently traces the history and varieties of the *nerdiludium* (a name of Persic etymology) from Ireland to

" sure road to wealth and reputation. A master
" of that sublime science, who, in a supper or
" assembly, is placed below a magistrate, dis-
" plays in his countenance the surprise and in-
" dignation, which Cato might be supposed to
" feel, when he was refused the pretorship by
" the votes of a capricious people. The acqui-
" sition of knowledge seldom engages the curi-
" osity of the nobles, who abhor the fatigue,
" and disdain the advantages, of study; and
" the only books which they peruse are the sa-
" tires of Juvenal, and the verbose and fabulous
" histories of Marius Maximus.* The libraries
" which they have inherited from their fathers,
" are secluded, like dreary sepulchres, from the
" light of day.ᵇ But the costly instruments of
" the theatre, . flutes, and enormous lyres, and
" hydraulic organs, are constructed for their
" use; and the .harmony of vocal and instru-
" mental music is incessantly repeated in the
" palaces of Rome. In those places, sound is
" preferred to sense, and the care of the body
" to that of the mind. It is allowed as a salu-
" tary maxim, that the light and frivolous sus-

to Japan, pours forth, on the trifling subject, a copious torrent of
classic and oriental learning. See Syntagma Dissertat. tom. ii, p
217-405.

ᵃ Marius Maximus, homo omnium verbosissimus, qui, et mithisto-
ricis so voluminibus implicavit. Vopiscus, in Hist. August. p. 242.
He wrote the lives of the emperors, from Trajan to Alexander Severus.
See Gerard, Vossius de Historicis Latin. l. ii, c. 3, in his works, vol.
iv, p. 57.

ᵇ This satire is probably exaggerated. The Saturnalia of Macrobius, and the epistles of Jerom, afford satisfactory proofs, that Christian
theology, and classic literature, were studiously cultivated by several
Romans, of both sexes, and of the highest rank.

" picion of a contagious malady, is of sufficient
" weight to excuse the visits of the most inti-
" mate friends ; and, even the servants, who are
" despatched to make the decent inquiries, are
" not suffered to return home, till they have
" undergone the ceremony of a previous ablu-
" tion.   Yet this selfish and unmanly delicacy
" occasionally yields to the more imperious
" passion of avarice.   The prospect of gain will
" urge a rich and gouty senator as far as Spoleto ;
" every sentiment of arrogance and dignity is
" subdued by the hopes of an inheritance, or
" even of a legacy ; and a wealthy, childless
" citizen is the most powerful of the Romans.
" The art of obtaining the signature of a favour-
" able testament, and sometimes of hastening
" the moment of its execution, is perfectly un-
" derstood ; and it has happened, that in the
" same house, though in different apartments,
" a husband and a wife, with the laudable de-
" sign of over-reaching each other, have sum-
" moned their respective lawyers, to declare, at
" the same time, their mutual, but contradic-
" tory intentions.   The distress which follows
" and chastises extravagant luxury, often re-
" duces the great to the use of the most humi-
" liating expedients.   When they desire to
" borrow, they employ the base and supplicat-
" ing style of the slave in the comedy ; but
" when they are called upon to pay, they as-
" sume the royal and tragic declamation of the
" grandsons of Hercules.   If the demand is
" repeated, they readily procure some trusty

" sycophant, instructed to maintain a charge of
" poison, or magic, against the insolent credi-
" tor; who is seldom released from prison, till
" he has signed a discharge of the whole debt.
" These vices, which degrade the moral charac-
" ter of the Romans, are mixed with a puerile
" superstition, that disgraces their understand-
" ing.   They listen with confidence to the pre-
" dictions of haruspices, who pretend to read,
" in the entrails of victims, the signs of future
" greatness and prosperity ; and there are many
" who do not presume either to bathe, or to dine,
" or to appear in public, till they have diligent-
" ly consulted, according to the rules of astro-
" logy, the situation of Mercury, and the as
" pect of the moon.[c]   It is singular enough,
" that this vain credulity may often be disco-
" vered among the profane sceptics, who im-
" piously doubt, or deny, the existence of a
" celestial power."

State and
character
of the peo-
ple of
Rome.
In populous cities, which are the seat of commerce and manufactures, the middle ranks of
inhabitants, who derive their subsistence from
the dexterity, or labour, of their hands, are
commonly the most prolific, the most useful,
and, in that sense, the most respectable,
part of the community.   But the plebeians of
Rome, who disdained such sedentary and
servile arts, had been oppressed, from the
earliest times, by the weight of debt and
usury ; and the husbandman, during the term

[c] Macrobius, the friend of these Roman nobles, considered the stars
as the cause, or at least the signs, of future events, (de Somn. Scipion.
l i, c 19, p. 68).

of his military service, was obliged to abandon the cultivation of his farm.[d] The lands of
Italy, which had been originally divided among
the families of free and indigent proprietors,
were insensibly purchased, or usurped, by the
avarice of the nobles; and in the age which
preceded the fall of the republic, it was computed, that only two thousand citizens were
possessed of any independent subsistence.[e]
Yet as long as the people bestowed, by their
suffrages, the honours of the state, the command of the legions, and the administration of
wealthy provinces, their conscious pride alleviated, in some measure, the hardships of poverty;
and their wants were seasonably supplied by
the ambitious liberality of the candidates, who
aspired to secure a venal majority in the thirty-
five tribes, or the hundred and ninety-three
centuries, of Rome. But when the prodigal
commons had imprudently alienated not only
the *use*, but the *inheritance*, of power, they sunk,
under the reign of the Cæsars, into a vile and
wretched populace, which must, in a few generations, have been totally extinguished, if it
had not been continually recruited by the ma-

[d] The histories of Livy (see particularly vi, 36) are full of the
extortions of the rich, and the sufferings of the poor debtors. The
melancholy story of a brave old soldier, (Dionys. Hal. l. vi, c. 26,
p. 347, edit. Hudson, and Livy, ii, 23), must have been frequently
repeated in those primitive times, which have been so undeservedly
praised.

[e] Non esse in-civitate duo millia hominum qui rem haberent. Cicero. offic. ii, 21, and Comment. Paul. Manut. in edit. Græv. This
vague computation was made A. U. C. 649, in a speech of the tribune
Phillippus; and it was his object, as well as that of the Gracchi, (see
Plutarch), to deplore, and perhaps to exaggerate, the misery of the
common people.

mumission of slaves, and the influx of strangers. As early as the time of Hadrian, it was the just complaint of the ingenuous natives, that the capital had attracted the vices of the universe, and the manners of the most opposite nations. The intemperance of the Gauls, the cunning and levity of the Greeks, the savage obstinacy of the Egyptians and Jews, the servile temper of the Asiatics, and the dissolute, effeminate prostitution of the Syrians, were mingled in the various multitude; which, under the proud and false denomination of Romans, presumed to despise their fellow-subjects, and even their sovereigns, who dwelt beyond the precincts of the ETERNAL CITY.[f]

Public distribution of bread, bacon, oil, wine, &c.

Yet the name of that city was still pronounced with respect: the frequent and capricious tumults of its inhabitants were indulged with impunity; and the successors of Constantine, instead of crushing the last remains of the democracy, by the strong arm of military power, embraced the mild policy of Augustus, and studied to relieve the poverty, and to amuse the idleness, of an innumerable people.[g]   I. For the

---

[f] See the third Satire (60-125) of Juvenal, who indignantly complains,

————Quamvis quota portio fæcis Achæi !
Jampridem Syrus in Tiberim defluxit Orontes;
Et linguam et mores, &c.

Seneca, when he proposes to comfort his mother (Consolat. ad Helv. c. 6) by the reflection, that a great part of mankind were in a state of exile, reminds her how few of the inhabitants of Rome were born in the city.

[g] Almost all that is said of the bread, bacon, oil, wine, &c. may be found in the fourteenth book of the Theodosian Code; which expressly treats of the *police* of the great cities. See particularly the titles iii, iv, xv, xvi, xvii, xxiv. The collateral testimonies are produced in Godefroy's

convenience of the lazy plebeians, the monthly distributions of corn were converted into a daily allowance of bread; a great number of ovens was constructed and maintained at the public expence; and at the appointed hour, each citizen, who was furnished with a ticket, ascended the flight of steps, which had been assigned to his peculiar quarter or division, and received, either as a gift, or at a very low price, a loaf of bread, of the weight of three pounds, for the use of his family. II. The forests of Lucania, whose acorns fattened large droves of wild hogs,[h] afforded, as a species of tribute, a plentiful supply of cheap and wholesome meat. During five months of the year, a regular allowance of bacon was distributed to the poorer citizens; and the annual consumption of the capital, at a time when it was much declined from its former lustre, was ascertained, by an edict of Valentinian III, at three millions six hundred and twenty-eight thousand pounds.[i] III. In the manners of antiquity, the use of oil was indispensible for the lamp, as well as for

froy's Commentary, and it is needless to transcribe them. According to a law of Theodosius, which appretiates in money the military allowance, a piece of gold (eleven shillings) was equivalent to eighty pounds of bacon, or to eighty pounds of oil, or to twelve modii (or pecks) of salt. (Cod. Theod. l. viii, tit. iv, leg. 17). This equation, compared with another of seventy pounds of bacon for an *amphora*, (Cod. Theod. l. xiv, tit. iv, leg. 4), fixes the price of wine at about sixteen pence the gallon.

[h] The annonymous author of the Description of the World, (p. 14, in tom. iii, Geograph. Minor, Hudson), observes of Lucania, in his barbarous Latin, Regio obtima, et ipsa omnibus habundans, et lardum multum foras emittit. Propter quod est in montibus, cujus æscam animalium variam, &c.

[i] See Novell. ad calcem Cod. Theod. D. Valet. l. i, tit. xv. This law was published at Rome, June 29, A. D. 452.

the bath; and the annual tax, which was imposed on Africa for the benefit of Rome, amounted to the weight of three millions of pounds, to the measure, perhaps, of three hundred thousand English gallons. IV. The anxiety of Augustus to provide the metropolis with sufficient plenty of corn, was not extended beyond that necessary article of human subsistence; and when the popular clamour accused the dearness and scarcity of wine, a proclamation was issued, by the grave reformer, to remind his subjects, that no man could reasonably complain of thirst, since the aqueducts of Agrippa had introduced into the city so many copious streams of pure and salubrious water.[k] This rigid sobriety was insensibly relaxed; and, although the generous design of Aurelian[l] does not appear to have been executed in its full extent, the use of wine was allowed on very easy and liberal terms. The administration of the public cellars was delegated to a magistrate of honourable rank; and a considerable part of the vintage of Campania was reserved for the fortunate inhabitants of Rome.

Use of the
public
baths.
The stupendous aqueducts, so justly celebrated by the praises of Augustus himself, replenished the *Thermæ*, or baths, which had been constructed in every part of the city, with

[k] Sueton. in August. c. 42. The utmost debauch of the emperor himself, in his favourite wine of Rhætia, never exceeded a *sextarius*, (an English pint). Id. c. 77. Torrentius ad Loc. and Arbuthnot's Tables, p. 86.

[l] His design was to plant vineyards along the sea-coast of Hetruria, (Vopiscus, in Hist. August. p. 225); the dreary unwholesome, uncultivated *Maremme* of modern Tuscany.

imperial magnificence. The baths of Antoninus Caracalla, which were open, at stated
hours, for the indiscriminate service of the senators and the people, contained above sixteen
hundred seats of marble; and more than three
thousand were reckoned in the baths of Diocletian.[m] The walls of the lofty apartments
were covered with curious mosaics, that imitated the art of the pencil in the elegance of design, and the variety of colours. The Egyptian
granite was beautifully incrusted with the precious green marble of Numidia; the perpetual
stream of hot water was poured into the capacious basons, through so many wide mouths of
bright and massy silver; and the meanest Roman could purchase, with a small copper coin,
the daily enjoyment of a scene of pomp and luxury, which might excite the envy of the kings of
Asia.[n] From these stately palaces issued a
swarm of dirty and ragged plebeians, without
shoes, and without a mantle; who loitered away
whole days in the street or Forum, to hear news,
and to hold disputes; who dissipated, in extravagant gaming, the miserable pittance of
their wives and children; and spent the hours
of the night in obscure taverns, and brothels,

[m] Olymplodor. apud Phot. p. 197.

[n] Seneca (epistol, lxxxvi) compares the baths of Scipio Africanus, at
his villa of Liternum, with the magnificence (which was continually increasing) of the public baths of Rome, long before the stately Thermæ
of Antoninus and Diocletian were erected. The *quadrans* paid for
admission was the quarter of the *as*, about one-eighth of an English
penny.

in the indulgence of gross and vulgar sensua-
lity.° ᷍

Games
and spec-
tacles. ⁄ But the most lively and splendid amusement
of the idle multitude, depended on the frequent
exhibitions of public games and spectacles. The
piety of Christian princes had suppressed the
inhuman combats of gladiators; but the Roman
people still considered the Circus as their home,
their temple, and the seat of the republic. The
impatient crowd rushed at the dawn of day to
secure their places, and there were many who
passed a sleepless and anxious night in the adjacent porticos. From the morning to the evening, careless of the sun, or of the rain, the spectators, who sometimes amounted to the number
of four hundred thousand, remained in eager
attention; their eyes fixed on the horses and
charioteers; their minds agitated with hope and
fear, for the success of the *colours* which they
espoused: and the happiness of Rome appeared to hang on the event of a race.ᴾ The same
immoderate ardour inspired their clamours, and
their applause, as often as they were entertained with the hunting of wild beasts, and the various modes of theatrical representation. These
representations in modern capitals may deserve

° Ammianus, (l. xiv, c. 6, and l. xxviii, c. 4), after describing the
luxury and pride of the nobles of Rome, exposes, with equal indignation, the vices and follies of the common people.
ᴾ Juvenal. Satir, xi, 191, &c. The expressions of the historian Ammianus are not less strong and animated than those of the satirist; and
both the one and the other painted from the life: The numbers which
the great Circus was capable of receiving, are taken from the *original
Notitia* of the city. The differences between them prove that they did
not transcribe each other; but the sum may appear incredible, though
the country on these occasions flocked to the city.

to be considered as a pure and elegant school of taste, and perhaps of virtue. But the Tragic and Comic Muse of the Romans, who seldom aspired beyond the imitation of Attic genius,[q] had been almost totally silent since the fall of the republic;[r] and their place was unworthily occupied by licentious farce, effeminate music, and splendid pageantry. The pantomimes,[s] who maintained their reputation from the age of Augustus to the sixth century, expressed, without the use of words, the various fables of the gods and heroes of antiquity; and the perfection of their art, which sometimes disarmed the gravity of the philosopher, always excited the applause and wonder of the people The vast and magnificent theatres of Rome were filled by three thousand female dancers, and by three thousand singers, with the masters of the respective chorusses. Such was the popular favour which they enjoyed, that, in a time of

[q] Sometimes indeed they composed original pieces.
————Vestigia Græca
Ausi deserere et celebrare domestica facta.
Horat. Epistol. ad Pisones, 285, and the learned, though perplexed, note of Dacier, who might have allowed the name of tragedies to the *Brutus* and the *Decius* of Pacuvius, or to the *Cato* of Maternus. The *Octavia*, ascribed to one of the Senecas, still remains a very unfavourable specimen of Roman tragedy.

[r] In the time of Quintilian and Pliny, a tragic poet was reduced to the imperfect method of hiring a great room, and reading his play to the company, whom he invited for that purpose, (see Dialog. de Oratoribus, c. 9, 11, and Plin. Epistol. vii, 17).

[s] See the Dialogue of Lucian, entitled, de Saltatione, tom. ii, p. 265-317, edit. Reitz. The pantomimes obtained the honourable name of χειροσοφοι ; and it was required, that they should be conversant with almost every art and science. Barette (in the Memoires de l'Academie des Inscriptions, tom. i, p. 127, &c.) has given a short history of the art of pantomimes.

scarcity, when all strangers were banished from the city, the merit of contributing to the public pleasures, exempted *them* from a law, which was strictly executed against the professors of the liberal arts.[t]

It is said, that the foolish curiosity of Elagabalus attempted to discover, from the quantity of spiders webs, the number of the inhabitants of Rome.   A more rational method of inquiry might not have been undeserving of the attention of the wisest princes, who could easily have resolved a question so important for the Roman government, and so interesting to succeeding ages.   The births and deaths of the citizens were duly registered ; and if any writer of antiquity had condescended to mention the annual amount; or the common average, we might now produce some satisfactory calculation, which would destroy the extravagant assertions of critics, and perhaps confirm the modest and probable conjectures of philosophers.[u] The most diligent researches have colected only the following circumstances; which, slight and imperfect as they are, may tend, in some degree, to illustrate the question of

[t] Ammianus, l. xiv, c. 6.   He complains, with decent indignation, that the streets of Rome were filled with crowds of females, who might have given children to the state, but whose only occupation was to curl and dress their hair, and jactari volubilibus gyris, dum exprimunt innumera simulacra, quæ finxere fabulæ theatrales.

[u] Lipsius, (tom. iii, p. 423, de Magnitud. Romanâ, l. iii, c. 3), and Issac Vossius, (Observat. Var. p. 26-34), have indulged strange dreams of four, or eight, or fourteen millions in Rome.   Mr. Hume, (Essays, vol. i, p. 450-457), with admirable good sense and scepticism, betrays some secret disposition to extenuate the populousness of ancient times.

the populousness of ancient Rome. I. When
the capital of the empire was besieged by the
Goths, the circuit of the walls was accurately
measured, by Ammonius, the mathematician,
who found it equal to twenty-one miles.[x] It
should not be forgotten, that the form of the
city was almost that of a circle; the geometri-
cal figure which is known to contain the largest
space within any given circumference. II. The
architect Vitruvius, who flourished in the Augustan age, and whose evidence, on this occasion, has peculiar weight and authority, observes, that the innumerable habitations of the
Roman people would have spread themselves
far beyond the narrow limits of the city; and
that the want of ground, which was probably
contracted on every side by gardens and villas,
suggested the common, though inconvenient,
practice of raising the houses to a considerable
height in the air.[y] But the loftiness of these
buildings, which often consisted of hasty work,
and insufficient materials, was the cause of frequent and fatal accidents; and it was repeatedly enacted by Augustus, as well as by Nero,
that the height of private edifices, within the
walls of Rome, should not exceed the measure

---

[x] Olympiodor. ap. Phot. p. 197. See Fabricius, Bibl. Græc. tom.
ix, p. 400.

[y] In eâ autem majestate urbis, et civium infinitâ frequentiâ innumer-
abiles habitationes opus fuit explicare. Ergo cum recipere non posset
area plana tantam multitudinem in urbe, ad auxilium altitudinis ædifi-
ciorum res ipsa coëgit devenire. Vitruv. ii, 8. This passage, which
I owe to Vossius, is clear, strong, and comprehensive.

of seventy feet from the ground.[a] III. Juvenal[b] laments, as it should seem from his own experience, the hardships of the poorer citizens, to whom he addresses the salutary advice of emigrating, without delay, from the smoke of Rome, since they might purchase, in the little towns of Italy, a cheerful commodious dwelling, at the same price which they annually paid for a dark and miserable lodging. House-rent was therefore immoderately dear: the rich acquired, at an enormous expence, the ground, which they covered with palaces and gardens; but the body of the Roman people was crowded into a narrow space; and the different floors, and apartments, of the same house, were divided, as it is still the custom of Paris, and other cities, among several families of plebeians. IV. The total number of houses in the fourteen regions of the city, is accurately stated in the description of Rome, composed under the reign of Theodosius, and they amount to forty-eight thousand three hun-

---

[a] The successive testimonies of Pliny, Aristides, Claudian, Rutilius, &c. prove the insufficiency of these restrictive edicts. See Lipsius, de Magnitud. Romanâ, l. iii, c. 4.

————Tabulata tibi jam tertia fumant
Tu nescis; nam si gradibus trepidatur ab imis
Ultimus ardebit, quem tegula sola tuetur
A pluvia.

                          Juvenal. Satir. iii, 199.

[b] Read the whole third satire, but particularly 166, 223, &c. The description of a crowded *insula*, or lodging-house, in Petronius, (c. 95, 97), perfectly tallies with the complaints of Juvenal; and we learn from legal authority, that in the time of Augustus, (Heinneccius, Hist. Juris. Roman. e. iv, p. 181), the ordinary rent of the several *cænacula*, or apartments of an *insula*, annually produced forty thousand sesterces, between three and four hundred pounds sterling. (Pandect. l. xix, tit. ii, No. 30); a sum which proves at once the large extent, and high value, of those common buildings.

dred and eighty-two.[b] The two classes of *domus* and of *insulæ*, into which they are divided, include all the habitations of the capital, of every rank and condition, from the marble palace of the Anicii, with a numerous establishment of freedmen and slaves, to the lofty and narrow lodging-house, where the poet Codrus, and his wife, were permitted to hire a wretched garret immediately under the tiles. If we adopt the same average, which, under similar circumstances, has been found applicable to Paris,[c] and indifferently allow about twenty-five persons for each house, of every degree, we may fairly estimate the inhabitants of Rome at twelve hundred thousand: a number which cannot be thought excessive for the capital of a mighty empire, though it exceeds the populousness of the greatest cities of modern Europe.[d]

Such was the state of Rome under the reign of Honorius; at the time when the Gothic army formed the siege, or rather the blockade, of the city.[e] By a skilful disposition of his numerous

[b] This sum total is composed of 1780 *domus*, or great houses, of 46,602 *insulæ*, or plebeian habitations, (see Nardini, Roma Antica. l. iii, p. 88); and these numbers are ascertained by the agreement of the texts of the different *Notitiæ*. Nardini, l. viii, p. 498, 500.

[c] See that accurate writer M. de Messance, Recherches sur la Population, p. 175-187. From probable, or certain grounds, he assigns to Paris 23,565 houses, 71,114 families, and 576,630 inhabitants.

[d] This computation is not very different from that which M. Brotier, the last editor of Tacitus (tom. ii, p. 380), has assumed from similar principles; though he seems to aim at a degree of precision, which it is neither possible nor important to obtain.

[e] For the events of the first siege of Rome, which are often confounded with those of the second and third, see Zosimus, l. v, p. 350-354.

forces, who impatiently watched the moment of
an assault, Alaric encompassed the walls, commanded the twelve principal gates, intercepted
all communication with the adjacent country,
and vigilantly guarded the navigation of the
Tiber, from which the Romans derived the surest
and most plentiful supply of provisions. The
first emotions of the nobles, and of the people,
were those of surprise and indignation, that a
vile barbarian should dare to insult the capital
of the world : but their arrogance was soon
humbled by misfortune; and their unmanly
rage, instead of being directed against an enemy in arms, was meanly exercised on a defenceless and innocent victim. Perhaps in the
person of Serena, the Romans might have respected the niece of Theodosius, the aunt, nay
even the adopted mother, of the reigning emperor : but they abhorred the widow of Stilicho; and they listened with credulous passion
to the tale of calumny, which accused her of
maintaining a secret and criminal correspondence with the Gothic invader. Actuated, or
overawed, by the same popular frenzy, the senate, without requiring any evidence of her guilt,
pronounced the sentence of her death. Serena was ignominiously strangled ; and the infa-
tuated multitude were astonished to find, that
this cruel act of injustice did not immediately
produce the retreat of the barbarians, and the
deliverance of the city. That unfortunate city

254. Sozomen, l. ix, c. 6. Olympiodorus, ap. Phot. p. 180. Philostorgius, l. xii, c. 3 ; and Godefroy, Dissertat. p. 467-475.

gradually experienced the distress of scarcity, and at length the horrid calamities of famine. The daily allowance of three pounds of bread was reduced to one-half, to one-third, to nothing; and the price of corn sill continued to rise in a rapid and extravagant proportion. The poorer citizens, who were unable to purchase the necessaries of life, solicited the precarious charity of the rich; and for a while the public misery was alleviated by the humanity of Læta, the widow of the emperor Gratian, who had fixed her residence at Rome, and consecrated to the use of the indigent, the princely revenue, which she annually received from the grateful successors of her husband.* But these private and temporary donatives were insufficient to appease the hunger of a numerous people; and the progress of famine invaded the marble palaces of the senators themselves. The persons of both sexes, who had been educated in the enjoyment of ease and luxury, discovered how little is requisite to supply the demands of nature; and lavished their unavailing treasures of gold and silver, to obtain the coarse and scanty sustenance which they would formerly have rejected with disdain. The food the most repugnant to sense or imagination, the aliments the most unwholesome and pernicious to the constitution, were eagerly devoured, and fiercely disputed, by the rage of hunger. A dark suspicion was entertained, that some desperate

---

* The mother of Læta was named Pissumena. Her father, family, and country, are unknown. Ducange, Fam. Byzantin. p. 59.

wretches fed on the bodies of their fellow-creatures, whom they had secretly murdered; and even mothers, (such was the horrid conflict of the two most powerful instincts implanted by nature in the human breast), even mothers are said to have tasted the flesh of their slaughtered infants![e] Many thousands of the inhabitants of Rome expired in their houses, or in the streets, for want of sustenance; and as the public sepulchres without the walls were in the power of the enemy, the stench, which arose from so many putrid and unburied carcasses, infected the air; and the miseries of famine were suc-

Plague.
ceeded and aggravated by the contagion of a pestilential disease. The assurances of speedy and effectual relief, which were repeatedly transmitted from the court of Ravenna, supported, for some time, the fainting resolution of the Romans, till at length the despair of any human aid tempted them to accept the offers

Superstition.
of a preternatural deliverance. Pompeianus, prefect of the city, had been persuaded, by the art or fanaticism of some Tuscan diviners, that, by the mysterious force of spells and sacrifices, they could extract the lightning from the clouds, and point those celestial fires against the camp of the barbarians.[h] The important secret was

[e] Ad nefandos cibos erupit esurientium rabies, et sua invicem membra laniarunt, dum mater non parcit lactenti infantiæ; et recipit utero, quem paullò ante effuderat. Jerom ad Principiam, tom. i. p. 121. The same horrid circumstance is likewise told of the sieges of Jerusalem and Paris. For the latter, compare the tenth book of the Henriade, and the Journal de Henry IV, tom. i, p, 47-83; and observe that a plain narrative of facts is much more pathetic, than the most laboured descriptions of epic poetry.

[h] Zosimus (l. v, p. 355, 356) speaks of these ceremonies, like a

communicated to Innocent, the bishop of Rome; and the successor of St. Peter is accused, perhaps without foundation, of preferring the safety of the republic to the rigid severity of the Christian worship. But when the question was agitated in the senate; when it was proposed, as an essential condition, that those sacrifices should be performed in the Capitol, by the authority, and in the presence, of the magistrates; the majority of that respectable assembly, apprehensive either of the divine, or of the imperial, displeasure, refused to join in an act, which appeared almost equivalent to the public restoration of paganism.[1]

The last resource of the Romans was in the clemency, or at least in the moderation, of the king of the Goths. The senate, who in this emergency assumed the supreme powers of government, appointed two ambassadors to nego-

Greek unacquainted with the national superstition of Rome and Tuscany. I suspect, that they consisted of two parts, the secret, and the public; the former were probably an imitation of the arts and spells, by which Numa had drawn down Jupiter and his thunder, on Mount Aventine.

——————Quid agant laqueis, quæ carmina dicant
Quâque trahant superis sedibus arte Jovem
Scire nefas homini.

The ancilia, or shields of Mars, the pignora Imperii, which were carried in solemn procession on the calends of March, derived their origin from this mysterious event, (Ovid. Fast. iii, 259-398). It was probably designed to revive this ancient festival, which had been suppressed by Theodosius. In that case, we recover a chronological date, (March 1, A. D. 409), which has not hitherto been observed.

[1] Sozomen (l. ix, c. 6) insinuates, that the experiment was actually, though unsuccessfully, made; but he does not mention the name of Innocent: and Tillemont (Mem. Eccles. tom. x, p. 645) is determined not to believe, that a pope could be guilty of such impious condescension.

tiate with the enemy. This important trust was delegated to Basilius, a senator, of Spanish extraction, and already conspicuous in the administration of provinces; and to John, the first tribune of the notaries, who was peculiarly qualified, by his dexterity in business, as well as by his former intimacy with the Gothic prince. When they were introduced into his presence, they declared, perhaps in a more lofty style than became their abject condition, that the Romans were resolved to maintain their dignity, either in peace or war; and that, *if* Alaric refused them a fair and honourable capitulation, he might sound his trumpets, and prepare to give battle to an innumerable people, exercised in arms, and animated by despair. " The thicker the hay, the easier it is mowed," was the concise reply of the barbarian; and this rustic metaphor was accompanied by a loud and insulting laugh, expressive of his contempt for the menaces of an unwarlike populace, enervated by luxury before they were emaciated by famine. He then condescended to fix the ransom, which he would accept as the price of his retreat from the walls of Rome: *all* the gold and silver in the city, whether it were the property of the state, or of individuals; *all* the rich and precious moveables; and *all* the slaves who could prove their title to the name of *barbarians*. The ministers of the senate presumed to ask, in a modest and suppliant tone,— " If such, O King! are your demands, what do " you intend to leave us?" " YOUR LIVES;" replied the haughty conqueror. They trembled,

and retired. Yet before they retired, a short
suspension of arms was granted, which allowed some time for a more temperate negotiation. The stern features of Alaric were insensibly relaxed; he abated much of the rigour of his terms; and at length consented to raise the siege, on the immediate payment of five thousand pounds of gold, of thirty thousand pounds of silver, of four thousand robes of silk, of three thousand pieces of fine scarlet cloth, and of three thousand pounds weight of pepper.[x] But the public treasury was exhausted; the annual rents of the great estates in Italy and the provinces, were intercepted by the calamities of war; the gold and gems had been exchanged during the famine, for the vilest sustenance; the hoards of secret wealth were still concealed by the obstinacy of avarice; and some remains of consecrated spoils afforded the only resource that could avert the impending ruin of the city. As soon as the Romans had satisfied the rapacious demands of Alaric, they were restored, in some measure, to the enjoyment of peace and plenty. Several of the gates were cautiously opened; the importation of provisions from the river, and the adjacent country, was no longer obstructed by the Goths; the citizens resorted in crowds to the free market,

[x] Pepper was a favourite ingredient of the most expensive Roman cookery, and the best sort commonly sold for fifteen denarii, or ten shillings, the pound. See Pliny, Hist. Natur. xii, 14. It was brought from India; and the same country, the coast of Malabar, still affords the greatest plenty : but the improvement of trade and navigation has multiplied the quantity, and reduced the price. See Histoire Politique et Philosophique, &c. tom. i, p. 457.

CHAP.
XXXI.

which was held during three days in the suburbs; and while the merchants who undertook
this gainful trade, made a considerable profit,
the future subsistence of the city was secured
by the ample magazines which were deposited
in the public and private granaries. A more
regular discipline, than could have been expected, was maintained in the camp of Alaric; and
the wise barbarian justified his regard for the
faith of treaties, by the just severity with which
he chastised a party of licentious Goths, who
had insulted some Roman citizens on the road
to Ostia. His army, enriched by the contributions of the capital, slowly advanced into the
fair and fruitful province of Tuscany, where he
proposed to establish his winter-quarters; and
the Gothic standard became the refuge of forty
thousand barbarian slaves, who had broke their
chains, and aspired, under the command of
their great deliverer, to revenge the injuries,
and the disgrace, of their cruel servitude. About
the same time, he received a more honourable
reinforcement of Goths and Huns, whom Adolphus,[1] the brother of his wife, had conducted,
at his pressing invitation, from the banks of the
Danube to those of the Tiber, and who had cut
their way, with some difficulty and loss, through
the superior numbers of the imperial troops.
A victorious leader, who united the daring spirit of a barbarian with the art and discipline

[1] This Gothic chieftain is called by Jornandes and Isidore, *Athaul-
phus*; by Zosimus and Orosius, *Ataulphus*; and by Olympiodorus,
Aduoulphus. I have used the celebrated name of *Adolphus*, which seems
to be authorized by the practice of the Swedes, the sons or brothers of
the ancient Goths.

of a Roman general, was at the head of an
hundred thousand fighting men ; and Italy pronounced, with terror and respect, the formidable name of Alaric.[m]

At the distance of fourteen centuries, we may
be satisfied with relating the military exploits
of the conquerors of Rome, without presuming
to investigate the motives of their political conduct.   In the midst of his apparent prosperity,
Alaric was conscious, perhaps, of some secret
weakness, some internal defect ; or perhaps the
moderation which he displayed, was intended
only to deceive and disarm the easy credulity
of the ministers of Honorius.   The king of the
Goths repeatedly declared, that it was his desire
to be considered as the friend of peace, and of
the Romans.   Three senators, at his earnest
request, were sent ambassadors to the court of
Ravenna, to solicit the exchange of hostages,
and the conclusion of the treaty ; and the proposals, which he more clearly expressed during
the course of the negotiations, could only inspire a doubt of his sincerity, as they might
seem inadequate to the state of his fortune.
The barbarian still aspired to the rank of master-general of the armies of the West ; he stimulated an annual subsidy of corn and money ;
and he chose the provinces of Dalmatia, Noricum, and Venetia, for the seat of his new kingdom, which would have commanded the important communication between Italy and the

---

[m] The treaty between Alaric and the Romans, &c. is taken from
Zosimus, l. v, p. 354, 355, 358, 359, 3C2, 268.   The additional circumstances are too few and trifling to require any other quotation.

CHAP.
XXXI.

Danube. If these modest terms should be rejected, Alaric shewed a disposition to relinquish his pecuniary demands, and even to content himself with the possession of Noricum; an exhausted and impoverished country, perpetually exposed to the inroads of the barbarians of Germany.[*] But the hopes of peace were disappointed by the weak obstinacy, or interested views, of the minister Olympius. Without listening to the salutary remonstrances of the senate, he dismissed their several ambassadors under the conduct of a military escort, too numerous for a retinue of honour, and too feeble for an army of defence. Six thousand Dalmatians, the flower of the imperial legions, were ordered to march from Ravenna to Rome, through an open country, which was occupied by the formidable myriads of the barbarians. These brave legionaries, encompassed and betrayed, fell a sacrifice to ministerial folly; their general, Valens, with an hundred soldiers, escaped from the field of battle; and one of the ambassadors, who could no longer claim the protection of the law of nations, was obliged to purchase his freedom with a ransom of thirty thousand pieces of gold. Yet Alaric, instead of resenting this act of impotent hostility, immediately renewed his proposals of peace; and the second embassy of the Roman senate, which derived weight and dignity from the presence of Innocent, bishop of the city, was guarded from

[*] Zosimus, l. v, p. 367, 368, 369.

the dangers of the road by a detachment of Gothic soldiers. [o]

CHAP.
XXXI.

Change
and suc-
cession of
ministers.

Olympius[p] might have continued to insult the just resentment of a people, who loudly accused him as the author of the public calamities; but his power was undermined by the secret intrigues of the palace. The favourite eunuchs transferred the government of Honorius, and the empire, to Jovius, the pretorian prefect; an unworthy servant, who did not atone, by the merit of personal attachment, for the errors and misfortunes of his administration. The exile, or escape, of the guilty Olympius, reserved him for more vicissitudes of fortune: he experienced the adventures of an obscure and wandering life; he again rose to power; he fell a second time into disgrace; his ears were cut off; he expired under the lash; and his ignominious death afforded a grateful spectacle to the friends of Stilicho. After the removal of Olympius, whose character was deeply tainted with religious fanaticism, the pagans and heretics were delivered from the impolitic proscription, which excluded them from the dignities of the state. The brave Gennerid,[q] a soldier of barbarian origin, who still

---

[o] Zosimus, l. v, p. 360, 361, 362. The bishop, by remaining at Ravenna, escaped the impending calamities of the city. Orosius, l. vii, c. 39, p. 573.

[p] For the adventures of Olympius, and his successors in the ministry, see Zosimus, l. v, p. 363, 365, 366, and Olympiodor. ap. Phot. p. 180, 181.

[q] Zosimus (l. v, p. 364) relates this circumstance with visible complacency, and celebrates the character of Gennerid as the last glory of expiring

adhered to the worship of his ancestors, had been obliged to lay aside the military belt: and though he was repeatedly assured by the emperor himself, that laws were not made for persons of his rank or merit, he refused to accept any partial dispensation, and persevered in honourable disgrace, till he had extorted a general act of justice from the distress of the Roman government. The conduct of Gennerid, in the important station, to which he was promoted or restored, of master-general of Dalmatia, Pannonia, Noricum, and Rhætia, seemed to revive the discipline and spirit of the republic. From a life of idleness and want, his troops were soon habituated to severe exercise, and plentiful subsistence; and his private generosity often supplied the rewards, which were denied by the avarice, or poverty, of the court of Ravenna. The valour of Gennerid, formidable to the adjacent barbarians, was the firmest bulwark of the Illyrian frontier; and his vigilant care assisted the empire with a reinforcement of ten thousand Huns, who arrived on the confines of Italy, attended by such a convoy of provisions, and such a numerous train of sheep and oxen, as might have been sufficient, not only for the march of an army, but for the settlement of a colony. But the court and councils of Honorius still remained a scene of weakness and distraction, of corruption and anarchy.

expiring paganism. Very different were the sentiments of the council of Carthage, who deputed four bishops to the court of Ravenna, to complain of the law, which had been just enacted, that all conversions to Christianity should be free and voluntary. See Baronius, Annal. Eccles. A. D. 409, No. 12; A. D. 410, No. 47 48 ·

Instigated by the prefect Jovius, the guards rose in furious mutiny, and demanded the heads of two generals, and of the two principal eunuchs. The generals, under a perfidious promise of safety, were sent on ship-board, and privately executed; while the favour of the eunuchs procured them a mild and secure exile at Milan and Constantinople. Eusebius the eunuch, and the barbarian Allobich, succeeded to the command of the bed-chamber and of the guards; and the mutual jealousy of these subordinate ministers was the cause of their mutual destruction. By the insolent order of the count of the domestics, the great chamberlain was shamefully beaten to death with sticks, before the eyes of the astonished emperor; and the subsequent assassination of Allobich, in the midst of a public procession, is the only circumstance of his life, in which Honorius discovered the faintest symptom of courage or resentment. Yet before they fell, Eusebius and Allobich had contributed their part to the ruin of the empire, by opposing the conclusion of a treaty which Jovius, from a selfish, and perhaps a criminal, motive, had negotiated with Alaric, in a personal interview under the walls of Rimini. During the absence of Jovius, the emperor was persuaded to assume a lofty tone of inflexible dignity, such as neither his situation, nor his character, could enable him to support: and a letter, signed with the name of Honorius, was immediately despatched to the pretorian prefect, granting him a free permission to dispose of the public money, but sternly refusing to prostitute the military honours of Rome to the proud demands of a barbarian.' This letter was imprudently communicated to Alaric himself; and the Goth, who in the whole transaction had behaved with temper and decency, expressed, in the most outrageous language, his lively sense of the insult so wantonly offered to his person, and to his nation. The conference of Rimini was hastily interrupted; and the prefect Jovius, on his return to Ravenna, was compelled to adopt, and even to encourage, the fashionable opinions of the court. By his advice and example, the principal officers of the state and army were obliged to swear, that, without listening, in *any* circumstances, to *any* conditions of peace, they would still persevere in perpetual and implacable war against the enemy of the republic. This rash engagement opposed an insuperable bar to all future negotiation. The ministers of Honorius were heard to declare, that, if they had only invoked the name of the Deity, they would consult the public safety, and trust their souls to the mercy of Heaven: but they had sworn by the sacred head of the emperor himself; they had touched, in solemn ceremony, that august seat of majesty and wisdom; and the violation of their oath would expose them to the temporal penalties of sacrilege and rebellion.'

r Zosimus, l. v, p. 367, 368, 369. This custom of swearing by the head, or life, or safety, or genius, of the sovereign, was of the highest antiquity, both in Egypt (Genesis, xlii, 15) and Scythia. It was soon transferred, by flattery, to the Cæsars; and Tertullian complains, that it was the only oath which the Romans of his time affected to reverence.

CHAP.
XXXI.

Second
siege of
Rome by
the Goths,
A. D. 409.

While the emperor and his court enjoyed, with sullen pride, the security of the marshes and fortifications of Ravenna, they abandoned Rome, almost without defence, to the resentment of Alaric. Yet such was the moderation which he still preserved, or affected, that, as he moved with his army along the Flaminian way, he successively despatched the bishops of the towns of Italy to reiterate his offers of peace, and to conjure the emperor, that he would save the city and its inhabitants from hostile fire, and the sword of the barbarians.* These impending calamities were however averted, not indeed by the wisdom of Honorius, but by the prudence or humanity of the Gothic king; who employed a milder, though not less effectual, method of conquest. Instead of assaulting the capital, he successively directed his efforts against the *Port* of Ostia, one of the boldest and most stupendous works of Roman magnificence.* The accidents to which the precarious subsistence of the city was continually exposed in a winter navigation, and an open road,

ence. See an elegant Dissertation of the Abbé Massieu on the Oaths of the Ancients, in the Mem. de l'Academie des Inscriptions, tom. i, p. 208, 209.

* Zosimus, l. v, p. 368, 369. I have softened the expressions of Alaric, who expatiates, in too florid a manner, on the history of Rome.

: See Sueton. in Claud. c. 20; Dion. Cassius, l. lx, p. 949, edit. Reimar, and the lively description of Juvenal, Satir. xii, 75, &c. In the sixteenth century, when the remains of this Augustan port were still visible, the antiquarians sketched the plan, (see d'Anville, Mem. de l'Academie des Inscriptions, tom. xxx, p. 198), and declared, with enthusiasm, that all the monarchs of Europe would be unable to execute so great a work, (Bergier, Hist. des grands Chemins de Romains, tom. ii, p. 356).

had suggested to the genius of the first Cæsar the useful design, which was executed under the reign of Claudius. The artificial moles, which formed the narrow entrance, advanced far into the sea, and firmly repelled the fury of the waves, while the largest vessels securely rode at anchor within three deep and capacious basons, which received the northern branch of the Tiber, about two miles from the ancient colony of Ostia." The Roman *Port* insensibly swelled to the size of an episcopal city,ˣ where the corn of Africa was deposited in spacious granaries for the use of the capital. As soon as Alaric was in possession of that im-

---

" The *Ostia Tyberina*, (see Cluver. Italia Antiq. l. iii, p. 870-879). In the plural number, the two mouths of the Tiber, were separated by the Holy Island, an equilateral triangle, whose sides were each of them computed at about two miles. The colony of Ostia was founded immediately beyond the left, or southern, and the *Port* immediately beyond the right, or northern, branch of the river; and the distance between their remains measures something more than two miles on Cingolani's map. In the time of Strabo, the sand and mud deposited by the Tiber, had choaked the harbour of Ostia; the progress of the same cause had added much to the size of the Holy Island, and gradually left both Ostia and the Port at a considerable distance from the shore. The dry channels, (fiumi morti), and the large estuaries, (stagno di Ponente, de Levante), mark the changes of the river, and the efforts of the sea. Consult, for the present state of this dreary and desolate tract, the excellent map of the ecclesiastical state by the mathematicians of Benedict XIV; an actual survey of the *Argo Romano*, in six sheets, by Cingolani, which contains 113,819 *rubbia*, (about 570,000 acres); and the large topographical map of Ameti, in eight sheets.

ˣ As early as the third, (Lardner's Credibility of the Gospel, part ii, vol. iii, p. 89-92), or at least the fourth, century, (Carol. a Sancto Paulo, Notit. Eccles. p. 47), the port of Rome was an episcopal city, which was demolished, as it should seem, in the ninth century, by pope Gregory IV, during the incursions of the Arabs. It is now reduced to an inn, a church, and the house, or palace, of the bishop; who ranks as one of six cardinal bishops of the Roman church. See Eschinard, Descrizione di Roma et dell' Argo Romano, p. 328.

portant place, he summoned the city to surrender at discretion; and his demands were enforced by the positive declaration, that a refusal, or even a delay, should be instantly followed by the destruction of the magazines, on which the life of the Roman people depended. The clamours of that people, and the terror of famine, subdued the pride of the senate; they listened, without reluctance, to the proposal of placing a new emperor on the throne of the unworthy Honorius; and the suffrage of the Gothic conqueror bestowed the purple on Attalus, prefect of the city. The grateful monarch immediately acknowledged his protector as master-general of the armies of the West; Adolphus, with the rank of count of the domestics, obtained the custody of the person of Attalus; and the two hostile nations seemed to be united in the closest bands of friendship and alliance.[y]

The gates of the city were thrown open, and the new emperor of the Romans, encompassed on every side by the Gothic arms, was conducted, in tumultuous procession, to the palace of Augustus and Trajan. After he had distributed the civil and military dignities among his favourites and followers, Attalus convened an assembly of the senate; before whom, in a formal and florid speech, he asserted his resolution of restoring the majesty of the republic, and of uniting to the empire the provinces of

Attalus is created emperor by the Goths at Romans.

[y] For the elevation of Attalus, consult Zosimus, l. vi, p. 377-380; Sozomen, l. ix, c. 8, 9; Olympiodor. ap. Phot. p. 180, 181; Philostorg. l. xii, c. 3, and Godefroy, Dissertat. p. 470.

Egypt and the East, which had once acknowledged, the sovereignty of Rome. Such extravagant promises inspired every reasonable citizen with a just contempt for the character of
an unwarlike usurper whose elevation was the
deepest and most ignominious wound which the
republic had yet sustained from the insolence
of the barbarians. But the populace with their
usual levity, applauded the change of masters.
The public discontent was favourable to the
rival of Honorius; and the sectaries, oppressed
by his persecuting edicts, expected some degree
of countenance, or at least of toleration, from a
prince, who, in his native country of Ionia, had
been educated in the pagan superstition, and
who had since received the sacrament of baptism from the hands of an Arian bishop. The
first days of the reign of Attalus were fair and
prosperous. An officer of confidence was sent
with an inconsiderable body of troops to secure
the obedience of Africa ; the greatest part of
Italy submitted to the terror of the Gothic
powers ; and though the city of Bologna made
a vigorous and effectual resistance, the people
of Milan, dissatisfied perhaps with the absence
of Honorius, accepted, with loud acclamations,
the choice of the Roman senate. At the head
of a formidable army, Alaric conducted his
royal captive almost to the gates of Ravenna ;

* We may admit the evidence of Sozomen for the Arian baptism,
and that of Philostorgius for the pagan education, of Attalus. The
visible joy of Zosimus, and the discontent which he imputes to the
Anician family, are very unfavourable to the Christianity of the new
emperor.

and a solemn embassy of the principal ministers of Jovius, the pretorian prefect, of Valens, master of the cavalry, and infantry, of the questor Potamius, and of Julian, the first of the notaries, was introduced, with martial pomp, into the Gothic camp. In the name of their sovereign, they consented to acknowledge the lawful election of his competitor, and to divide the provinces of Italy and the West between the two emperors. Their proposals were rejected with disdain; and the refusal was aggravated by the insulting clemency of Attalus, who condescended to promise, that, if Honorius would instantly resign the purple, he should be permitted to pass the remainder of his life in the peaceful exile of some remote island.[a] So desperate, indeed, did the situation of the son of Theodosius appear, to those who were the best acquainted with his strength and resources, that Jovius and Valens, his minister and his general, betrayed their trust, infamously deserted the sinking cause of their benefactor, and devoted their treacherous allegiance to the service of his more fortunate rival. Astonished by such examples of domestic treason, Honorius trembled at the approach of every servant, at the arrival of every messenger. He dreaded the secret enemies, who might lurk in his capital, his palace, his bed-chamber; and some ships

---

[a] He carried his insolence so far, as to declare that he should mutilate Honorius before he sent him into exile. But this assertion of Zosimus is destroyed by the more impartial testimony of Olympiodorus, who attributes the ungenerous proposal (which was absolutely rejected by Attalus) to the baseness, and perhaps the treachery, of Jovius.

CHAP.
XXXI.
lay ready in the harbour of Ravenna, to transport the abdicated monarch to the dominions
of his infant nephew, the emperor of the East.

He is de-
graded by
Alaric,
A. D. 410.
But there *is* a providence (such at least was
the opinion of the historian Procopius[b]) that
watches over innocence and folly; and the pretensions of Honorius to its peculiar care cannot
reasonably be disputed. At the moment when
his despair, incapable of any wise or manly
resolution, meditated a shameful flight, a seasonable reinforcement of four thousand veterans
unexpectedly landed in the port of Ravenna.
To these valiant strangers, whose fidelity had
not been corrupted by the factions of the court,
he committed the walls and gates of the city;
and the slumbers of the emperor were no longer disturbed by the apprehension of imminent
and internal danger. The favourable intelligence which was received from Africa, suddenly
changed the opinions of men, and the state of
public affairs. The troops and officers, whom
Attalus had sent into that province, were defeated and slain; and the active zeal of Heraclian
maintained his own allegiance, and that of his
people. The faithful count of Africa transmitted a large sum of money, which fixed the
attachment of the imperial guards; and his vigilance, in preventing the exportation of corn and
oil, introduced famine, tumult, and discontent,
into the walls of Rome. The failure of the
African expedition, was the source of mutual
complaint and recrimination in the party of At-

---

[b] Procop. de Bell. Vandal. l. i, c. 2.

talus; and the mind of his protector was insensibly alienated from the interest of a prince, who wanted spirit to command, or docility to obey. The most imprudent measures were adopted, without the knowledge, or against the advice, of Alaric; and the obstinate refusal of the senate, to allow, in the embarkation, the mixture even of five hundred Goths, betrayed a suspicious and distrustful temper, which, in their situation, was neither generous nor prudent. The resentment of the Gothic king was exasperated by the malicious arts of Jovius, who had been raised to the rank of patrician, and who afterwards excused his double perfidy, by declaring, without a blush, that he had only *seemed* to abandon the service of Honorius, more effectually to ruin the cause of the usurper. In a large plain near Rimini, and in the presence of an innumerable multitude of Romans and barbarians, the wretched Attalus was publicly despoiled of the diadem and purple; and those ensigns of royalty were sent by Alaric, as the pledge of peace and friendship, to the son of Theodosius.[c] The officers who returned to their duty, were reinstated in their employments, and even the merit of a tardy repentance was graciously allowed: but the degraded emperor of the Romans, desirous of life, and insensible of disgrace, implored the per-

---

[c] See the cause and circumstances of the fall of Attalus in Zosimus, l. vi, p. 380-383. Sozomen, l. ix, c. 8. Philostorg. l. xii, c. 3. The two acts of indemnity in the Theodosian Code, l. ix, tit. xxxviii, leg. 11, 22, which were published the 12th of February, and the 8th of August, A. D. 410, evidently relate to this usurper.

CHAP XXXI.

Third siege and sack of Rome by the Goths, A. D. 410, Aug. 24.

mission of following the Gothic camp, in the train of a haughty and capricious barbarian.[d]

The degradation of Attalus removed the only real obstacle to the conclusion of the peace; and Alaric advanced within three miles of Ravenna, to press the irresolution of the imperial ministers, whose insolence soon returned with the return of fortune. His indignation was kindled by the report, that a rival chieftain, that Sarus, the personal enemy of Adolphus, and the hereditary foe of the house of Balti, had been received into the palace. At the head of three hundred followers, that fearless barbarian immediately sallied from the gates of Ravenna; surprised, and cut in pieces, a considerable body of Goths; re-entered the city in triumph; and was permitted to insult his adversary, by the voice of a herald, who publicly declared that the guilt of Alaric had for ever excluded him from the friendship and alliance of the emperor.[e] The crime and folly of the court of Ravenna was expiated, a third time, by the calamities of Rome. The king of the Goths, who no longer dissembled his appetite for plunder and revenge, appeared in arms under the walls of the capital; and the trembling senate, without any hopes of relief, prepared, by a des-

[d] In hoc, Alaricus, imperatore, facto, infecto, refecto, ac defecto. . . . Mimum risit, et ludum spectavit imperii. Orosius, l. vii, c. 42, p. 582.

[e] Zosimus, l. vi, p. 384. Sozomen, l. ix, c. 9. Philostorgius, l. xii, c. 3. In this place the text of Zosimus is mutilated, and we have lost the remainder of his sixth and last book, which ended with the sack of Rome. Credulous and partial as he is, we must take our leave of that historian with some regret.

perate resistance, to delay the ruin of their country.   But they were unable to guard against the
secret conspiracy of their slaves and domestics;
who, either from birth or interest, were attached
to the cause of the enemy.   At the hour of midnight, the Salarian gate was silently opened, and
the inhabitants were awakened by the tremen-
dous sound of the Gothic trumpet.   Eleven
hundred and sixty-three years after the foundation of Rome, the imperial city, which had
subdued and civilized so considerable a part
of mankind, was delivered to the licentious fury
of the tribes of Germany and Scythia.[f]

The proclamation of Alaric, when he forced
his entrance into a vanquished city, discovered,
however, some regard for the laws of humanity
and religion.   He encouraged his troops boldly
to seize the rewards of valour, and to enrich
themselves with the spoils of a wealthy and effeminate people : but he exhorted them, at the
same time, to spare the lives of the unresisting
citizens, and to respect the churches of the
apostles St. Peter and St. Paul, as holy and in-
violable sanctuaries.   Amidst the horrors of a
nocturnal tumult, several of the Christian Goths
displayed the fervour of a recent conversion;
and some instances of their uncommon piety

---

[f] Adest Alaricus, trepidam Romam obsidet, turba, irrumpit.   Orosius, l. vii, c. 39, p. 573.   He despatches this great event in seven words;
but he employs whole pages in celebrating the devotion of the Goths.
I have extracted from an improbable story of Procopius, the circumstances which had an air of probability.   Procop. de Bell. Vandal. l.
i, c. 2.   He supposes, that the city was surprised while the senators
slept in the afternoon; but Jerom, with more authority and more reason, affirms, that it was in the night, nocte Moab capta est; nocte ceci-
dit murus ejus, tom. i, p. 121, ad Principiam.

and moderation are related, and perhaps adorned, by the zeal of ecclesiastical writers.[s] While
the barbarians roamed through the city in quest
of prey, the humble dwelling of an aged virgin,
who had devoted her life to the service of the
altar, was forced open by one of the powerful
Goths. He immediately demanded, though in
civil language, all the gold and silver in her possession; and was astonished at the readiness
with which she conducted him to a splendid
hoard of massy plate, of the richest materials,
and the most curious workmanship. The barbarian viewed with wonder and delight this valuable acquisition, till he was interrupted by
a serious admonition, addressed to him in the
following words.—" These," said she, " are the
" consecrated vessels belonging to St. Peter; if
" you presume to touch them, the sacrilegious
" deed will remain on your conscience. For
" my part, I dare not keep what I am unable to
" defend." The Gothic captain, struck with
reverential awe, despatched a messenger to inform the king of the treasure which he had discovered; and received a peremptory order from
Alaric, that all the consecrated plate and ornaments should be transported, without damage
or delay, to the church of the apostle. From

[s] Orosius (l. vii, c. 39, p. 573-576) applauds the piety of the Christian Goths, without seeming to perceive that the greatest part of them
were Arian heretics. Jornandes, (c. 30, p. 653), and Isidore of Seville,
(Chron. p. 714, edit. Grot.) who were both attached to the Gothic cause,
have repeated and embellished these edifying tales. According to
Isidore, Alaric himself was heard to say, that he waged war with the
Romans, and not with the apostles. Such was the style of the seventh
century; two hundred years before, the fame and merit had been ascribed, not to the apostles, but to Christ.

the extremity, perhaps, of the Quirinal hill, to
the distant quarter of the Vatican, a numerous
detachment of Goths, marching in order of battle through the principal streets, protected,
with glittering arms, the long train of their devout companions, who bore aloft, on their heads,
the sacred vessels of gold and silver; and the
martial shouts of the barbarians were mingled
with the sound of religious psalmody. From
all the adjacent houses, a crowd of Christians
hastened to join this edifying procession; and
a multitude of fugitives, without distinction of
age, or rank, or even of sect, had the good fortune to escape to the secure and hospitable sanctuary of the Vatican. The learned work, concerning the *City of God*, was professedly composed by St. Augustin, to justify the ways of Providence in the destruction of the Roman greatness. He celebrates, with peculiar satisfaction, this memorable triumph of Christ; and
insults his adversaries, by challenging them to
produce some similar example, of a town taken
by storm, in which the fabulous gods of antiquity had been able to protect either themselves, or their deluded votaries.[h]

In the sack of Rome, some rare and extraor- Pillage
dinary examples of barbarian virtue had been and fire
deservedly applauded. But the holy precincts of Rome.
of the Vatican, and the apostolic churches, could
receive a very small proportion of the Roman
people: many thousand warriors, more especially of the Huns, who served under the stand-

[h] See Augustin, de Civitat. Dei, l. i, c. 1-6. He particularly appeals
to the examples of Troy, Syracuse, and Tarentum.

CHAP.
XXXI.

ard of Alaric, were strangers to the name, or at least to the faith, of Christ; and we may suspect, without any breach of charity or candour, that, in the hour of savage license, when every passion was inflamed, and every restraint was removed, the precepts of the gospel seldom influenced the behaviour of the Gothic Christians. The writers, the best disposed to exaggerate their clemency, had freely confessed, that a cruel slaughter was made of the Romans;[1] and that the streets of the city were filled with dead bodies, which remained without burial during the general consternation. The despair of the citizens was sometimes converted into fury; and whenever the barbarians were provoked by opposition, they extended the promiscuous massacre to the feeble, the innocent, and the helpless. The private revenge of forty thousand slaves was exercised without pity or remorse; and the ignominious lashes, which they had formerly received, were washed away in the blood of the guilty, or obnoxious, families. The matrons and virgins of Rome were exposed to injuries more dreadful in the apprehension of chastity, than death itself; and the ecclesiastical historian has selected an example of fe-

---

[1] Jerom (tom. i, p. 121, ad Principiam) has applied to the sack of Rome all the strong expressions of Virgil.—

     Quis cladem illius noctis, quis funera fando,

     Explicet, &c.

Procopius (l. i, c. 2) positively affirms that great numbers were slain by the Goths. Augustin (de Civ. Dei, l. i, c. 12, 13) offers Christian comfort for the death of those, whose bodies (*multa corpora*) had remained (*in tantá strage*) unburied. Baronius, from the different writings of the Fathers, has thrown some light on the sack of Rome. Anual. Eccles. A. D 410, No. 16-44.

male virtue, for the admiration of future ages.[k] A Roman lady, of singular beauty and orthodox faith, had excited the impatient desires of a young Goth, who, according to the sagacious remark of Sozomen, was attached to the Arian heresy. Exasperated by her obstinate resistance, he drew his sword, and, with the anger of a lover, slightly wounded her neck. The bleeding heroine still continued to brave his resentment, and to repel his love, till the ravisher desisted from his unavailing efforts, respectfully conducted her to the sanctuary of the Vatican, and gave six pieces of gold to the guards of the church, on condition that they should restore her inviolate to the arms of her husband. Such instances of courage and generosity were not extremely common. The brutal soldiers satisfied their sensual appetites, without consulting either the inclination, or the duties, of their female captives : and a nice question of casuistry was seriously agitated, Whether those tender victims, who had inflexibly refused their consent to the violation which they sustained, had lost, by their misfortune, the glorious crown of virginity?[l] There were

---

[k] Sozomen, l. ix, c. 10. Augustin (de Civitat. Dei, l. i, c. 17) intimates, that some virgins or matrons actually killed themselves to escape violation ; and though he admires their spirit, he is obliged, by his theology, to condemn their rash presumption. Perhaps the good bishop of Hippo, was too easy in the belief, as well as too rigid in the censure, of this act of female heroism. The twenty maidens, (if they ever existed), who threw themselves into the Elbe, when Magdeburgh was taken by storm, have been multiplied to the number of twelve hundred. See Harte's History of Gustavus Adolphus, vol. i, p. 308.

[l] See Augustin, de Civitat. Dei, l. i, c. 16, 18. He treats the subject
with

other losses indeed of a more substantial kind, and more general concern. It cannot be presumed, that all the barbarians were at all times capable of perpetrating such amorous outrages; and the want of youth, or beauty, or chastity, protected the greatest part of the Roman women from the danger of a rape. But avarice is an insatiate and universal passion; since the enjoyment of almost every object that can afford pleasure to the different tastes and tempers of mankind, may be procured by the possession of wealth. In the pillage of Rome, a just preference was given to gold and jewels, which contain the greatest value in the smallest compass and weight: but, after these portable riches had been removed by the more diligent robbers, the palaces of Rome were rudely stripped of their splendid and costly furniture. The sideboards of massy plate, and the variegated wardrobes of silk and purple, were irregularly piled in the waggons, that always followed the march of a Gothic army. The most exquisite works of art were roughly handled, or wantonly destroyed; many a statue was melted for the sake of the precious materials; and many a vase, in the division of the spoil, was shivered into fragments by the stroke of a battle-axe. The ac-

with remarkable accuracy; and after admitting that there cannot be any crime, where there is no consent, he adds, Sed quia non solum quod ad dolorem, verum etiam quod ad libidinem, pertinet, in corpore alieno perpetrari potest; quicquid tale factum fuerit, etsi retentam constantissimo animo pudicitiam non excutit, pudorem tamen incutit, ne credatur factum cum mentis etiam voluntate, quod fieri fortasse sine carnis aliquâ voluptate non potuit. In c. 18, he makes some curious distinctions between moral and physical virginity.

quisition of riches served only to stimulate the avarice of the rapacious barbarians, who, proceeded, by threats, by blows, and by tortures, to force from their prisoners the confession of hidden treasure.[m] Visible splendour and expence were alleged as the proof of a plentiful fortune: the appearance of poverty was imputed to a parsimonious disposition; and the obstinacy of some misers, who endured the most cruel torments before they would discover the secret object of their affection, was fatal to many unhappy wretches, who expired under the lash, for refusing to reveal their imaginary treasures. The edifices of Rome, though the damage has been much exaggerated, received some injury from the violence of the Goths. At their entrance through the Salarian gate, they fired the adjacent houses to guide their march, and to distract the attention of the citizens: the flames which encountered no obstacle in the disorder of the night, consumed many private and public buildings; and the ruins of the palace of Sallust[n] remained, in the age of Justinian, a stately monument of the Gothic

[m] Marcella, a Roman lady, equally respectable for her rank, her age, and her piety, was thrown on the ground, and cruelly beaten and whipped, cæsam fustibus flagellisque, &c. Jerom. tom. i, p. 121, ad Principiam. See Augustin, de Civ. Dei, l. i, c. 10. The modern Sacco di Roma, p. 208, gives an idea of the various methods of torturing prisoners for gold.

[n] The historian Sallust, who usually practised the vices which he has so eloquently censured, employed the plunder of Numidia to adorn his palace and gardens on the Quirinal hill. The spot where the house stood, is now marked by the church of St. Susanna, separated only by a street from the baths of Diocletian, and not far distant from the Salarian gate. See Nardini, Roma Antica, p. 192, 193, and the great Plan of Modern Rome, by Nolli.

conflagration.[o] Yet a contemporary historian has observed, that fire could scarcely consume the enormous beams of solid brass, and that the strength of man was insufficient to subvert the foundations of ancient structures. Some truth may possibly be concealed in his devout assertion, that the wrath of Heaven supplied the imperfections of hostile rage; and that the proud Forum of Rome, decorated with the statues of so many gods and heroes, was levelled in the dust by the stroke of lightning.[p]

Captives
and fugi-
tives.
Whatever might be the numbers of equestrian, or plebeian rank, who perished in the massacre of Rome, it is confidently affirmed, that only one senator lost his life by the sword of the enemy.[q] But it was not easy to compute the

[o] The expressions of Procopius are distinct and moderate, (de Bell. Vandal. l. i, c. 2). The Chronicle of Marcellinus speaks too strong, partem urbis Romæ cremavit; and the words of Philostorgius, (εν ερειπιοις δε τας πολεως κειμενης, l. xii, c. 3), convey a false and exaggerated idea. Bargæus has composed a particular dissertation, (see tom. iv, Antiquit. Rom. Græv.) to prove that the edifices of Rome were not subverted by the Goths and Vandals.

[p] Orosius, l. ii, c. 19, p. 143. He speaks as if he disapproved all statues; vel Deum vel hominem mentiuntur. They consisted of the kings of Alba and Rome from Æneas, the Romans, illustrious either in arms or arts, and the deified Cæsars. The expression which he uses of Forum is somewhat ambiguous, since there existed five principal Fora; but as they were all contiguous and adjacent, in the plain which is surrounded by the Capitoline, the Quirinal, the Esquiline, and the Palatine hills, they might fairly be considered as one. See the Roma Antiqua of Donatus, p. 162-201, and the Roma Antica of Nardini, p. 212-273. The former is more useful for the ancient descriptions, the latter for the actual topography.

[q] Orosius (l. ii, c. 19, p. 142) compares the cruelty of the Gauls and the clemency of the Goths. Ibi vix quemquam inventum senatorem, qui vel absens evaserit; hic vix quemquam requiri, qui forte ut latens perierit. But there is an air of rhetoric, and perhaps of falsehood, in this antithesis; and Socrates (l. vii, c. 10) affirms, perhaps by an opposite exaggeration, that many senators were put to death with various and exquisite tortures.

multitudes, who, from an honourable station, and a prosperous fortune, were suddenly reduced to the miserable condition of captives and exiles. As the barbarians had more occasion for money than for slaves, they fixed, at a moderate price, the redemption of their indignant prisoners; and the ransom was often paid by the benevolence of their friends, or the charity of strangers.[r] The captives who were regularly sold, either in open market, or by private contract, would have legally regained their native freedom, which it was impossible for a citizen to lose, or to alienate.[s] But as it was soon discovered, that the vindication of their liberty would endanger their lives; and that the Goths, unless they were tempted to sell, might be provoked to murder, their useless prisoners; the civil jurisprudence had been already qualified by a wise regulation, that they should be obliged to serve the moderate term of five years, till they had discharged by their labour the price of their redemption.[t] The nations who invaded the Roman empire, had driven before them, into Italy, whole troops of hungry and affrighted provincials, less apprehensive of servitude than of famine. The calamities of Rome and Italy dispersed the inhabitants to the most lonely, the most secure, the most distant places

[r] Multi . . . Christiani in captivitatem ducti sunt. Augustin. de Civ. Dei, l. i, c. 14; and the Christians experienced no peculiar hardships.

[s] See Heineccius, Antiquitat. Juris Roman. tom. i, p. 96.

[t] Appendix Cod. Theodos. xvi, in Sirmond. Opera, tom. i, p. 735. This edict was published the 11th of December, A. D. 408, and is more reasonable than properly belonged to the ministers of Honorius.

of refuge. While the Gothic cavalry spread terror and desolation along the sea-coast of Campania and Tuscany, the little island of Igilium, separated by a narrow channel from the Argentarian promontory, repulsed, or eluded, their hostile attempts; and at so small a distance from Rome, great numbers of citizens were securely concealed in the thick woods of that sequestered spot." The ample patrimonies, which many senatorian families possessed in Africa, invited them, if they had time, and prudence, to escape from the ruin of their country; and to embrace the shelter of that hospitable province. The most illustrious of these fugitives was the noble and pious Proba,[x] the widow of the prefect Petronius. After the

" Eminus Igilii sylvosa caeumina miror;
    Quem fraudare nefas laudis honore suæ
Hæc proprios nuper tutata est insula saltus;
    Sive loci ingenio, seu Domini genio.
Gurgite cum modico victricibus obstitit armis
    Tanquam longinquo dissociata mari.
Hæc multos laceræ suscepit ab urbe fugatos,
    Hic fessis posito certa timore salus.
Plurima terreno populaverat æquora bello,
    Contra naturam classe timendus eques
Unum, mira fides, vario discrimine portum!
    Tam prope Romanis, tam procul esse Getis.
                            Rutilius, in Itinerar. l. i, 325.

The island is now called Giglio. See Cluver. Ital. Antiq. l. ii, p. 502.

[x] As the adventures of Proba and her family are connected with the life of St. Augustin, they are diligently illustrated by Tillemont, Mem. Eccles. tom. xiii, p. 620-635. Sometime after their arrival in Africa, Demetrias took the veil, and made a vow of virginity; an event which was considered as of the highest importance to Rome and to the world. All the *Saints* wrote congratulatory letters to her; that of Jerom is still extant, (tom. i, p. 62-73, and Demetriad. de servandâ Virginitat.) and contains a mixture of absurd reasoning, spirited declamation, and curious facts, some of which relate to the siege and sack of Rome.

death of her husband, the most powerful subject of Rome, she had remained at the head of
the Anician family, and successively supplied,
from her private fortune, the expence of the
consulships of her three sons. When the city
was besieged and taken by the Goths, Proba
supported, with Christian resignation, the loss
of immense riches ; embarked in a small vessel,
from whence she beheld, at sea, the flames of
her burning palace, and fled with her daughter
Læta, and her grand-daughter, the celebrated
virgin, Demetrias, to the coast of Africa. The
benevolent profusion with which the matron
distributed the fruits, or the price, of her estates,
contributed to alleviate the misfortunes of exile
and captivity. But even the family of Proba
herself was not exempt from the rapacious oppression of Count Heraclian, who basely sold,
in matrimonial prostitution, the noblest maidens
of Rome, to the lust or avarice of the Syrian
merchants. The Italian fugitives were dispersed through the provinces, along the coast of
Egypt and Asia, as far as Constantinople and
Jerusalem ; and the village of Bethlem, the solitary residence of St. Jerom and his female
converts, was crowded with illustrious beggars
of either sex, and every age, who excited the
public compassion by the remembrance of their
past fortune.[y] This awful catastrophe of Rome
filled the astonished empire with grief and ter-
tor. So interesting a contrast of greatness and
ruin, disposed to the fond credulity of the people

---

[y] See the pathetic complaint of Jerom, (tom. v. p. 400), in his pre-
face to the second book of his Commentaries on the prophet Ezekiel.

to deplore, and even to exaggerate, the afflictions of the queen of cities. The clergy, who applied to recent events the lofty metaphors of oriental prophecy, were sometimes tempted to confound the destruction of the capital, and the dissolution of the globe.

Sack of
Rome by
the troops
of Charles
V.
There exists in human nature a strong propensity to depreciate the advantages, and to magnify the evils, of the present times. Yet, when the first emotions had subsided, and a fair estimate was made of the real damage, the more learned and judicious contemporaries were forced to confess, that infant Rome had formerly received more essential injury from the Gauls, than she had now sustained from the Goths in her declining age.[a] The experience of eleven centuries has enabled posterity to produce a much more singular parallel; and to affirm with confidence, that the ravages of the barbarians, whom Alaric had led from the banks of the Danube, were less destructive, than the hostilities exercised by the troops of Charles V, a catholic prince, who styled himself emperor of the Romans.[b] The Goths evacuated the

[a] Orosius, though with some theological partiality, states this comparison, l. ii, c. 19, p. 142; l. vii, c. 39, p. 575. But, in the history of the taking of Rome by the Gaul, every thing is uncertain, and perhaps fabulous. See Beaufort sur l'Incertitude, &c. de l'Histoire Romaine, p. 356; and Melot, in the Mem. de l'Academie des Inscript. tom. xv, p. 1-21.
[b] The reader who wishes to inform himself of the circumstances of this famous event, may peruse an admirable narrative in Dr. Robertson's History of Charles V, vol. ii, p. 283; or consult the Annali d'Italia of the learned Muratori, tom. xiv, p. 230-244, octavo edition. If he is desirous of examining the originals, he may have resource to the eighteenth book of the great, but unfinished, history of Guicciardini.
                                                                                But

city at the end of six days, but Rome remained above nine months in the possession of the imperialists; and every hour was stained by some atrocious act of cruelty, lust, and rapine. The authority of Alaric preserved some order and moderation among the ferocious multitude, which acknowledged him for their leader and king: but the constable of Bourbon had gloriously fallen in the attack of the walls; and the death of the general removed every restraint of discipline, from an army which consisted of three independent nations, the Italians, the Spaniards, and the Germans. In the beginning of the sixteenth century, the manners of Italy exhibited a remarkable scene of the depravity of mankind. They united the sanguinary crimes that prevail in an unsettled state of society, with the polished vices that spring from the abuse of art and luxury; and the loose adventurers, who had violated every prejudice of patriotism and superstition to assault the palace of the Roman pontiff, must deserve to be considered as the most profligate of the *Italians*. At the same era, the *Spaniards* were the terror both of the Old and New World: but their high-spirited valour was disgraced by gloomy pride, rapacious avarice, and unrelenting cruelty. Indefatigable in the pursuit of fame and riches, they had improved, by repeated practice, the

But the account which most truly deserves the name of authentic and original, is a little book, entitled, *Il Sacco di Roma*, composed, within less than a month after the assault of the city, by the *brother* of the historian Guicciardini, who appears to have been an able magistrate, and a dispassionate writer.

most exquisite and effectual methods of torturing their prisoners; many of the Castillians, who
pillaged Rome, were familiars of the holy inquisition; and some volunteers, perhaps, were
lately returned from the conquest of Mexico.
The *Germans* were less corrupt than the Italians, less cruel than the Spaniards; and the
rustic, or even savage, aspect of those *Tramon-
tane* warriors, often disguised a simple and merciful disposition. But they had imbibed, in
the first fervour of the reformation, the spirit,
as well as the principles, of Luther. It was
their favourite amusement to insult, or destroy,
the consecrated objects of catholic superstition;
they indulged, without pity or remorse, a devout hatred against the clergy of every denomination and degree, who form so considerable
a part of the inhabitants of modern Rome; and
their fanatic zeal might aspire to subvert the
throne of Antichrist, to purify, with blood and
fire, the abominations of the spiritual Babylon.[b]

Alaric eva-
cuates
Rome, and
ravages
Italy,
A. D. 410,
Aug. 29.
The retreat of the victorious Goths, who evacuated Rome on the sixth day,[c] might be the
result of prudence; but it was not surely the
effect of fear.[d] At the head of an army, encum-

[b] The furious spirit of Luther, the effect of temper and enthusiasm,
has been forcibly attacked, (Bossuet, Hist. des Variations des Eglises
Protestantes, livre i, p. 20-36), and feebly defended, (Seckendorf,
Comment. de Lutheranismo, especially l. i, No. 78, p. 120, and l. iii,
No. 122, p. 556).

[c] Marcellinus, in Chron. Orosius, (l. vii, c. 39, p. 575), asserts, that
he left Rome on the *third* day; but this difference is easily reconciled
by the successive motions of great bodies of troops.

[d] Socrates (l. vii, c. 10) pretends, without any colour of truth, or reason, that Alaric fled on the report, that the armies of the eastern empire
were in full march to attack him.

bered with rich and weighty spoils, their intrepid leader advanced along the Appian way into the southern provinces of Italy, destroying whatever dared to oppose his passage, and contenting himself with the plunder of the unresisting country. The fate of Capua, the proud and luxurious metropolis of Campania, and which was respected, even in its decay, as the eighth city of the empire,[a] is buried in oblivion; whilst the adjacent town of Nola[f] has been illustrated, on this occasion, by the sanctity of Paulinus,[g] who was successively a consul, a monk, and a bishop. At the age of forty, he renounced the enjoyment of wealth and honour, of society and literature, to embrace a life of solitude and penance; and the loud applause of the clergy encouraged him to despise the reproaches of his worldly friends, who ascribed this desperate act to some disorder of the mind, or body.[h] An early and passionate attachment determined him to fix his humble dwelling in

[a] Ausonius de Claris Urbibus, p. 233, edit. Toll. The luxury of Capua had formerly surpassed that of Sybaris itself. See ..... us Deipnosophist. l. xii, p. 528, edit. Casaubon.

[f] Forty-eight years before the foundation of Rome, (about 800 before the Christian era), the Tuscans built Capua and Nola, at the distance of twenty-three miles from each other; but the latter of the ... never emerged from a state of mediocrity.

[g] Tillemont (Mem. Eccles. tom. xiv, p. 1-146) has compiled, with his usual diligence, all that relates to the life and writings of Paulinus, whose retreat is celebrated by his own pen, and by the praises of St. Ambrose, St. Jerom, St. Augustin, Sulpicius Severus, &c. his Christian friends and contemporaries.

[h] See the affectionate letters of Ausonius (epist, xix-xxv, p. 650-698, edit. Toll.) to his colleague, his friend, and his disciple, Paulinus. The religion of Ausonius is still a problem, (see ... de l'Academie des Inscriptions, tom. xv, p. 123-138). I believe ... was such in his own time, and consequently, that in his heart he was a pagan.

one of the suburbs of Nola, near the miraculous tomb of St. Fælix, which the public
devotion had already surrounded with five
large and populous churches. The remains
of his fortune, and of his understanding, were
dedicated to the service of the glorious martyr; whose praise, on the day of his festival, Paulinus never failed to celebrate by a
solemn hymn; and in whose name he erected a
sixth church, of superior elegance and beauty,
which was decorated with many curious pictures,
from the History of the old and New Testament.
Such assiduous zeal secured the favour of the
saint,[1] or at least of the people; and, after
fifteen years retirement, the Roman consul was
compelled to accept the bishopric of Nola, a
few months before the city was invested by the
Goths. During the siege, some religious persons were satisfied that they had seen, either in
dreams or visions, the divine form of their tutelar patron; yet it soon appeared by the event,
that Fælix wanted power, or inclination, to preserve the flock, of which he had formerly been
the shepherd. Nola was not saved from the
general devastation;[k] and the captive bishop
was protected only by the general opinion of
his innocence and poverty. About four years
elapsed from the successful invasion of Italy by
the arms of Alaric, to the voluntrary retreat of

[1] The humble Paulinus once presumed to say, that he believed St.
Fælix would love him; at least, as a master loves his little dog.
     Jornandes, de Reb. Get. c. 30, p. 653. Philostorgius, l. xii,
c. — Augustin, de Civ. Dei, l. i, c. 10. Baronius, Annal. Eccles.
A. D. 410, No. 45, 46.

the Goths under the conduct of his successor
Adolphus; and, during the whole time, they
reigned without controul over a country, which,
in the opinion of the ancients, had united all the
various excellencies of nature and art. The prosperity, indeed, which Italy had attained in the
auspicious age of the Antonines, had gradually
declined with the decline of the empire. The
fruits of a long peace perished under the rude
grasp of the barbarians; and they themselves
were incapable of tasting the more elegant refinement of luxury, which had been prepared
for the use of the soft and polished Italians.
Each soldier, however, claimed an ample portion of the substantial plenty, the corn and cattle, oil and wine, that was daily collected, and
consumed, in the Gothic camp; and the principal warriors insulted the villas, and gardens,
once inhabited by Lucullus and Cicero, along
the beauteous coast of Campania. Their trembling captives, the sons and daughters of Roman senators, presented, in goblets of gold and
gems, large draughts of Falernian wine, to the
haughty victors; who stretched their huge
limbs under the shade of plane-trees,[1] artificially
disposed to exclude the scorching rays, and to
admit the genial warmth, of the sun. There

---

[1] The *platanus*, or plane-tree, was a favourite of the ancients; by
whom it was propagated, for the sake of shade, from the East to Gaul.
Pliny, Hist. Natur. xii, 3, 4, 5. He mentions several of an enormous
size; one in the imperial villa at Velitræ, which Caligula called his
nest, as the branches were capable of holding a large table, the upper
attendants, and the emperor himself, whom Pliny quaintly styled *umbra*; an expression which might, with equal reason, be applied to
Alaric.

CHAP.
XXXI.

delights were enhanced by the memory of past hardships; the comparison of their native soil, the bleak and barren hills of Scythia, and the frozen banks of the Elbe, and Danube, added new charms to the felicity of the Italian climate.[m]

Death of
Alaric,
A. D. 410.

Whether fame, or conquest, or riches, were the object of Alaric, he pursued that object with an indefatigable ardour, which could neither be quelled by adversity, nor satiated by success. No sooner had he reached the extreme land of Italy, than he was attracted by the neighbouring prospect of a fertile and peaceful island. Yet even the possession of Sicily he considered only as an intermediate step to the important expedition, which he already meditated against the continent of Africa. The straits of Rhegium and Messina[n] are twelve miles in length, and, in the narrowest passage, about one mile and a half broad; and the fabulous monsters of the deep, the rocks of Scylla, and the whirlpool of Charybdis could terrify none but the most timid and unskilful mariners. Yet as

[m] The prostrate South to the destroyer yields
    Her boasted titles, and her golden fields:
    With grim delight the brood of winter view
    A brighter day, and skies of azure hue;
    Scent the new fragrance of the opening rose,
    And quaff the pendant vintage as it grows.

See Gray's Poems, published by Mr. Mason, p. 197. Instead of compiling tables of chronology and natural history, why did not Mr. Gray apply the powers of his genius to finish the philosophic poem, of which he has left such an exquisite specimen?

[n] For the perfect description of the Straits of Messina, Scylla, Charybdis, &c. see Cluverius, (Ital. Antiq. l. iv, p. 1293), and Sicilia Antiq. l. i, p. 60-76), who had diligently studied the ancients, and surveyed with a curious eye the actual face of the country.

soon as the first division of the Goths had embarked, a sudden tempest arose, which sunk, or scattered, many of the transports; their courage was daunted by the terrors of a new element; and the whole design was defeated by the premature death of Alaric, which fixed, after a short illness, the fatal term of his conquests. The ferocious character of the barbarians was displayed, in the funeral of a hero, whose valour, and fortune, they celebrated with mournful applause. By the labour of a captive multitude, they forcibly diverted the course of the Busentinus, a small river that washes the walls of Consentia. The royal sepulchre, adorned with the splendid spoils, and trophies, of Rome, was constructed in the vacant bed; the waters were then restored to their natural channel; and the secret spot, where the remains of Alaric had been deposited, was for ever concealed by the inhuman massacre of the prisoners, who had been employed to execute the work.[o]

The personal animosities, and hereditary feuds of the barbarians, were suspended by the strong necessity of their affairs; and the brave Adolphus, the brother-in-law of the deceased monarch, was unanimously elected to succeed to his throne. The character and political system of the new king of the Goths, may be best understood from his own conversation with an illustrious citizen of Narbonne; who afterwards, in a pilgrimage to the Holy Land, related it to

Adolphus king of the Goths, concludes a peace with the empire, and marches into Gaul, A. D. 412.

[o] Jornandes, de Reb. Get. c. 30, p. 654.

CHAP.
XXXI.

St. Jerom, in the presence of the historian Oro
sius. "In the full confidence of valour and
" victory, I once aspired (said Adolphus) to
" change the face of the universe; to obliterate
" the name of Rome; to erect on its ruins the
" dominion of the Goths; and to acquire, like
" Augustus, the immortal fame of the founder
" of a new empire. By repeated experiments,
" I was gradually convinced, that laws are
" essentially necessary to maintain and regu-
" late a well-constituted state; and that the
" fierce untractable humour of the Goths was
" incapable of bearing the salutary yoke of
" laws, and civil government. From that mo-
" ment I proposed to myself a different object
" of glory and ambition; and it is now my sin
" cere wish, that the gratitude of future ages
" should acknowledge the merit of a stranger,
" who employed the sword of the Goths, not to
" subvert, but to restore and maintain, the pros-
" perity of the Roman empire."[p] With these
pacific views, the successor of Alaric suspended
the operations of war; and seriously negotiated
with the imperial court a treaty of friendship
and alliance. It was the interest of the ministers of Honorius, who were now released from
the obligation of their extravagant oath, to deliver Italy from the intolerable weight of the
Gothic powers; and they readily accepted their
service against the tyrants and barbarians who

[p] Orosius l. vii, c. 43, p. 584, 585. He was sent by St. Augustin, in
the year 415, from Africa to Palestine, to visit St. Jerom, and to consult with him on the subject of the Pelagian controversy.

infested the provinces beyond the Alps.[q] Adolphus, assuming the character of a Roman general, directed his march from the extremity of Campania to the southern provinces of Gaul. His troops, either by force or agreement, immediately occupied the cities of Narbonne, Thoulouse, and Bourdeaux; and though they were repulsed by Count Boniface from the walls of Marseilles, they soon extended their quarters from the Mediterranean to the Ocean. The oppressed provincials might exclaim, that the miserable remnant, which the enemy had spared, was cruelly ravished by their pretended allies; yet some specious colours were not wanting to palliate, or justify, the violence of the Goths. The cities of Gaul, which they attacked, might perhaps be considered as in a state of rebellion against the government of Honorius; the articles of the treaty, or the secret instructions of the court, might sometimes be alleged in favour of the seeming usurpations of Adolphus; and the guilt of any irregular, unsuccessful, act of hostility, might always be imputed, with an appearance of truth, to the ungovernable spirit of a barbarian host, impatient of peace or discipline. The luxury of Italy had been less effectual to soften the temper, than to relax the courage, of the Goths; and

[q] Jornandes supposes, without much probability, that Adolphus visited and plundered Rome a second time, (more cocustarum erasit). Yet he agrees with Orosius in suppposing, that a treaty of peace was concluded between the Gothic prince and Honorius. See Oros. l. vii, c. 43, p. 581, 585. Jornandes, de Reb. Geticis, c. 31, p. 654, 655.

CHAP.
XXXI.

His mar-
riage with
Placidia,
A. D. 414.

they had imbibed the vices, without imitating the arts and institutions, of civilized society.[r]

The professions of Adolphus were probably sincere, and his attachment to the cause of the republic was secured by the ascendant which a Roman princess had acquired over the heart and understanding of the barbarian king. Placidia,[s] the daughter of the great Theodosius, and of Galla, his second wife, had received a royal education in the palace of Constantinople; but the eventful story of her life is connected with the revolutions which agitated the western empire under the reign of her brother Honorius. When Rome was first invested by the arms of Alaric, Placidia, who was then about twenty years of age, resided in the city; and her ready consent to the death of her cousin Serena has a cruel and ungrateful appearance, which, according to the circumstances of the action, may be aggravated, or excused, by the consideration of her tender age.[t] The victorious barbarians detained, either as a hostage or a captive,[u] the sister of Honorius; but, while she was disposed to the disgrace of following round Italy the motions of a Gothic camp, she experienced,

[r] The retreat of the Goths from Italy, and their first transactions in Gaul, are dark and doubtful. I have derived much assistance from Mascou, (Hist. of the ancient Germans, l. viii, c. 29, 35, 36, 37), who has illustrated, and connected, the broken chronicles and fragments of the times.

[s] See an account of Placidia in Ducange, Fam. Byzant. p. 72; and Tillemont, Hist. des Empereurs, tom. v, p. 260, 386, &c. tom. vi, p. 240.

[t] Zosim. l. v, p. 350.

[u] Zosim. l. vi, p. 383. Orosius (l. vii, c. 40, p. 576), and the Chronicles of Marcellinus and Idatius, seem to suppose, that the Goths did not carry away Placidia till after the last siege of Rome.

however, a decent and respectful treatment. The authority of Jornandes, who praises the beauty of Placidia, may perhaps be counterbalanced by the silence, the expressive silence, of her flatterers; yet the splendour of her birth, the bloom of youth, the elegance of manners, and the dexterous insinuation which she condescended to employ, made a deep impression on the mind of Adolphus; and the Gothic king aspired to call himself the brother of the emperor. The ministers of Honorius rejected with disdain the proposal of an alliance, so injurious to every sentiment of Roman pride; and repeatedly urged the restitution of Placidia, as an indispensable condition of the treaty of peace. But the daughter of Theodosius submitted, without reluctance, to the desires of the conqueror, a young and valiant prince, who yielded to Alaric in loftiness of stature, but who excelled in the more attractive qualities of grace and beauty. The marriage of Adolphus and Placidia[x] was consummated before the Goths retired from Italy; and the solemn, perhaps the anniversary, day of their nuptials was afterwards celebrated in the house of Ingenuus, one of the most illustrious citizens of Narbonne in Gaul. The bride, attired and adorned like a

[x] See the pictures of Adolphus and Placidia, and the account of their marriage in Jornandes, de Reb. Geticis, c. 31, p. 654, 655. With regard to the place where the nuptials were stipulated, or consummated, or celebrated, the mss. of Jornandes vary between two neighbouring cities, Forli and Imola, (Forum Livii and Forum Cornelii). It is fair and easy to reconcile the Gothic historian with Olympiodorus, (see Mascon, l. viii, c. 46): but Tillemont grows peevish, and swears, that it is not worth while to try to conciliate Jornandes with any good authors.

Roman empress, was placed on a throne of state; and the king of the Goths, who assumed, on this occasion, the Roman habit, contented himself with a less honourable seat by her side. The nuptial gift, which, according to the custom of his nation,[7] was offered to Placidia, consisted of the rare and magnificent spoils of her country. Fifty beautiful youths, in silken robes, carried a basin in each hand; and one of these basins was filled with pieces of gold, the other with precious stones of an inestimable value. Attalus, so long the sport of fortune, and of the Goths, was appointed to lead the chorus of the Hymeneal song; and the degraded emperor might aspire to the praise of a skilful musician. The barbarians enjoyed the insolence of their triumph; and the provincials rejoiced in this alliance, which tempered, by the mild influence of love and reason, the fierce spirit of their Gothic lord.[a]

The Gothic treasures

The hundred basins of gold and gems, presented to Placidia at her nuptial feast, formed an inconsiderable portion of the Gothic trea-

[7] The Visigoths (the subjects of Adolphus) restrained, by subsequent laws, the prodigality of conjugal love. It was illegal for a husband to make any gift or settlement for the benefit of his wife during the first year of their marriage; and his liberality could not at any time exceed the tenth part of his property. The Lombards were somewhat more indulgent: they allowed the *morgingcap* immediately after the wedding night; and this famous gift, the reward of virginity, might equal the fourth part of the husband's substance. Some cautious maidens, indeed, were wise enough to stipulate beforehand a present, which they were too sure of not deserving. See Montesquieu, Espirit des Loix, l. xix, c. 25. Muratori, delle Antichità Italiane. tom. i; Dissertazion xx, p. 243:

[a] We owe the curious detail of this nuptial feast to the historian Olympiodorus, ap. Photium, p. 185-186.

sures; of which some extraordinary specimens may be selected from the history of the successors of Adolphus. Many curious and costly ornaments of pure gold, enriched with jewels, were found in their palace of Narbonne, when it was pillaged, in the sixth century, by the Franks: sixty cups, or chalices; fifteen *patens*, or plates, for the use of the communion; twenty boxes, or cases, to hold the books of the gospels: this consecrated wealth* was distributed by the son of Clovis among the churches of his dominions, and his pious liberality seems to upbraid some former sacrilege of the Goths. They possessed, with more security of conscience, the famous *missorium*, or great dish for the service of the table, of massy gold, of the weight of five hundred pounds, and of far superior value, from the precious stones, the exquisite workmanship, and the tradition that it had been presented by Ætius the patrician, to Torismond king of the Goths. One of the successors of Torismond purchased the aid of the French monarch by the promise of this magnificent gift. When he was seated on the throne of Spain, he delivered it with reluctance to the ambassadors of Dagobert; despoiled them on the road; stipulated, after a long negotiation, the inadequate ransom of two hundred thousand pieces of gold; and preserved the *misso-*

* See in the great collection of the historians of France by Dom. Bouquet, tom. ii, Greg. Turonens, l. iii, c. 10, p. 191. Gesta Regum Francorum, c. 23, p. 567. The anonymous writer, with an ignorance worthy of his times, supposes that these instruments of Christian worship had belonged to the temple of Solomon. If he has any meaning, it must be, that they were found in the sack of Rome.

CHAP.
XXXI.

rium, as the pride of the Gothic treasur
When that treasury, after the conquest of Spain,
was plundered by the Arabs, they admired, and
they have celebrated, another object still more
remarkable; a table of considerable size, of one
single piece of solid emerald,* encircled with
three rows of fine pearls, supported by three
hundred and sixty-five feet of gems and massy
gold, and estimated at the price of five hundred
thousand pieces of gold.* Some portion of the
Gothic treasures might be the gift of friendship,
or the tribute of obedience: but the far greater
part had been the fruits of war and rapine, the
spoils of the empire, and perhaps of Rome.

Laws for
the relief
of Italy
and Rome,
A. D. 410-
417.

After the deliverance of Italy from the oppression of the Goths, some secret counsellor was
permitted, amidst the factions of the palace, to
heal the wounds of that afflicted country.* By a

* Consult the following original testimonies in the Historians of
France, tom. ii. Fredegarii Scholastici Chron. c. 73, p. 441. Frede-
gar. Fragment. iii, p. 463. Gesta Regis Dagobert c. 29, p. 587. The
accession of Sisenand, to the throne of Spain, happened A. D. 631. The
200,000 pieces of gold were appropriated by Dagobert to the foundation of the church of St. Denys.

c The president Goguet (Origine des Loix, &c. tom. ii, p. 239) is of
opinion, that the stupendous pieces of emerald, the statues, and columns, which antiquity has placed in Egypt, at Gades, at Constantinople, were in reality artificial compositions of coloured glass. The famous emerald dish, which is shewn at Genoa, is supposed to countenance
the suspicion.

d Elmacin. Hist. Saracenica, l. i, p. 85. Roderic. Tolet. Hist. Arab.
c. 9. Cardonne, Hist. de l'Afrique et de l'Espagne sons les Arabes, tom.
i, p. 83. It was called the table of Solomon, according to the custom
of the orientals, who ascribe to that prince every ancient work of knowledge and magnificence.

e His three laws are inserted in the Theodosian Code, l. xi, tit. xxviii,
leg. 7; l. xiii, tit. xi, leg. 12; l. xv, tit. xiv, leg. 14. The expressions
of the last are very remarkable; since they contain not only a pardon,
but an apology.

wise and humane regulation, the eight provinces which had been the most deeply injured, Campania, Tuscany, Picenum, Samnium, Apulia, Calabria, Bruttium, and Lucania, obtained an indulgence of five years: the ordinary tribute was reduced to one-fifth, and even that fifth was destined to restore, and support, the useful institution of the public posts. By another law, the lands, which had been left without inhabitants or cultivation, were granted, with some diminution of taxes, to the neighbours who should occupy, or the strangers who should solicit them: and the new possessors were secured against the future claims of the fugitive proprietors. About the same time a general amnesty was published in the name of Honorius, to abolish the guilt and memory of all the *involuntary* offences, which had been committed by his unhappy subjects, during the term of the public disorder and calamity. A decent and respectful attention was paid to the restoration of the capital; the citizens were encouraged to rebuild the edifices which had been destroyed or damaged by hostile fire; and extraordinary supplies of corn were imported from the coast of Africa. The crowds that so lately fled before the sword of the barbarians, were soon recalled by the hopes of plenty and pleasure; and Albinus, prefect of Rome, informed the court, with some anxiety and surprise, that, in a single day, he had taken an account of the arrival of fourteen thousand strangers.[f] In less than

---

[f] Olympiodorus, ap. Phot. p. 188. Philostorgius (l. xii, c. 5) observes.

CHAP.
XXXI.
seven years, the vestiges of the Gothic invasion
were almost obliterated ; and the city appeared
to resume its former splendour and tranquillity. The venerable matron replaced her crown
of laurel, which had been ruffled by the storms
of war : and was still amused, in the last moment of her decay, with the prophecies of revenge, of victory, and of eternal dominion.[e]

Revolt
and de-
feat of He-
raclian,
count of
Africa,
A. D. 413.
This apparent tranquillity was soon disturbed by the approach of an hostile armament from
the country which afforded the daily subsistence of the Roman people. Heraclian, count
of Africa, who, under the most difficult and
distressful circumstances, had supported, with
active loyalty, the cause of Honorius, was tempted, in the year of his consulship, to assume the
character of a rebel, and the title of emperor.
The ports of Africa were immediately filled
with the naval forces, at the head of which he
prepared to invade Italy : and his fleet, when
it cast anchor at the mouth of the Tiber, indeed
surpassed the fleets of Xerxes and Alexander,
if *all* the vessels, including the royal galley,
and the smallest boat, did actually amount to

serves, that when Honorius made his triumphal entry, he encouraged
the Romans with his hand and voice, (χειρι και γλωττη), to rebuild their
city; and the Chronicle of Prosper commends Heraclian, qui in Romanæ
urbis reparationem strenuum exhibuerat ministerium.

   [e] The date of the voyage of Claudius Rutilius Numatianus, is
clogged with some difficulties ; but Scaliger has deduced, from astro-
nomical characters, that he left Rome the 24th of September, and
embarked at Porto the 9th of October, A. D. 416. See Tillemont,
Hist. des Empereurs, tom. v, p. 820. In this poetical Itinerary,
Rutilius (l. i, 115, &c.) addresses Rome in a high strain of congratu-
lation.—

      Erige crinales lauros, seniumque sacrati
      Verticis in virides Roma recinge comas, &c.

the incredible number of three thousand two hundred.[h] Yet with such an armament, which might have subverted, or restored, the greatest empire of the earth, the African usurper made a very faint and feeble impression on the provinces of his rival. As he marched from the port, along the road which leads to the gates of Rome, he was encountered, terrified, and routed, by one of the imperial captains; and the lord of this mighty host, deserting his fortune and his friends, ignominiously fled with a single ship.[i] When Heraclian landed in the harbour of Carthage, he found that the whole province, disdaining such an unworthy ruler, had returned to their allegiance. The rebel was beheaded in the ancient temple of Memory; his consulship was abolished;[k] and the remains of his private fortune, not exceeding the moderate sum of four thousand pounds of gold, were granted to the brave Constantius, who had already defended the throne, which he afterwards shared with his feeble sovereign. Honorius viewed, with supine indifference, the calamities

---

[h] Orosius composed his history in Africa, only two years after the events; yet his authority seems to be overbalanced by the improbability of the fact. The Chronicle of Marcellinus gives Heraclian 700 ships and 3000 men; the latter of these numbers is ridiculously corrupt; but the former would please me very much.

[i] The Chronicle of Idatius affirms, without the least appearance of truth, that he advanced as far as Otriculum, in Umbria, where he was overthrown in a great battle, with the loss of fifty thousand men.

[k] See Cod. Theod. l. xv, tit. xiv, leg. 13 The legal acts performed in his name, even the manumission of slaves, were declared invalid, till they had been formally repealed.

of Rome and Italy;[l] but the rebellious attempts of Attalus and Heraclian, against his personal safety, awakened, for a moment, the torpid instinct of his nature. He was probably ignorant of the causes and events which preserved him from these impending dangers; and as Italy was no longer invaded by any foreign or domestic enemies, he peaceably existed in the palace of Ravenna, while the tyrants beyond the Alps were repeatedly vanquished in the name, and by the lieutenants, of the son of Theodosius.[m] In the course of a busy and interesting narrative, I might possibly forget to mention the death of such a prince: and I shall therefore take the precaution of observing, in this place, that he survived the last siege of Rome about thirteen years.

Revolutions of Gaul and Spain, A. D. 409. 413.
The usurpation of Constantine, who received the purple from the legions of Britain, had been successful; and seemed to be secure. His title was acknowledged, from the wall of Antoninus to the columns of Hercules; and, in the midst of the public disorder, he shared the dominion, and the plunder, of Gaul and Spain, with the

[l] I have disdained to mention a very foolish, and probably a false, report, (Procop. de Bell. Vandal. l. i, c. 2), that Honorius was alarmed by the *loss* of Rome, till he understood that it was not a favourite chicken of that name, but only the capital of the world, which had been lost. Yet even this story is some evidence of the public opinion.

[m] The materials for the lives of all these tyrants are taken from six contemporary historians, two Latins, and four Greeks: Orosius, l. vii, c. 42, p. 581, 582, 583; Renatus Profuturus Frigeridus, apud Gregor. Turon. l. ii, c. 9, in the historians of France, tom. ii, p. 165, 166; Zosimus, l. vi, p. 370, 371; Olympiodorus, apud Phot. p. 180, 181, 184, 185; Sozomen, l. ix, c. 12, 13, 14, 15; and Philostorgius, l. xi, c. 5, 6, with Godefroy's Dissertations, p. 447-481; besides the four Chronicles of Prosper Tyro, Prosper of Aquitain, Idatius, and Marcellinus.

tribes of barbarians, whose destructive progress was no longer checked by the Rhine or Pyrenees. Stained with the blood of the kinsmen of Honorius, he extorted, from the court of Ravenna, with which he secretly corresponded, the ratification of his rebellious claims. Constantine engaged himself, by a solemn promise, to deliver Italy from the Goths; advanced as far as the banks of the Po; and after alarming, rather than assisting, his pusillanimous ally, hastily returned to the palace of Arles, to celebrate, with intemperate luxury, his vain and ostentatious triumph. But this transient prosperity was soon interrupted and destroyed by the revolt of Count Gerontius, the bravest of his generals; who, during the absence of his son Constans, a prince already invested with the imperial purple, had been left to command in the provinces of Spain. For some reason, of which we are ignorant, Gerontius, instead of assuming the diadem, placed it on the head of his friend Maximus, who fixed his residence at Tarragona, while the active count pressed forwards, through the Pyrenees, to surprise the two emperors, Constantine and Constans, before they could prepare for their defence The son was made prisoner at Vienna, and immediately put to death; and the unfortunate youth had scarcely leisure to deplore the elevation of his family; which had tempted, or compelled, him sacrilegiously to desert the peaceful obscurity of the monastic life. The father maintained a siege within the walls of Arles; but those walls must have yielded to

the assailants, had not the city been unexpectedly relieved by the approach of an Italian
army. The name of Honorius, the proclamation
of a lawful emperor, astonished the contending
parties of the rebels. Gerontius, abandoned
by his own troops, escaped to the confines of
Spain; and rescued his name from oblivion, by
the Roman courage which appeared to animate
the last moments of his life. In the middle of
the night, a great body of his perfidious soldiers
surrounded, and attacked, his house, which he
had strongly barricaded. His wife, a valiant
friend of the nation of the Alani, and some faithful slaves, were still attached to his person; and
he used, with so much skill and resolution, a
large magazine of darts and arrows, that above
three hundred of the assailants lost their lives in
the attempt. His slaves, when all the missile
weapons were spent, fled at the dawn of day;
and Gerontius, if he had not been restrained by
conjugal tenderness, might have imitated their
example; till the soldiers provoked by such
obstinate resistance, applied fire on all sides to
the house. In this fatal extremity, he complied
with the request of his barbarian friend, and
cut off his head. The wife of Gerontius, who
conjured him not to abandon her to a life of
misery and disgrace, eagerly presented her
neck to his sword; and the tragic scene was
terminated by the death of the count himself,
who, after three ineffectual strokes, drew a short
dagger, and sheathed it in his heart." The un-

* The praises which Sozomen has bestowed on this act of despair,
appear

protected Maximus, whom he had invested
with the purple, was indebted for his life to
the contempt that was entertained of his power
and abilities. The caprice of the barbarians,
who ravaged Spain, once more seated, this
imperial phantom on the throne: but they soon
resigned him to the justice of Honorius; and
the tyrant Maximus, after he had been shewn to
the people of Ravenna and Rome, was publicly
executed.

The general, Constantius was his name, who
raised by his approach the siege of Arles, and
dissipated the troops of Gerontius, was born
a Roman: and this remarkable distinction is
strongly expressive of the decay of military spirit
among the subjects of the empire. The strength
and majesty which were conspicuous in the person of that general, [o] marked him, in the popular opinion, as a candidate worthy of the throne,
which he afterwards ascended. In the familiar
intercourse of private life, his manners were
cheerful and engaging: nor would he sometimes
disdain, in the license of convivial mirth, to vie
with the pantomimes themselves, in the exercises
of their ridiculous profession. But when the
trumpet summoned him to arms; when he
mounted his horse, and, bending down (for such

Character and victories of the general Constantius.

appear strange and scandalous in the mouth of an ecclesiastical historian. He observes, (p. 379), that the wife of Gerontius was a
Christian; and that her death was worthy of her religion and of immortal fame.

[o] Ειδος αξιον τυραννιδος, is the expression of Olympiodorus, which he
seems to have borrowed from Æolus, a tragedy of Euripides, of which
some fragments only are now extant, (Euripid. Barnes, tom. ii, p. 443,
ver. 38). This allusion may prove, that the ancient tragic poets were
still familiar to the Greeks of the fifth century.

CHAP
XXXI.
was his singular practice) almost upon the neck, fiercely rolled his large animated eyes round the field, Constantius then struck terror into his foes, and inspired his soldiers with the assurance of victory. He had received from the court of Ravenna the important commission of extirpating rebellion in the provinces of the West; and the pretended emperor, Constantine, after enjoying a short and anxious respite, was again besieged in his capital by the arms of a more formidable enemy. Yet this interval allowed time for a successful negotiation with the Franks and Alemanni; and his ambassador, Edobic, soon returned, at the head of an army, to disturb the operations of the siege of Arles. The Roman general, instead of expecting the attack in his lines, boldly, and perhaps wisely, resolved to pass the Rhone, and to meet the barbarians. His measures were conducted with so much skill and secrecy, that, while they engaged the infantry of Constantius in the front, they were suddenly attacked, surrounded, and destroyed by the cavalry of his lieutenant Ulphilas, who had silently gained an advantageous post in their rear. The remains of the army of Edobic were preserved by flight or submission, and their leader escaped from the field of battle to the house of a faithless friend; who too clearly understood, that the head of his obnoxious guest would be an acceptable and lucrative present to the imperial general. On this occasion, Constantius behaved with the magnanimity of a genuine Roman. Subduing, or suppressing,

every sentiment of jealousy, he publicly acknowledged the merit and services of Ulphilas: but he turned with horror from the assassin of Edobic; and sternly intimated his commands, that the camp should no longer be polluted by the presence of an ungrateful wretch, who had violated the laws of friendship and hospitality. The usurper, who beheld, from the walls Arles, the ruin of his last hopes, was tempted to place some confidence in so generous a conqueror. He required a solemn promise for his security; and after receiving, by the imposition of hands, the sacred character of a Christian presbyter, he ventured to open the gates of the city. But he soon experienced, that the principles of honour and integrity, which might regulate the ordinary conduct of Constantius, were superseded by the loose doctrines of political morality. The Roman general, indeed, refused to sully his laurels with the blood of Constantine; but the abdicated emperor, and his son Julian, were sent under a strong guard into Italy; and before they reached the palace of Ravenna, they met the ministers of death.

Death of the usurper Constantine, A. D. 411, Nov. 28.

At a time when it was universally confessed, that almost every man in the empire was superior in personal merit to the princes whom the accident of their birth had seated on the throne, a rapid succession of usurpers, regardless of the fate of their predecessors, still continued to arise. This mischief was peculiarly felt in the provinces of Spain and Gaul, where the principles of order and obedience had been extin-

Fall of the usurpers, Jovinus, Sebastian, and Attalus, A. D 411-416.

guished by war and rebellion. Before Constantine resigned the purple, and in the fourth month of the siege of Arles, intelligence was received in the imperial camp, that Jovinus had assumed the diadem at Mentz, in the Upper Germany, at the instigation of Goar, king of the Alani, and of Guntiarius, king of the Burgundians; and that the candidate, on whom they had bestowed the empire, advanced with a formidable host of barbarians, from the banks of the Rhine to those of the Rhone. Every circumstance is dark and extraordinary in the short history of the reign of Jovinus. It was natural to expect, that a brave and skilful general, at the head of a victorius army, would have asserted, in a field of battle, the justice of the cause of Honorius. The hasty retreat of Constantius might be justified by weighty reasons; but he resigned, without a struggle, the possession of Gaul : and Dardanus, the pretorian prefect, is recorded as the only magistrate who refused to yield obedience to the usurper.[p] When the Goths, two years after the siege of Rome, established their quarters in Gaul, it was natural to suppose that their inclination could be divided only between the emperor Honorius, with whom they had formed a recent alliance,

---

[p] Sidonius Apollinaris (l. v, epist. 9, p. 139, and Not. Sirmond, p. 58), after stigmatizing the *inconstancy* of Constantine, the *facility* of Jovinus, the *perfidity* of Gerontius, continues to observe, that *all* the vice of those tyrants were united in the person of Dardanus. Yet the prefect supported a respectable character in the world, and even in the church; held a devout correspondence with St. Augustin and St Jerom; and was complimented by the latter (tom. iii, p. 66) with the epithets of Christianorum Nobilissime, and Nobilium Christianissime.

and the degraded Attalus, whom they reserved in their camp for the occasional purpose of acting the part of a musician or a monarch. Yet in a moment of disgust, (for which it is not easy to assign a cause, or a date), Adolphus connected himself with the usurper of Gaul; and imposed on Attalus the ignominious task of negotiating the treaty, which ratified his own disgrace. We are again surprised to read, that, instead of considering the Gothic alliance as the firmest support of his throne, Jovinus upbraided, in dark and ambiguous language, the officious importunity of Attalus; that, scorning the advice of his great ally, he invested with the purple his brother Sebastian; and that he most imprudently accepted the service of Sarus, when that gallant chief, the soldier of Honorius, was provoked to desert the court of a prince, who knew not how to reward, or punish. Adolphus, educated among a race of warriors, who esteemed the duty of revenge as the most precious and sacred portion of their inheritance, advanced with a body of ten thousand Goths to encounter the hereditary enemy of the house of Balti. He attacked Sarus at an unguarded moment, when he was accompanied only by eighteen or twenty of his valiant followers. United by friendship, animated by despair, but at length oppressed by multitudes, this band of heroes deserved the esteem, without exciting the compassion, of their enemies; and the lion was no sooner taken in the toils,[q] than he was

[q] The expression may be understood almost literally; Olympiodorus says,

CHAP.
XXXI.

instantly despatched. The death of Sarus dissolved the loose alliance which Adolphus still maintained with the usurpers of Gaul. He again listened to the dictates of love and prudence; and soon satisfied the brother of Placidia, by the assurance that he would immediately transmit, to the palace of Ravenna, the heads of the two tyrants, Jovinus and Sebastian. The king of the Goths executed his promise without difficulty or delay: the helpless brothers, unsupported by any personal merit, were abandoned by their barbarian auxiliaries; and the short opposition of Valentia was expiated by the ruin of one of the noblest cities of Gaul. The emperor, chosen by the Roman senate, who had been promoted, degraded, insulted, restored, again degraded, and again insulted, was finally abandoned to his fate: but when the Gothic king withdrew his protection, he was restrained, by pity or contempt, from offering any violence to the person of Attalus. The unfortunate Attalus, who was left without subjects or allies, embarked in one of the ports of Spain, in search of some secure and solitary retreat; but he was intercepted at sea, conducted to the presence of Honorius, led in triumph through the streets of Rome or Ravenna, and publicly exposed to the gazing multitude, on the second step of the throne of his *invincible* conqueror. The same

says, μολις σακκοις εζωγρησαν. Σακκος (or σακος) may signify a sack, or a loose garment; and this method of entangling and catching an enemy, laciniis contortis, was much practised by the Huns, (Ammian. xxxi, 2). Il fut pris vif avec des filets, is the translation of Tillemont, **Hist des Empereurs,** tom. v, p. 608.

measure of punishment, with which, in the days
of his prosperity, he was accused of menacing
his rival, was inflicted on Attalus himself: he
was condemned, after the amputation of two
fingers, to a perpetual exile in the isle of Lipa-
ri, where he was supplied with the decent necessaries of life. The remainder of the reign of
Honorius was undisturbed by rebellion; and
it may be observed, that, in the space of five
years, seven usurpers had yielded to the fortune of a prince, who was himself incapable
either of counsel or of action.

The situation of Spain, separated, on all Invasion
of Spain
by the
Suevi,
Vandals,
Alani, &c.
A. D. 409,
Oct. 13.
sides, from the enemies of Rome, by the sea,
by the mountains, and by intermediate provinces, had secured the long tranquillity of
that remote and sequestered country; and we
may observe, as a sure symptom of domestic
happiness, that in a period of four hundred
years, Spain furnished very few materials to
the history of the Roman empire. The footsteps of the barbarians, who, in the reign of
Gallienus, had penetrated beyond the Pyrenees,
were soon obliterated by the return of peace;
and in the fourth century of the Christian era,
the cities of Emerita, or Merida, of Corduba,
Seville, Bracara, and Tarragona, were numbered with the most illustrious of the Roman
world. The various plenty of the animal, the
vegetable and the mineral kingdoms, was improved and manufactured by the skill of an industrious people; and the peculiar advantages of
naval stores contributed to support an extensive

and profitable trade.[r] The arts and sciences
flourished under the protection of the emperors; and if the character of the Spaniards was
enfeebled by peace and servitude, the hostile approach of the Germans, who had spread terror
and desolation from the Rhine to the Pyrenees,
seemed to rekindle some sparks of military ardour.   As long as the defence of the mountains
was intrusted to the hardy and faithful militia
of the country, they successfully repelled the
frequent attempts of the barbarians. But no
sooner had the national troops been compelled
to resign their post to the Honorian bands, in
the service of Constantine, than the gates of
Spain were treacherously betrayed to the public
enemy, about ten months before the sack of
Rome by the Goths.[s] The consciousness of
guilt, and the thirst of rapine, prompted the
mercenary guards of the Pyrenees to desert their
station; to invite the arms of the Suevi, the
Vandals, and the Alani; and to swell the torrent which was poured with irresistible violence
from the frontiers of Gaul to the sea of Africa.
The misfortunes of Spain may be described in
the language of its most eloquent historian, who

[r] Without recurring to the more ancient writers, I shall quote three
respectable testimonies which belong to the fourth and seventh centuries; the Expositio totius Mundi, (p. 16, in the third volume of Hudson's Minor Geographers); Ansonius, (de Claris Urbibus, p. 242, edit.
Toll.) and Isidore of Seville, (Præfat. ad Chron. ap Grotium, Hist.
Goth. p. 707)   Many particulars relative to the fertility and trade of
Spain, may be found in Nonnius, Hispania Illustrata, and in Huet. Hist.
du Commerce des Anciens, c. 40, p. 228-234.

[s] The date is accurately fixed in the Fasti, and the Chronicle of Idatius.   Orosius (i. vii, c. 40, p. 578) imputes the loss of Spain to the treachery of the Honorians · while Sozomen (l. ix, c. 12) accuses only their
negligence.

has so concisely expressed the passionate, and
perhaps exaggerated, declamations of contemporary writers.[t] " The irruption of these nations
" was followed by the most dreadful calamities:
" as the barbarians exercised their indiscrimi-
" nate cruelty on the fortunes of the Romans
" and the Spaniards; and ravaged with equal
" fury the cities and the open country. The
" progress of famine reduced the miserable in-
" habitants to feed on the flesh of their fellow-
" creatures; and even the wild beasts, who
" multiplied, without controul, in the desert,
" were exasperated, by the taste of blood, and
" the impatience of hunger, boldly to attack
" and devour their human prey. Pestilence
" soon appeared, the inseparable companion of
" famine; a large proportion of the people was
" swept away; and the groans of the dying ex-
" cited only the envy of their surviving friends.
" At length the barbarians, satiated with car-
" nage and rapine, and afflicted by the contagi-
" ous evils which they themselves had intro-
" duced, fixed their permanent seats in the
" depopulated country. The ancient Gallicia,
" whose limits included the kingdom of Old
" Castille, was divided between the Suevi and
" the Vandals; the Alani were scattered over the
" provinces of Carthagena and Lusitania, from
" the Mediterranean to the Atlantic ocean; and
" the fruitful territory of Bœtico was allotted to
" the Silingi, another branch of the Vandalic

[t] Idatius wishes to apply the prophecies of Daniel to these national calamities; and is, therefore, obliged to accommodate the circumstances of the event to the terms of the prediction.

"nation. After regulating this partition, the
"conquerors contracted with their new sub-
"jects some reciprocal engagements of protec-
"tion and obedience: the lands were again cul-
"tivated; and the towns and villages were
"again occupied by a captive people. The
"greatest part of the Spaniards was even dis-
"posed to prefer this new condition of poverty
"and barbarism, to the severe oppressions of
"the Roman government; yet there were many
"who still asserted their native freedom; and
"who refused, more especially in the moun-
"tains of Gallicia, to submit to the barbarian
"yoke."[u]

Adolphus
king of the
Goths,
marches
into Spain,
A. D. 414

The important present of the heads of Jovinus
and Sebastian, had approved the friendship of
Adolphus, and restored Gaul to the obedience of
his brother Honorius. Peace was incompatible
with the situation and temper of the king of the
Goths. He readily accepted the proposal of
turning his victorious arms against the barbarians of Spain: the troops of Constantius intercepted his communication with the sea-ports of
Gaul, and gently pressed his march towards
the Pyrenees:[x] he passed the mountains, and
surprised, in the name of the emperor, the city
of Barcelona. The fondness of Adolphus for

---

[u] Mariana de Rebus Hispanicis, l. v, c. 1, tom. i, p. 148. Hag.
Comit. 1733. He had read in Orosius (l. vii, c. 41, p. 579), that the
barbarians had turned their swords into ploughshares; and that many
of the provincials preferred inter barbaros pauperem libertatem quam
inter Romanos tributariam solicitudinem sustinere.

[x] This mixture of force and persuasion may be fairly inferred from
comparing Orosius and Jornandes, the Roman and the Gothic historian.

his Roman bride, was not abated by time or possession; and the birth of a son, surnamed, from his illustrious grandsire, Theodosius, appeared to fix him for ever in the interest of the republic.   The loss of that infant, whose remains were deposited in a silver coffin in one of the churches near Barcelona, afflicted his parents; but the grief of the Gothic king was suspended by the labours of the field; and the course of his victories was soon interrupted by domestic treason.   He had imprudently received into his service one of the followers of Sarus; a barbarian of a daring spirit, but of a diminutive stature; whose secret desire of revenging the death of his beloved patron, was continually irritated by the sarcasms of his insolent master. Adolphus was assassinated in the palace of Barcelona; the laws of the succession were violated by a tumultuous faction;[7] and a stranger to the royal race, Singeric, the brother of Sarus himself, was seated on the Gothic throne.   The first act of his reign was the inhuman murder of the six children of Adolphus, the issue of a former marriage, whom he tore, without pity, from the feeble arms of a venerable bishop.[8] The unfortunate Placidia, instead of the respectful compassion, which she might have excited in the most savage breasts, was treated with cruel and wanton insult.   The daughter

His death, A. D. 415, August.

---

[7] According to the system of Jornandes (c. 33, p. 659), the true hereditary right to the Gothic sceptre was vested in the *Amali*; but those princes, who were the vassals of the Huns, commanded the tribes of the Ostrogoths in some distant parts of Germany or Scythia.

[8] The murder is related by Olympiodorus; but the number of the children is taken from an epitaph of suspected authority.

of the emperor Theodosius, confounded among a crowd of vulgar captives, was compelled to march on foot above twelve miles, before the horse of a barbarian, the assassin of an husband whom Placidia loved and lamented.[a]

The Goths conquer and restore Spain, A. D. 415-418. But Placidia soon obtained the pleasure of revenge; and the view of her ignominious sufferings might rouse an indignant people against the tyrant, who was assassinated on the seventh day of his usurpation. After the death of Singeric, the free choice of the nation bestowed the Gothic sceptre on Wallia; whose warlike and ambitious temper appeared, in the beginning of his reign, extremely hostile to the republic. He marched in arms, from Barcelonia to the shores of the Atlantic Ocean, which the ancients revered and dreaded as the boundary of the world. But when he reached the southern promontory of Spain,[b] and, from the rock now covered by the fortress of Gibraltar, contemplated the neighbouring and fertile coast of Africa, Wallia resumed the designs of conquest, which had been interrupted by the death of Alaric. The winds and waves again disappointed the enterprise of the Goths; and the minds of a superstitious people were deeply affected by the repeated

---

[a] The death of Adolphus was celebrated at Constantinople with illuminations and Circensian games. (See Chron. Alexandrin). It may seem doubtful, whether the Greeks were actuated, on this occasion, by their hatred of the Barbarians, or of the Latins.

[b] Quòd *Tartessiacis* avus hujus Vallia *terris*
Vandalicas turmas, et juncti Martis Alanos
Stravit, et occiduam texère cadavera *Calpen*.
Sidon, Apollinar. in Panegyr. Anthem. 362.
p. 300, edit. Sirmond

disasters of storms and shipwrecks. In this disposition, the successor of Adolphus no longer refused to listen to a Roman ambassador, whose proposals were enforced by the real, or supposed, approach of a numerous army, under the conduct of the brave Constantius. A solemn treaty was stipulated and observed: Placidia was honourably restored to her brother; six hundred thousand measures of wheat were delivered to the hungry Goths;[c] and Wallia engaged to draw his sword in the service of the empire. A bloody war was instantly excited among the barbarians of Spain; and the contending princes are said to have addressed their letters, their ambassadors, and their hostages, to the throne of the western emperor, exhorting him to remain a tranquil spectator of their contest; the events of which must be favourable to the Romans, by the mutual slaughter of their common enemies.[d] The Spanish war was obstinately supported, during three campaigns, with desperate valour, and various success; and the martial achievements of Wallia diffused through the empire the superior renown of the Gothic hero. He exterminated the Silingi, who

[c] This supply was very acceptable; the Goths were insulted by the Vandals of Spain with the epithet of *Truli*, because, in their extreme distress, they had given a piece of gold for a *trula*, or about half a pound, of flour. Olympiod. apud Phot. p. 189.

[d] Orosius inserts a copy of these pretended letters. Tu cum omnibus pacem habe, omniumque obsides accipe; nos nobis confligimus, nobis perimus, tibi vincimus; immortalis vero quæstus erat Reipublicæ tuæ, si utrique pereamus. The idea is just; but I cannot persuade myself that it was entertained, or expressed, by the barbarians.

had irretrievably ruined the elegant plenty of
the province of Bœtica.   He slew, in battle, the
king of the Alani; and the remains of those
Scythian wanderers, who escaped from the
field, instead of choosing a new leader, humbly
sought a refuge under the standard of the Vandals, with whom they were ever afterwards
confounded.   The Vandals themselves, and the
Suevi, yielded to the efforts of the invincible
Goths.   The promiscuous multitude of barbarians, whose retreat had been intercepted, were
driven into the mountains of Gallicia; where
they still continued, in a narrow compass, and
on a barren soil, to exercise their domestic and
implacable hostilities.   In the pride of Victory,
Wallia was faithful to his engagements: he restored his Spanish conquests to the obedience
of Honorius; and the tyranny of the imperial
officers soon reduced an oppressed people to
regret the time of their barbarian servitude.
While the event of the war was still doubtful,
the first advantages obtained by the arms of
Wallia, had encouraged the court of Ravenna
to decree the honours of a triumph to their feeble sovereign.   He entered Rome like the ancient conquerors of nations; and if the monuments of servile corruption had not long
since met with the fate which they deserved,
we should probably find that a crowd of poets,
and orators, of magistrates, and bishops, applauded the fortune, the wisdom, and the invincible courage, of the emperor Honorius.*'

* Romam triumphans ingreditur, is the formal expression of Prosper's
                                                                Chronicle.

Such a triumph might have been justly claimed by the ally of Rome, if Wallia, before he repassed the Pyrenees, had extirpated the seeds of the Spanish war. His victorious Goths, forty-three years after they had passed the Danube, were established, according to the faith of treaties, in the possession of the second Aquitain; a maritime province between the Garonne and the Loire, under the civil and ecclesiastical jurisdiction of Bourdeaux. That metropolis, advantageously situated for the trade of the ocean, was built in a regular and elegant form; and its numerous inhabitants were distinguished among the Gauls by their wealth, their learning, and the politeness of their manners. The adjacent province, which has been fondly compared to the garden of Eden, is blessed with a fruitful soil, and a temperate climate: the face of the country displayed the arts and the rewards of industry; and the Goths, after their martial toils, luxuriously exhausted the rich vineyards of Aquitain.[f] The Gothic limits were enlarged by the additional gift of some neighbouring dioceses; and the successors of Alaric fixed their royal residence at Thoulouse, which included five populous quarters, or cities, within the spacious circuit of its walls. About the same time, in the last years of the reign of

Chronicle. The facts which relate to the death of Adolphus, and the exploits of Wallia, are related from Olympiodorus (apud Phot. p. 183), Orosius (l. vii, c. 43, p. 584. 587). Jornandes (de Rebus Geticis, c. 31, 32), and the Chronicles of Idatius and Isidore.

[f] Ausonius (de Claris Urbibus, p. 257-262), celebrates Bourdeaux with the partial affection of a native. See in Salvian (de Gubern. Dei, p. 228. Paris, 1608), a florid description of the provinces of Aquitain and Novempopulania.

CHAP
XXXI.

The Bur-
gundians.

Honorius, the GOTHS, the BURGUNDIANS, and the FRANKS, obtained a permanent seat and dominion in the provinces of Gaul. The liberal grant of the usurper Jovinus to his Burgundian allies, was confirmed by the lawful emperor; the lands of the First, or Upper, Germany, were ceded to those formidable barbarians; and they gradually occupied, either by conquest or treaty, the two provinces which still retain, with the titles of *Duchy* and of *County*, the national appellation of Burgundy.[s] The Franks, the valiant and faithful allies of the Roman republic, were soon tempted to imitate the invaders, whom they had so bravely resisted. Treves, the capital of Gaul, was pillaged by their lawless bands; and the humble colony, which they so long maintained in the district of Toxandria, in Brabant, insensibly multiplied along the banks of the Meuse and Scheld, till their independent power filled the whole extent of the Second, or Lower Germany. These facts may be sufficiently justified by historic evidence; but the foundation of the French monarchy by Pharamond, the conquests, the laws, and even the existence, of that hero, have been justly arraigned by the impartial severity of modern criticism.[t]

[s] Orosius (l. vii, c. 32, p. 550), commends the mildness and modesty of these Burgundians, who treated their subjects of Gaul as their Christian brethren. Mascou has illustrated the origin of their kingdom in the four first annotations at the end of his laborious History of the Ancient Germans, vol. ii, p. 555-572, of the English translation.

[t] See Mascou, l. viii, c. 43, 44, 45. Except in a short and suspicious line of the Chronicle of Prosper, (in tom. i, p. 638), the name of Pharamond is never mentioned before the seventh century. The author

The ruin of the opulent provinces of Gaul may be dated from the establishment of these barbarians, whose alliance was dangerous and oppressive, and who were capriciously impelled, by interest or passion, to violate the public peace. A heavy and partial ransom was imposed on the surviving provincials, who had escaped the calamities of war; the fairest and most fertile lands were assigned to the rapacious strangers, for the use of their families, their slaves, and their cattle; and the trembling natives relinquished with a sigh the inheritance of their fathers. Yet these domestic misfortunes, which are seldom the lot of a vanquished people, had been felt and inflicted by the Romans themselves, not only in the insolence of foreign conquest, but in the madness of civil discord. The Triumvirs proscribed eighteen of the most flourishing colonies of Italy; and distributed their lands and houses to the veterans who revenged the death of Cæsar, and oppressed the liberty of their country. Two poets of unequal fame, have deplored, in similar circumstances, the loss of their patrimony; but the legionaries of Augustus appear to have surpassed, in violence and injustice, the barbarians, who invaded Gaul, under the reign of Honorius. It was not without the utmost difficulty that Virgil escaped from the sword of the centurion, who had usurped his farm in the neighbourhood of Man-

thor of the Gesta Francorum (in tom. ii, p. 543) suggests, probably enough, that the choice of Pharamond, or at least of a king was recommended to the Franks by his father Marcomir, who was an exile in Tuscany.

tua; but Paulinus of Bourdeaux received a sum of money from his Gothic purchaser, which he accepted with pleasure and surprise; and, though it was much inferior to the real value of his estate, this act of rapine was disguised by some colours of moderation and equity.[k] The odious name of conquerors, was softened into the mild and friendly appellation of the *guests* of the Romans; and the barbarians of Gaul, more especially the Goths, repeatedly declared, that they were bound to the people by the ties of hospitality, and to the emperor by the duty of allegiance and military service. The title of Honorius and his successors, their laws, and their civil magistrates, were still respected in the provinces of Gaul, of which they had resigned the possession to the barbarian allies; and the kings, who exercised a supreme and independent authority over their native subjects, ambitiously solicited the more honourable rank of master-general of the imperial armies.[l] Such was the involuntary reverence

[i] O Lycida, vivi pervenimus: advena nostri
(Quod nunquam veriti sumus) ut possessor agelli
Diceret: Hæc mea sunt; veteres migrate coloni.
Nunc victi tristes, &c.

See the whole of the 9th eclogue, with the useful Commentary of Servius. Fitteen miles of the Mantuan territory were assigned to the veterans, with a reservation, in favour of the inhabitants, of three miles round the city. Even in this favour they were cheated by Alfenus Varus, a famous lawyer, and one of the commissioners, who measured eight hundred paces of water and morass.

[k] See the remarkable passage of the Eucharisticon of Paulinus, 575, apud Mascou, l. viii, c. 42.

[l] This important truth is established by the accuracy of Tillemont (Hist. des Emp. tom. v, p. 641), and by the ingenuity of the Abbé Dubos (Hist. de l'Etablissement de la Monarchie Françoise dans les Gauls, tom. i, p. 259).

which the Roman name still impressed on the minds of those warriors, who had borne away in triumph the spoils of the capitol.

Whilst Italy was ravaged by the Goths, and a succession of feeble tyrants oppressed the provinces beyond the Alps, the British island separated itself from the body of the Roman empire. The regular forces, which guarded that remote province, had been gradually withdrawn; and Britain was abandoned, without defence, to the Saxon pirates, and the savages of Ireland and Caledonia. The Britons, reduced to this extremity, no longer relied on the tardy and doubtful aid of a declining monarchy. They assembled in arms, repelled the invaders, and rejoiced in the important discovery of their own strength.[m] Afflicted by similar calamities, and actuated by the same spirit, the Armorican provinces (a name which comprehended the maritime countries of Gaul between the Seine and the Loire.[n]) resolved to imitate the example of the neighbouring island. They expelled the Roman magistrates, who acted under the authority of the usurper Constantine; and a free government was established among a people who had so long been subject to the arbitrary will of a master. The inde-

---

[m] Zosimus (l. vi, p. 376, 383), relates in a few words the revolt of Britain and Armorica. Our antiquarians, even the great Cambden himself, have been betrayed into many gross errors, by their imperfect knowledge of the history of the continent.

[n] The limits of Armorica are defined by two national geographers, Messieurs de Valois and d'Anville, in their *Notitias* of Ancient Gaul. The word had been used in a more extensive, and was afterwards contracted to a much narrower, signification.

pendence of Britain and Armorica was soon
confirmed by Honorius himself, the lawful emperor of the West; and the letters, by which
he committed to the new states the care of their
own safety, might be interpreted as an absolute
and perpetual abdication of the exercise and
rights of sovereignty.   This interpretation was,
in some measure, justified by the event.   After
the usurpers of Gaul had successively fallen,
the maritime provinces were restored to the
empire.   Yet their obedience was imperfect
and precarious: the vain, inconstant, rebellious
disposition of the people, was incompatible either with freedom or servitude;[o] and Armorica, though it could not long maintain the form
of a republic,[p] was agitated by frequent and
destructive revolts.   Britain was irrecoverably
lost.[q]   But as the emperors wisely acquiesced

[o] Gens inter geminos notissima clauditur amnes,
Armoricana prius veteri cognomine dicta
Torva, ferox, ventosa, procax, incauta, rebellis ;
Inconstans, disparque sibi novitatis amore ;
Prodiga verborum, sed non et prodiga facti.
Erricus, Monach. in Vit. St. Germani, l. v, apud Vales. Notit. Gallia-
rum. p. 43. Valesius alleges several testimonies to confirm this character;
to which I shall add the evidence of the presbyter Constantine, (A. D.
488), who, in the life of St. Germain, calls the Armorican rebels mobi-
lem et indisciplinatum populum.   See the Historians of France, tom.
i, p. 643.

[p] I thought it necessary to enter my protest against this part of the
system of the Abbé Dubos, which Montesquieu has so vigorously opposed.   See Esprit des Loix, l. xxx, c. 24.

[q] Βρεταννιαν μεν τοι Ρωμαιοι ανασωσασθαι ικετι εχον, are the words of Procopius, (de Bell. Vandal. l. i, c. 2, p. 181, Louvre edition), in a very
important passage, which has been too much neglected.   Even Bede
(Hist. Gent. Anglican. l. i, c. 12, p. 50, edit. Smith) acknowledges that
the Romans finally left Britain in the reign of Honorius.   Yet our modern historians and antiquaries extend the term of their dominion ; and
there are some who allow only the interval of a few months between
their departure and the arrival of the Saxons.

in the independence of a remote province, the separation was not embittered by the reproach of tyranny or rebellion ; and the claims of allegiance and protection were succeeded by the mutual and voluntary offices of national friendship.[r]

This revolution dissolved the artificial fabric of civil and military government, and the independent country, during a period of forty years, till the descent of the Saxons, was ruled by the authority of the clergy, the nobles, and the municipal towns.[s] I. Zosimus, who alone has preserved the memory of this singular transaction, very accurately observes, that the letters of Honorius were addressed to the *cities* of Britain.[t] Under the protection of the Romans, ninety-two considerable towns had arisen in the several parts of that great province; and, among these, thirty-three cities were distinguished above the rest, by their superior privileges and importance.[u] Each of these cities, as in all the other provinces of the empire, formed a legal corpo-

CHAP.
XXXI.

State of
Britain,
A. D. 409.
449.

---

[r] Bede has not forgot the occasional aid of the legions against the Scots and Picts ; and more authentic proof will hereafter be produced, that the independent Britains raised 12,000 men for the service of the emperor Anthemius, in Gaul.

[s] I owe to myself, and to historic truth, to declare that some *circumstances* in this paragraph are founded only on conjecture and analogy. The stubbornness of our language has sometimes forced me to deviate from the *conditional* into the *indicative* mood.

[t] Προς τας ω Βρεταννια πολεις. Zosimus, l. vi, p. 383.

[u] Two cities of Britain were *municipia*, nine *colonies*, ten *Latii jure donatæ*, twelve *stipendiariæ* of eminent note. This detail is taken from Richard of Cirencester, de Situ Britanniæ, p. 36 ; and though it may not seem probable, that he wrote from the MSS. of a Roman general, he shews a genuine knowledge of antiquity, very extraordinary for a monk of the fourteenth century.

ration, for the purpose of regulating their domestic policy; and the powers of municipal government were distributed among annual magistrates, a select senate, and the assembly of the
people, according to the original model of the
Roman constitution.[x] The management of a
common revenue, the exercise of civil and criminal jurisdiction, and the habits of public
counsel and command, were inherent to these
petty republics; and when they asserted their
independence, the youth of the city, and of the
adjacent districts, would naturally range themselves under the standard of the magistrate.
But the desire of obtaining the advantages, and
of escaping the burthens, of a political society,
is a perpetual and inexhaustible source of discord; nor can it reasonably be presumed, that
the restoration of British freedom was exempt
from tumult and faction. The pre-eminence of
birth and fortune must have been frequently
violated by bold and popular citizens; and the
haughty nobles, who complained that they were
become the subjects of their own servants,[y]
would sometimes regret the reign of an arbitrary monarch. II. The jurisdiction of each
city over the adjacent country, was supported
by the patrimonial influence of the principal
senators; and the smaller towns, the villages,
and the proprietors of land, consulted their own
safety by adhering to the shelter of these rising

[x] See Maffei Verona Illustrata, part i, l. v, p. 83-106.
[y] Leges restituit, libertatemque reducit,
Et servos famulis non finit erse suis,
Itinerar. Rutil. l. i, 215.

republics. The sphere of their attraction was proportioned to the respective degrees of their wealth and populousness; but the hereditary lords of ample possessions, who were not oppressed by the neighbourhood of any powerful city, aspired to the rank of independent princes, and boldly exercised the rights of peace and war. The gardens and villas, which exhibited some faint imitation of Italian elegance, would soon be converted into strong castles, the refuge, in time of danger, of the adjacent country:[x] the produce of the land was applied to purchase arms and horses; to maintain a military force of slaves, of peasants, and of licentious followers; and the chieftain might assume, within his own domain, the powers of a civil magistrate. Several of these British chiefs might be the genuine posterity of ancient kings; and many more would be tempted to adopt this honourable genealogy, and to vindicate their hereditary claims, which had been suspended by the usurpation of the Cæsars.[x] Their situation, and their hopes, would dispose them to affect the dress, the language, and the customs of their ancestors. If the *princes* of Britain relapsed into barbarism, while the *cities* studi-

---

[x] An inscription (apud Sirmond, Not. ad Sidon. Apollinar. p. 59), describes a castle, cum muris et portis, tuitioni omnium, erected by Dardanus on his own estate, near Sisteron, in the second Narbonnese, and named by him Theopolis.

[x] The establishment of their power would have been easy indeed, if we could adopt the impracticable scheme of a lively and learned antiquarian; who supposes, that the British monarchs of the several tribes continued to reign, though with subordinate jurisdiction, from the time of Claudius to that of Honorius. See Whitaker's History of Manchester, vol. i, p 247-257

CHAP.
XXXI.

ously preserved the laws and manners of Rome, the whole island must have been gradually divided by the distinction of two national parties; again broken into a thousand subdivisions of war and faction, by the various provocations of interest and resentment. The public strength, instead of being united against a foreign enemy, was consumed in obscure and intestine quarrels; and the personal merit which had placed a successful leader at the head of his equals, might enable him to subdue the freedom of some neighbouring cities; and to claim a rank among the *tyrants,*[b] who infested Britain after the dissolution of the Roman government. III. The British church might be composed of thirty or forty bishops,[c] with an adequate proportion of the inferior clergy; and the want of riches (for they seem to have been 'poor') would compel them to deserve the public esteem, by a decent and exemplary behaviour. The interest, as well as the temper, of the clergy, was favourable to the peace and union of their distracted country; those salutary lessons might be frequently inculcated in their popular discourses; and the episcopal synods were the only councils that could pretend to the weight and authority of a na-

[b] Αλλ' οσα υπο τυραννις απ' αυτη εμασι. Procopius, de Bell. Vandal. l. i, c. 2, p. 181. Britaunia fertilis provincia tyrannorum, was the expression of Jerom, in the year 415, (tom. ii, p. 255, ad Ctesiphont). By the pilgrims, who resorted every year to the Holy Land, the monk of Bethelem received the earliest and most accurate intelligence.

[c] See Bingham's Eccles. Antiquities, vol. i, l. ix, c. 6, p. 394.

[d] It is reported of *three* British bishops who assisted at the council of Rimini, A. D. 859, tam pauperes fuisse ut nihil haberent. Sulpicius Severus, Hist. Sacra, l. ii, p. 420. Some of their brethren, however, were in better circumstances.

tional assembly. In such councils, where the princes and magistrates sat promiscuously with the bishops, the important affairs of the state, as well as of the church, might be freely debated; differences reconciled, alliances formed, contributions imposed, wise resolutions often concerted, and sometimes executed; and there is reason to believe, that, in moments of extreme danger, a *Pendragon*, or Dictator, was elected by the general consent of the Britons. These pastoral cares, so worthy of the episcopal character, were interrupted, however, by zeal and superstition; and the British clergy incessantly laboured to eradicate the Pelagian heresy, which they abhorred, as the peculiar disgrace of their native country.[*]

It is somewhat remarkable, or rather it is extremely natural, that the revolt of Britain and Armorica should have introduced an appearance of liberty into the obedient provinces of Gaul. In a solemn edict,[f] filled with the strongest assurances of that paternal affection which princes so often express, and so seldom feel, the emperor Honorius promulgated his intention of convening an annual assembly of the *seven provinces*: a name peculiarly appropriated to Aquitain, and the ancient Narbonnese, which had long since exchanged their Celtic rudeness for the useful and elegant arts of

---

[*] Consult Usher, de Antiq. Eccles. Britannicar. c. 8-12.

[f] See the correct text of this edict, as published by Sirmond, Not. ad Sidon. Apollin. p. 147). Hincmar, of Rheims, who assigns a place to the *bishops*, had probably seen (in the ninth century) a more perfect copy. Dubos, Hist. Critique de la Monarchie Françoise, tom. i, p. 241-255.

CHAP.
XXXI.

Italy.[s]   Arles, the seat of government and commerce, was appointed for the place of the assembly; which regularly continued twenty-eight days, from the fifteenth of August to the thirteenth of September, of every year.   It consisted of the pretorian prefect of the Gauls; of seven provincial governors, one consular and six presidents; of the magistrates, and perhaps the bishops, of about sixty cities; and of a competent, though indefinite, number of the most honourable and opulent *possessors* of land, who might justly be considered as the representatives of their country.   They were empowered to interpret and communicate the laws of their sovereign; to expose the grievances and wishes of their constituents; to moderate the excessive or unequal weight of taxes; and to deliberate on every subject of local or national importance, that could tend to the restoration of the peace and prosperity of the seven provinces.   If such an institution, which gave the people an interest in their own government, had been universally established by Trajan or the Antonines, the seeds of public wisdom and virtue might have been cherished and propagated in the empire of Rome.   The privileges of the subject would have secured the throne of the monarch; the abuses of an arbitrary administration might have been prevented, in some degree, or corrected, by the interposition of these representative as-

---

[s] It is evident from the *Notitia*, that the seven provinces were the Viennensis, the maritime Alps, the first and second Narbonnese, Novempopulania, and the first and second Aquitain.   In the room of the first Aquitain, the Abbé Dubos, on the authority of Hincmar. desires to introduce the first Lugdunensis, or Lyonnese.

semblies; and the country would have been defended against a foreign enemy by the arms of
natives and freemen. Under the mild and generous influence of liberty, the Roman empire
might have remained invincible and immortal ;
or if its excessive magnitude, and the instability
of human affairs, had opposed such perpetual
continuance, its vital and constituent members
might have separately preserved their vigour
and independence. But in the decline of the
empire, when every principle of health and life
had been exhausted, the tardy application of
this partial remedy was incapable of producing
any important or salutary effects. The emperor
Honorius expresses his surprise, that he must
compel the reluctant provinces to accept a privilege which they should ardently have solicited. A fine of three, or even five, pounds of
gold, was imposed on the absent representatives; who seem to have declined this imaginary gift of a free constitution, as the last and
most cruel insult of their oppressors.

CHAP. XXXII.

*Arcadius emperor of the East—Administration
and disgrace of Eutropius—Revolt of Gainas
—Persecution of St. John Chrysostom—Theodosius II. emperor of the East—His sister Pulcheria—His wife Eudocia—The Persian war,
and division of Armenia.*

CHAP.
XXXII.
- - - - - - - -
The em-
pire of the
East,
A. D. 395
1453.
Reign of
Arcadius,
A. D. 395-
408.

THE division of the Roman world between the
sons of Theodosius, marks the final establishment of the empire of the East, which, from
the reign of Arcadius to the taking of Constantinople by the Turks, subsisted one thousand and fifty-eight years, in a state of premature and perpetual decay. The sovereign of
that empire assumed, and obstinately retained,
the vain, and at length fictitious, title of Emperor of the ROMANS; and the hereditary appellations of CÆSAR and AUGUSTUS continued
to declare that he was the legitimate successor
of the first of men, who had reigned over the
first of nations. The palace of Constantinople
rivalled, and perhaps excelled, the magnificence
of Persia; and the eloquent sermons of St.
Chrysostom * celebrate, while they condemn,

* Father Montfaucon, who, by the command of his Benedictine superiors, was compelled (see Longueruana, tom. i, p. 205) to execute the
laborious edition of St. Chrysostom, in thirteen volumes in folio, (Paris
1738), amused himself with extracting from that immense collection of
morals, some curious *antiquities*, which illustrate the manners of the
Theodosian age, (see Chrysostom. Opera, tom. xiii, p. 192-196), and his
French Dissertation, in the Memoires de l'Acad. des Inscriptions, tom.
xiii, p. 474-490.

the pompous luxury of the reign of Arcadius.
" The emperor," says he, " wears on his head
" either a diadem, or a crown of gold, decorat-
" ed with precious stones of inestimable value.
" These ornaments, and his purple garments,
" are reserved for his sacred person alone; and
" his robes of silk are embroidered with the
" figures of golden dragons. His throne is of
" massy gold. Whenever he appears in pub-
" lic, he is surrounded by his courtiers, his
" guards, and his attendants. Their spears,
" their shields, their cuirasses, the bridles and
" trappings of their horses, have either the sub-
" stance, or the appearance, of gold; and the
" large splendid boss in the midst of their
" shield, is encircled with smaller bosses, which
" represent the shape of the human eye. The
" two mules that draw the chariot of the mo-
" narch, are perfectly 'white, and shining all
" over with gold. The chariot itself, of pure
" and solid gold, attracts the admiration of the
" spectators, who contemplate the purple cur-
" tains, the snowy carpet, the size of the pre-
" cious stones, and the resplendent plates of
" gold, that glitter as they are agitated by the
" motion of the carriage. The imperial pictures
" are white, on a blue ground; the emperor
" appears seated on his throne, with his arms,
" his horses, and his guards beside him; and his
" vanquished enemies in chains at his feet."
The successors of Constantine established their
perpetual residence in the royal city, which he

had erected on the verge of Europe and Asia. Inaccessible to the menaces of their enemies, and perhaps to the complaints of their people, they received, with each wind, the tributary productions of every climate; while the impregnable strength of their capital continued for ages to defy the hostile attempts of the barbarians. Their dominions were bounded by the Hadriatic and the Tigris; and the whole interval of twenty-five days navigation, which separated the extreme cold of Scythia from the torrid zone of Æthiopia,* was comprehended within the limits of the empire of the East. The populous countries of that empire were the seat of art and learning, of luxury and wealth; and the inhabitants, who had assumed the language and manners of Greeks, styled themselves, with some appearance of truth, the most enlightened and civilized portion of the human species. The form of government was a pure and simple monarchy; the name of the ROMAN REPUBLIC, which so long preserved a faint tradition of freedom, was confined to the Latin provinces; and the princes of Constantinople measured their greatness by the servile obedience of their people. They were ignorant how

* According to the loose reckoning, that a ship could sail, with a fair wind, 1000 stadia, or 125 miles, in the revolution of a day and night; Diodorus Siculus computes ten days from the Palus Mœotis to Rhodes; and ,four days from Rhodes to Alexandria. The navigation of the Nile, from Alexandria to Syrene, under the tropic of Cancer, required, as it was against the stream, ten days more. Diodor. Sicul. tom. i, l. iii, p. 200, edit. Wesseling. He might, without much impropriety, measure the extreme heat from the verge of the torrid zone; but he speaks of the Mœotis in the 47th degree of northern latitude, as if it lay within the polar circle,

much this passive disposition enervates and degrades every faculty of the mind. The subjects, who had resigned their will to the absolute commands of a master, were equally incapable of guarding their lives and fortunes against the assaults of the barbarians, or of defending their reason from the terrors of superstition.

The first events of the reign of Arcadius and Honorius are so intimately connected, that the rebellion of the Goths, and the fall of Rufinus, have already claimed a place in the history of the West. It has already been observed, that Eutropius,[*] one of the principal eunuchs of the palace of Constantinople, succeeded the haughty minister whose ruin he had accomplished, and whose vices he soon imitated. Every order of the state bowed to the new favourite; and their tame and obsequious submission encouraged him to insult the laws, and, what is still more difficult and dangerous, the manners of his country. Under the weakest of the predecessors of Arcadius, the reign of the eunuchs had been secret and almost invisible. They insinuated themselves into the confidence of the prince; but their ostensible functions were confined to the menial service of the wardrobe and imperial bed-chamber. They might direct, in a whisper, the public counsels, and blast, by

[*] Barthius, who adored his author with the blind superstition of a commentator, gives the preference to the two books which Claudian composed against Eutropius, above all his other productions, (Baillet, Jugemens des Savans, tom. iv, p. 227). They are indeed a very elegant and spirited satire; and would be more valuable in an historical light, if the invective were less vague, and more temperate.

their malicious suggestions, the fame and fortunes of the most illustrious citizens; but they
never presumed to stand forward in the front
of empire,[4] or to prophane the public honours
of the state. Eutropius was the first of his
artificial sex, who dared to assume the character of a Roman magistrate and general.[*] Sometimes, in the presence of the blushing senate,
he ascended the tribunal, to pronounce judgment, or to repeat elaborate harangues; and
sometimes appeared on horseback, at the head
of his troops, in the dress and armour of a hero.
The disregard of custom and decency always
betrays a weak and ill-regulated mind; nor
does Eutropius seem to have compensated for
the folly of the design, by any superior merit
or ability in the execution. His former habits
of life had not introduced him to the study of
the laws, or the exercises of the field; his awkward and unsuccessful attempts provoked the

---

[4] After lamenting the progress of the eunuchs in the Roman palace,
and defining their proper functions, Claudian adds,

—————A fronte recedant
      Imperii.
                    In Eutrop. i, 422.
Yet it does not appear that the eunuch had assumed any of the effi-
cient offices of the empire, and he is styled only Præpositus sacri cu-
biculi, in the edict of his banishment. See Cod. Theod. l. ix, tit. xl,
leg. 17.

[*] Jamque oblita sui, nec sobria divitiis mens
  In miseras leges hominumque negotia ludit;
  Judicat eunuchus . . . . .
  Arma etiam violare parat. . .

Claudian (i, 229-270), with that mixture of indignation and humour,
which always pleases in a satiric poet, describes the insolent folly of the
eunuch, the disgrace of the empire and the joy of the Goths.

—————Gaudet, cum viderit hostis.
  Et sentit jam deesse viros.

secret contempt of the spectators; the Goths expressed their wish, that *such* a general might always command the armies of Rome; and the name of the minister was branded with ridicule, more pernicious perhaps than hatred, to a public character. The subjects of Arcadius were exasperated by the recollection, that this deformed and decrepid eunuch,[f] who so perversely mimicked the actions of a man, was born in the most abject condition of servitude; that, before he entered the imperial palace, he had been successively sold, and purchased, by an hundred masters, who had exhausted his youthful strength in every mean and infamous office, and at length dismissed him, in his old age, to freedom and poverty.[g] While these disgraceful stories were circulated, and perhaps exaggerated, in private conversations, the vanity of the favourite was flattered with the most extraordinary honours. In the senate, in the capital, in the provinces, the statues of Eutropius were erected, in brass, or marble, decorated

[f] The poet's lively description of his deformity, (i, 110-125), is confirmed by the authentic testimony of Chrysostom, (tom. iii, p. 384, edit. Montfaucon); who observes, that when the paint was washed away, the face of Eutropius appeared more ugly and wrinkled than that of an old woman. Claudian remarks, (i, 469), and the remark must have been founded on experience, that there was scarcely any interval between the youth and the decrepid age of an eunuch.

[g] Eutropius appears to have been a native of Armenia or Assyria. His three services, which Claudian more particularly describes, were these. 1. He spent many years as the catamite of Ptolemy, a groom or soldier of the imperial stables. 2. Ptolemy gave him to the old general Arintheus, for whom he very skilfully exercised the profession of a pimp. 3. He was given, on her marriage, to the daughter of Arintheus; and the future consul was employed to comb her hair, to present the silver ewer, to wash and to fan his mistress in hot weather. See l. i. 31-137.

with the symbols of his civil and military virtues, and inscribed with the pompous title of the third founder of Constantinople. He was promoted to the rank of *patrician*, which began to signify, in a popular, and even legal, acceptation, the father of the emperor ; and the last year of the fourth century was polluted by the *consulship* of an eunuch, and a slave. This strange and inexpiable prodigy [h] awakened, however, the prejudices of the Romans. The effeminate consul was rejected by the West, as an indelible stain to the annals of the republic; and, without invoking the shades of Brutus and Camillus, the colleague of Eutropius, a learned and respectable magistrate,[i] sufficiently represented the different maxims of the two administrations.

His venality and injustice ; The bold and vigorous mind of Rufinus seems to have been actuated by a more sanguinary and revengeful spirit; but the avarice of the eunuch was not less insatiate than that of the prefect.[k] As long as he despoiled the oppressors, who had enriched themselves with the plunder of the

[h] Claudian (l. i, in Eutrop. 1-22) after enumerating the various prodigies of monstrous births, speaking animals, showers of blood or stones, double suns, &c. adds, with some exaggeration,
Omnia cesserunt eunucho consule monstra.
The first book concludes with a noble speech of the goddess of Rome to her favourite Honorius, deprecating the new ignominy to which she was exposed.

[i] Fl. Mallius Theodorus, whose civil honours, and philosophical works, have been celebrated by Claudian in a very elegant panegyric

[k] Μεθυων δε πλη τω πλωτω, drunk with riches, is the forcible expression of Zosimus (l. v, p. 301); and the avarice of Eutropius is equally execrated in the Lexicon of Suidas, and the Chronicle of Marcellinus. Chrysostom had often admonished the favourite, of the vanity and danger of immoderate wealth, (tom. iii, p. 381.)

people, Eutropius might gratify his covetous disposition without much envy or injustice: but the progress of his rapine soon invaded the wealth which had been acquired by lawful inheritance, or laudable industry. The usual methods of extortion were practised and improved; and Claudian has sketched a lively and original picture of the public auction of the state. " The impotence of the eunuch" (says that agreeable satirist) " has served only to " stimulate his avarice : the same hand which, " in his servile condition, was exercised in petty " thefts, to unlock the coffers of his master, " now grasps the riches of the world; and this " infamous broker of the empire appretiates and " divides the Roman provinces, from mount " Hæmus to the Tigris. One man, at the ex- " pence of his villa, is made proconsul of Asia; " a second purchases Syria with his wife's jew- " els; and a third laments, that he has ex- " changed his paternal estate for the govern- " ment of Bithynia. In the anti-chamber of " Eutropius, a large tablet is exposed to public " view, which marks the respective prices of " the provinces. The different value of Pon- " tus, of Galatia, of Lydia, is accurately dis- " tinguished. Lycia may be obtained for so " many thousand pieces of gold; but the opu- " lence of Phrygia will require a more consider- " able sum. The eunuch wishes to obliterate, " by the general disgrace, his personal ignominy; " and as he has been sold himself, he is desirous " of selling the rest of mankind. In the eager

" contention, the balance, which contains the
" fate and fortunes of the provinces, often trem-
" bles on the beam ; and till one of the scales is
" inclined, by a superior weight, the mind of the
" impartial judge remains in anxious suspense.'
" Such" (continues the indignant poet) " are the
" fruits of Roman valour, of the defeat of An-
" tiochus, and of the triumph of Pompey."
This venal prostitution of public honours secured the impunity of *future* crimes ; but the
riches, which Eutropius derived from confiscation, were *already* stained with injustice ; since
it was decent *to* accuse, and to condemn, the
proprietors of the wealth which he was impatient
to confiscate. Some noble blood was shed by
the hand of the executioner ; and the most
inhospitable extremities of the empire were fil-
Ruin of
Abundan-
tius;
led with *innocent and illustrious exiles.* Among
the generals and consuls of the East, Abun-
dantius^m had reason to dread the first effects
of the resentment of Eutropius. He had been
guilty of the unpardonable crime of introducing that abject slave to the palace of
Constantinople : and some degree of praise
must be allowed to a powerful and ungrateful

<hr />

'   ———certantum sæpe duorum
   Diversum suspendit onus : cum pondere judex
   Vergit, et in geminas nutat provincia lances.
Claudian (i, 192-209) so curiously distinguishes the circumstances of the
sale, that they all seem to allude to particular anecdotes.

   ^m Claudian (i, 154-170) mentions the *guilt* and exile of Abundantius
nor could he fail to quote the example of the artist, who made the
first trial of the brazen bull, which he presented to Phalaris. See Zosimus, l. v, p. 302   Jerom. tom. i, p. 26.   The difference of place is
easily reconciled ; but the decisive authority of Asterius of Amasia,
(Orat. iv, p. 76, apud Tillemont, Hist. des Empereurs, tom. v, p. 435)
must turn the scale in favour of Pityus.

favourite, who was satisfied with the disgrace of his benefactor. Abundantius was stripped of his ample fortunes by an imperial rescript, and banished to Pityus, on the Euxine, the last frontier of the Roman world; where he subsisted by the precarious mercy of the barbarians, till he could obtain, after the fall of Eutropius, a milder exile at Sidon in Phœnicia. The destruction of Timasius[n] required a more serious and regular mode of attack. That great officer, the master-general of the armies of Theodosius, had signalized his valour by a decisive victory, which he obtained over the Goths of Thessaly; but he was too prone, after the example of his sovereign, to enjoy the luxury of peace, and to abandon his confidence to wicked and designing flatterers. Timasius had despised the public clamour, by promoting an infamous dependant to the command of a cohort; and he deserved to feel the ingratitude of Bargus, who was secretly instigated by the favourite to accuse his patron of a treasonable conspiracy. The general was arraigned before the tribunal of Arcadius himself; and the principal eunuch stood by the side of the throne to suggest the questions and answers of his sovereign. But as this form of trial might be deemed partial and

of Timasius.

[n] Suidas (most probably from the history of Eunapius) has given a very unfavourable picture of Timasius. The account of his accuser, the judges, trial, &c. is perfectly agreeable to the practice of ancient and modern courts. (See Zosimus, l. v, p. 298, 299, 300). I am almost tempted to quote the romance of a great master, (Fielding's Works, vol. iv, p. 49, &c. 8vo. edit.) which may be considered as the history of human nature.

arbitrary, the further inquiry into the crimes of Timasius was delegated to Saturninus and Procopius; the former of consular rank, the latter still respected as the father-in-law of the emperor Valens. The appearances of a fair and legal proceeding were maintained by the blunt honesty of Procopius; and he yielded with reluctance to the obsequious dexterity of his colleague, who pronounced a sentence of condemnation against the unfortunate Timasius. His immense riches were confiscated, in the name of the emperor, and for the benefit of the favourite; and he was doomed to perpetual exile at Oasis, a solitary spot in the midst of the sandy deserts of Libya.° Secluded from all human converse, the master-general of the Roman armies was lost for ever to the world; but the circumstances of his fate have been related in a various and contradictory manner. It is insinuated, that Eutropius despatched a private order for his secret execution.ᵖ It was reported, that, in attempting to escape from Oasis, he perished in the desert, of thirst and hunger; and that his dead body was found on the sands

° The great Oasis was one of the spots in the sands of Libya, watered with springs, and capable of producing wheat, barley, and palm-trees. It was about three days journey from north to south, about half a day in breadth, and at the distance of about five days march to the west of Abydus, on the Nile. See d'Anville, Description de l'Egypte, p. 186, 187, 188. The barren desert which encompasses Oasis, (Zosimus, l. v, p. 300), has suggested the idea of comparative fertility, and even the epithet of the *happy island*, (Herodot. iii, 26).

ᵖ The line of Claudian, in Eutrop. l. i, 180,
Marmaricus claris violatur cædibus Hammon,
evidently alludes to *his* persuasion of the death of Timasius.

of Libya.[q] It has been asserted, with more con- fidence, that his son Syagrius, after success- fully eluding the pursuit of the agents and emis- saries of the court, collected a band of African robbers; that he rescued Timasius from the place of his exile; and that both the father and son disappeared from the knowledge of man- kind.[r] But the ungrateful Bargus, instead of being suffered to possess the reward of guilt, was soon afterwards circumvented and destroy- ed, by the more powerful villany of the minister himself; who retained sense and spirit enough to abhor the instrument of his own crimes.

The public hatred, and the despair of indi- viduals, continually threatened, or seemed to threaten, the personal safety of Eutropius; as well as of the numerous adherents, who were attached to his fortune, and had been promoted by his venal favour. For their mutual defence, he contrived the safeguard of a law, which vio- lated every principle of humanity and justice.[s] I. It is enacted, in the name and by the autho- rity, of Arcadius, that all those who shall con- spire, either with subjects, or with strangers, against the lives of any of the persons whom the

A cruel and unjust law of treason, A. D. 397, Sept. 4.

---

[q] Sozomen, l. viii, c. 7. He speaks from report, ὡς τινες ἐπύθομεν.

[r] Zosimus, l. v, p. 309. Yet he seems to suspect that this rumour was spread by the friends of Eutropius.

[s] See the Theodosian Code, l. ix, tit. 14, ad legem Corneliam de Sicariis, leg. 3, and the Code of Justinian. l. ix, tit. viii, ad legem Juliam de Majestate, leg. 5. The alteration of the *title*, from murder to treason, was an improvement of the subtle Tribonian. Godefroy, in a formal dissertation, which he has inserted in his Commentary, illustrates this law of Arcadius, and explains all the difficult passages which had been perverted by the jurisconsults of the darker ages. See tom. iii, p. 88—111.

emperor considers as the members of his own body, shall be punished with death and confiscation. This species of fictitious and metaphorical treason is extended to protect not only the *illustrious* officers of the state and army, who are admitted into the sacred consistory, but likewise the principal domestics of the palace, the senators of Constantinople, the military commanders, and the civil magistrates of the provinces; a vague and indefinite list, which, under the successors of Constantine, included an obscure and numerous train of subordinate ministers. II. This extreme severity might perhaps be justified, had it been only directed to secure the representatives of the sovereign from any actual violence in the execution of their office. But the whole body of imperial dependants claimed a privilege, or rather impunity, which screened them, in the loosest moments of their lives, from the hasty, perhaps the justifiable, resentment of their fellow-citizens: and, by a strange perversion of the laws, the same degree of guilt and punishment was applied to a private quarrel, and to a deliberate conspiracy against the emperor and the empire. The edict of Arcadius most positively and most absurdly declares, that in such cases of treason, *thoughts* and *actions* ought to be punished with equal severity; that the knowledge of a mischievous intention, unless it be instantly revealed, becomes equally criminal with the intention itself;' and that those rash men, who shall pre-

---

' Bartolus understands a simple and naked consciousness, without
any

sume to solicit the pardon of traitors, shall themselves be branded with public and perpetual infamy. III. " With regard to the sons of " the traitors," (continues the emperor), " although they ought to share the punishment, " since they will probably imitate the guilt, of " their parents; yet, by the special effect of our " imperial lenity, we grant them their lives; but, " at the same time, we declare them incapable " of inheriting, either on the father's or on the " mother's side, or of receiving any gift or le- " gacy, from the testament either of kinsmen or " of strangers. Stigmatized with hereditary " infamy, excluded from the hopes of honours " or fortune, let them endure the pangs of po- " verty and contempt, till they shall consider " life as a calamity, and death as a comfort and " relief." In such words, so well adapted to insult the feelings of mankind, did the emperor, or rather his favourite eunuch, applaud the moderation of a law, which transferred the same unjust and inhuman penalties to the children of all those who had seconded, or who had not disclosed, these fictitious conspiracies. Some of the noblest regulations of Roman jurisprudence have been suffered to expire; but this edict, a convenient and forcible engine of ministerial tyranny, was carefully inserted in the

any sign of approbation or concurrence. For this opinion, says Baldus, he is now roasting in hell. For my own part, continues the discreet Heineccius, (Element. Jur. Civil. l. iv, p. 411), I must approve the theory of Bartolus; but in practice I should incline to the sentiment of Baldus. Yet Bartolus was gravely quoted by the lawyers of Cardinal Richelieu; and Eutropius was indirectly guilty of the murder of the virtuous de Thou.

codes of Theodosius and Justinian; and the same maxims have been revived in modern ages, to protect the electors of Germany, and the cardinals of the church of Rome."

Rebellion
of Tribi-
gild,
A. D. 399.
Yet these sanguinary laws, which spread terror among a disarmed and dispirited people, were of too weak a texture to restrain the bold enterprise of Tribigild* the Ostrogoth. The colony of that warlike nation, which had been planted by Theodosius in one of the most fertile districts of Phrygia,** impatiently compared the slow returns of laborious husbandry with the successful rapine and liberal rewards of Alaric; and their leader resented, as a personal affront, his own ungracious reception in the palace of Constantinople. A soft and wealthy province, in the heart of the empire, was astonished by the sound of war; and the faithful vassal, who had been disregarded or oppressed, was again respected, as soon as he resumed the hostile character of a barbarian. The vineyards and fruitful fields, between the rapid

---

" Godefroy, tom. iii, p. 89. It is, however, suspected, that this law, so repugnant to the maxims of Germanic freedom, has been surreptitiously added to the golden bull.

* A copious and circumstantial narrative (which he might have reserved for more important events) is bestowed by Zosimus (l. v, p. 304-312) on the revolt of Tribigild and Gainas. See likewise Socrates, l. vi, c. 6, and Sozomen, l. viii, c. 4. The second book of Claudian against Eutropius, is a fine, though imperfect, piece of history.

** Claudian (in Eutrop. l. ii, 237-250) very accurately observes, that the ancient name and nation of the Phrygians extended very far on every side, till their limits were contracted by the colonies of the Bithynians of Thrace, of the Greeks, and at last of the Gauls. His description (ii, 257-272) of the fertility of Phrygia, and of the four rivers that produced gold, is just and picturesque.

Marsyas and the winding Mæander,[a] were consumed with fire; the decayed walls of the city crumbled into dust, at the first stroke of an enemy; the trembling inhabitants escaped from a bloody massacre to the shores of the Hellespont; and a considerable part of Asia Minor was desolated by the rebellion of Tribigild. His rapid progress was checked by the resistance of the peasants of Pamphylia; and the Ostrogoths, attacked in a narrow pass, between the city of Selgæ,[b] a deep morass, and the craggy cliffs of Mount Tarus, were defeated with the loss of their bravest troops. But the spirit of their chief was not daunted by misfortune; and his army was continually recruited by swarms of barbarians and outlaws, who were desirous of exercising the profession of robbery, under the more honourable names of war and conquest. The rumours of the success of Tribigild might for some time be suppressed by fear, or disguised by flattery; yet they gradually alarmed both the court and the capital. Every misfortune was exaggerated in dark and doubtful hints; and the future designs of the rebels became the subject of anxious conjecture. Whenever Tribigild advanced into the inland country, the Romans were inclined to

---

[a] Xenophon. Anabasis, l. i, p. 11, 12, edit. Hutchinson. Strabo, l. xii, p. 865, edit. Amstel. Q. Curt. l. iii, c. 1. Claudian compares the junction of the Marsyas and Mæander to that of the Saone and the Rhône; with this difference, however, that the smaller of the Phrygian rivers is not accelerated, but retarded, by the larger.

[b] Selgæ a colony of the Lacedæmonians, had formerly numbered twenty thousand citizens; but in the age of Zosimus it was reduced to a πολιχνη, or small town. See Cellarius, Geograph. Antiq. tom. ii, p. 117.

CHAP. XXXII. suppose that he meditated the passage of Mount Taurus, and the invasion of Syria. If he descended towards the sea, they imputed, and perhaps suggested, to the Gothic chief, the more dangerous project of arming a fleet in the harbours of Ionia, and of extending his depradations along the maritime coast, from the mouth of the Nile to the port of Constantinople. The approach of danger, and the obstinacy of Tribigild, who refused all terms of accommodation, compelled Eutropius to summon a council of war.[b] After claiming for himself the privilege of a veteran soldier, the eunuch intrusted the guard of Thrace and the Hellespont to Gainas the Goth; and the command of the Asiatic army to his favourite Leo; two generals, who differently, but effectually, promoted the cause of the rebels. Leo,[c] who, from the bulk of his body, and the dulness of his mind, was surnamed the Ajax of the East, had deserted his original trade, of a woolcomber, to exercise, with much less skill and success, the military profession; and his uncertain operations were capriciously framed and executed, with an ignorance of real difficulties, and a timorous neglect of every favourable opportunity. The rashness of the

[b] The council of Eutropius, in Claudian, may be compared to that of Domitian in the fourth satire of Juvenal. The principal members of the former were, juvenes protervi lascivique senes; one of them had been a cook, a second a woolcomber. The language of their original profession exposes their assumed dignity; and their trifling conversation about tragedies, dancers, &c. is made still more ridiculous by the importance of the debate.

[c] Claudian (l. ii, 376-461) has branded him with infamy; and Zosimus, in more temperate language, confirms his reproaches, (l. v, p. 305).

Ostrogoths had drawn them into a disadvantageous position between the rivers Melas and Eurymedon, where they were almost besieged by the peasants of Pamphylia; but the arrival of an imperial army, instead of completing their destruction, afforded the means of safety and victory. Tribigild surprised the unguarded camp of the Romans, in the darkness of the night; seduced the faith of the greater part of the barbarian auxiliaries, and dissipated, without much effort, the troops, which had been corrupted by the relaxation of discipline, and the luxury of the capital. The discontent of Gainas, who had so boldly contrived and executed the death of Rufinus, was irritated by the fortune of his unworthy successor; he accused his own dishonourable patience under the servile reign of an eunuch; and the ambitious Goth was convicted, at least in the public opinion, of secretly fomenting the revolt of Tribigild, with whom he was connected by a domestic, as well as by a national, alliance.⁴ When Gainas passed the Hellespont, to unite under his standard the remains of the Asiatic troops, he skilfully adapted his motions to the wishes of the Ostrogoths; abandoning, by his retreat, the country which they desired to invade; or facilitating, by his approach, the desertion of the barbarian auxiliaries. To the imperial

---

⁴ The *conspiracy* of Gainas and Tribigild, which is attested by the Greek historian, had not reached the ears of Claudian, who attributes the revolt of the Ostrogoths to his own *martial* spirit, and the advice of his wife.

VOL. V.   C C

court he repeatedly magnified the valour, the genius, the inexhaustible resources of Tribigild ; confessed his own inability to prosecute the war; and extorted the permission of negotiating with his invincible adversary. The conditions of peace were dictated by the haughty rebel ; and the peremptory demand of the head of Eutropius, revealed the author and the design of this hostile conspiracy.

The bold satirist, who has indulged his discontent by the partial and passionate censure of the Christian emperors, violates the dignity, rather than the truth, of history, by comparing the son of Theodosius to one of those harmless and simple animals, who scarcely feel that they are the property of their shepherd. Two passions, however, fear and conjugal affection, awakened the languid soul of Arcadius ; he was terrified by the threats of a victorious barbarian ; and he yielded to the tender eloquence of his wife Eudoxia, who, with a flood of artificial tears, presenting her infant children to their father, implored his justice for some real or imaginary insult,* which she imputed to the audacious eunuch. The emperor's hand was directed to sign the condemnation of Eutropius ; the magic spell, which during four years had bound the prince and the people, was instantly dissolved ; and the acclamations, that so lately hailed the merit and fortune of the favourite, were converted into the clamours of

* This anecdote, which Philostorgius alone has preserved, (l. xi, c. 6, and Gothofred. Dissertat. p. 451-456), is curious and important; since it connects the revolt of the Goths with the secret intrigues of the palace.

the soldiers and people, who reproached his crimes, and pressed his immediate execution. In this hour of distress and despair, his only refuge was in the sanctuary of the church, whose privileges he had wisely, or profanely, attempted to circumscribe; and the most eloquent of the saints, John Chrysostom, enjoyed the triumph of protecting a prostrate minister, whose choice had raised him to the ecclesiastical throne of Constantinople. The archbishop, ascending the pulpit of the cathedral, that he might be distinctly seen and heard by an innumerable crowd of either sex and of every age, pronounced a seasonable and pathetic discourse on the forgiveness of injuries, and the instability of human greatness. The agonies of the pale and affrighted wretch who lay grovelling under the table of the altar, exhibited a solemn and instructive spectacle; and the orator, who was afterwards accused of insulting the misfortunes of Eutropius, laboured to excite the contempt, that he might assuage the fury, of the people.' The powers of humanity, of superstition, and of eloquence, prevailed. The empress Eudoxia was restrained, by her own prejudices, or by those of her subjects, from violating the sanctuary of the church; and Eutropius was tempted

CHAP. XXXII.

See the Homily of Chrysostom, tom. iii, p. 381-386, of which the exordium is particularly beautiful. Socrates, l. vi, c. 5; Sozomen, l. viii, c. 7. Montfaucon (in his life of Chrysostom, tom. xiii, p. 135) too hastily supposes that Tribigild was *actually* in Constantinople; and that he commanded the soldiers who were ordered to sieze Eutropius. Even Claudian, a pagan poet, (Præfat. ad l. ii, in Eutrop. 27), has mentioned the flight of the eunuch to the sanctuary.

Suppliciterque pias humilis prostratus ad aras
Mitigat iratas voce tremente nurus.

to capitulate, by the milder arts of persuasion, and by an oath, that his life should be spared.[e] Careless of the dignity of their sovereign, the new ministers of the palace immediately published an edict, to declare, that his late favourite had disgraced the names of consul and patrician, to abolish his statues, to confiscate his wealth, and to inflict a perpetual exile in the island of Cyprus.[h] A despicable and decrepid eunuch could no longer alarm the fears of his enemies; nor was he capable of enjoying what yet remained, the comforts of peace, of solitude, and of a happy climate. But their implacable revenge still envied him the last moments of a miserable life, and Eutropius had no sooner touched the shores of Cyprus, than he was hastily recalled. The vain hope of eluding, by a change of place, the obligation of an oath, engaged the empress to transfer the scene of his trial and execution, from Constantinople to the adjacent suburb of Chalcedon. The consul Aurelian pronounced the sentence; and the motives of that sentence expose the jurisprudence of a despotic government. The crimes

---

[e] Chrysostom, in another homily, (tom. iii, p. 386), affects to declare, that Eutropius would not have been taken, had he not deserted the church. Zosimus, (l. v, p. 313), on the contrary, pretends, that his enemies forced him (εξαρπασαντες αυτον) from the sanctuary. Yet the promise is an evidence of some treaty; and the strong assurance of Claudian, (Præfat. ad l. ii, 46),

   Sed tamen exemplo non feriere tuo,

may be considered as an evidence of some promise.

[h] Cod. Theod. l. ix, tit. xi, leg. 14. The date of that law (Jan. 17, A. D. 399) is erroneous and corrupt; since the fall of Eutropius could not happen till the autumn of the same year. See Tillemont, Hist. des Empereurs, tom. v, p. 780.

which Eutropius had committed against the
people, might have justified his death; but he
was found guilty of harnessing to his chariot
the *sacred* animals, who, from their breed, or
colour, were reserved for the use of the emperor
alone.[i]

While this domestic revolution was transacted, Gainas[k] openly revolted from his allegiance; united his forces, at Thyatira in Lydia,
with those of Tribigild; and still maintained
his superior ascendant over the rebellious leader
of the Ostrogoths. The confederate armies
advanced, without resistance, to the straits of
the Hellespont, and the Bosphorus; and Arcadius was instructed to prevent the loss of his
Asiatic dominions, by resigning his authority
and his person to the faith of the barbarians.
The church of the holy martyr Euphemia, situate on a lofty eminence near Chalcedon,[l] was
chosen for the place of the interview. Gainas
bowed, with reverence, at the feet of the emperor, whilst he required the sacrifice of Aurelian and Saturninus, two ministers of consular
rank; and their naked necks were exposed, by
the haughty rebel, to the edge of the sword,

---

[i] Zosimus, l. v, p. 813. Philostorgius, l. xi, c. 6.

[k] Zosimus, (l. v, p. 813-823); Socrates, (l. vi, c. 4); Sozomen,
(l. viii, c. 4), and Theodoret, (l. v, c. 32, 33), represent, though with
some various circumstances, the conspiracy, defeat, and death of
Gainas.

[l] Οσιας Ευφημιας μαρτυριον, is the expression of Zosimus himself, (l. v,
p. 814), who inadvertently uses the fashionable language of the Christians. Evagrius describes (l. ii, c. 3) the situation, architecture, relics,
and miracles of that celebrated church, in which the general council of
Chalcedon was afterwards held.

till he condescended to grant them a precarious and disgraceful respite. The Goths, according to the terms of the agreement, were immediately transported from Asia into Europe; and their victorious chief, who accepted the title of master-general of the Roman armies, soon filled Constantinople with his troops, and distributed among his dependants, the honours and rewards of the empire. In his early youth, Gainas had passed the Danube as a suppliant, and a fugitive: his elevation had been the work of valour and fortune; and his indiscreet, or perfidious, conduct, was the cause of his rapid downfal. Notwithstanding the vigorous opposition of the archbishop, he importunately claimed, for his Arian sectaries, the possession of a peculiar church; and the pride of the catholics was offended by the public toleration of heresy.[m] Every quarter of Constantinople was filled with tumult and disorder; and the barbarians gazed with such ardour on the rich shops of the jewellers, and the tables of the bankers, which were covered with gold and silver, that it was judged prudent to remove those dangerous temptations from their sight. They resented the injurious precaution; and some alarming attempts were made, during the night, to attack and destroy with fire the imperial palace.[n] In this state of

---

[m] The pious remonstrances of Chrysostom, which do not appear in his own writings, are strongly urged by Theodoret; but his insinuation, that they were successful, is disproved by facts. Tillemont (Hist. des Empereurs, tom. v, 863) has discovered, that the emperor, to satisfy the rapacious demands of Gainas, was obliged to melt the plate of the church of the Apostles.

[n] The ecclesiastical historians, who sometimes guide, and sometimes follow

mutual and suspicious hostility, the guards, and the people of Constantinople, shut the gates, and rose in arms to prevent, or to punish, the conspiracy of the Goths. During the absence of Gainas, his troops were surprised and oppressed; seven thousand barbarians perished in this bloody massacre. In the fury of the pursuit, the catholics uncovered the roof, and continued to throw down flaming logs of wood, till they over-whelmed their adversaries, who had retreated to the church or conventicle of the Arians. Gainas was either innocent of the design, or too confident of his success: he was astonished by the intelligence, that the flower of his army had been ingloriously destroyed; that he himself was declared a public enemy; and that his countryman, Fravitta, a brave and loyal confederate, had assumed the management of the war by sea and land. The enterprises of the rebel, against the cities of Thrace, were encountered by a firm and well-ordered defence: his hungry soldiers were soon reduced to the grass that grew on the margin of the fortifications; and Gainas, who vainly regretted the wealth and luxury of Asia, embraced a desperate resolution of forcing the passage of the Hellespont. He was destitute of vessels; but the woods of the Chersonesus afforded materials for rafts, and his intrepid barbarians did not refuse to trust themselves to the waves. But Fravitta attentively watched the progress of their undertaking. As soon as they had gained

follow, the public opinion, most confidently assert that the palace of Constantinople was guarded by legions of angels.

CHAP.
XXXII.
~~~~~~~~

the middle of the stream, the Roman galleys,[*]
impelled by the full force, of oars, of the current, and of a favourable wind, rushed forwards
in compact order, and with irresistible weight;
and the Hellespont was covered with the fragments of the Gothic shipwreck. After the destruction of his hopes, and the loss of many
thousands of his bravest soldiers, Gainas, who
could no longer aspire to govern, or to subdue,
the Romans, determined to resume the independence of a savage life. A light and active
body of barbarian horse, disengaged from their
infantry and baggage, might perform, in eight
or ten days, a march of three hundred miles
from the Hellespont to the Danube;[p] the garrisons of that important frontier had been gradually annihilated; the river, in the month of
December, would be deeply frozen; and the
unbounded prospect of Scythia was opened to
the ambition of Gainas. This design was secretly communicated to the national troops,
who devoted themselves to the fortunes of their
leader; and before the signal of departure was

[*] Zosimus (l. v, p. 319) mentions these galleys by the name of
Liburnians, and observes, that they were as swift (without explaining
the difference between them) as the vessels with fifty oars; but that
they were far inferior in speed to the *triremes*, which had been long
disused. Yet he reasonably concludes, from the testimony of Polybius, that galleys of a still larger size had been constructed in the
Punic-wars. Since the establishment of the Roman empire over the
Mediterranean, the useless art of building large ships of war had probably been neglected, and at length forgotten.

[p] Chishull (Travels, p. 61-63, 72 76) proceeded from Gallipoli, through
Hadrianople, to the Danube, in about fifteen days. He was in the train
of an English ambassador, whose baggage consisted of seventy-one
waggons. That learned traveller has the merit of tracing a curious and
unfrequented route.

given, a great number of provincial auxiliaries, CHAP.
whom he suspected of an attachment to their XXXII.
native country, were perfidiously massacred.
The Goths advanced, by rapid marches,
through the plains of Thrace; and they were
soon delivered from the fear of a pursuit, by the
vanity of Fravitta, who, instead of extinguish-
ing the war, hastened to enjoy the popular applause, and to assume the peaceful honours of
the consulship. But a formidable ally appeared in arms to vindicate the majesty of the empire, and to guard the peace and liberty of
Scythia.[q] The superior forces of Uldin, king
of the Huns, opposed the progress of Gainas;
an hostile and ruined country prohibited his
retreat; he disdained to capitulate; and after
repeatedly attempting to cut his way through
the ranks of the enemy, he was slain, with his
desperate followers, in the field of battle.
Eleven days after the naval victory of the Hel- A. D. 431,
lespont, the head of Gainas, the inestimable January 3
gift of the conqueror, was received at Constantinople, with the most liberal expressions of
gratitude; and the public deliverance was celebrated by festivals and illuminations. The
triumphs of Arcadius became the subject of

[q] The narrative of Zosimus, who actually leads Gainas beyond the
Danube, must be corrected by the testimony of Socrates, and Sozomen,
that he was killed in *Thrace*; and by the precise and authentic dates of
the Alexandrian, or Paschal Chronicle, p. 307. The naval victory of
the Hellespont is fixed to the month Apellæus, the tenth of the calends
of January, (December 23); the head of Gainas was brought to Constantinople the third of the nones of January, (January 3), in the month
Audynæus.

epic poems;[r] and the monarch, no longer oppressed by any hostile terrors, resigned himself
to the mild and absolute dominion of his wife,
the fair and artful Eudoxia, who has sullied
her fame by the persecution of St. John Chrysostom.

Election
and merit
of Chry-
sostom,
A. D. 398.
Feb. 26.

After the death of the indolent Nectarius, the
successor of Gregory Nazianzen, the church of
Constantinople was distracted by the ambition
of rival candidates, who were not ashamed to
solicit, with gold or flattery, the suffrage of
the people, or of the favourite. On this occasion, Eutropius seems to have deviated
from his ordinary maxims; and his uncor-
rupted judgment was determined only by
the superior merit of a stranger. In a late
journey into the East, he had admired the
sermons of John, a native and presbyter of Antioch, whose name has been distinguished by the
epithet of Chrysostom, or the Golden Mouth.[s]

---

[r] Eusebius Scholasticus acquired much fame by his poem on the
Gothic war, in which he had served. Near forty years afterwards,
Ammonius recited another poem on the same subject, in the presence
of the emperor Theodosius. See Socrates, l. vi, c. 6.

[s] The sixth book of Socrates, the eighth of Sozomen, and the fifth of
Theodoret, afford curious and authentic materials for the life of John
Chrysostom. Besides those general historians, I have taken for my
guides the four principal biographers of the saint. 1. The author of a
partial and passionate Vindication of the Archbishop of Constantinople, composed in the form of a dialogue, and under the name of his
zealous partizan, Palladius, bishop of Helenopolis, (Tillemont, Mem.
Eccles. tom. xi, p. 500 533). It is inserted among the works of Chrysostom, tom. xiii, p. 1-90, edit. Montfaucon. 2. The moderate Erasmus, (tom. iii. epist. MCL, p. 1331-1347, edit. Ludg. Bat). His vivacity
and good sense were his own; his errors, in the uncultivated state of
ecclesiastical antiquity, were almost inevitable. 3. The learned Tillemont, (Mem. Ecclesiastiques, tom. xi, p. 1-405, 547-626, &c. &c.) who
compiles the lives of the saints with incredible patience, and religious
accuracy.

A private order was despatched to the governor of Syria; and as the people might be unwilling to resign their favourite preacher, he was transported with speed and secrecy, in a post-chariot, from Antioch to Constantinople. The unanimous and unsolicited consent of the court, the clergy, and the people, ratified the choice of the minister; and, both as a saint and as an orator, the new archbishop surpassed the sanguine expectations of the public. Born of a noble and opulent family, in the capital of Syria, Chrysostom had been educated, by the care of a tender mother, under the tuition of the most skilful masters. He studied the art of rhetoric in the school of Libanius: and that celebrated sophist, who soon discovered the talents of his disciple, ingenuously confessed, that John would have deserved to succeed him, had he not been stolen away by the Christians. His piety soon disposed him to receive the sacrament of baptism; to renounce the lucrative and honourable profession of the law, and to bury himself in the adjacent desert, where he subdued the lusts of the flesh by an austere penance of six years. His infirmities compelled him to return to the society of mankind; and the authority of Meletius devoted his talents to the service of the church: but in the midst of his family, and afterwards on the archiepiscopal throne, Chrysostom still perse-

accuracy. He has minutely searched the voluminous works of Chrysostom himself. 4. Father Montfaucon; who has perused these works with the curious diligence of a editor, discovered several new homilies, and again reviewed and composed the life of Chrysostom, (Opera Chrysostom. tom. xiii, p. 91-177).

CHAP. vered in the practice of the monastic virtues.
XXXII. The ample revenues, which his predecessors
had consumed in pomp and luxury, he diligently applied to the establishment of hospitals ;
and the multitudes, who were supported by his
charity, preferred the eloquent and edifying
discourses of their archbishop, to the amusements of the theatre, or the circus. The monuments of that eloquence, which was admired
near twenty years at Antioch and Constantinople, have been carefully preserved ; and the
possession of near one thousand sermons, or
homilies, has authorized the critics' of succeeding times to appretiate the genuine merit of
Chrysostom. They unanimously attribute to
the Christian orator, the free command of an
elegant and copious language; the judgment to
conceal the advantages which he derived from
the knowledge of rhetoric and philosophy; an
inexhaustible fund of metaphors and simili-
tudes, of ideas and images, to vary and illustrate the most familiar topics ; the happy art
of engaging the passions in the service of virtue ; and of exposing the folly, as well as the
turpitude, of vice, almost with the truth and
spirit of a dramatic representation.

The pastoral labours of the archbishop of
Constantinople provoked, and gradually united

---

* As I am *almost* a stranger to the voluminous sermons of Chrysostom, I have given my confidence to the two most judicious and mod-
rate of the ecclesiastical critics, Erasmus, (tom. iii, p. 1344) and Du-
pin, (Bibliotheque Ecclesiastique, tom. iii, p. 38) : yet the good taste
of the former is sometimes vitiated by an excessive love of antiquity ;
and the good sense of the latter is always restrained by prudential considerations.

against him, two sorts of enemies; the aspiring clergy, who envied his success, and the obstinate sinners, who were offended by his reproofs. When Chrysostom thundered, from the pulpit of St. Sophia, against the degeneracy of the Christians, his shafts were spent among the crowd, without wounding, or even marking, the character of any individual. When he declaimed against the peculiar vices of the rich, poverty might obtain a transient consolation from his invectives: but the guilty were still sheltered by their numbers; and the reproach itself was dignified by some ideas of superiority, and enjoyment. But as the pyramid rose towards the summit, it insensibly diminished to a point; and the magistrates, the ministers, the favourite eunuchs, the ladies of the court," the empress Eudoxia herself, had a much larger share of guilt, to divide among a smaller proportion of criminals. The personal applications of the audience were anticipated, or confirmed, by the testimony of their own conscience; and the intrepid preacher assumed the dangerous right of exposing both the offence, and the offender, to the public abhorrence. The secret resentment of the court encouraged the discontent of the clergy and monks of Constantinople, who were

CHAP.
XXXII.

His administration and defects,
A. D. 398.
403.

" The females of Constantinople distinguished themselves by their enmity or their attachment to Chrysostom. Three noble and opulent widows, Marsa, Castricia, and Eugraphia, were the leaders of the persecution, (Pallad. Dialog. tom. xiii, p. 14). It was impossible that they should forgive a preacher, who reproached their affectation to conceal, by the ornaments of dress, their age and ugliness, (Pallad. p. 27). Olympius, by equal zeal, displayed in a more pious cause, has obtained the title of saint. See Tillemont, Mem. Eccles. tom. xi, 416-440.

CHAP. too hastily reformed by the fervent zeal of their
XXXII. archbishop.   He had condemned, from the
pulpit, the domestic females of the clergy of
Constantinople, who, under the names of servants, or sisters, afforded a perpetual occasion
either of sin, or of scandal.   The silent and solitary ascetics, who had secluded themselves
from the world, were entitled to the warmest
approbation of Chrysostom; but he despised
and stigmatized, as the disgrace of their holy
profession, the crowd of degenerate monks, who,
from some unworthy motives of pleasure or
profit, so frequently infested the streets of the
capital.   To the voice of persuasion, the archbishop was obliged to add the terrors of authority; and his ardour, in the exercise of ecclesiastical jurisdiction, was not always exempt
from passion; nor was it always guided by
prudence.   Chrysostom was naturally of a
choleric disposition.[x] Although he struggled, according to the precepts of the gospel, to love
his private enemies, he indulged himself in the
privilege of hating the enemies of God, and of
the church; and his sentiments were sometimes
delivered with too much energy of countenance
and expression.   He still maintained, from some
considerations of health, or abstinence, his former habits of taking his repasts alone; and this

---

[x] Sozomen, and more especially Socrates, have defined the real
character of Chrysostom with a temperate and impartial freedom, very
offensive to his blind admirers.   Those historians lived in the next generation, when party violence was abated, and had conversed with many
persons intimately acquainted with the virtues and imperfections of the
saint.

inhospitable custom,[y] which his enemies imputed to pride, contributed, at least, to nourish the infirmity of a morose and unsocial humour. Separated from that familiar intercourse, which facilitates the knowledge and the despatch of business, he reposed an unsuspecting confidence in his deacon Serapion; and seldom applied his speculative knowledge of human nature to the particular characters, either of his dependants, or of his equals., Conscious of the purity of his intentions, and perhaps of the superiority of his genius, the archbishop of Constantinople extended the jurisdiction of the imperial city, that he might enlarge the sphere of his pastoral labours; and the conduct which the profane imputed to an ambitious motive, appeared to Chrysostom himself in the light of a sacred and indispensible duty. In his visitation through the Asiatic provinces, he deposed thirteen bishops of Lydia and Phrygia; and indiscreetly declared, that a deep corruption of simony and licentiousness had infected the whole episcopal order.[z] If those bishops were innocent, such a rash and unjust condemnation must excite a well-grounded discontent. If they were guilty, the numerous associates of their guilt would

[y] Palladius (tom. xiii, p. 40, &c.) very seriously defends the archbishop. 1. He never tasted wine. 2. The weakness of his stomach required a peculiar diet. 3. Business, or study, or devotion, often kept him fasting till sun-set. 4. He detested the noise and levity of great dinners. 5. He saved the expence for the use of the poor. 6. He was apprehensive, in a capital like Constantinople, of the envy and reproach of partial invitations.

[z] Chrysostom declares his free opinion, (tom. ix, hom. iii, in Act Apostol. p. 29), that the number of bishops, who might be saved, bore a very small proportion to those who would be damned.

soon discover, that their own safety depended on the ruin of the archbishop; whom they studied to represent as the tyrant of the eastern church.

Chrysostom is persecuted by the empress Eudoxia,
A. D. 403.

This ecclesiastical conspiracy was managed by Theophilus,[a] archbishop of Alexandria, an active and ambitious prelate, who displayed the fruits of rapine in monuments of ostentation His national dislike to the rising greatness of a city, which degraded him from the second, to the third, rank, in the Christian world, was exasperated by some personal disputes with Chrysostom himself.[b] By the private invitation of the empress, Theophilus landed at Constantinople, with a stout body of Egyptian mariners, to encounter the populace; and a train of dependant bishops, to secure, by their voices, the majority of a synod. The synod[c] was convened in the suburb of Chalcedon, surnamed the *Oak*, where Rufinus had erected a stately church and monastery; and their proceedings were continued during fourteen days, or sessions. A bishop and a deacon accused the archbishop of Constantinople; but the frivolous or improbable nature of the forty-seven articles

[a] See Tillemont, Mem. Eccles. tom. xi, p. 441-500.

[b] I have purposely omitted the controversy which arose among the monks of Egypt, concerning Origenism and Antropomorphism; the dissimulation and violence of Theophilus; his artful management of the simplicity of Epiphanius; the persecution and flight of the *long*, or tall, brothers; the ambiguous support which they received at Constantinople from Chrysostom, &c. &c.

[c] Photius (p. 53-60) has preserved the original facts of the synod of the Oak; which destroy the false assertion, that Chrysostom was condemned by no more than thirty-six bishops, of whom twenty-nine were Egyptians. Forty-five bishops subscribed his sentence. See Tillemont, Mem. Eccles. tom. xi, p. 595.

CHAP.
XXXII.
~~~~~~~~~~

Character
and ad-
ventures
of the em-
press Eu-
docia,
A. D. 421.
460.

throne, might be deemed an incredible romance, if such a romance had not been verified in the marriage of Theodosius. The celebrated Athenais* was educated by her father Leontius in the religion and sciences of the Greeks; and so advantageous was the opinion which the Athenian philosopher entertained of his contemporaries, that he divided his patrimony between his two sons, bequeathing to his daughter a small legacy of one hundred pieces of gold, in the lively confidence that her beauty and merit would be a sufficient portion. The jealousy and avarice of her brothers soon compelled Athenais to seek a refuge at Constantinople; and, with some hopes, either of justice or favour, to throw herself at the feet of Pulcheria. That sagacious princess listened to her eloquent complaint; and secretly destined the daughter of the philosopher Leontius for the future wife of the emperor of the East, who had now attained the twentieth year of his age. She easily excited the curiosity of her brother, by an interesting picture of the charms of Athenais; large eyes, a well-proportioned nose, a fair complex-

---

* Socrates, (l. vii, c. 21) mentions her name, (Athenais the daughter of Leontius, an Athenian sophist), her baptism, marriage, and poetical genius. The most ancient account of her history is in John Malala, (part ii, p. 20, 21, edit. Venet. 1743), and in the Paschal Chronicle, (p. 311, 312). Those authors had probably seen original pictures of the empress Eudocia. The modern Greeks, Zonaras, Cedrenus, &c. have displayed, the love, rather than the talent, of fiction. From Nicephorus, indeed, I have ventured to assume her age. The writer of a romance would not have *imagined*, that Athenais was near twenty-eight years old when she inflamed the heart of a young emperor.

ion, golden locks, a slender person, a graceful
demeanour, an understanding improved by
study, and a virtue tried by distress. Theodosius, concealed behind a curtain in the apartment of his sister, was permitted to behold the
Athenian virgin: the modest youth immediately declared his pure and honourable love; and
the royal nuptials were celebrated amidst the
acclamations of the capital and the provinces.
Athenais, who was easily persuaded to renounce
the errors of paganism, received at her baptism
the Christian name of Eudocia; but the cautious
Pulcheria withheld the title of Augusta, till the
wife of Theodosius had approved her fruitfulness by the birth of a daughter, who espoused,
fifteen years afterwards, the emperor of the
West. The brothers of Eudocia obeyed, with
some anxiety, her imperial summons; but as
she could easily forgive their fortunate un-
kindness, she indulged the tenderness, or perhaps the vanity, of a sister, by promoting them
to the rank of consuls and prefects. In the
luxury of the palace, she still cultivated those
ingenious arts, which had contributed to her
greatness; and wisely dedicated her talents to
the honour of religion, and of her husband.
Eudocia composed a poetical paraphrase of the
first eight books of the Old Testament, and of
the prophecies of Daniel and Zachariah; a
cento of the verses of Homer, applied to the life
and miracles of Christ, the legend of St. Cyprian, and a panegyric on the Persian victories
of Theodosius: and her writings, which were

applauded by a servile and superstitious age, have not been disdained by the candour of impartial criticism.[f] The fondness of the emperor was not abated by time and possession ; and Eudocia, after the marriage of her daughter, was permitted to discharge her grateful vows by a solemn pilgrimage to Jerusalem. Her ostentatious progress through the East may seem inconsistent with the spirit of Christian humility : she pronounced, from a throne of gold and gems, an eloquent oration to the senate of Antioch, declared her royal intention of enlarging the walls of the city, bestowed a donative of two hundred pounds of gold to restore the public baths, and accepted the statues, which were decreed by the gratitude of Antioch. In the Holy Land, her alms and pious foundations exceeded the munificence of the great Helena; and though the public treasure might be impoverished by this excessive liberality, she enjoyed the conscious satisfaction of returning to Constantinople, with the chains of St. Peter, the right arm of St. Stephen, and an undoubted picture of the Virgin, painted by St. Luke.[s] But this pilgrimage was the fatal term of the glories of Eudocia. Satiated with empty pomp, and un-

[f] Socrates, l. vii, c. 21. Photius, p. 413-420. The Homeric cento is still extant, and has been repeatedly printed, but the claim of Eudocia to that insipid performance is disputed by the critics. See Fabricius, Biblioth. Græc. tom. i, p. 357. The *Ionia*, a miscellaneous dictionary of history and fable, was compiled by another empress of the name of Eudocia, who lived in the eleventh century; and the work is still extant in manuscript.

[s] Baronius (Annal. Eccles. A. D. 438, 439) is copious and florid; but he is accused of placing the lives of different ages on the same level of authenticity.

CHAP.
XXXII.
----

mindful, perhaps, of her obligations to Pulcheria, she ambitiously aspired to the government of the eastern empire; the palace was distracted by female discord; but the victory was at last decided, by the superior ascendant of the sister of Theodosius. The execution of Paulinus, master of the offices, and the disgrace of Cyrus, pretorian prefect of the East, convinced the public that the favour of Eudocia was insufficient to protect her most faithful friends; and the uncommon beauty of Paulinus, encouraged the secret rumour, that his guilt was that of a successful lover.[a] As soon as the empress perceived that the affection of Theodosius was irretrievably lost, she requested the permission of retiring to the distant solitude of Jerusalem. She obtained her request; but the jealousy of Theodosius, or the vindictive spirit of Pulcheria, pursued her in her last retreat; and Saturninus, count of the domestics, was directed to punish with death two ecclesiastics, her most favoured servants. Eudocia instantly revenged them by the assassination of the count; the furious passions, which she indulged on this suspicious occasion, seemed to justify the severity of Theodosius; and the empress, ignominiously stript of the honours of her rank,[1] was

[a] In this short view of the disgrace of Eudocia, I have imitated the caution of Evagrius, (l. i, c. 21), and count Marcellinus, (in Chron. A. D. 440 and 444). The two authentic dates assigned by the latter, overturn a great part of the Greek fictions; and the celebrated story of the apple, &c. is fit only for the Arabian Nights, where something not very unlike it may be found.

[1] Priscus, (in Excerpt. Legat. p. 69), a contemporary, and a courtier, dryly mentions her pagan and Christian names, without adding any title of honour or respect.

disgraced, perhaps unjustly, in the eyes of the world. The remainder of the life of Eudocia, about sixteen years, was spent in exile and devotion; and the approach of age, the death of Theodosius, the misfortunes of her only daughter, who was led a captive from Rome to Carthage, and the society of the holy monks of Palestine, insensibly confirmed the religious temper of her mind. After a full experience of the vicissitudes of human life, the daughter of the philosopher Leontius expired, at Jerusalem, in the sixty-seventh year of her age; protesting, with her dying breath, that she had never transgressed the bounds of innocence and friendship.[k]

The gentle mind of Theodosius was never inflamed by the ambition of conquest, or military renown; and the slight alarm of a Persian war scarcely interrupted the tranquillity of the East. The motives of this war were just and honourable. In the last year of the reign of Jezdegerd, the supposed guardian of Theodosius, a bishop, who aspired to the crown of martyrdom, destroyed one of the fire-temples of Susa.[l]

The Persian war, A. D. 422

[k] For the *two* pilgrimages of Eudocia, and her long residence at Jerusalem, her devotion, alms, &c. see Socrates (l. vii, c. 47), and Evagrius, (l. i, c. 20, 21, 22). The Paschal Chronicle may sometimes deserve regard; and, in the domestic history of Antioch, John Malala becomes a writer of good authority. The Abbé Guenée, in a memoir on the fertility of Palestine, of which I have only seen an extract, calculates the gifts of Eudocia at 20,488 pounds of gold, above 800,000 pounds sterling.

[l] Theodoret, l. v, c. 39. Tillemont, Mem. Eccles. tom. xii, p. 356-364. Assemanni, Bibliot, Oriental. tom. iii, p. 396; tom. iv, p 61. Theodoret blames the rashness of Abdas, but extols the constancy of his martyrdom. Yet I do not clearly understand the casuistry which prohibits our repairing the damage which we have unlawfully committed.

CHAP.
XXXII.
His zeal and obstinacy were revenged on his brethren : the Magi excited a cruel persecution ; and the intolerant zeal of Jezdegerd was imitated by his son Vararanes, or Bahram, who soon afterwards ascended the throne. Some Christian fugitives, who escaped to the Roman frontier, were sternly demanded, and generously refused ; and the refusal, aggravated by commercial disputes, soon kindled a war between the rival monarchies. The mountains of Armenia, and the plains of Mesopotamia, were filled with hostile armies; but the operations of two successive campaigns were not productive of any decisive or memorable events. Some engagements were fought, some towns were besieged, with various and doubtful success ; and if the Romans failed in their attempt to recover the long-lost possession of Nisibis, the Persians were repulsed from the walls of a Mesopotamian city, by the valour of a martial bishop, who pointed his thundering engine in the name of St. Thomas the apostle. Yet the splendid victories, which the incredible speed of the messenger Palladius repeatedly announced to the palace of Constantinople, were celebrated with festivals and panegyrics. From these panegyrics the historians[m] of the age might borrow their extraordinary, and, perhaps, fabulous, tales ; of the proud challenge of a Persian hero, who was entangled by the net, and despatched by the sword, of Areobindus the Goth ;

[m] Socrates (l. vii, c. 18, 19, 20, 21) is the best author for the Persian war. We may likewise consult the three Chronicles, the Paschal, and those of Marcellinus and Malala.

of the ten thousand *Immortals*, who were slain in the attack of the Roman camp; and of the hundred thousand Arabs, or Saracens, who were impelled by a panic terror to throw themselves headlong into the Euphrates. Such events may be disbelieved, or disregarded; but the charity of a bishop, Acacius of Amida, whose name might have dignified the saintly calendar, shall not be lost in oblivion. Boldly declaring that vases of gold and silver are useless to a god who neither eats nor drinks, the generous prelate sold the plate of the church of Amida; employed the price in the redemption of seven thousand Persian captives; supplied their wants with affectionate liberality; and dismissed them to their native country, to inform the king of the true spirit of the religion which he persecuted. The practice of benevolence in the midst of war must always tend to assuage the animosity of contending nations; and I wish to persuade myself, that Acacius contributed to the restoration of peace. In the conference which was held on the limits of the two empires, the Roman ambassadors degraded the personal character of their sovereign, by a vain attempt to magnify the extent of his power; when they seriously advised the Persians to prevent, by a timely accommodation, the wrath of a monarch, who was yet ignorant of this distant war. A truce of one hundred years was solemnly ratified; and, although the revolutions of Armenia might threaten the public tranquillity, the essential conditions of this treaty were

Armenia
divided
between
the Per-
sians and
the Ro-
mans.
A. D. 431-
440.

respected near fourscore years by the successors of Constantine and Artaxerxes.

Since the Roman and Parthian standards first encountered on the banks of the Euphrates, the kingdom of Armenia[a] was alternately oppressed by its formidable protectors; and, in the course of this History, several events, which inclined the balance of peace and war, have been already related. A disgraceful treaty had resigned Armenia to the ambition of Sapor; and the scale of Persia appeared to preponderate. But the royal race of Arsaces impatiently submitted to the house of Sassan; the turbulent nobles asserted, or betrayed, their hereditary independence; and the nation was still attached to the *Christian* princes of Constantinople. In the beginning of the fifth century, Armenia was divided by the progress of war and faction;[b] and the unnatural division precipitated the downfal of that ancient monarchy. Chosroes, the Persian vassal, reigned over the eastern and most extensive portion of the country; while the

[a] This account of the ruin and division of the kingdom of Armenia is taken from the third book of the Armenian history of Moses of Chorene. Deficient as he is in every qualification of a good historian, his local information, his passions, and his prejudices, are strongly expressive of a native and contemporary. Procopius (de Edificiis, l. xiii, c. i, 5) relates the same facts in a very different manner; but I have extracted the circumstances the most probable in themselves, and the least inconsistent with Moses of Chorene.

[b] The western Armenians used the Greek language and characters in their religious offices; but the use of that hostile tongue was prohibited by the Persians in the eastern provinces, which were obliged to use the Syriac, till the invention of the Armenian letters by Mesrobes, in the beginning of the fifth century, and the subsequent version of the bible into the Armenian language; an event which relaxed the connection of the church and nation with Constantinople.

which they presented against him, may justly
be considered as a fair and unexceptionable
panegyric. Four successive summons were
signified to Chrysostom; but he still refused to
trust either his person, or his reputation, in the
hands of his implacable enemies, who, prudently declining the examination of any particular
charges, condemned his contumacious disobedience, and hastily pronounced a sentence of
deposition. The synod of the *Oak* immediately addressed the emperor to ratify and execute
their judgment, and charitably insinuated, that
the penalties of treason might be inflicted on the
audacious preacher, who had reviled, under
the name of Jezebel, the empress Eudoxia herself. The archbishop was rudely arrested, and
conducted through the city, by one of the imperial messengers, who landed him, after a short
navigation, near the entrance of the Euxine;
from whence, before the expiration of two days,
he was gloriously recalled.

The first astonishment of his faithful people
had been mute and passive: they suddenly
rose with unanimous and irresistible fury.
Theophilus escaped; but the promiscuous
crowd of monks and Egyptian mariners were
slaughtered without pity in the streets of Constantinople.[c] A seasonable earthquake justi-

---

[c] Palladius owns, (p. 30), that if the people of Constantinople had
found Theophilus, they would certainly have thrown him into the sea.
Socrates mentions (l. vi, c. 17) a battle between the mob and the sailors
of Alexandria, in which many wounds were given, and some lives
were

fied the interposition of heaven; the torrent of sedition rolled forwards to the gates of the palace; and the empress, agitated by fear or remorse, threw herself at the feet of Arcadius, and confessed, that the public safety could be purchased only by the restoration of Chrysostom. The Bosphorus was covered with innumerable vessels; the shores of Europe and Asia were profusely illuminated; and the acclamations of a victorious people accompanied, from the port to the cathedral, the triumph of the archbishop; who, too easily, consented to resume the exercise of his functions, before his sentence had been legally reversed by the authority of an ecclesiastical synod. Ignorant, or careless, of the impending danger, Chrysostom indulged his zeal, or perhaps his resentment; declaimed with peculiar asperity against *female* vices; and condemned the profane honours which were addressed, almost in the precincts of St. Sophia, to the statue of the empress. His imprudence tempted his enemies to inflame the haughty spirit of Eudoxia, by reporting, or perhaps inventing, the famous exordium of a sermon, " Herodias is again furi-" ous; Herodias again dances: she once more " requires the head of John;" an insolent allusion, which as a woman and a sovereign, it was impossible for her to forgive.[e] The short inter-

were lost. The massacre of the monks is observed only by the pagan Zosimus, (l. v, p. 324), who acknowledges that Chrysostom had a singular talent to lead the illiterate multitude, ην γαρ ο ανθρωπος αλογον οχλον επαγαγεσθαι δεινος.

[e] See Socrates, l. vi, c. 18; Sozomen l. viii, c. 20. Zosimus, (l. v, p. 324,

val of a perfidious truce was employed to con-
cert more effectual measures for the disgrace
and ruin of the archbishop. A numerous council of the eastern prelates, who were guided from
a distance by the advice of Theophilus, confirmed the validity, without examining the justice, of the former sentence; and a detachment
of barbarian troops was introduced into the
city, to suppress the emotions of the people.
On the vigil of Easter, the solemn administration of baptism was rudely interrupted by the
soldiers, who alarmed the modesty of the naked
catechumens, and violated, by their presence,
the awful mysteries of the Christian worship.
Arsacius occupied the church of St. Sophia,
and the archiepiscopal throne. The catholics
retreated to the baths of Constantine, and afterwards to the fields: where they were still
pursued and insulted by the guards, the bishops, and the magistrates. The fatal day of the
second and final exile of Chrysostom was marked by the conflagration of the cathedral, of the
senate-house, and of the adjacent buildings;
and this calamity was imputed, without proof,
but not without probability, to the despair of
a persecuted faction.[f]

Cicero might claim some merit, if his voluntary banishment preserved the peace of the re-

324, 327) mentions, in general terms, his invectives against Eudoxia.
The homily, which begins with those famous words, is rejected as
spurious. Montfaucon, tom. xiii, p. 151. Tillemont, Mem. Eccles.
tom. xi, p. 603.

[f] We might naturally expect such a charge from Zosimus, (l. v, p.
327); but it is remarkable enough, that it should be confirmed by Socrates, l. vi, c. 18, and the Paschal Chronicle, p. 307.

CHAP.
XXXII.

Exile of
Chrysos-
tom,
A. D. 404,
June 20.

public ;[g] but the submission of Chrysostom was
the indispensable duty of a Christian and a
subject. Instead of listening to his humble
prayer, that he might be permitted to reside at
Cyzicus, or Nicomedia, the inflexible empress
assigned for his exile the remote and desolate
town of Cucusus, among the ridges of Mount
Taurus, in the Lesser Armenia. A secret hope
was entertained, that the archbishop might
perish in a difficult and dangerous march of
seventy days, in the heat of summer, through
the provinces of Asia Minor, where he was
continually threatened by the hostile attacks of
the Isaurians, and the more implacable fury of
the monks. Yet Chrysostom arrived in safety
at the place of his confinement; and the three
years, which he spent at Cucusus, and the
neighbouring town of Arabissus, were the last
and most glorious of his life. His character
was consecrated by absence and persecution;
the faults of his administration were not long
remembered; but every tongue repeated the
praises of his genius and virtue: and the respectful attention of the Christian world was
fixed on a desert spot among the mountains of
Taurus. From that solitude, the archbishop,
whose active mind was invigorated by misfortunes, maintained a strict and frequent correspondence[h] with the most distant provinces;

[g] He displays those specious motives (Post Reditum, c. 13, 14) in the
language of an orator and a politician.
[h] Two hundred and forty-two of the epistles of Chrysostom are still
extant, (Opera, tom. iii, p. 528-736). They are addressed to a great
variety

exhorted the separate congregation of his faithful adherents to persevere in their allegiance; urged the destruction of the temples of Phœnicia, and the extirpation of heresy in the isle of Cyprus; extended his pastoral care to the missions of Persia and Scythia; negotiated, by his ambassadors, with the Roman pontiff, and the emperor Honorius; and boldly appealed, from a partial synod, to the supreme tribunal of a free and general council. The mind of the illustrious exile was still independent; but his captive body was exposed to the revenge of the oppressors, who continued to abuse the name and authority of Arcadius.[1] An order was despatched for the instant removal of Chrysostom to the extreme desert of Pityus: and his guards so faithfully obeyed their cruel instructions, that, before he reached the sea-coast of the Euxine, he expired at Comana, in Pontus, in the sixtieth year of his age. The succeeding generation acknowledged his innocence and merit. The archbishops of the East, who might blush that their predecessors had been the enemies of Chrysostom, were gradually disposed,

CHAP. XXXII.

His death A. D. 407, Sept. 14.

variety of persons, and shew a firmness of mind, much superior to that of Cicero in his exile. The fourteenth epistle contains a curious narrative of the dangers of his journey.

[1] After the exile of Chrysostom, Theophilus published an *enormous* and *horrible* volume against him, in which he perpetually repeats the polite expressions of hostem humanitatis, sacrilegorum principem, immundum dæmonem; he affirms, that John Chrysostom had delivered his soul to be adulterated by the devil; and wishes that some farther punishment, adequate (if possible) to the magnitude of his crimes, may be inflicted on him. St. Jerom, at the request of his friend Theophilus, translated this edifying performance from Greek into Latin. See Facundus Hermian. Defens. pro iii, Capitul. l. vi, c. 5, published by Sirmond. Opera, tom. ii, p. 595, 596, 597.

CHAP.
XXXII.

His relics
transport-
ed to Con-
stantino-
ple,
A. D. 438.
Jan. 27.

by the firmness of the Roman pontiff, to restore the honours of that venerable name.[k] At the pious solicitation of the clergy and people of Constantinople, his relics, thirty years after his death, were transported from their obscure sepulchre to the royal city.[l] The emperor Theodosius advanced to receive them as far as Chalcedon; and, falling prostrate on the coffin implored, in the name of his guilty parents, Arcadius and Eudoxia, the forgiveness of the injured saint.[m]

The death
of Arca-
dius,
A. D. 408,
May 1.

Yet a reasonable doubt may be entertained, whether any stain of hereditary guilt could be derived from Arcadius to his successor. Eudoxia was a young and beautiful woman, who indulged her passions, and despised her husband: Count John enjoyed, at least, the familiar confidence of the empress: and the public named him as the real father of Theodosius the younger.[n] The birth of a son was accepted,

[k] His name was inserted by his successor Atticas in the Dyptics of the church of Constantinople, A. D. 418. Ten years afterwards he was revered as a saint. Cyril, who inherited the place, and the passions, of his uncle, Theophilus, yielded with much reluctance. See Facund. Hermian. l. iv, c. 1. Tillemont, Mem. Eccles. tom. xiv, p. 277–283.

[l] Socrates, l. vii, c. 45. Theodoret, l. v, c. 36. This event reconciled the Joannites, who had hitherto refused to acknowledge his successors. During his lifetime, the Joannites were respected by the catholics, as the true and orthodox communion of Constantinople. Their obstinacy gradually drove them to the brink of schism.

[m] According to some accounts, (Baronius, Annal. Eccles. A. D. 438, No. 9, 10), the emperor was forced to send a letter of invitation and excuses before the body of the ceremonious saint could be moved from Comana.

[n] Zosimus, l. v, p. 315. The chastity of an empress should not be impeached without producing a witness; but it is astonishing, that the witness should write and live under a prince, whose legitimacy he
dared

however, by the pious husband, as an event the most fortunate and honourable to himself, to his family, and to the eastern world: and the royal infant, by an unprecedented favour, was invested with the titles of Cæsar and Augustus. In less than four years afterwards, Eudoxia, in the bloom of youth, was destroyed by the consequences of a miscarriage; and this untimely death confounded the prophecy of a holy bishop,[*] who, amidst the universal joy, had ventured to foretel, that she should behold the long and auspicious reign of her glorious son. The catholics applauded the justice of heaven, which avenged the persecution of St. Chrysostom; and perhaps the emperor was the only person who sincerely bewailed the loss of the haughty and rapacious Eudoxia. Such a domestic misfortune afflicted *him* more deeply than the public calamities of the East;[p] the licentious excursions from Pontus to Palestine, of the Isaurian robbers, whose impunity accused the weakness of the government; and the earthquakes, the conflagrations, the famine, and the flights of locusts,[q] which the popular discontent

dared to attack. We must suppose that his history was a party libel, privately read and circulated by the pagans. Tillemont (Hist. des Empereurs, tom. v, p. 782) is not averse to brand the reputation of Eudoxia.

[*] Porphyry of Gaza. His zeal was transported by the order which he had obtained for the destruction of eight pagan temples of that city. See the curious details of his life, (Baronius, A. D. 401, No. 17–51), originally written in Greek, or perhaps in Syriac, by a monk, one of his favourite deacons.

[p] Philostorg. l. xi, c. 8, and Godefroy, Dissertat. p. 457.

[q] Jerom (tom. vi, p. 73, 76) describes, in lively colours, the regular and destructive march of the locusts, which spread a dark cloud
between

was equally disposed to attribute to the incapacity of the monarch.   At length, in the thirty-
first year of his age, after a reign (if we may
abuse that word) of thirteen years three months
and fifteen days, Arcadius expired in the palace
of Constantinople.   It is impossible to delineate
his character, since, in a period very copiously
furnished with historical materials, it has not
been possible to remark one action that properly belongs to the son of the great Theodosius. ;

His sup-
posed tes-
tament.
The historian Procopius[r] has indeed illuminated the mind of the dying emperor with a ray
of human prudence, or celestial wisdom.   Arcadius considered, with anxious foresight, the
helpless condition of his son Theodosius, who
was no more than seven years of age, the dangerous factions of a minority, and the aspiring
spirit of Jezdegerd, the Persian monarch.   Instead of tempting the allegiance of an ambitious
subject, by the participation of supreme power,
he boldly appealed to the magnanimity of a
king; and placed, by a solemn testament, the
sceptre of the East in the hands of Jezdegerd
himself.   The royal guardian accepted and discharged this honourable trust with unexampled
fidelity ; and the infancy of Theodosius was
protected by the arms and councils of Persia.
Such is the singular narrative of Procopius ;

between heaven and earth, over the land of Palestine.   Seasonable
winds scattered them, partly into the Dead Sea, and partly into the
Mediterranean.

[r] Procopius, de Bell. Persic. i. l, c. 2, p. 8, edit. Louvre.

and his veracity is not disputed by Agathias,[1] while he presumes to dissent from his judgment, and to arraign the wisdom of a Christian emperor, who so rashly, though so fortunately, committed his son and his dominions to the unknown faith of a stranger, a rival, and a heathen. At the distance of one hundred and fifty years, this political question might be debated in the court of Justinian; but a prudent historian will refuse to examine the *propriety*, till he has ascertained the *truth*, of the testament of Arcadius. As it stands without a parallel in the history of the world, we may justly require, that it should be attested by the positive and unanimous evidence of contemporaries. The strange novelty of the event, which excites our distrust, must have attracted their notice; and their universal silence annihilates the vain tradition of the succeeding age.

The maxims of Roman jurisprudence, if they could be fairly transferred from private property to public dominion, would have adjudged to the emperor Honorius the guardianship of his nephew, till he had attained, at least, the fourteenth year of his age. But the weakness of Honorius, and the calamities of his reign, disqualified him from prosecuting this natural claim; and such was the absolute separation of

---

[1] Agathias, l. iv, p. 136, 137. Although he confesses the prevalence of the tradition, he asserts that Procopius was the first who had committed it to writing. Tillemont, (Hist. des Empereurs, tom. v, p. 597) argues very sensibly on the merits of this fable. His criticism was not warped by any ecclesiastical authority: both Procopius and Agathias are half pagans.

CHAP.
XXXII.

the two monarchies, both in interest and affection, that Constantinople would have obeyed, with less reluctance, the orders of the Persian, than those of the Italian, court. Under a prince, whose weakness is disguised by the external signs of manhood and discretion, the most worthless favourites may secretly dispute the empire of the palace; and dictate to submissive provinces the commands of a master, whom they direct and despise. But the ministers of a child, who is incapable of arming them with the sanction of the royal name, must acquire and exercise an independent authority. The great officers of the state and army, who had been appointed before the death of Arcadius, formed an aristocracy, which might have inspired them with the idea of a free republic; and the government of the eastern empire was fortunately assumed by the prefect Anthemius,[*] who obtained, by his superior abilities, a lasting ascendant over the minds of his equals. The safety of the young emperor proved the merit and integrity of Anthemius: and his prudent firmness sustained the force and reputation of an infant reign. Uldin, with a formidable host of barbarians, was encamped in the heart of Thrace: he proudly rejected all terms of accommodation; and pointing to the rising sun, declared to the Roman ambassadors, that

[*] Socrates, l. vii, c. 1. Anthemius was the grandson of Philip, one of the ministers of Constantius, and the grandfather of the emperor Anthemius. After his return from the Persian embassy, he was appointed consul and pretorian prefect of the East, in the year 405; and held the prefecture about ten years. See his honours and praises in Godefroy, Cod. Theod. tom. vi, p. 350. Tillemont, Hist. des Emp. tom. vi, p. 1, &c.

the course of that planet should alone terminate the conquests of the Huns. But the desertion of his confederates, who were privately convinced of the justice and liberality of the imperial ministers, obliged Uldin to repass the Danube: the tribe of the Scyrri, which composed his rear-guard, was almost extirpated; and many thousand captives were dispersed to cultivate, with servile labour, the fields of Asia.[u] In the midst of the public triumph Constantinople was protected by a strong inclosure of new and more extensive walls; the same vigilant care was applied to restore the fortifications of the Illyrian cities; and a plan was judiciously conceived, which, in the space of seven years, would have secured the command of the Danube, by establishing on that river a perpetual fleet of two hundred and fifty armed vessels.[x]

But the Romans had so long been accustomed to the authority of a monarch, that the first, even among the females, of the imperial family, who displayed any courage or capacity, was permitted to ascend the vacant throne of Theodosius. His sister Pulcheria,[y] who was only two years older than himself, received, at the age of sixteen, the title of *Augusta;* and though her

Character
and admi-
nistration
of Pul-
cheria,
A. D. 414-
45?.

[u] Sozomen, l. ix, c. 5. He saw some Scyrri at work near Mount Olympus, in Bithynia, and cherished the vain hope that those captives were the last of the nation.

[x] Cod. Theod. l. vii. tit. xvii; l. xv, tit. i, leg. 49.

[y] Sozomen has filled three chapters with a magnificent panegyric of Pulcheria, (l. ix, c. 1, 2, 3); and Tillemont (Memoires Eccles. tom. xv, p. 171-184) has dedicated a separate article to the honour of St. Pulcheria, virgin and empress.

favour might be sometimes clouded by caprice or intrigue, she continued to govern the eastern empire near forty years; during the long minority of her brother, and, after his death, in her own name, and in the name of Marcian, her nominal husband. From a motive, either of prudence, or religion, she embraced a life of celebacy; and notwithstanding some aspersions on the chastity of Pulcheria,[a] this resolution, which she communicated to her sisters Arcadia and Marina, was celebrated by the Christian world, as the sublime effort of heroic piety. In the presence of the clergy and people, the three daughters of Arcadius[b] dedicated their virginity to God; and the obligation of their solemn vow was inscribed on a tablet of gold and gems; which they publicly offered in the great church of Constantinople. Their palace was converted into a monastery; and all males, except the guides of their conscience, the saints who had forgotten the distinction of sexes, were scrupulously excluded from the holy threshold. Pulcheria, her two sisters, and a chosen train of favourite damsels, formed a religious community: they renounced the vanity of dress; interrupted, by frequent fasts, their simple and frugal diet; allotted a portion of their time to

[a] Suidas (Excerpta, p. 68, in Script. Byzant.) pretends on the credit of the Nestorians, that Pulcheria was exasperated against their founder, because he censured her connection with the beautiful Paulinus, and her incest with her brother Theodosius.

[b] See Ducange, Famil. Byzantin. p. 70. Flaccilla, the eldest daughter, either died before Arcadius, or, if she lived till the year 431, (Marcellin. Chron.) some defect of mind or body must have excluded her from the honours of her rank.

works of embroidery; and devoted several hours of the day and night to the exercises of prayer and psalmody. The piety of a Christian virgin was adorned by the zeal and liberality of an empress. Ecclesiastical history describes the splendid churches, which were built at the expence of Pulcheria, in all the provinces of the East; her charitable foundations for the benefit of strangers and the poor; the ample donations which she assigned for the perpetual maintenance of monastic societies; and the active severity with which she laboured to suppress the opposite heresies of Nestorius and Eutyches. Such virtues were supposed to deserve the peculiar favour of the Deity: and the relics of martyrs, as well as the knowledge of future events, were communicated in visions and revelations to the imperial saint.[b] Yet the devotion of Pulcheria never diverted her indefatigable attention from temporal affairs; and she alone, among all the descendants of the great Theodosius, appears to have inherited any share of his manly spirit and abilities. The elegant and familiar use which she had acquired, both of the Greek and Latin languages, was readily applied to the various occasions of speak-

[b] She was admonished, by repeated dreams, of the place where the relics of the forty martyrs had been buried. The ground had successively belonged to the house and garden of a woman of Constantinople, to a monastery of Macedonian monks, and to a church of St. Thyrsus, erected by Cæsarius, who was consul A. D. 397; and the memory of the relics was almost obliterated. Notwithstanding the charitable wishes of Dr. Jortin, (Remarks, tom. iv, p. 234), it is not easy to acquit Pulcheria of some share in the pious fraud; which must have been transacted when she was more than five and thirty years of age.

ing, or writing, on public business; her deliberations were maturely weighed; her actions
were prompt and decisive; and, while she
moved without noise or ostentation the wheel
of government, she discreetly attributed to the
genius of the emperor, the long tranquillity of
his reign. · In the last years of his peaceful life,
Europa was indeed afflicted by the arms of
Attila; but the more extensive provinces of
Asia still continued to enjoy a profound and
permanent repose. Theodosius the younger
was never reduced to the disgraceful necessity
of encountering and punishing a rebellious subject: and since we cannot applaud the vigour,
some praise may be due to the mildness, and
prosperity, of the administration of Pulcheria.

Education
and cha-
racter of
Theodo-
sius the
younger.
The Roman world was deeply interested in
the education of its master. A regular course
of study and exercise was judiciously instituted; of the military exercises of riding, and
shooting with the bow; of the liberal studies
of grammar, rhetoric, and philosophy: the most
skilful masters of the East ambitiously solicited the attention of their royal pupil; and several noble youths were introduced into the
palace, to animate his diligence by the emulation of friendship. Pulcheria alone discharged
the important task of instructing her brother in
the arts of government; but her precepts may
countenance some suspicion of the extent of
her capacity, or of the purity of her intentions.
She taught him to maintain a grave and majestic deportment; to walk, to hold his robes, to
seat himself on his throne, in a manner worthy

of a great prince; to abstain from laughter; to listen with condescension; to return suitable answers; to assume, by turns, a serious or a placid countenance; in a word, to represent with grace and dignity the external figure of a Roman emperor. But Theodosius[c] was never excited to support the weight and glory of an illustrious name; and instead of aspiring to imitate his ancestors, he degenerated (if we may presume to measure the degrees of incapacity) below the weakness of his father and his uncle. Arcadius and Honorius had been assisted by the guardian care of a parent, whose lessons were enforced by his authority, and example. But the unfortunate prince, who is born in the purple, must remain a stranger to the voice of truth; and the son of Arcadius was condemned to pass his perpetual infancy, encompassed only by a servile train of women and eunuchs. The ample leisure, which he acquired by neglecting the essential duties of his high office, was filled by idle amusements, and unprofitable studies. Hunting was the only active pursuit that could tempt him beyond the limits of the palace; but he most assiduously laboured, sometimes by the light of

[c] There is a remarkable difference between the two ecclesiastical historians, who in general bear so close a resemblance. Sozomen (l. ix, c. 1) ascribes to Pulcheria the government of the empire, and the education of her brother; whom he scarcely condescends to praise. Socrates, though he affectedly disclaims all hopes of favour or fame, composes an elaborate panegyric on the emperor, and cautiously suppresses the merits of his sister, (l. vii, c. 22, 42). Philostorgius (l. xii, c. 7) expresses the influence of Pulcheria in gentle and courtly language, τας βασιλικας σημειωσις υπηρετουμενη και διαθεουσα. Suidas (Excerpt. p. 53) gives a true character of Theodosius; and I have followed the example of Tillemont (tom. vi, p. 25) in borrowing some strokes from the modern Greeks.

a midnight lamp, in the mechanic occupations of painting and carving; and the elegance with which he transcribed religious books, entitled the Roman emperor to the singular epithet of *Calligraphes,* or a fair writer. Separated from the world by an impenetrable veil, Theodosius trusted the persons whom he loved; he loved those who were accustomed to amuse and flatter his indolence; and as he never perused the papers that were presented for the royal signature, the acts of injustice the most repugnant to his character, were frequently perpetrated in his name. The emperor himself was chaste, temperate, liberal, and merciful; but these qualities, which can only deserve the name of virtues, when they are supported by courage, and regulated by discretion, were seldom beneficial, and they sometimes proved mischievous, to mankind. His mind, enervated by a royal education, was oppressed and degraded by abject superstition: he fasted, he sung psalms, he blindly accepted the miracles and doctrines, with which his faith was continually nourished. Theodosius devoutly worshipped the dead and living saints of the catholic church; and he once refused to eat, till an insolent monk, who had cast an excommunication on his sovereign, condescended to heal the spiritual wound which he had inflicted.[a]

The story of a fair and virtuous maiden, exalted from a private condition to the imperial

[a] Theodoret, l. v, c. 37. The bishop of Cyrrhus, one of the first men of his age for his learning and piety, applauds the obedience of Theodosius to the divine laws.

western province acknowledged the jurisdiction of Arsaces, and the supremacy of the emperor Arcadius. After the death of Arsaces, the Romans suppressed the regal government, and imposed on their allies the condition of subjects. The military command was delegated to the count of the Armenian frontier; the city of Theodosiopolis[p] was built and fortified in a strong situation, on a fertile and lofty ground, near the sources of the Euphrates, and the dependant territories were ruled by five satraps, whose dignity was marked by a peculiar habit of gold and purple. The less fortunate nobles, who lamented the loss of their king, and envied the honours of their equals, were provoked to negotiate their peace and pardon at the Persian court; and returning, with their followers, to the palace of Artaxata, acknowledged Chosroes for their lawful sovereign. About thirty years afterwards, Artasires, the nephew and successor of Chosroes, fell under the displeasure of the haughty and capricious nobles of Armenia; and they unanimously desired a Persian governor in the room of an unworthy king. The answer of the archbishop Isaac, whose sanction they earnestly solicited, is expressive of the character of a superstitious people. He deplored the manifest and inexcusable vices of Artasires; and declared, that he should not hesitate

[p] Moses Choren. l. iii, c. 59, p. 309 and p. 358. Procopius, de Edificiis, l. iii, c. 5. Theodosiopolis stands, or rather stood, about thirty-five miles to the east of Arzeroum, the modern capital of Turkish Armenia. See d'Anville, Geographie Ancienne, tom. ii, p. 99, 100.

CHAP.
XXXII. to accuse him before the tribunal of a Christian emperor, who would punish without destroying, the sinner. " Our king," continued Isaac, " is too much addicted to licentious " pleasures, but he has been purified in the " holy waters of baptism. He is a lover of " women, but he does not adore the fire or the " elements. He may deserve the reproach of " lewdness, but he is an undoubted catholic; " and his faith is pure, though his manners are " flagitious. I will never consent to abandon " my sheep to the rage of devouring wolves; and " you would soon repent your rash exchange of " the infirmities of a believer, for the specious " virtues of an heathen."ᵠ Exasperated by the firmness of Isaac, the factious nobles accused both the king and the archbishop as the secret adherents of the emperor: and absurdly rejoiced in the sentence of condemnation, which, after a partial hearing, was solemnly pronounced by Bahram himself. The descendants of Arsaces were degraded from the royal dignity,ʳ which they had possessed above five hundred and sixty years;ˢ and the dominions of the unfortunate

---

ᵠ Moses Choren. l. iii, c. 63, p. 316. According to the institution of St. Gregory the apostle of Armenia, the archbishop was always of the royal family; a circumstance which, in some degree, corrected the influence of the sacerdotal character, and united the mitre with the crown.

ʳ A branch of the royal house of Arsaces still subsisted with the rank and possessions (as it should seem) of Armenian satraps. See Moses Choren. l. iii, c. 65, p. 321.

ˢ Valarsaces was appointed king of Armenia by his brother the Parthian monarch, immediately after the defeat of Antiochus Sidetes (Moses Choren. l. ii, c. 2, p. 85), one hundred and thirty years before Christ. Without depending on the various and contradictory periods of the reigns

Artasires, under the new and significant appellation of Persarmenia, were reduced into the form of a province. This usurpation excited the jealousy of the Roman government; but the rising disputes were soon terminated by an amicable, though unequal, partition of the ancient kingdom of Armenia; and a territorial acquisition, which Augustus might have despised, reflected some lustre on the declining empire of the younger Theodosius.

reigns of the last king, we may be assured, that the ruin of the Armenian kingdom happened after the council of Chalcedon, A. D. 431, (l. iii, c. 61, p 312); and under Veramus, or Bahram, king of Persia, (l. iii, c. 64, p. 317), who reigned from A. D. 420 to 440. See Assemanni, Bibliot. Oriental. tom. iii, p. 396.

END OF THE FIFTH VOLUME.

Plummer and Brewis, Printers, Love-Lane, Little-Eastcheap.